D1046898

PLAYS FOR ACTRESSES

PLAYS FOR ACTRESSES

EDITED BY *Eric Lane*
AND *Nina Shengold*

VINTAGE BOOKS
A DIVISION OF RANDOM HOUSE, INC. NEW YORK

Copyright © 1997 by Eric Lane and Nina Shengold

All rights reserved under International and Pan-American Copyright Conventions. Published in the United States by Vintage Books, a division of Random House, Inc., New York, and simultaneously in Canada by Random House of Canada Limited, Toronto.

ISBN 0-679-77281-2

Pages 629–630 constitute an extension of this copyright page

Book design by Mia Risberg

Printed in the United States of America

CONTENTS

INTRODUCTION

Gather any group of actresses, from students to stars, and you will hear the same refrain: "Where are all the great roles? Why do men get to work all the time? Why aren't there more plays for us?"

Plays for Actresses offers seventeen outstanding plays with all-female casts. (The only two male roles are silent, in *Three Tall Women* and *The Winged Man,* and an off-stage male voice in *Poof!*) You'll find full-length plays and one-acts, comedies and dramas, works of well-known and emerging playwrights (both women and men). Above all, you'll find wonderful *roles*—dozens of juicy and challenging parts for actresses of all ages and types.

The seven full-length plays in this anthology are astoundingly varied. Their voices range from the brilliant theatricality of *Three Tall Women,* Edward Albee's Pulitzer Prize-winning study of youth, maturity and old age, to the nuanced naturalism of Lee Blessing's *Independence,* a family portrait of a mentally ill woman and her three daughters that brings insight and depth to the archetypal roles of black sheep, dutiful daughter, and rebel.

Laura Cunningham's *Beautiful Bodies,* a darkly hilarious vision of a NoHo baby shower run amok, features plum roles for no fewer than six women; four actresses double as schoolgirls and nuns in *Catholic School Girls,* Casey Kurtti's pitch-perfect evocation of growing up Catholic in the '60s. (As a further bonus, both of these plays contain marvelous monologues.)

Velina Hasu Houston's exquisite, heartbreaking *Tea* is a portrait of Japanese war brides estranged not just from their homeland, but from one another. Sherry Kramer's breathtakingly original *David's Redhaired Death* is a metaphysical tour de force about two women whose love for each other is cut short by tragedy. And Paula Vogel's bawdy romp *Desdemona* inventively reinterprets the women of Shakespeare's *Othello,* examining stereotypical female roles—then and now—in the process.

This collection also includes ten one-acts of varying lengths. Actresses looking for one-woman plays will be thrilled with Craig Lucas's offbeat and lyrical *Credo* and Wendy Wasserstein's *Workout,* which deftly skewers the overachieving, have-it-all mythos of women in the '90s. Two longer one-acts explore issues of women's self-image: Tina Howe's giddily slapstick *Appearances,* set in a department store dressing room, and Madeleine George's unique and disturbing *The Most Massive Woman Wins,* set in the waiting room of a liposuction clinic.

Raptures of the deep haunt a Y.M.C.A. kiddie pool in Adam LeFevre's enigmatic *Waterbabies,* winner of the Actors Theatre of Louisville's 1995 Heideman Award for Best Ten-Minute Play. An African-American woman gets sweet revenge on her abusive husband in Lynn Nottage's *Poof!* Mary Gallagher's *Bedtime* poignantly explores childhood fears and the bond between sisters. José Rivera's *The Winged Man* blends magic realism and street smarts in an unconventional tale of teen pregnancy. Two more ten-minute plays, *The Role of Della* and *Lives of the Great Waitresses,* weave comic variations on those perennial nightmares of actresses lives, auditions and restaurant work.

When we first decided to assemble a collection of plays with all-female casts, we wondered whether we'd find enough good ones to fill a book. We sent queries to playwrights, theatres, and agents. In no time at all, we were flooded with wonderful scripts—so many that our toughest challenge as editors was winnowing hundreds of choices down to a mere seventeen. The more we read, the more shocked we became that these plays are not better known and more widely produced.

In fact, it's amazing to us that this anthology is (as far as we know) the first of its kind. It seems that nearly every theatre group—from high school drama club to Equity rep—includes more women than men, competing for roles in plays that require more men than women. If your local producers continue to offer an unbalanced diet of *Henry IV* parts I and II, *Glengarry Glen Ross* and *A Few Good Men,* choose a play that you love and produce it yourself. Do an evening of one-acts or scenes. Stage a reading. Find ways to find work.

Whether you're seeking a script to produce, a scene for acting class or a new audition speech, this book will provide you with a wealth of wonderful roles. It will also, and not incidentally, introduce you to some of the finest playwrights working today. Enjoy their words.

—Nina Shengold and Eric Lane

ACKNOWLEDGMENTS

We'd like to thank the following individuals for their invaluable contributions to this anthology: Linda Driekonski; Elenore Speert at Dramatists Play Service; Michael Bigelow Dixon at Actors Theatre of Louisville; John McCormack; David Robinson; Tom Szentgyorgyi at Denver Center Theatre; Peter Franklin, Matthew Lewis, and Eric Zohn at William Morris; Florence Eichen at NAL; Peter Hagen at Writers & Artists; Ron Gwiazda at Rosenstone/Wender; Mary Harden at Harden/Curtis; Yaddo; and as always, our families and friends.

Special thanks to our agents Susie Perlman and Phyllis Wender for their extraordinary efforts and skill. Also our editor at Vintage, LuAnn Walther, for the opportunity to publish this book. And most of all, the playwrights for their wonderful plays, and the actresses who bring their works to life.

PLAYS FOR ACTRESSES

THREE TALL WOMEN

Edward Albee

THREE TALL WOMEN was produced by Vineyard Theatre (Douglas Aibel, Artistic Director; John Nakagawa, Managing Director) in New York City in January 1994, and later moved to the Promenade Theatre (produced by Elizabeth I. McCann, Jeffrey Ash, and Daryl Roth, in association with Leavitt/Fox/Manges). It was directed by Lawrence Sacharow; the set design was by James Noone; the costume design was by Muriel Stockdale; the lighting design was by Phil Monat, and the production stage manager was Elizabeth M. Berther. The cast was as follows:

A	Myra Carter
B	Marian Seldes
C	Jordon Baker
THE BOY	Michael Rhodes

THE CHARACTERS

A: a very old woman; thin, autocratic, proud, as together as the ravages of time will allow. Nails scarlet, hair nicely done, wears makeup. Lovely nightgown and dressing gown.

B: looks rather as A would have at 52; plainly dressed.

C: looks rather as B would have at 26.

THE BOY: 23 or so; preppy dress (jacket, tie, shirt, jeans, loafers, etc.)

PLACE

A "wealthy" bedroom, French in feeling. Pastels, with blue predominant. A bed upstage center, with a small bench at its foot. Lacy pillows, a lovely spread. Nineteenth-century French paintings. Two light armchairs, beautifully covered in silk. If there is a window, silk swags. Pastel carpeted floor. Two doors, one left, one right. Archways for both.

ACT ONE

At rise, A *is in the left armchair,* B *is in the right one,* C *on the bed-foot bench.*

It is afternoon.

Some silence.

A: (*An announcement from nowhere; to no one in particular.*) I'm ninety-one.

B: (*Pause.*) Is that so?

A: (*Pause.*) Yes.

C: (*Small smile*) You're ninety-*two.*

A: (*Longer pause; none too pleasant.*) Be that as it *may.*

B: (*To* C.) Is that so?

C: (*Shrugs; indicates papers.*) Says so here.

B: (*Pause; stretching.*) Well . . . what does it matter?

C: Vanity is amazing.

B: So's forgetting.

A: (*General.*) I'm ninety-one.

B: (*Accepting sigh.*) O.K.

C: (*Smaller smile.*) You're ninety-*two.*

B: (*Unconcerned.*) Oh . . . let it alone.

C: No! It's important. Getting things . . .

B: It doesn't matter!

C: (*Sotto voce.*) It does to *me.*

A: (*Pause.*) I know because he says, You're exactly thirty years older than I am; I know how old I am because I know how old *you* are, and if you ever forget how old you are ask me how old *I* am, and then you'll know. (*Pause.*) Oh, he's said that a lot.

C: What if he's wrong?

A: (*From a distance; curiously lighter, higher voice.*) What?

B: Let it *be.*

C: (*Still to* A.) What if he's wrong? What if he's not thirty years younger than you?

A: (*Oddly loud, tough.*) You'd think he'd know how old he is!

C: No, I mean . . . what if he's wrong about how old *you* are.

A: (*Pause.*) Don't be silly. How couldn't he be thirty years younger than me when I'm thirty years older than he is? He's said it over and over. (*Pause.*) Every time he comes to see me. What is today?

B: It's [*whatever day it is in reality*].

A: You see?!

C: (*A bit as if to a child.*) Well, one of you might be wrong, and it might not be him.

B: (*Small sneer.*) *He.*

C: (*Quick smile.*) Yes; I know.

A: Don't be stupid. *What* is it? *What day* is it?

B: It's [*ibid.*].

A: (*Shakes her head.*) No.

C: (*Interested.*) No what?

A: No it *isn't.*

B: O.K.

C: (*To* A.) What day do you *think* it is?

A: (*Confusion.*) What day is it? What day do I . . . ? (*Eyes narrowing.*) Why, it's today, of course. What day do you *think* it is!? (*Turns to* B; *cackles.*)

B: Right on, girl!

C: (*Scoffs.*) What an answer! What a dumb . . .

A: Don't you talk to me that way!

C: (*Offended.*) Well! I'm sorry!

A: I pay you, don't I? You can't talk to me that way.

C: In a way.

A: (*A daring tone.*) What!?

C: Indirectly. You pay someone who pays me, someone who . . .

A: Well; there; you see? You can't talk to me that way.

B: She isn't talking to you that way.

A: What?

B: She isn't *talking* to you that way.

A: (*Dismissive laugh.*) I don't know what you're talking about. (*Pause.*) Besides. (*Silence; then* A *cries. They let her. It begins in self-pity, proceeds to crying for crying's sake, and concludes with rage and self-loathing at having to cry. It takes quite a while.*)

B: (*When it's over.*) There. Feel better?

C: (*Under her breath.*) Honestly.

B: (*To* A.) A good cry lets it all out.

A: (*Laughs; sly.*) What does a *bad* one do? (*She laughs again;* B *joins her.*)

C: (*Shakes her head in admiration.*) Sometimes you're so . . .

A: (*Ugly; suddenly.*) What!?

C: (*Tiny pause.*) Never *mind.* I was going to say something *nice.* Never *mind.*

A: (*To* B.) What did she say!? She mumbles all the time.

C: I don't mumble! (*Annoyance at herself.*) Never mind!

A: How is anybody expected to hear what she says!?

B: (*Placating.*) She didn't finish her sentence. It doesn't matter.

A: (*Small, smug triumph.*) I'll *bet* it doesn't.

C: (*Dogged, but not unpleasant.*) What I meant was you may have been incorrect about your age for so long—may have made up the fiction so many years ago, though why anyone would lie about one year . . .

B: (*Weary.*) Let her alone; let her have it if she wants to.

C: I will *not.*

A: Have what!?

C: Why you would lie about one *year.* I can imagine taking off ten—or *trying* to. Though more probably seven, or five—good and tricky—but *one!?* Taking off *one year?* What kind of vanity is *that?*

B: (*Clucks.*) How you go *on.*

A: (*Imitation.*) How you go *on.*

C: (*Purrs.*) How I go on. So, I can understand ten, or five, or seven, but not one.

B: How you *do.*

A: (*To* C.) How you *do.* (*To* B.) How *what!?*

B: How she goes on.

A: (*Cheerful.*) Yes! How you go *on!*

C: (*Smiles.*) Yes; I do.

A: (*Suddenly, but not urgently.*) I want to go.

C: On?

A: (*More urgently.*) I want to go. I want to go.

B: You want to go? (*Rises.*) You want the pan? Is it number one? Do you want the pan?

A: (*Embarrassed to discuss it.*) No. . . . Noooo!

B: Ah. (*Moves to* A.) All right. Can you walk?

A: (*Weepy.*) I don't know!

B: Well, we'll try you. O.K.? (*Indicates walker.*) You want the walker?

A: (*Near tears.*) I want to walk! I don't know! Anything! I have to *go!* (*Starts to fret-weep.*)

B: All right! (B *moves* A *to a standing position. We discover* A*'s left arm is in a sling, useless.*)

A: You're hurting me!! You're hurting me!!

B: All right; I'm being careful!

A: No, you're *not!!*

B: Yes, I am!

A: No, you're *not!!!*

B: (*Angry.*) Yes, I *am!*

A: No, you're *not!* (*On her feet, weeping, shuffling off with* B*'s help.*) You're trying to hurt me; you know I hurt!!

B: (*To* C, *as they exit.*) Hold the fort.

C: I will. I will hold the fort. (*Muffled exchanges offstage.* C *looks toward them, shakes her head, looks back down. Continued; both to herself and to be heard.*) I suppose one could lie about one year—some kind of one-upmanship, a private vengeance, perhaps, some tiny victory, maybe. (*Shrugs.*) I don't know, maybe these things get important. (*She sits in* A*'s chair.*) Why can't I be nice?

B: (*Reenters.*) Made it that time. (*Sighs.*) And so it goes.

C: Not always, eh?

B: In the morning, when she wakes up she wets—a kind of greeting to the day, I suppose: the sphincter and the cortex not in sync. Never during the *night,* but *as* she wakes.

C: Good morning to the morning, eh?

B: Something to something.

C: Put a diaper on her.

B: (*Shakes her head.*) She won't have it. I'm working on it, but she won't have it.

C: Rubber sheet?

B: Won't have it. Get her up, put her in the chair and she does the other. Give her a cup of coffee . . .

C: Black.

B: (*Chuckles.*) Half cream and all that sugar! Three spoons! How has she lived this long? Give her her cup of coffee, put her in her chair, give her her cup of coffee and place your bets.

C: (*Looks at the chair she is in.*) *What* chair!? *This* chair!?

B: (*Laughs.*) You got it. Don't worry.

C: It must be awful.

B: (*Deprecating.*) *For whom?*

C: (*Rising to it.*) For her! You're paid. It's probably awful for you, too, but you're paid.

B: As she never ceases to inform me . . . *and* you.

C: To begin to lose it, I mean—the control, the loss of dignity, the . . .

B: Oh, stop it! It's downhill from sixteen on! For all of us!

C: Yes, but . . .

B: What *are* you, twenty-something? Haven't you figured it out yet? (*Demonstrates.*) You take the breath in . . . you let it out. The first one you take in you're upside down and they slap you into it. The last one . . . well, the last one you let it all out . . . and that's it. You start . . . and then you stop. Don't be so soft. I'd like to see children learn it—have a six-year-old say, "I'm dying" and know what it means.

C: You're horrible!

B: Start in young; make 'em aware they've got only a little time. Make 'em aware that they're dying from the minute they're alive.

C: Awful!

B: Grow up! Do *you* know it? Do *you* know you're dying?

C: Well, of course, but . . .

B: (*Ending it.*) Grow up.

A: (*Wobbling, shuffling in.*) A person could die in there and nobody'd care.

B: (*Bright.*) Done already!

A: A person could die! A person could fall down and break something! A person could die! Nobody would care!

B: (*Going to her.*) Let me help you.

A: (*Good arm flailing.*) Get your *hands* off me! A person could die for all anybody'd care.

C: (*To herself, but to be overheard.*) Who is this . . . "person"? A person could do this, a person could do . . .

B: It's a figure of speech.

C: (*Mildly sarcastic.*) No. Really?

B: (*Not rising to it.*) So they tell me.

A: (*Flailing about.*) Hold *on* to me! Do you want me to fall!? You want me to *fall!*

B: Yes, I want you to fall; I want you to fall and shatter in . . . ten pieces.

C: Or five, or seven.

A: Where's my chair! (*Sees it perfectly well.*) Where's my chair gone to?

B: (*Playing the game.*) Goodness, where's her chair *gone* to!? Somebody's taken her *chair!*

C: (*Realizing.*) What!?

A: (*Does she know? Probably.*) Who's got my chair?

C: (*High horse.*) I'm sorry! (*Gets up quickly; moves away.*) Your majesty!

B: (*Placating.*) There's your chair. Do you want your pillow? Shall I get you your pillow? (*To* C.) Fetch her pillow.

A: I want to sit *down.*

B: Yes, yes. Here we go. (B *gently lowers* A *into the vacated armchair.*)

C: (*At bed.*) Which *pillow?*

B: (*To* A.) Are you comfortable? Do you want your pillow?

A: (*Petulant.*) Of *course* I'm not comfortable; of *course* I want my pillow.

C: (*Still at the bed; to* B.) I don't know which one!

B: (*Moving to the bed.*) It's two, actually, one for the back (*Takes it.*) and this one for the arm. (*Takes it; moves toward* A.) Here we are; lean forward. (*Positions back pillow.*) That's a girl.

A: My arm! My arm! Where's the pillow!?

B: Here we go. (*Arranges arm pillow.*) All comfy? (*Silence. Continued.*) All comfy?

A: What?

B: Nothing. (*A knowing smile to* C.)

C: And so it goes?

B: Un-huh.

C: What a production.

B: You haven't seen anything.

C: I bet!

A: (*To* B.) You can't just leave me in there like that. What if I fell? What if I died?

B: (*Considers it; calm.*) Well . . . if you fell I'd either hear you or you'd raise a racket, and if you died what would it matter?

A: (*Pause; then she laughs; true enjoyment.*) You can say that again! (*Amused at seeing* C *not amused.*) What's the matter with you?

C: (*Small silence, until she realizes she's being talked to.*) Who!? Me!?

A: Yes. You.

C: What's the *matter* with me?

B: (*Amused.*) That's what she *said.*

A: That's what I *said.*

C: (*Panicking a little.*) What are you all doing—ganging up on me?

B: (*To* A.) Is that what we're doing?

A: (*Enjoying it greatly.*) *May*be!

C: (*To defend herself.*) There's *nothing* the matter with me.

B: (*Sour smile.*) Well . . . you just *wait.*

A: What did she say?

B: She says there's nothing the matter with her—Miss Perfect over there.

C: I didn't *say* that; that's not what I . . . !!

A: (*To* B; *sincere.*) Why is she *yelling* at me!?

B: She's *not.*

C: I'm *not!*

B: *Now* you are.

A: You see!? (*Confused.*) What day is it?

B: It's *[whatever day it is in reality].*

A: Will he come today? Is today the day he comes?

B: No; not today.

A: (*Whining.*) Why not!?

B: (*Making nothing of it.*) Oh, he probably has something else to do; he probably has a full schedule.

A: (*Teary.*) He never comes to see me, and when he does he

never stays. (*A sudden shift in tone to hatred.*) *I'll* fix him; I'll fix *all* of 'em. They all think they can treat me like this. You all think you can get away with anything. I'll fix you all.

C: (*To* B; *an aside.*) Is it always like this?

B: (*Overly patient.*) No . . . it's often very pleasant.

C: Huh!

A: (*Muttering now.*) You all want something; there's nobody doesn't want something. My mother taught me that; be careful, she said; they all want something; she taught me what to expect, me and my sister. She prepared us and somebody had to. I mean, we were girls and that was way back then, and it was different then. We didn't have a lot, and being a girl wasn't easy. We knew we'd have to make our own way, and being a girl back then . . . why am I talking about this!?

B: Because you want to.

A: That's right. She tried to prepare us . . . for going out in the world, for men, for making our own way. Sis couldn't do it; that's too bad. *I* could; *I* did. I met him at a party, and he said he'd seen me before. He'd been married twice—the first one was a whore, the second one was a drunk. He was funny! He said, let's go riding in the park, and I said all right . . . scared to death. I lied; I said I rode. *He* didn't care; he wanted me; I could tell that. It only took six weeks.

B: Good girl!

A: We had horses when we were married; we had a stable; we had saddle horses; we rode.

C: (*Mildly.*) Hoity-toity.

A: I learned to ride and I was very good.

B: (*Encouraging.*) I'm sure!

C: (*Mildly contemptuous.*) *How* are you sure!?

B: Shhhhhhh.

A: (*Childlike enthusiasm.*) I rode sidesaddle and I rode astride, and I drove ponies—hackneys—and I loved it all. He would go with me and we would ride every morning, and the Dalmatian would go with us—what was her name . . . Suzie? No. We had good horses and we showed them and we won all the ribbons, and we kept them in a big case down in the . . . no, that was the other house. We kept them. (*Pause; reinvigorating herself.*) And cups. All the silver cups we won, and bowls, and platters. We knew all the judges but that's not why we would win: we won because we were the best.

C: (*Under her breath.*) Of course.

B: (*Sotto voce.*) Be decent.

A: (*Dismissive.*) Oh, she'll learn. (*Back to the memory.*) We had horses! I knew all the judges, and I'd go in the ring when we were in the championships, and I'd sit there and I'd watch the horses—I never rode when we were in the championships; Earl did that; he was our rider. I would sit there and watch with the judges. They all knew me; we were famous; we had a famous stable, and when the judging was done they'd tell me if we'd won, and we almost always did, and if they told me, and they almost always did, I'd signal. I'd take my hat off and I'd touch my hair. (*Does it: touches hair.*) and that way they'd know we'd won.

C: (*To* B; *whispers.*) Who!? (B *shrugs, keeps her eyes on* A.)

A: (*Very rational; explaining.*) Everyone in our box. (*Childish again.*) Oh, I used to love it, riding in the morning, going to the stable in the station wagon in my coat and jodhpurs and my derby, and petting . . . what was her name?, the Dalmatian—Suzie, I think . . . no—and mounting and riding off. Sometimes he came with me and sometimes he didn't. Sometimes I went off alone.

C: (*To* B.) Who?

B: Her husband, most likely. (*To* A.) Did you ride when you were little?

A: (*A little deprecating laugh.*) No. We were poor.

C: (*To* A.) Poor? Really . . . "poor"?

A: Well, no; not really poor; my father was an architect; he designed furniture; he made it.

C: That's not an architect, that's . . .

B: Let it be.

A: He made such beautiful furniture; he was an architect. Strict, but fair. No, my *mother* was strict. No, they were *both* strict. *And* fair. (*This confuses her; she cries.*)

B: Now, now.

A: I don't know what I'm saying! What am I *saying*?

B: (*Comforting.*) You're talking about horses; you were talking about riding, and we asked: when you were a little girl . . .

A: (*Rational; tough.*) We never rode; the neighbors had a horse but we never rode it. I don't think my sister ever rode. But I can't swim. (*Conspiratorial whisper.*) She drank.

C: When she was a little girl?

B: Oh, please!

A: (*Truly innocent.*) What? What are we talking about?

B: Horses. You didn't ride when you were a little girl.

A: You rode if you were a farmer or if you were rich.

C: (*Mildly mocking.*) Or if you were a rich *farmer.*

B: Shhhhhhh.

A: (*Of* C, *to* B.) She'll learn. (*To* C; *ominous.*) *Won't* you?!

C: (*Flustered laugh.*) Well, I dare *say.*

A: (*Story again.*) I wasn't rich until I got married, and I wasn't really right then till later. It all adds up. We had saddle horses; we rode. I learned to ride and I was very good. I rode sidesaddle and I rode astride, and I drove ponies—hackneys . . .

C: . . . and you loved it all.

B: Shhhhhh.

A: And I what?

C: You loved it all.

B: You loved it all.

A: I did?

B: So you say.

A: (*Laughs.*) Well, then, it must be true. I didn't like sex much, but I had an affair.

C: (*Interested.*) Oh?

A: (*Suddenly suspicious.*) What! What do you want!?

B: *She* doesn't want anything.

A: (*Off again.*) We used to ride. *He* would go with me—not all the time. Sometimes I would go off alone, or with the dog, part way, never too far from the stable; she had a cat she was in love with. She'd go back, but I'd go on. I had my jodhpurs and my coat and my switch and my derby hat. I always rode in all my costume. Never go out except you're properly dressed, I always say. I'd drive the station wagon from the house—I loved to drive. I was good at it. I was good at everything; I *had* to be; *he* wasn't. I'd drive in the station wagon to the stable, and Earl would be there, or . . . or one of the stable boys: Tom . . . or Bradley. (*Long pause.*) Am I doing in my panties!? (*Starts to cry.*)

B: (*Leisurely.*) Well . . . let's see. (*Goes to* A.) Upseedaisey! (B *raises* A, *who whimpers; cries more.* B *feels under her. Continued.*) Nope, but I bet you're going to. Off you go. (B *helps* A *off.*)

C: Hold the fort? (C *goes to window; looks out; looks at bed; goes to it; smooths the covers.* B *reenters. Continued.*) Why am I doing this?

B: Because it's unnecessary? Because I've already done it?

C: The princess and the pea, maybe? What's wrong with her arm?

B: She fell and broke it. It didn't heal. Mostly they don't at that age. They put pins in it, metal pins; the bone disintegrates around the pins and the arm just hangs there. They want to take it off.

C: What!?

B: (*Matter of fact.*) The arm; they want to take the *arm* off.

C: (*Protest.*) No!

B: (*Shrugs.*) It hurts.

C: Still!

B: She won't *let* them.

C: I shouldn't *think* so.

B: What do *you* know? She makes us go into the city once a week—to see the surgeon, the one who set it, the one who wants to take it off. God!, he's almost as old as she is. She trusts him, she says. She goes in once a week, and she makes them x-ray it, and *look* at it, and each time the pins are looser, and the bone is gone more, and she tells the old guy—the surgeon—it's so much better, and she wants him to agree, and he waffles, and he looks at me and I'm no help, and she makes him promise that he'll never take the arm off, and won't let anyone *else* do it either, and he promises—assuming she'll forget? Probably; but she won't. There are some things she never forgets. "He promised me; you were there; you heard him." I think she says that every other day: "He promised me; you were there; you heard him." (*A crack of glass from offstage. Continued.*) Oh, God! (*She exits. From offstage now.*) Now, why did you do that!?You naughty, naughty girl! Bad, bad girl! (*Offstage,* A *hoots and cackles. Continued, offstage.*) What do I have to do—take everything away from you? Huh!? (A *appears onstage again, hooting and giggling, followed by* B.)

A: (*Drifting, hobbling; very happy; to* C.) I broke the glass! I took the glass and I threw it down in the sink! I broke the glass and now she has to clean it up! (B *has reentered.*)

B: Bad girl!

A: I broke the glass! I broke the glass! (*Giggles; suddenly her face collapses and she cries; then.*) I have to sit down! I can't sit down by my*self!* Why won't somebody help me!?

B: (*Helping her.*) Now, now; here we go.

A: Ow! Ow!

B: *All* right, now.

C: (*Under her breath.*) Jesus!

B: (*To* C; *settling* A.) *You're* a big help.

C: (*Cold.*) I didn't know I was supposed to be.

B: (*Sneers.*) Just here from the lawyer, eh?

C: Yes; just here from the lawyer.

A: (*Suddenly suspiciously alert.*) What? What did you say?

B: (*Matter of fact.*) I said—well, what I implied was, since she's here from the lawyer, why should she behave like a human being; why should she be any help; why should she . . .

A: (*To* C; *happy.*) You're from Harry?

C: No; Harry's dead; Harry's been dead for years.

A: (*Tears again.*) Harry's *dead?* When did *Harry* die?

C: (*Loud.*) Thirty years ago!

A: (*Tiny pause; crying stops.*) Well, *I* knew *that*. What are you talking about *Harry* for?

C: You asked if I'd come from Harry; you asked . . .

A: I wouldn't do anything that *stupid*.

B: (*Amused; for* C.) And so it goes.

A: (*Clarifying it for the world.*) Harry *used* to be my lawyer, but that was *years* ago. Harry died—what? Thirty years ago?—Harry died. Now his son's the lawyer. I go to *him;* well, he comes to me; *some*times I go to him.

C: Yes; you do. *And* yes he does.

A: Why are *you* here?

C: (*Sighs.*) Some things have been . . . misplaced; aren't being done. Some things . . .

A: (*Panic.*) Somebody's stealing things!?

C: No no no no. We send you papers to sign and you don't sign them; we call you and you don't call back; we send you checks to sign and you don't sign them; things like that.

A: I don't know what you're talking about.

C: Well . . .

A: None of it's true! You're lying! Get Harry on the phone!

C: Harry is . . .

B: (*To* A.) Excuse me? The "I'll get to it" pile?

A: (*Suspicious of* B *now.*) What!?

B: (*Calm.*) The "I'll get to it" pile?

A: I don't know *what* you're talking about.

C: (*To* B.) Papers? Checks?

B: (*Broad.*) Oh . . . lots of stuff.

A: (*Adamant.*) There's *nothing!*

C: (*To* B.) What *is* there? What *is* it?

B: (*To* A; *patiently.*) You have a drawer full; the bills come and you look at them, and some of them you send on and they get paid, and some of them you say you can't remember and so you don't send them, and . . .

A: (*Defiant.*) Why would I send in a bill for something I never ordered?

B: (*Shuts eyes briefly.*) And they send you your checks—to sign? To pay bills? And some of them you sign because you remember what they were for, but some of them—some of the checks—you can't remember?

A: I *what!?*

B: (*Smiles tolerantly.*) . . . you don't remember what they're for and so you don't sign them and you put them in the drawer.

A: So?

B: (*Shrugs.*) These things pile up.

C: I *see;* I *see.*

A: Everybody out there's ready to rob me blind. I'm not made of money, you know.

B: (*Laughs.*) Yes, you *are.* (*To* C.) Isn't she?

C: (*Smiles.*) More or less.

A: (*Conspiratorially.*) They'd steal you blind if you didn't pay attention: the help, the stores, the markets, that little Jew makes my furs—what's her name? She's nice. They all rob you blind if you so much as turn your back on them. All of them!

C: We've asked you: let all your bills come to us; we'll know what to do; let me *bring* you your checks every month; I'll stay here while you sign them. Whatever you like.

A: (*A superior smile, but hesitant around the edges.*) None of you think I can handle my own affairs? I've done it for . . . when he was so sick I did it all; I did all the bills; I did all the checks; I did everything.

C: (*Gentle.*) But now you don't *have* to.

A: (*Proud.*) I didn't have to then: I *wanted* to. I wanted everything to be *right;* and I do now; I still do!

C: Well, of *course* you do.

B: Of *course* you do.

A: (*Ending it; superior.*) And so I'll handle my own affairs, thank you.

C: (*Defeated; shrugs.*) Well; certainly.

B: And *I'll* watch you *pretend* to handle them.

A: And I watch you, every one of you. I used to love horses.

B: It's just people you don't like.

A: (*Noncommittal.*) Oh? Is that it? We rode Western saddle, too. It was when he almost died—the first time, the first time I was with him. He had a blood infection. He was hunting, they were all hunting, and a gun went off and it hit him in the arm, the shoulder. (*Touches hers; realizes the parallel; smiles sadly.*) My God! (*Pause.*) They shot him in the shoulder, and they didn't get all the bullet out, and it got infected and his arm swelled up like a balloon and they lanced it and it burst and there was pus all over . . .

C: Stop!

B: (*Cold.*) Why? What's it to you? (C *shudders.*)

A: . . . and they put drains in it and there weren't any medicines then . . .

B: No antibiotics, you mean.

A: What?

B: No antibiotics.

A: Yes, and it wouldn't go away and it would get worse, and everybody said he was going to die, but I wouldn't let him! I said No! he is not going to die! I told that to the doctors, and I told him that, too, and he said all right, he would try, if I would sleep with him, if I wouldn't leave him alone at night, be next to him, and I did and it smelled so awful—the pus, the rot, the . . .

C: Don't! Please!

A: . . . and they said take him to the desert, bake his arm in the hot sun, and so we went there—we went to Arizona—and he sat in the baking sun all day—his arm oozing, and stinking, and splitting and . . . in six months it went away and the arm went down in size and there was no more pus and he was saved—except for the scars, all the scars, and I learned to ride Western saddle.

B: My, my.

A: And it was outside of Phoenix—Camelback Mountain; we used to ride out into the desert. And the movie star was there—the one who married the young fellow who ran the studio; she had eyes of a different color.

C: (*Small pause.*) She had *what?*

A: She had eyes of a different color: one eye was blue, or something, and the other one was green, I think.

C: (*To* B.) Who *was* this? (B *shrugs.*)

A: Oh, she was a big star; she was tiny and she had a very big head. I think *she* drank too.

B: You think *everyone* drinks. Merle Oberon?

A: No; of course not! *You* know!

B: (*Enjoying this a little.*) How long ago *was* this? Claire Trevor?

A: Oh . . . when I was there; when we were there. She was tiny! She had two eyes!

B: In the thirties?

A: Probably. She had a son; she cooked an egg on the sidewalk; it was so hot. He *told* me.

C: (*Lost.*) Her . . . son . . . told you?

A: No! Ours! He was a little boy, too; he played with all the other children: the chewing-gum twins; *that* one.

B: That must have been before the *war.*

C: Which one!?

B: Civil.

A: (*Triumphant.*) Thalberg! *That's* who she married. Arnold Thalberg; he was a real smart little Jew.

B: (*To* C; *ironic.*) All smart Jews are *little.* Have you noticed? (To A.) Irving; *Irving* Thalberg.

C: (*Cold.*) I'm a democrat; I notice a lot of things.

B: Most of us *are;* most of us *do.* But still, it's fascinating, isn't it—grisly, but fascinating. She doesn't *mean* anything by it—or if she did, once, she doesn't now. It just falls out.

A: (*Joyous.*) Norma Shearer!

B: Of course!

C: Who?

A: (*Laughs.*) What's the matter with all you people!?

C: (*Explaining.*) We're democrats.

A: What?

C: Well, you asked what the matter was.

A: Don't you get fresh!

B: My God! I haven't heard that in a long time. (*Imitates.*) "Don't you get fresh!"

A: My mother would say that to me all the time: don't you get fresh! To Sis and me. She made us eat everything she put before us, and wash the dishes; she made us know what being a grownup was. She was strict but fair. No, that was our father; no, that was both of them. (*A little girl whine.*) They're dead; Sis, they're dead!

C: A small little Jew?

B: At least she didn't say kike.

A: (*Back to her memory.*) She would make us write thank-you notes, and take little gifts whenever we went somewhere, and made us wash everything we wore the night we wore it, by hand, before we went to bed. Sometimes Sis wouldn't and I had to do hers, too. She made us be proper young ladies.

C: And go to church twice a day? And pray a lot?

A: What? Oh, yes, we went to church but we didn't talk about it very much. We took it for granted, I suppose. (*To* B.) How much did you *steal?*

B: (*Not rising to it.*) When?

A: Whenever.

B: (*Drawling.*) Well, I waited until you were asleep . . .

A: I never sleep.

B: . . . until you were pretending to be asleep, and then I went into the silver closet and took down all the big silver bowls, and I stuck them up under my skirt, and I waddled out into the hall . . .

A: Joke about it if you want to. (*A sudden fit of giggles.*) You must have looked *funny!*

B: (*Playing along.*) Well, I suppose.

A: Waddling out like that; you probably clanked, too.

B: Yes; I'm sure I did. Clank, clank.

A: (*Hoots.*) Clank, clank! (*Notices* C *isn't amused; tough.*) You don't think *any*thing's funny, do you?

C: Oh, yes; I'm just trying to decide what I think's really the most hilarious—unpaid bills, anti-Semitism, senility, or . . .

B: Now, now. Play in your own league, huh?

C: (*Miffed.*) Well! I'm *sorry!*

A: (*Looks right at* C.) I'll have to talk to Harry about you.

B: Harry's dead; Harry's been dead for years.

A: (*With increasing self-absorption.*) I know; so's everybody. I don't have any friends anymore; most of them are dead, and the ones aren't dead are dying, and the ones aren't dying have moved away or I don't see anymore.

B: (*Comforting.*) Well, what does it matter? You don't like any of them anymore anyway.

A: (*Uncomplicated agreement.*) That's true. But you're supposed to like them, to have them with you. Isn't it a contract? You take people as friends and you spend time at it, you put effort in it, and it doesn't matter if you don't like them anymore—who likes anybody anymore?—you've put in all that time, and what right do they have to . . . to . . .

C: (*Incredulous.*) To die?!

A: What!?

C: What right do they have to die?

A: No! To not be what they were.

C: To change, you mean?

B: (*Gently.*) Let her alone.

A: No! No right! You count on them! And they change. The Bradleys! The Phippses! They die; they go away. And family dies; family goes away. Nobody should *do* this! Look at Sis!

B: What about her?

A: My sister was a drunk. (*Not friendly.*) She was smarter than me . . . no: brighter, two years younger.

C: (*Smiles.*) Or five, or seven.

A: What!?

C: Nothing.

A: She always got better grades, had more beaux—when we were growing up. Only then; she missed more boats than you can shake a stick at.

C: (*Examining her nails.*) I've never shook a stick at a boat.

B: (*Dry.*) Well, maybe you should give it a try. Shaken; not shook.

A: We came to the city together, after she finished school, and we had a tiny little apartment, and our mother and our father came to see it, to be sure it was all right, not dangerous, I suppose. It was furnished, but he didn't like it, so he gave us some of theirs, some from the garage. He made the most beautiful furniture: he was an architect. We went out all the time—looking for jobs, jobs that a young lady could accept—being escorted out at night. We were the same size, so we could wear each other's clothes; *that* saved money. We had a little allowance, but a very little one, nothing to spoil us. She was a little shorter, but not much. We kept a list so the boys—the young men, the men—who took us out—we went out with them together a lot—wouldn't know we were wearing each other's. Is that what I mean?

B: Yes; I think so; most probably.

C: Keep awake.

A: "No, no, I wore that at the Plaza; don't you remember? You'd better wear the beads." We had a regular list. We had big feet. (*Silence.*)

B: (*About the non sequitur.*) What!?

C: They had big *feet.*

A: We had big feet. I still do . . . I guess. (*To* B.) Do I still have big feet?

B: Yes; yes, you do.

A: Well, I'd never know. I think we liked each other. We used to confide a lot, and laugh, and. . . . Mother made us write twice a week or call, later. We tried sending letters together—one letter together—but she'd make us send two—each of us one. They had to be newsy, and long, and she'd send them back to us with things like "That's not true," or "Don't abbreviate," or "Your sister said the same thing," if she didn't like them. Or spelling. Sis couldn't spell. She drank.

C: (*Incredulous.*) Your mother!?

A: What!? No, of course not. My *sister!*

B: Of course.

C: Even then?

A: When?

C: When you . . . when you first came to the city.

A: No, of course not! Later. Well, we'd have champagne when we went out—before the speakeasies. We would drink champagne and nibble on candied orange rind. *He* brings me some, sometimes, when he comes. Or flowers—freesia, when they're in season. It's the least he can do. And he *knows* it!

C: (*To* B; *an aside.*) Who? Who *is* this?

B: (*Absorbed with* A.) Shhhhhhh. Her son. He brings her pretty things.

A: We'd go out, but we didn't take each other's boyfriends. She was prim; I liked . . . wilder men, I suppose.

C: Tsk, tsk, tsk.

B: (*To* C; *amused.*) Why? Don't you?

A: We never liked the same boys . . . men. I don't think she liked men very much. Well, I *know* she didn't—sex, anyway. We had to make her get married, when she was almost forty—*get* someone for her. I don't think she wanted him; he was a wop.

C: (*Shakes her head.*) I don't believe it sometimes.

B: (*Sharp, as* A *tries to adjust herself in her chair.*) Why not? Wop, nigger, kike? I told you: it doesn't *mean* anything. It's the way she learned things.

C: From these strict but fair parents. (B *shrugs.*)

A: (*She has heard.*) I have Jewish friends and I have Irish friends, and I have South American friends—I *did*. Not Puerto Rican, or like that, but Venezuelan, and Cuban. Oh, we loved to go to Havana.

C: (*To* B, *more or less.*) Another world, eh?

B: Uh-huh.

A: I've never known any colored—well, *help,* yes. In Pinehurst they had colored help and we used to visit them there. They knew their place; they were polite, and well-behaved; none of those uppity niggers, the city ones.

C: (*Dismay.*) Oh, Jesus Christ!

A: He keeps telling me I can't say these things. I don't know what things he means. He said once he wouldn't come to see me anymore if I said those things. I don't know what things he means. What did he mean?

B: Don't worry yourself. Your sister married an *Italian*.

A: (*Confused.*) She did . . . what? Oh, that was later. I always had my eye out for the right man.

C: And she didn't?

A: No; she always thought everything would fall right into her lap. And it *did;* a *lot*. I had to work for *everything;* nothing came my way. I was tall and handsome; she was tall and pretty, tall but shorter, not as tall as I am . . . was. (*Weeps.*) I've shrunk! I'm not tall! I used to be so tall! Why have I shrunk!?

B: (*To* A; *patient.*) It happens with time: we get shorter. It happens every day, too: we're taller in the morning than we are at night.

A: (*Still weeping.*) How!?

B: The spine compresses as the day goes on.

A: (*Even weepier.*) I don't *have* one. I used to have a spine; I don't have one anymore!

C: (*To* B; *sotto voce.*) What does she mean?

B: She means osteoporosis.

A: (*To* C; *ugly; weeping down to sniveling.*) It hasn't happened to you yet? You wait!

B: . . . the spine collapses; you can fracture it by walking, turning around . . . whatever.

A: (*Weepy again.*) I used to be *tall!* I've shrunk!

C: (*To* B.) I know. (B *smiles.*)

A: (*Off again.*) *He* was *short*. A lot of my beaux were tall, but he was short.

C: (*Sotto voce; to* B.) Who *is* this?

B: (*Also sotto voce.*) Her husband, I think.

C: Oh; that's a long time ago.

A: Oh, I knew such tall boys, such dancers. Sis and I would dance all night with all the tall boys. Some of them were show boys—they were fairies—but some of them were regular. We would dance the night away; and sometimes I'd go off.

B: (*Smiling.*) Naughty girl!

A: I was the wild one. Sis would say to me, How can you *do* that!? and I'd laugh and I'd say, Oh, come on! I liked to have a good time, but I had my eye out. I always had my eye out. (*A shift of tone toward bitter.*) If I don't have my eye out, who will? I've always had to be on my toes, them sneaking around, stealing and . . . conniving. If I didn't keep my eye out we wouldn't have had *any*thing. His *sister!* That one she married? The first one! The dumpy little . . . dentist was he? What did *he* know about running an office? What did *he* know about handling money? Enough to steal! Enough to line his *own* pockets. And of course the old man kept his head turned the other way because the—what's his name, the dentist—was married to his precious daughter! Oh *that* one! Whining and finagling, wrapping him around her little finger! I had to stay one step ahead of *all* of them. I fixed 'em.

B: (*Proud of her.*) *Did* you?

A: (*Confused.*) What!?

B: *Did* you fix them?

A: (*Panicking.*) Who!? Who are you talking about!?

B: The ones you fixed.

A: How do *I* know? I don't know what you're talking about! Fix who!?

B: I don't *know.*

C: (*To help.*) The ones who were robbing you blind.

B: (*To* A.) Yes: those.

A: (*Grim.*) *Every*body's robbing me—right and left. Everybody steals. Everybody steals *some*thing.

B: (*Without comment.*) Including me? Do *I* steal?

A: (*Nervous laugh.*) I don't know. How would I know? He says I should have more money.

B: (*To* C.) Doesn't your office . . . ?

C: We deal with what comes *in*. There's more than one handles her money. There's plenty of chance, if anyone *wanted* to.

A: Sis used to envy me after I married. She never *did* well. I always had my eye out.

C: You use all your income as far as *I* can see.

A: Well, why not? It's mine.

C: Well, just don't complain. If you wanted an increase in principal, you'd have to . . .

A: *I* don't complain: I *never* complain. I have you, and I have her, (*Points to* B.) and I have the chauffeur, and I have this place here, and I have to look pretty, and sometimes I have the nurses—though they're black. Why *is* that?—and I have all those things . . . I have the cook, I have the . . .

C: I know; I know.

A: They all steal; every one of them.

B: (*After a pause; a sigh.*) Ah, well.

A: Sis didn't have her eye out; not like I did. I married him. He was short; he had one eye; one was glass; a golf ball hit him there; they took it out; he had a glass one.

C: Which eye?

B: (*To* C; *chiding.*) Oh, *come* on!

C: (*Amused.*) No, I want to know. (To A.) Which eye? Which eye was glass?

A: Which eye was . . . ? Well, I don't . . . (*Becomes weepy.*) I can't remember! I don't know which eye was the glass one! (*Full weep.*) I . . . can't . . . remember. I . . . can't . . . remember!

B: (*Moves to* A; *to comfort.*) Now, now; now, now.

A: I can't remember! (*Sudden venom.*) Get your *hands* off me! How *dare* you!

B: (*Retreating.*) Sorry; sorry.

A: (*To* B; *tearful again.*) Why can't I re*mem*ber anything?

B: I think you remember everything; I think you just can't bring it to mind all the time.

A: (*Quieting.*) Yes? Is that it?

B: Of course!

A: I remember everything?

B: Somewhere in there.

A: (*Laughs.*) My gracious! (*To* C.) I remember everything!

C: Gracious. That must be a burden.

B: *Be* nice.

C: Isn't salvation forgetting? Lethe, and all?

A: Who?

B: No one.

C: Lethe.

A: I don't *know* her. Well, maybe I do, I just don't have it right now. (*To* B.) Is that right?

B: That's *right*.

A: I *loved* my husband. (*Silly, remembering smile.*)

B: I bet you *did*.

A: He gave me pretty things; he gave me jewelry.

B: *Them's* pretty.

A: My God, he said, you're so big, so tall, you'll cost me a fortune! I can't give you little things. And he *couldn't.* I liked pearls and diamonds best.

C: No kidding!

B: (*Amused.*) Oh, hush!

A: I had my pearls, and I had some bracelets, and he wanted me to have another—he'd found one without telling me. We wore wide bracelets back then—diamond ones—wide, *this* wide. (*She demonstrates: two inches, or so.*) Flat and wide, the stones in designs, very . . . what? Very what?

B: Ornate.

A: Yes, ornate . . . and wide. We had been out—I'll never forget it, I'll never forget this—we'd been to a party, and we'd had champagne, and we were . . . what? Tipsy?, a little I suppose. And we came home and we were on the way to bed. We had our big bedroom, and it had its separate dressing rooms, and—you know—its separate bathrooms—and we were undressing; we were getting ready for bed. I was at my table, and I'd taken off my clothes—my shoes, my dress, and my underthings—and I was sitting there at my dressing table (*She really enjoys telling this: laughs, giggles, etc.*) and I was . . . well, I was naked; I didn't have a stitch, except I had on all my jewelry. I hadn't take off my jewelry.

B: How wonderful!

A: Yes!, and there I was, all naked with my pearls—my necklace—and my bracelets, my diamond bracelets . . . two, no; three! Three! And in he walked, naked as a jaybird—he was funny when he wanted to be—we were naked a lot, early on, pretty early on. All that stopped. (*Pause.*) Where am I?

B: In your story?

A: What?

B: In your story. Where are you in your story?

A: Yes; of course.

C: You're naked at your dressing table, and *he* walks in, and *he's* naked, too.

A: . . . as a jaybird; yes! Oh, I shouldn't *tell* this!

B: Yes! Yes, you should!

C: Yes!

A: Yes? Oh . . . well, there I was, and I had my big powder puff, and I was powdering myself, and I was paying attention to *that.* I knew he was there, but I wasn't paying attention. I *have* something for you, he said, I *have* something for you. And I was sitting there, and I raised my eyes and looked in the mirror and . . . no! I can't tell this!

B and C: (*Silly schoolgirls; ad lib.*) Yes, yes; tell, tell. Tell us! Yes! Tell us!

A: And I looked and there he was, and his . . . his pee-pee was all hard, and . . . and hanging on it was a new bracelet.

C: (*Awe.*) Oh, my God! (B *smiles.*)

A: And it was on his pee-pee, and he came close and it was the most beautiful bracelet I'd ever seen; it was diamonds, and it was wide, so wide and . . . I thought you might like this, he said. Oh, my goodness, it's so beautiful, I said. Do you want it? he said. Yes, yes! I said, Oh, goodness, yes! (*Mood shifts a little toward darkness.*) And he came closer, and his pee-pee touched my shoulder—he was short, and I was tall, or something. Do you want it? he said, and he poked me with it, with his pee-pee, and I turned, and he had a little pee-pee. Oh, I shouldn't say that; that's terrible to say, but I *know.* He had a little . . . *you* know . . . and there was the bracelet on it, and he moved closer, to my face, and Do you want it? I thought you might like it. And I said, No! I can't *do* that! You *know* I can't *do* that! And I couldn't; I could *never* do that, and I said, No! I can't do that! And he stood there for . . . well, I don't know . . . and his pee-pee got . . . well, it started to go soft, and the bracelet slid off, and it fell into my lap. I was naked; deep into my lap. Keep it, he said, and he turned and walked out of my dressing room. (*Long silence; finally she weeps, slowly, conclusively.*)

B: (*Eventually.*) It's all right; it's all right. (*Goes and comforts* A.)

C: (*Kindly.*) The wild one.

B: (*Still comforting.*) It's all right; it's all right.

A: (*Little child.*) Take me to bed; take me to bed.

B: Sure. (*To* C.) Help me. (*They ease her up from her chair and to the bed during the following.*)

A: (*Screams.*) My arm! My arm!

C: (*Terrified.*) I'm sorry!

A: Bed! I wanna go to bed!

B: All right now; we're almost there. (*At bed.*) O.K. Here we are.

A: (*Full baby.*) I wanna go to bed! (*It hurts!*) Oh! Oh! Oh!

B: All right, now. (A *is now on the bed, under covers, sitting up part way. Continued.*) There. Comfy?

C: (*To* B.) I'm sorry; I didn't mean to . . .

B: (*To* C.) It's all right. (*To* A.) Comfy?

A: (*Tiny voice.*) Yes. Thank you.

B: (*As she moves away from the bed.*) You're welcome.

C: I'm not good at . . . all that.

B: You'll get there.

C: I can't pro*ject.*

B: (*Comforting.*) Well, think of it this way: if you live long enough you won't have to; you'll be there.

C: Thanks.

B: And since it's the far past we're supposed to recall best—if we *get* to the future—you'll re*mem*ber not being able to project.

C: As I said: thanks.

B: (*Pause; sighs.*) *A*-ha.

C: (*Pause.*) What happens now?

B: (*Eyes closed.*) You tell *me.*

C: *You're* the one works here.

B: (*Smiles; eyes still closed.*) As I said: *you* tell *me.* (*Silence.*)

A: (*Propped up; eyes opening and closing from time to time, eyes wandering; very stream of consciousness.*) The things we're able to do and the things we're *not.* What we remember doing and what we're not sure. What do I re*mem*ber? I remember being *tall.* I remember first it making me unhappy, being taller in my class, taller than the boys. I remember, and it comes and goes. I think they're all robbing me. I *know* they are, but I can't prove it. I think I know, and then I can't remember what I know. (*Cries a little.*) He never comes to see me.

B: (*Mildly.*) *Yes,* he does.

A: When he has to; now and then.

B: More than most; he's a good son.

A: (*Tough.*) Well, I don't know about that. (*Softer.*) He brings me things; he brings me flowers—orchids, freesia, those big violets . . . ?

B: African.

A: Yes. He brings me those, and he brings me chocolates—

orange rind in chocolate, that dark chocolate I like; he does *that.* But he doesn't love me.

B: Oh, now.

A: He doesn't! He loves his . . . he loves his boys, those boys he has. You don't know! He doesn't love me and I don't know if I love him. I can't *remember!*

B: *He* loves you.

A: (*Near tears.*) I can't remember; I can't remember what I can't remember. (*Suddenly alert and self-mocking.*) Isn't *that* something!

B: (*Nicely.*) It certainly *is.*

A: (*Rambling again.*) There's so much: holding on; fighting for everything; *he* wouldn't do it; *I* had to do *everything*; tell him how handsome he was, clean up his blood. Everything came on *me:* Sis being that way, hiding her bottles in her night-things where she thought I wouldn't find them when she came to stay with me for a little; falling . . . falling down the way she did. Mother coming to stay, to live with us; he *said* she could; where else could she go? Did we like each other even? At the end? Not at the end, not when she hated me. I'm helpless she . . . she screamed; I hate you! She stank; her room stank; she stank; I hate you, she screamed at me. I think they all hated me, because I was strong, because I *had* to be. Sis hated me; Ma hated me; all those others, *they* hated me; *he* left home; he ran away. Because I was strong. I was tall and I was strong. *Somebody* had to be. If I wasn't, then . . . (*Silence;* A *is still, eyes open. Has she shuddered a little before her silence? After a bit* B *and* C *look at one another.* B *rises, goes to the bed, leans over, gazes at* A, *feels her pulse.*)

C: (*Looks over after a little.*) Is she . . . oh, my God, is she dead?

B: (*After a little.*) No. She's alive. I think she's had a stroke.

C: Oh, my God!

B: You better call her son. I'll call her doctor. (C *rises, exits right, looking at* A *as she exits;* B *strokes* A*'s head, exits left.* A *alone; still; silence.*)

END OF ACT ONE

ACT TWO

"A" *is propped up in bed.* (*Actually, a dummy with an exact life mask of the actress playing* A; *same costume as* A*'s in Act One. We must believe it to be* A; *a breathing mask over nose and mouth helps this.*)

Some silence. B *and* C *enter, opposite from their exits at the end of Act One and dressed differently from the way they were.* C *seats herself.* B *goes to the bed, looks at* "A."

B: (*General.*) No change.

C: (*Wistful.*) No?

B: That's the way it goes.

C: (*Shudders.*) Yes?

B: (*Grim.*) Something to look forward to. (*No response from* C. *Continued.*) No?

C: (*Hard.*) I don't want to *talk* about it; I don't want to *think* about it. Let me alone.

B: (*Sharp.*) It's worth thinking about—even at *your* age.

C: Let me *alone!*

B: (*Wandering about; touching things.*) It's got to be *some* way . . . stroke, cancer or, as the lady said, "heading in to the mountain with a jet." No? (*No response. Continued.*) *Or* . . . walking off a curb into a sixty-mile-an-hour wall . . .

C: *Stop* it!

B: Or . . . even worse; *think* about this . . . home alone in the evening, servants off, him out, at the Club, sitting home alone, the window jimmied, *they* get in, little cat feet and all, *find* you, sitting there in the upstairs sitting room . . .

C: I said: *stop* it!

B: (*Smiles.*) . . . find me sitting there in the upstairs sitting room, going over invitations, or whatever . . . bills; come up behind me, slit my throat, me thinking, Oh, my God, my throat's being slit, *if* that, if there's *time* for that.

C: (*Animal growl of protest.*) Arghhhhhhhh!

B: (*Tranquil.*) I'm almost done. Or I hear them . . . you hear them, turn around, see them—how many? Two? Three?—fall apart, start screaming, so they have to slit your throat, my throat, though they may not have planned it that way. All that blood on the Chinese rug. My, my.

C: (*Pause; curious.*) Chinese rug?

B: (*Very natural.*) Yes, beige, with rose embroidery all around the edges. We get it at auction.

C: I wouldn't know.

B: (*Momentary surprise.*) No; of course not; you *wouldn't*. You will, though—the rug, I mean. Clearly nobody slits your throat, or mine, for that matter. (*Considers it.*) Might be better.

C: (*Rue and helplessness.*) You have things to tell me, I suppose.

B: Oh, I certainly do. But, then again, I don't know everything either, *do* I?! (*Gestures towards* "A.")

C: (*She looks, too.*) I'll do a will; I'll do some paper won't let me go on if I get like that.

B: There *aren't* any . . . *weren't* any then, I tried. You can't get your way in this world. (A *enters during this next, from left.* A *is dressed in a lovely, lavender dress; sling gone.*)

C: There *must* be one. You have your way in everything and then you can't at the last? There *must* be!

A: There *must* be what? (*She is thoroughly rational during this Act.* B *and* C *are not surprised to see her.*)

C: A living will.

A: (*Observing* "A.") I was going to, but then I forgot, or it's slipped my mind, or something. He kept saying, Make one! He has one for himself, he says. I meant to; nothing much to do about it now. Any change?

B: No, we're . . . just as we were; no change.

A: I wonder how long *this'll* go on. I hope it's quick. What's her name took six years; not a move, not a blink, hooked up, breathed for, pissed for.

B: Do I know her?

A: No; after your time, so to speak.

B: A-*ha*.

A: A lot of money—a *lot*. The kids—hah! Fifty the youngest—the "kids" disagreed. They wanted to see the will first, the lawyer wouldn't *show* it to 'em, they came down on both sides—*kill* her off! *keep* her going! Not pretty.

C: (*Really beside herself.*) Stop it! Stop it!

A: (*To a naughty child.*) *Grow . . . up.*

B: (*Smiles.*) She will; she does.

A: Well; yes; of course. And so do *you*.

C: (*Rage.*) I will not become . . . *that!* (*Points to* "A.")

A: (*"Come off it."*) Oh, *really.*

B: (*"Oh, really!"*) Come *off* it.

C: I *won't.*

B: (*Smiles.*) What do you plan to *do* about it?

A: (*Amused.*) Yes; *that's* interesting.

C: (*To* A; *pointing to* B.) Nor will I become *this.*

B: (*A hoot.*) Hah! (C *comes down front and speaks to the audience.* A *and* B *relax, comment from time to time, react with each other, etc.*)

C: I *won't.* I *know* I won't—*that's* what I mean. That . . . (*Points to* "A.") . . . *thing* there? I'll never be like that. (B *hoots;* A *shakes her head, chuckles. Continued.*) *Nobody* could. I'm twenty-six; I'm a *good* girl; my mother was strict but fair—she still *is;* she *loves* me; she loves me and Sis, and she wants the very best for us. We have a *nice* little apartment, Sis and I, and at night we go out with our beaux, and I *do* have my eye out for . . . for what—"the man of my dreams"? And so does Sis, I *guess.* I don't think I've been in love, but I've been loved—by a couple of them, but they weren't the right ones.

B: (*Rue; to herself.*) They never *are.*

A: (*Purring.*) Hmmmm.

C: Mother taught us what the right one would be. We have fun with the others—dancing, staying out late, seeing the sun up sometimes. Things get a little . . . involved now and again, and that's fun too, though Sis doesn't think so as much as I do. They get involved, but they never get very . . . *serious.* I have my eye out, and we do have our *jobs.* We're mannequins: the fanciest shop in town!

B: I don't want that *known!*

A: (*To* B; *pleasantly chiding.*) Oh, stop; it was fun.

C: We go into work and we put on these lovely frocks, and we walk elegantly around the store, (*Imitates.*) among the ladies shopping, sometimes with their men, sometimes not, and we stop, and they touch our dresses—the silk, the fabric—and they ask us questions, and then we pass on to another group, to another section. We twirl, we . . . sashay. (*She does so;* B *imitates;* A, *too, but sitting. Continued; to* A *and* B.) We *do!*

B: Oh, I *know.*

A: Yes, we *know;* do *we know.*

C: (*To the audience again.*) Don't look at them; don't . . . listen to them. (A *and* B *laugh a little. Continued.*) We wear our beautiful evening gowns, and we parade about, and we know there are people looking at us, studying us, and we smile, and we . . . well, I suppose we flirt a little with the men who are doing it—the husbands, or whatever.

B: (*To* A; *mock astonishment.*) Flirt?! You!?

A: Me!? Flirt!?

B: (*Sashays; twirls.*) Wheeeeee!

A: (*Claps with one hand; her knee, probably.*) Brava! Brava!

B: (*Still sashaying.*) Wheeeeee!

C: Stop it! *Stay* out of my life!

B: Oh! My dear!

A: (*To* C.) I remember it differently, little one. I remember more . . . design. I remember a little calculation.

B: Oh, yes; a little calculation; a little design.

C: (*To audience.*) Don't listen to them. Design? What are they talking about?

B: (*Cheerful.*) Never mind.

C: (*To audience.*) They don't *know* me!

B: (*Looking at* A; *mocking.*) Nooooooooo!

C: *Remember* me!

A: (*Also mocking.*) Nooooooooo! (C *claps her hands over her ears, shuts her eyes. Continued.*) Oh, all right, dear; go on. (C *can't hear. Continued; louder.*) I said, go *on!*

B: (*Loud.*) She says go *on!*, honestly.

C: I am a . . . good . . . girl.

B: (*To* A.) Well, yes; I suppose so.

A: And not dumb.

C: I'm a good girl. I know how to attract *men*. I'm *tall;* I'm striking; *I* know how to do it. Sis slouches and caves her front in; I stand tall, breasts out, chin up, hands . . . just so. I walk between the aisles and they know there's somebody coming, that there's somebody *there.* But, I'm a *good girl.* I'm not a virgin, but I'm a good girl. The boy who took me was a good boy. (C *does not necessarily hear—or, at least, notice—the asides to come.*)

B: Oh, yes, he *was.*

A: Yes? Was he?

B: *You* remember.

A: (*Laughs.*) Well, it *was* a *while* ago.

B: But you *do* remember.

A: *Oh* yes, I remember him. He was . . .

C: . . . sweet and handsome; no, not handsome: beautiful. He was beautiful!

A: (*To* B.) He was; yes.

B: (*To* A *and herself.*) Yes.

C: He has coal-black hair and violet eyes and such a smile!

A: Ah!

B: Yes!

C: His body was . . . well, it was thin, but *hard;* all sinew and muscle; he fenced, he told me, and he was the one with the megaphone on the crew. When I held him when we danced, there was only sinew and muscle. We dated a lot; I liked him; I didn't tell Mother, but I liked him a lot. I like him, Sis, I said; I really like him. Have you told Mother? No, and don't *you;* I like him a lot, but I don't *know.* Has he? . . . *you* know. No, I said; no, he hasn't. But then he did. We were dancing—slowly—late, the end of the evening, and we danced so close, all . . . pressed, and . . . we were pressed, and I could feel that he was hard, *that* muscle and sinew, pressed against me while we danced. We were the same height and he looked into my eyes as we danced, slowly, and I felt the pressure up against me, and he tensed it and I felt it move against me.

B: (*Dreamy.*) Whatever is *that,* I said.

A: Hmmmmmmmm.

C: Whatever is *that,* I said. I *knew,* but whatever is that, I said, and he smiled, and his eyes shone, and it's me in love with you, he said. You have an interesting way of showing it, I said. Appropriate, he said, and I felt the muscle move again, and . . . well, I knew it was time; I knew I was ready, and I knew I wanted him—whatever that *meant*—that I wanted *him,* that I wanted *it.*

B: (*Looking back; agreeing.*) Yes; oh, yes.

A: Hmmmmmmmm.

C: Remember, don't give it away, Mother said; don't give it away like it was nothing.

B: (*Remembering.*) They won't respect you for it and you'll get known as a loose girl. *Then* who will you marry?

A: (*To* B.) Is that what she said? I can't remember.

B: (*Laughs.*) *Yes* you can.

C: They won't respect you for it and you'll get known as a loose girl. *Then* who will you marry? But he was pressed against me, exactly against where he wanted to be—we were the same height—and he was *so* beautiful, and his eyes shone, and he smiled at me and he moved his hips as we danced, so slowly, as we danced, and he breathed on my neck and he said, you don't want me to embarrass myself right here on the dance floor, do you?

B: (*Remembering.*) No, no; of course not.

C: I said, no, no; of course not. Let's go to my place, he said, and I heard myself saying (*Incredulous.*) I'm not that kind of girl? I mean, as soon as I said it I blushed: it was so . . . stupid, so . . . expected. Yes, you are, he said; *you're* that kind of girl.

B: And I was, and my God it was wonderful.

A: It hurt! (*Afterthought; to* B.) Didn't it?

B: (*Admonishing.*) Oh . . . well, a little.

C: You're that kind of girl, and I guess I was. We did it a lot. (*Shy.*) I know it's trite to say your first time is your best, but he was wonderful, and I know I'm only twenty-six now and there've been a few others, and I imagine I'll marry, and I'll be very happy.

B: (*Grudging.*) Well . . .

A: We'll talk about happy sometime.

C: I *know* I'll be very happy, but will I ever *not* think about him? He was long and thick and knew what I wanted, what I needed, and while I couldn't do . . . you know: the thing he wanted . . . I just *couldn't:* I *can't.*

B: (*Stretches.*) Nope; never could.

A: (*Sort of dreamy.*) I wonder why.

C: (*Very agitated; upset.*) I tried! I wanted to do what . . . but I choked, and I . . . (*Whispered.*) I threw up. I just . . . couldn't.

A: (*To* C.) Don't worry about it; don't worry about what can't be helped.

B: *And* . . . there's more than one way to skin a cat.

A: (*Puzzles that.*) Why?

B: Hm?

A: *Why* is there more than one way to skin a *cat?*

B: (*Puzzles that.*) Why not?

A: Who needs it!? Isn't one way *enough?*

C: (*To the audience; still; simply.*) I just want you to know that I'm a good girl, that I was a good girl.

B: (*To* C.) You meet him in two years.

C: (*Self-absorbed.*) What? Who?

B: (*Pleasant.*) Your husband. We're what—twenty-six? We'll meet him in two years.

C: (*Making light of it.*) The man of my dreams?

B: Well, a man you'll *dream* about.

A: For a long, long time.

C: Like the boy I was . . .

A: Well, yes, he was wonderful, but then there's life.

B: (*To* A.) *How* long?

A: Hm?

B: How *long?*

A: *Long* enough. (*To* B.) You're . . . what?!

B: Fifty-two.

A: (*Calculating.*) I marry when I'm twenty-eight; you're sixty-six when he dies. (*To* C; *smiles.*) We have him a good long time.

B: (*Musing.*) Another fourteen years.

A: Yes, but the last *six* aren't much fun.

C: That's almost forty years with one man.

B: (*To* C; *chuckles.*) Well, more or less: more or less one man. (*To* A.) No? Not much fun?

A: Not much.

C: How *is* he? Have I *met* him?

B: The one-eyed man? The little one; the little one-eyed man?

A: (*Chuckles.*) Oh, now.

C: (*Confused.*) What?

B: The one we meet at the party—Sis and me. Sis is with him, but I see him looking over at me.

A: (A *pleased recalling.*) Yes!

B: Sis doesn't much care, I don't think.

C: More or less? What is this more or less?

A: Hm?

B: (*Mildly annoyed.*) I beg your pardon?

C: I said almost forty years with one man; you said, more or less; more or less one man.

B: Oh? Ah! Well, what are you expecting? Monogamy or something?

C: Yes! If I care: yes!

B: (*To* A.) Remember monogamy?

A: (*Pretends to puzzle it.*) No. (*New tone; to* B.) *You* can talk about monogamy, if you like—pro and con, if you like. Leave me out of *that* one.

B: (*General.*) Infidelity is a matter of spirit—isn't that what they say? Aside from bad taste, disease, confusion as to where you live, having to lie all the time—*and* remember the lies! (*To* A.) God, remember the lies?

A: Hmmmm. Well, there wasn't much, not *too* much.

B: Except for the groom, eh?

A: Oh, my! The groom.

C: Why do I marry him?

B: Who—the groom? (A *and* B *laugh.*)

C: The one-eyed man! I marry the one-eyed man!

B: Yes, you do.

C: Why!?

B: (*To* C.) Why do I *marry* him? (*To* A.) Why did I *marry* him?

A: (*To* B.) Why did I?

B: Hmmmmmmmm.

C: *Tell* me.

B: Because he makes me *laugh*. Because he's little and he's funny looking—and little like a penguin.

A: (*Has she thought this before?*) Yes! Quite a bit like one.

B: (*Generous.*) Well . . . especially in his bib and tucker.

C: (*Some panic.*) Why would I marry him if I'm going to cheat on *him?*

A: (*Smiles.*) Why would you marry him if he's going to cheat on *you?*

C: I don't *know!*

B: Calm down; adjust; settle in. Men cheat; men cheat a *lot*. We cheat *less,* and we cheat because we're lonely; men cheat because they're men.

A: No. We cheat because we're bored, sometimes. We cheat to get back; we cheat because we don't know any better; we cheat because we're whores. *We* cheat for *lots* of reasons. Men cheat for only one—as you say, because they're men.

C: *Tell* me about him!

A: Don't you want to be surprised?

C: No!

B: You've seen him, or . . . he's seen *you*. I don't think you've met him. He's something of what they call a playboy—at least in *my* time, not yours. He's rich—or his father is—and he's divorcing his second wife; she's just plain bad; the first one drank; still does.

A: That one dies eventually—eighty, or something: pickled; preserved.

C: (*Timid again.*) What's he like?

B: (*Expansive.*) Well . . . he's short, and he has one eye, and he's a great dancer—'cept he keeps running into things, the eye, you know—and he sings like a dream! A lovely tenor—and he's funny! God, he's funny!

A: (*Wistful.*) Yes; yes, he was.

B: (*Pleased.*) And he likes tall women!

A: (*Still wistful.*) Yes; yes, he did.

C: (*Uncertain.*) I *have seen* him?

B: He tells me—I think I remember—he tells me he saw me with Sis before he dated her, that I was taller, that he had—you'll forgive the joke—his eye on me. (*To* A.) Didn't he tell you that—that he had his eye on us?

A: (*True.*) I can't remember. He was going with that comedienne did the splits, the eight-foot one.

B: Well, you put a stop to that soon enough.

A: Once you got your claws into him you mean?

C: (*Puzzling.*) Why did I *like* him? Is funny enough? Is having a voice, is dancing enough?

B: Don't forget one eye.

A: Oh, he was *nice;* we liked him a lot.

C: *Liked? Liked* him a lot.

B: (*Looking right at* C.) Oh, stop it! You're twenty-six years old, which is not a tot; there *is* the future to look out for . . .

A: . . . and he *is* rich, or is going to be: rich family.

C: I don't *believe* this.

A: (*Sharp.*) Our father *dies.*

B: (*About her father.*) I *loved him.*

C: No! He doesn't!

B: *Every*body does.

A: (*To herself.*) Except me, maybe.

B: (*To* C.) Except *us.*

C: I *love* him!

B: Well, that should be enough to keep the old heart going: Jesus, she loves me; how can I go and die on her?

C: Is it . . . quick?

A: (*Pensive.*) I don't remember.

B: Not bad: heart *failure,* fluid in the lungs, some bad breathing; oh, God, the terror in the eyes! (C *begins to weep;* B *notices. Continued.*) We did that, yes. We cried when Dad died. I cried; Sis cried; Mom went out on the porch and did it there.

A: (*Loss.*) I don't remember.

C: What happens to Ma?

B: She holds out; she stays on alone for almost twenty years, and then she moves in with us. (*To* A.) How does it *go?*

A: (*Toneless.*) What? She becomes an enemy. She dies when she's eighty-four—seventeen years of it, staying up in her room in the big house with us. The colitis, the cigarettes, the six or seven Pekingese she goes through. I stopped liking her.

C: I *couldn't!*

A: (*Shrugs.*) She becomes an enemy.

B: (*Interested, but not too much.*) How?

A: (*Sighs.*) She comes to resent me; she starts to resent getting old, getting . . . helpless—the eyes, the spine, the mind. She starts to resent that I have—we have—so much, and that I'm being generous—*we're* being generous. She snaps at everything; she sides with Sis; she criticizes me.

B: (*Some awe.*) She wasn't *like* that.

C: No! She *couldn't* be.

A: I don't care. Forget I told you. She never moved in; she's still alive up there in the country, in the same house, she's a hundred and thirty-seven now, does her own baking, jogs three times a week . . .

B: *All* right; *all* right.

A: (*To* B.) There's more. You want to hear it? (B *shakes her head. Continued; to* C.) Of course *you* don't. (C *shakes her head. Continued.*) No, of course not. Anyhow, you marry him.

C: (*Getting it straight.*) I do.

A: Yes; he's fun, and he's nice.

B: He sings . . .

A: He dances . . .

B: . . . and he's rich, or going to be . . .

A: . . . and he loves tall women.

B: And you suddenly realize you love short men.

A: Penguins. (A *and* B *both giggle.*)

B: (*Still to* C.) *And* it goes all right. His mother doesn't *like* me—doesn't *like* you—at all, but the old *man* does.

A: He certainly does! "You're tall; I bet you're hot stuff."

B: (*To* C.) You win him over. (*To* A.) You know, I think the old buzzard had letch for us?

A: Yes; *I* think so.

B: And, boy did he want a *grand*son.

A: Oh, that made him happy.

C: (*Wonder.*) I have children?

B: (*None too pleasant.*) We have one; we have a boy.

A: (*Same.*) Yes, we do. I have a son. (*He appears in the right archway, stands stock still, stares at "A" on the bed.*)

B: (*Seeing him; sneering.*) Well, fancy seeing you again. (*Sudden, and enraged, into his face.*) Get out of my house! (*He doesn't react.*)

C: (*Rising.*) Stop it! (*Moves toward him.*) Is . . . is that him?

B: I said, get out of my house!

A: (*To* B.) Do be quiet. (*To* C.) Let him alone; he's come to see me. (*He goes to "A," sits on a chair left of her, takes her left arm; his shoulders shake; he puts his forehead to her arm, or it to his forehead, becomes still. Does not react to anything about him until indicated. Continued.*) That's it; do your duty.

C: He's . . . my goodness. How nice; how handsome, how very . . .

B: You wouldn't say that if you knew!

A: Shhhhhhh.

B: (*To* A.) She wouldn't! (*To him.*) Filthy little . . . !

A: Shhhhhh. Shhhhhh. I don't want to think about *that*. He came back; he never loved me, he never loved us, but he came back. Let him alone.

C: He's so young.

A: Yes . . . well. This is how he looked when he went away, took his life and one bag and went off. (*To* B.) No?

B: (*To his back; less venom, but mixed with hurt.*) You wore that coat the day you left. I thought I told you to get your hair cut!

A: Yes; yes, he did; he wore that coat. I'm leaving, he said, and he took one bag. (*Pause.*) *And* his life.

C: (*Bewildered.*) He went away from me? Why?

B: (*Bitter.*) Maybe you changed; they say you changed; I haven't noticed. (*To* A.) He comes back? He comes back to me—to me? I let him?

A: Sure. We have a heart attack; they tell him; he comes back. Twenty-plus years? That's a long enough sulk—on both sides. He didn't come back when his father died.

B: (*Scathing.*) Of course not!

A: But he came to me. They call me up and they tell me he's coming to see me; they say he's going to call. He calls. I hear his voice and it all floods back, but I'm formal. Well, hello there, I say. Hello there to you, he says. Nothing about this shouldn't have happened. Nothing about I've missed you, not even that little lie. Sis is visiting; she's lying drunk and passed out upstairs and not even that little lie. I thought I'd come over. Yes, you do that. He comes; we look at each other and we both hold in whatever we've been holding in since that day he went away. You're looking well, he says; and you, too, I say. And there are no apologies, no recriminations, no tears, no hugs; dry lips on my dry cheeks; yes that. And we never discuss it? Never go into why? Never go beyond where we are? We're strangers; we're curious about each other; we leave it at that.

B: I'll *never* forgive him.

A: (*Wistful, sad.*) No; I never do. But we play the game. We dine; he takes me places—mother, son going to formal places. We never . . . reminisce. Eventually he lets me talk about when he was a little boy, but he never has an opinion on that; he doesn't seem to have an opinion on much of anything that has to do with us, with me.

B: (*Clenched teeth.*) Never!

A: (*To* B.) Or with *you*. (*To* C; *and sad smile.*) Or *you*.

C: Did we . . . did we drive him away? Did I change so?

B: (*Rage.*) He left!! He packed up his attitudes and he *left!!* And I never want to see him again. (*To him.*) Go away!! (*Angry, humiliated, tears.*)

A: (*Very calm; sad smile.*) Well, yes you *do*, you see. You *do* want to see him again. *Wait* twenty years. Be alone except for her upstairs passed out on the floor, and the piano top with the photos in the silver frames, and the butler, and . . . be all alone; you *do* want to see him again, but the terms are too hard. We never forgive him. We let him come, but we never forgive him. (*To him.*) I bet you don't know *that* . . . *do* you!?

C: (*To* A.) How did we change? (*To him.*) How did I change? (*He strokes "*A*'s" face, shudders a little.*)

B: Don't bother yourself. He *never* belonged.

C: (*Enraged.*) I don't believe it!

B: (*Furious.*) Let it *alone!*

C: No! How did I *change!?* What *happened* to me!?

A: (*Sighs.*) Oh, God.

C: (*Determined.*) How did I *change!?*

B: (*Sarcasm; to the audience.*) She wants to know how she *changed*. She wants to know how she turned into *me*. Next she'll want to know how I turned into *her.* (*Indicates* A.) No; I'll want to know *that; maybe* I'll want to know that.

A: Hahh!

B: *Maybe.* (To C.) You want to know how I changed?

C: (*Very alone.*) I don't know. *Do* I?

B: Twenty-six to fifty-two? Double it? Double your pleasure, double your fun? Try *this.* Try *this* on for size. They *lie* to you. You're growing up and they go out of their way to hedge, to qualify, to . . . to evade; to avoid—to *lie.* Never tell it how it is—how it's *going* to be—when a half-truth can be got in there. Never give the alternatives to the "pleasing prospects," the "what you have to look forward to." God, if they did the streets'd be littered with adolescent corpses! Maybe it's better they don't.

A: (*Mild ridicule.*) They? *They?*

B: Parents, teachers, all the others. You *lie* to us. You don't tell us things change—that Prince Charming has the morals of a sewer rat, that you're supposed to *live* with that . . . a*nd* like it, or give the ap*pear*ance of liking it. Chasing the chambermaid into closets, the kitchen maid into the root cellar, and God knows *what* goes on at the stag at the Club! They probably nail the whores to the billiard tables for easy access. Nobody *tells* you any of this.

A: (*Laying it on.*) Poor, poor you.

C: The root cellar?

B: (*To* A *and* C.) Hush. No wonder one day we come back from riding, the horse all slathered, snorting, and he takes the reins, the groom does, and he helps us dismount, the groom does, his hand touching the back of our thigh, and we notice, and he notices we notice, and we remember that we've noticed him before, most especially bare chested that day heaving the straw, those arms, that butt. And no wonder we smile in that way he understands so quickly, and no wonder he leads us into a further stall—into the fucking *hay,* for God's sake!—and down we go, and it's revenge and self-pity we're doing it for until we notice it turning into pleasure for its own sake, for *our* own sake, and we're dripping wet and he rides us like we've seen in the pornos and we actually scream, and then we lie there in the straw—which probably has shit on it—cooling down, and tells us he's wanted us a lot, that he likes big women, but he didn't dare, and will he get fired now? And I say, no, no of course you won't and for a month more of it I don't, but then I do; I do have him fired, because it's dangerous not to, because it's a good deal I've got with the penguin, a long-term deal in spite of the crap he pulls, and you'd better keep your nose clean—or polished, anyway—for the *real* battles—for the penguin's *other* lady folk, the *real* ones—the mother who just doesn't like you for no good reason except her daughter hates you, fears you and hates you—*envies* and therefore hates you—dumpy, stupid, whining little bitch! Just *doesn't* like you—maybe in part because she senses the old man's got the letch for you and besides, no girl's good enough for the penguin, not *her* penguin; the first two sure weren't and this one's not going to be either. Try to keep on the good side of the whole wretched family, stand up for your husband when he won't do it for himself, watch out for all the intrigue; start *really* worrying about your sister who's really stopped worrying about herself—about *anything;* watch your own mother begin to change even more than you're aware *you* are, and then try to raise that!? (*Points to him.*) That!?—gets himself thrown out of every school he can find, even one or two we haven't sent him to, sense he hates you, catch him doing it with your niece-in-law *and* your nephew-in-law the same week!? Start reading the letters he's getting from—how do they call it?—older friends?, telling him how to outwit *you,* how to survive living with his awful family; tell him you'll brain him with the fucking crystal ashtray if he doesn't stop getting letters, doesn't stop saying anything, doesn't stop . . . just . . . doesn't . . . stop? And he sneers, and he says very quietly that he can have me put in jail for opening his mail. Not while you're a minor, I tell him; you just wait, I tell him, you just wait; I'll have you thrown out of this house so quick it'll make your head spin. *You're* going to fire me, he says, quietly, smiling; You going to *fire* me too!? Just like you fired *him?* He's good in bed, *isn't* he!? Of course, *you* wouldn't know about *bed,* he says. He gets up, stops by me, touches my hair. I thought I saw some straw, he says; sorry. And he walks out of the solarium, out of the house, out of our lives. He doesn't say goodbye to either of us. He says goodbye to Mother, upstairs; he says goodbye to the Pekingese, too, I imagine. He packs one bag, and he leaves. (*To him; rage.*) Get out of my house!! (*Pause; to* C.) Does that tell you a little something about change? Does that tell you what you want to know?

C: (*Pause; softly.*) Yes. Thank you. (*Silence.*)

A: (*Curious.*) You want some more?

C: No, thank you.

B: I shouldn't *think* so.

A: Yes, you *do;* you *want* more.

C: (*Trying to stay polite.*) I said, no, thank you.

A: *That* doesn't cut any ice around here. (*Points to* B.) How you got to *her* is one thing; how you got to me is another. How do you put it . . . that *thing* there? (*Points to* "A.")

C: *I'm* sorry.

A: Well . . . maybe.

B: Yeah, I've got a few doubts about *that* route myself.

A: You!

B: *Yeah:* well. I'm not so bad. There's been shit, but there've been *good* times, too. Some of the best.

A: (*Oddly bright.*) Of course; there are always good times: like when we broke our back. (*To* C.) You break your back.

B: (*Laughs a little.*) Yeah; you sure *do.*

C: (*Scared of this.*) I do?

B: Snap!

A: (*Smiles.*) Well, not exactly. Snap! Really!

B: I should *know;* it was *only* ten years ago, and . . .

A: Riding, yes; jumping. We never liked jumping—hunters; saddle horse, yes, hunters, no. Brutes, every one of them, brutes or hysterics; but hunters it was *that* day, entertaining some damn fools. Brisk, burned leaves in the air, smell of burning, just dawn; mist on the ground, dawn all green and yellow. (*To* B.) We didn't like our *mount,* did we?

B: No.

A: No, I didn't *like* her; she was hysteric *and* a brute.

C: When do I learn to ride? I mean really *ride.*

B: It goes with the marriage.

A: Yes, I didn't trust her; I'd ridden her earlier that fall; she was stupid and cantankerous, shied at a moving shadow. (*To* C.) I said to him, you go on, I'll stay; you go on.

B: Yes.

A: But he looked so hurt I said, oh, all right, and off we went, into the wood, the green, the gold, the mist knee high to a . . . to your knees! Stupid *cow* of a horse! Couldn't she see the fence in the mist? Did she come on it too fast and shy like that? Over we *went!*

B: Over we *went.*

C: Oh, no!

A: (*To* B.) Could have broken my *neck,* I suppose. Lucky.

B: Well, yes, there *is* that.

A: (*To* B.) We never mounted a hunter again, did we?

B: Nope.

A: Damned cast weighed a ton! And you know what I thought about most?

B: (*Remembering.*) Who's he doing it with? who's he got cornered in what corner? what hallway? who he's poking his little dick into?

A: That he might leave us, that he might decide to get one isn't broken.

C: (*Awe.*) What kind of man *is* this!?

A: (*To* C.) Man-man.

B: (*To* C.) Man-man.

C: How was this happy time? Good times, you said?

B: (*To* C.) Oh, well, we proved we were human. (*To* A.) No?

A: (*To* B.) Of course. (*To* C.) We were fallible. Once you fall—whether you get up or not—once you fall, and they see it, they know you can be pushed. Whether you're made of crockery and smash into pieces, or you're bronze and you clang when you topple, it makes no never-mind; it's the plinth is important.

B: (*To* C.) To translate . . .

C: Thank you.

A: (*Sweet smile.*) Thank you.

B: To translate . . . you can go around fixing the *world*, patching everything up—*everyone*—and they're *grate*ful to you—grudgingly, but grateful—but once you fall yourself, prove you're not quite as *much* better than they are, than they thought, then they'll *let* you go right on doing everything for them, fixing the world, etcetera, but they won't hate you quite so much . . . because you're not perfect.

A: (*Very bright.*) And so everything's *better.* Nice and better. Doesn't that make it a good time? He *doesn't* leave you for something else; he's sweet and gives you a big diamond ring, and you don't have to get back up on a hunter anymore. Doesn't that make it a happy time?

C: Do I get to shoot the horse?

B: (*Laughs.*) I *beg* your pardon!?

A: (*Whoops!*) Whoooooo! Never occurred to me! (A *and* B *laugh together.*)

C: (*Grit.*) I'll never become you—either of you.

B: (*Looks at* C.) Oh, stop! (*To* A.) And the great ring—the big diamond? You don't wear it anymore?

A: (*Suddenly sober.*) Gone.

B: (*Sobered too.*) Oh?

A: I *sold* it.

B: Oh?

A: (*A little bitter.*) I've sold *everything.* Well, not everything . . . but most. Money doesn't go as far these days? Money doesn't go *anywhere!* I have no money. I have *money,* but I eat into it . . . every year; every year it's less.

B: We should cut back; we should . . .

A: Don't talk to me about cutting back! It's all paste! It's fake! All the jewelry sitting in the vault, in the bank? It's all fake!

C: Why is there? Why do you . . . why do we *bother?*

A: (*Contempt.*) Huh!

B: (*To* C, *then to* A.) Because we take it out and we wear it? Because the fake look as good as the real, even feels the same, and why should anybody know our business? (*Specifically to* A.) No?

C: Appearances?

B: Appearances? That which appears to be?

C: I mean, who are we trying to impress?

A: Ourselves. You'll learn. I took the big diamond in. When we bought it—when he brought it in for me, he said . . .

B: . . . this is a perfect stone; I've never seen a better one. You ever want to sell this you bring it back to me I'll give you better than you paid for it. He patted my hand. Pat-pat.

A: Pat-pat. And so I took it back—after he died, after the cancer and all, after all that. They looked at it; they said it was deeply flawed, or it was cloudy . . . or something.

B: Sons of bitches!

A: They offered me a third of what he paid for it, and the dollar wasn't worth half of what it had been?

C: (*To* A.) Didn't you sue? (*To* B.) I mean, what can we do? We just can't . . .

A: (*Accepting.*) What can you *do?* There's nothing you can *do.* You go *on;* you . . . eat *into* yourself. Starving people absorb their own bodies. The money's there—the investments are there, except less each year; it absorbs itself. It's all you've planned to *count* on *isn't;* the extras?

B: (*To* A.) The big diamond, eh?

A: The big diamond . . . *and* most of the rest. Well, what does it matter? It's all glitter.

C: (*Protest.*) No! It's more than that! It's tangible proof . . . that we're valuable . . . (*Embarrassed.*) that we're valued.

A: (*Shrugs.*) Well, it's gone; all the glitter's gone.

B: (*Rue.*) Yup. (*Waves.*) Bye.

C: Are there any *other* surprises?

B: (*Grating laugh.*) Oh, yeah; lots!

A: Oh, my dear; you just wait. (*Over toward the bed.*) She hides the money. Whatever she gets for the jewelry she keeps in cash, and spends a little whenever there isn't enough of the regular. There's a lot; she can't spend it all—without people knowing what she's doing, I mean. She hides it, and then eventually she can't remember where she hid it, and she can't find it . . . ever. And she can't tell anybody. (*Silence.*)

B: (*A little shy.*) Is the cancer bad?

A: When is it good?

C: *How* bad?

A: (*Mocking*). Fill me *in;* fill me in! (*To* C.) Pretty terrible! (*To* B; *softer tone.*) Six years; I told you that; it takes him six years from when he knows it—when they tell him he has it—to when he goes. Prostate—spreads to the bladder, spreads to the bone, spreads to the brain, and to the liver, of course; everything does—the *ancients* knew something. It's all right at first—except for the depression, *and* the fear—it's all right at first, but then the pain comes, slowly, growing, and then the day he screams in the bathroom, and I rush in; I expect to see him lying there, but no, he's standing at the toilet, and his face is filled with horror and he points to the bowl, and I look, and it's all pink in there, that the blood is coming with the urine now. And it's all downhill from there: the pink becomes red, and then there's blood in the bed, at night, as I'm lying with him, holding him; and then there's . . . no! Why go on with it!? (*To* C; *ugly.*) It's terrible! And there's nothing you can do to prepare yourself! I don't like you; you deserve it!

C: (*So softly.*) Thank you.

haven't happened yet. They're to *come.* Aren't they? Please? And . . . and whatever evil comes, whatever loss and taking away comes, won't it all be balanced out? Please? I'm not a fool, but there *is* a lot of happiness along the way. *Isn't* there!? And isn't it always ahead? Aren't I *right?* Aren't I? I mean . . . all along the way? No? Please? (B *comes to the right or left of* C, *leaving center free for* A *later.* B *shakes her head to* C, *not unkindly.*)

B: Silly, silly girl; silly baby. The happiest time? Now; now . . . always. This must be the happiest time: half of being adult done, the rest ahead of me. Old enough to be a *little* wise, past being *really* dumb . . . (*An aside to* C.) No offense.

C: (*Looking forward: tight smile.*) None taken.

B: Enough shit gone through to have a sense of the shit that's ahead, but way past sitting and *playing* in it. This *has* to be the happiest time—in theory, anyway. Things nibble away, of course; your job is to know *that,* too. The wood *may* be rotten under your feet—your nicely spread legs—and you'll be up to your ass in sawdust and dry rot before you know it, before you know it, before you can say this is the happiest time. Well, I can *live* with that, *die* with that. I mean, these things happen, but what I like most about being where I am—and fifty *is* a peak, in the sense of a mountain.

C: (*An aside.*) Fifty-two.

B: Yes, I know, thank you. What I like most about being where I am is that there's a lot I don't have to go through anymore, and that doesn't mean closing down—for *me,* at any rate. It opens up whole vistas—of decline, of obsolescence, peculiarity, but really *interesting!* Standing up here right on top of the middle of it *has* to be the happiest time. I mean, it's the only time you get a three-hundred-and-sixty-degree view—see in all directions. Wow! What a view! (A *moves to center,* B *and* C *stay where they are.*)

A: (*Shakes her head; chuckles; to* B *and* C.) You're both such children. The happiest moment of all? Really? The happiest moment? (*To the audience now.*) Coming to the end of it, I think, when all the waves cause the greatest woes subside, leaving breathing space, time to concentrate on the greatest woe of all—that blessed one—the end of it. Going through the whole thing and coming out . . . not out *beyond* it, of course, but sort of to . . . one side. None of that "further shore" nonsense, but to the point where you *can* think about yourself in the third person without being crazy. I've waked up in the morning, and I've thought, well, now, she's waking up, and now she's going to see what works—the eyes, for example. Can she *see?* She *can?* Well, good, I suppose; so much for that. Now she's going to test all the other stuff—the joints, the inside of the mouth, and now she's going to have to pee. What's she going to do—go for the walker. Lurch from chair to chair—pillar to post? Is she going to call for somebody—anybody . . . the tiniest thought there might be nobody there, that she's not making a sound, that maybe she's not alive—so's anybody'd notice, that is? *I* can do that. I can think about myself that way, which means, I suppose, that that's the way I'm *living*—beside myself, to one side. Is that what they mean by that? I'm beside myself? I don't think so, I think they're talking about *another* kind of joy. There's a difference between knowing you're going to *die* and *knowing* you're going to die. The second is better; it moves away from the theoretical. I'm rambling, aren't I?

B: (*Gently; face forward.*) A little.

A: (*To* B.) Well, we *do* that at ninety, or whatever I'm supposed to be; I mean, give a girl a break! (*To the audience again.*) Sometimes when I wake up and start thinking about myself like that—like I was watching—I really get the feeling that I *am dead*, but going on at the same time, and I wonder if she can talk and fear and . . . and then I wonder which has died—me, or the one I think about. It's a fairly confusing business. I'm rambling. (*She gestures to stop* B.) Yes; I know! (*Out.*) I was talking about . . . what: coming to the end of it; yes. So. There it is. You asked, after all. That's the happiest moment. (A *looks to* C *and* B, *puts her hands out, takes theirs. Continued.*) When it's all done. When we stop. When we can stop.

END OF PLAY

INDEPENDENCE

Lee Blessing

To Jeanne Blake,
the Eugene O'Neill
Theater Center,
and Actors Theatre of Louisville

INDEPENDENCE was given its professional premiere by the Actors Theatre of Louisville during its Eighth Annual Humana Festival of New American Plays in February 1984. It was directed by Patrick Tovatt; the scenery was designed by Paul Owen; the costumes were designed by Geoffrey T. Cunningham; and the sound design was by James M. Bay. The cast was as follows:

JO	Shelley Crandall
KESS	Deborah Hedwall
SHERRY	Gretchen West
EVELYN	Sylvia Gassell

CHARACTERS

EVELYN BRIGGS: 53
KESS: her daughter, 33
JO: her daughter, 25
SHERRY: her daughter, 19

TIME: Late May. The present.

PLACE: Independence, Iowa.

ACT ONE

Scene 1 Late Thursday afternoon
Scene 2 Saturday morning, two days later
Scene 3 The same day, around noon
Scene 4 Sunday evening, the next day

ACT TWO

Scene 1 Thursday evening, four days later
Scene 2 Friday afternoon, the next day
Scene 3 Late, the same night
Scene 4 Saturday afternoon, the next day
Scene 5 Sunday morning, the next day

ACT ONE

Scene One

Interior of an old frame house. Downstage is the living room, Upstage is the front porch. The effect should be of a dark room in the foreground, backed by the bright afternoon sunlight coming through the porch. Right is a door to SHERRY'S *room. Left, a door to the kitchen. Up Right, a hallway leads upstairs. Up Left, an archway leading to the dining room. The living room is filled with old-fashioned furniture: a couch, overstuffed chairs, etc. Well kept up.*

After a moment, JO *comes through the screen door, onto the porch. She wears an orthopedic collar.* KESS *follows, carrying a travel bag.*

JO: I can't believe it! You look incredible, you're so tan. How do you get so tan in Minneapolis?

KESS: Jo, shouldn't you be lying down?

JO: Oh, I'm fine. Here, let me take your bag . . .

KESS: That's OK. I've got it . . .

JO: (*Entering the living room.*) Well, come on in. Take a look at the old place. What do you think? After four years.

KESS: (*Remaining on the threshold.*) I think you should be lying down.

JO: Don't worry. This is my last day to wear this. The doctor said I'm fine if I don't move fast.

KESS: On the phone you said it was an emergency.

JO: It is an emergency.

KESS: You said you were laid up. I came down because I thought you couldn't get out of bed.

JO: I have been laid up. It's just that . . .

KESS: What do you mean? You're waltzing all over the room. If you've only got a minor injury . . .

JO: I broke my neck. Well . . . I chipped it. One of those little bones back there. The doctor said I could have been paralyzed for life. Really. I could have died. (*Of the collar.*) I've had to wear this for a week, I strained the muscles so bad.

KESS: You made me leave my work—you made me drive for hours—because you chipped your neck?

JO: Well . . . yes.

KESS: Why?

JO: Are you going to come in or not? (KESS *turns to go.*) Kess! That's not funny. (KESS *stops, looks at her.*) Please come in. (KESS *enters, stands uncomfortably in the room.*)

KESS: How'd you get hurt? (*A beat.* KESS *turns again for the door.*)

JO: Someone tried to kill me.

KESS: Kill you? Who?

JO: Mom.

KESS: Mom tried to . . . ? Why didn't you tell me on the phone?

JO: I couldn't say it over the phone . . .

KESS: She tried to *kill* you?

JO: Well, yes . . . in a way. She hit me. And I fell. I fell six feet. Into the street. You know—over by Duman's Drug? Where the street goes down? It's a six-foot drop from the sidewalk, and . . . she pushed me.

KESS: You said she hit you.

JO: She did hit me, but it was like a push. I mean, I fell over backwards. On my neck. I was almost hit by a Plymouth. I didn't wake up for a couple of minutes.

KESS: Did they see it? The person in the Plymouth?

JO: No, they were coming around the corner.

KESS: Did anybody see it?

JO: No, it was Sunday. The stores were closed. But it happened.

KESS: Why would Mom hit you?

JO: Because I'm pregnant. (*A beat.*) How do you like the house? We painted it last year. (KESS *moves to a chair, puts down her bag, but remains standing.*)

KESS: It's great to be home. I can only stay a couple days. I'm teaching three different courses . . .

JO: I don't expect you to stay long—honest. I just need you to be here awhile, for support. I need help with Mom, and . . . things. You know Mom.

KESS: Yes, I know Mom.

JO: I need you to . . . stand up to her. You know—like last time.

KESS: Last time I committed her for three months. Is that what you're talking about?

JO: Oh, no—no, no, no, no, no, no. No. I don't mean that. I just mean having you back would . . . help so much. You know, having *all* her daughters here for once, for her to . . .

KESS: Contend with.

JO: *No,* to . . . love. (SHERRY *enters from her room with a makeup kit.*)

SHERRY: Hey, is that big sister?

JO: Sherry—thought you were taking a shower.

SHERRY: I will tomorrow. (*Setting up a mirror, taking her brush out of the kit.*) Hi, Kess. How're you? Hope you don't mind if I do this while I say hello. I have to go to work. Nice to see you. (*She begins doing her makeup.*)

KESS: Nice to see you.

SHERRY: How you been the last four years?

KESS: Fine. You?

SHERRY: I'm getting out of school in a couple weeks. At long last. Would you believe it?

KESS: You look different.

SHERRY: I hope so. Christ, I was fifteen the last time you saw me. You just here for the day?

KESS: Well . . .

SHERRY: Stay long enough to catch Mom's act. She's really been lighting up the place lately. Ever since Jo got knocked up. Same routine as with me. Something about unmarried pregnant daughters just rings her bell. Check her out. She'll be back from work in a little while.

JO: (*Moving toward the kitchen.*) Kess, why don't we . . .

KESS: I didn't know she worked.

SHERRY: (*Laughs.*) Oh, yeah. She volunteers out at the MHI.

KESS: Since when?

SHERRY: Almost a year. Jo got her the job. Didn't you write her about that, Jo? Mom's like this model volunteer out there.

She made the local paper and everything. "Former Mental Patient Now Helps Others At Mental Health Institute." You know, one of those articles that makes you feel ten feet tall 'n shit? *Look* at this hair of mine. I gotta work tonight.

KESS: (*To* JO.) Mom's working with mental patients?

SHERRY: Don't worry. She won't hurt 'em. She's just in the craft center. They don't let her alone with anybody.

JO: She wanted to. I couldn't say no.

SHERRY: Hey, what do you think of the pregnant one here? She tell you all about it?

KESS: Not yet.

SHERRY: It's really ridiculous, believe me. I'm sorry, Jo, but it is. I mean, imagine this: Jo, who's been a virgin practically since pioneer days, finally decided to go out with someone. Did she write you about that? So guess what? She goes out with him and goes out with him. And in the course of human events, she gets pregnant.

JO: His name is Don Orbeck.

SHERRY: Deadeye Don Orbeck.

KESS: (*To* JO.) Well, what's he like?

SHERRY: He's got a Subaru—that's about it. So anyhow, he offers to marry Jo . . .

KESS: He wants to marry you?

SHERRY: *Did* want to. Jo said no.

KESS: You didn't want to marry him?

SHERRY: She turned him down.

JO: It would have been selfish. (*They look at her.*) To marry him and leave Mom all alone? He's not going to live with her, you know.

SHERRY: He's not completely stupid.

JO: Besides, I think he was just . . . offering. You know, 'cause he felt he had to. (SHERRY *has pulled hair out of her brush and thrown it on the floor.* KESS *bends to pick it up.*)

SHERRY: What are you doing?

KESS: Just . . .

SHERRY: Are you picking up after me?

KESS: You threw hair on the floor.

SHERRY: Put it back. (KESS *hesitates, then does so.*) I *have* a mother for that. So, anyway—like I say, now Jo's alone and pregnant, and there's this marksman walking around town, beginning to look for other targets.

JO: Sherry.

SHERRY: Well, he is. You know who he's showing up at Popeye's with now?

JO: Who?

SHERRY: You want to go insane? Heidi Joy Duckly.

JO: You're kidding.

SHERRY: Nope. Heidi Joy. (*To* KESS.) She's this blonde dwarf you wouldn't believe. I mean, Don was never too inventive, but *Heidi.* You know what Heidi once said to me out loud? "Women should never complain—that's the man's job." Really. I could've strangled the bitch. (KESS *has by now walked up to the front windows, and looks out.*) So what do you think of Jo's life? Screwed up, huh? And I thought I was in trouble when *I* had a kid . . .

JO: (*To* SHERRY.) You should have let me tell her about Don.

SHERRY: You would've taken all day. Hey, Kess. You like my hair this way?

KESS: What? Oh . . . sure.

SHERRY: You're not even looking. What are you looking at?

KESS: The traffic light.

SHERRY: *The* traffic light. That's about it. Independence, Iowa.

KESS: Same houses. Even the same billboards.

SHERRY: Only so many ways to sell herbicide. I'll be out of here so fast when I graduate. I'm nineteen years old and still in high school. That's the real cost of illegitimate kids, believe me. Jo, you were smart to wait.

KESS: I can see the MHI from here.

SHERRY: Second home to the demented of northeast Iowa. And I do mean Mom and Jo.

JO: Sherry . . .

SHERRY: (*Rising, after packing up her kit.*) I don't mean it. Just that anybody who works out there is bound to bring some of it home with her.

JO: I work in accounts. I never go near the patients.

KESS: (*Looking off to the side.*) Mrs. Anderberg's collection has grown.

SHERRY: Yeah. Lawn Ornament Land. She must have twenty of 'em out there. All the Iowa standards: stable boys, little fawns, sleeping Mexicans . . . Hey! You know what? I could use those in a sculpture, I bet. You know—just mush 'em all together some way? Shit, what a great idea. I wonder if I could buy some of them off her tomorrow? I'm an artist.

KESS: Oh? That's nice.

SHERRY: No, really. I won a thing at school. I'm a killer. Even my teacher thinks so.

KESS: That's excellent. I'm impressed.

SHERRY: "That's excellent. I'm impressed." Same old Kess.

JO: Sherry, aren't you late for work?

SHERRY: Don't you wish. Mom and Jo are officially ashamed of me, now that I'm a barmaid at Popeye's.

KESS: Popeye's? Doesn't the school get mad?

SHERRY: Nah. They're too desperate to get rid of me. I graduate in three weeks. (*Taking her kit into her room.*) Hey, how do you like this? I moved downstairs. It's not exactly a separate apartment, but almost. I still think my big mistake was not getting a separate apartment at birth.

KESS: Sherry?

SHERRY: (*Off.*) What?

KESS: How do you think Mom's doing?

SHERRY: (*Returning with a light jacket.*) Oh, fine. Never better. Last night she threw her shoe at my boyfriend. We were sitting in the den, watching TV. Mom was in there, sewing. Me and this guy were hugging and shit—nothing special. Suddenly she chucked her loafer at him. Then she went back to sewing, no explanation. She's great.

KESS: How did Jo get hurt?

JO: I told you . . .

SHERRY: Mom shoved her off the sidewalk or something, I don't know. Something lame like that. Hey, I gotta go work. Popeye's is sleazy, but it's all money. (*She moves toward the front door.*) Tell me about yourself sometime. See you later. 'Night. (*Stops again.*) This place seem any different to you?

KESS: Yes. A little.

SHERRY: It's not. (*She exits out the front door.*)

KESS: Well. She sure hasn't changed, has she?

JO: Not much. (JO *picks up the hair on the floor, disposes of it.*)

KESS: So. Mom is not happy.

JO: She's been terrible. Even after I told her I wasn't going to marry Don—that I was going to stay here. She acts like she doesn't believe me.

KESS: Do you think about leaving her?

JO: I couldn't leave her.

KESS: I did.

JO: You're you. You could do that.

KESS: Everyone does that. People grow up. They leave home. (*During* JO*'s next speech,* EVELYN *appears unnoticed in the dining room. She wears a coat. She stops when she sees* KESS.)

JO: They don't leave homes like this one. Mom needs more help than other people. She needs someone to be here. Steadily.

KESS: You, you mean?

JO: Well, yes me. If no one else is going to do it. (*A beat.*) I'm sorry. She still hasn't forgiven you, you know.

EVELYN: (*Moving into the living room.*) Who says I haven't forgiven her?

JO: Mom!

EVELYN: It's silly to say that I haven't forgiven Kess. Where did you get that idea?

JO: Well . . . you said . . .

EVELYN: (*Coming to* KESS.) I can't tell you how surprised I felt when Jo told me you were coming. I hope you'll feel comfortable here.

KESS: Thanks.

EVELYN: Do you want some tea?

KESS: No, thanks.

EVELYN: No? Coffee? Anything?

KESS: No.

EVELYN: Well, I'd like some tea. Jo, why don't you be good and make us some, all right? The way we like it?

JO: Oh . . . um, ok. (*She exits to the kitchen.*)

EVELYN: Have a seat.

KESS: In a minute.

EVELYN: (*Sitting near* KESS*'s bag.*) I will. I've been standing for hours. Out at the MHI. I work in the craft center, you know.

KESS: I heard.

EVELYN: I thought you'd be interested, since you were the one who brought me out there in the first place. Of course, now I'm helping other people, instead of being helped. They all like the projects I think up. Just simple things, really. Wood and yarn and paint and things. (EVELYN *opens* KESS*'s bag and rummages inside.*) How long are you staying? Did you bring a lot with you?

KESS: What are you doing?

EVELYN: Looking at your things. (*Holding up a book.*) What's this book? It's awfully thick.

KESS: It's a study of imagery in seventeenth-century Scottish Border Ballads.

EVELYN: What do you use it for? Do you read it?

KESS: I'm writing a book of my own.

EVELYN: Really? What's your book called?

KESS: "Imagery in Seventeenth-Century Scottish Border Ballads."

EVELYN: Isn't that the same thing?

KESS: It's my view.

EVELYN: (*Laughs, continues rummaging.*) I'll never understand it.

KESS: Mom, why are you going through my things?

EVELYN: I haven't seen you. I'm trying to get an idea of who you are. How you've changed, I mean.

KESS: (*Retrieving her bag, moving it away from her.*) I haven't.

EVELYN: You came back. How long are you staying?

KESS: Jo and I are still talking that one over.

EVELYN: I hope you stay a long time. It's exciting to have all you girls together again. It's a rare treat.

KESS: Jo said you tried to kill her.

EVELYN: Why don't you sit down?

KESS: I'll sit down when I want to sit down.

EVELYN: Are you afraid to sit down? (*A beat.* KESS *sits in a chair.*) You always used to sit there. (KESS *immediately rises.*) It's so hard to know what to start talking about after four years, isn't it? Are you still a homosexual?

KESS: (*A beat.*) Yes, Mother. I am still a homosexual.

EVELYN: I suppose that'll make it hard for you to give Jo much advice about this Don Orbeck fellow. She's awfully confused right now. She wanted to marry him, but I think I've pointed out the disadvantages of *that.*

KESS: What are they?

EVELYN: Oh—well, everyone counsels against getting married because of an inadvertent pregnancy. I mean, look at my own life. I married Henry Briggs just because we were expecting you, and that didn't work out so wonderfully, did it?

KESS: I guess not.

EVELYN: What is it about the women in this family? We get near a man, and the next thing we know we're pregnant. You're probably right to stay away from men.

KESS: Mom . . .

EVELYN: Are you sure you don't want to sit? I feel like I'm staring up at a big building.

KESS: I'll stand.

EVELYN: I hope you won't do any homosexual things while you're in town. I mean, it's your life, but . . .

KESS: (*Moving toward the kitchen.*) I wonder if Jo needs help?

EVELYN: Oh, she's gone down to the bakery for some rolls.

KESS: She has?

EVELYN: She always does when she makes tea. It's one of our little sins.

KESS: (*Sighs, perches on the back of a chair.*) Oh.

EVELYN: It's been so long since we've talked. I admit, I wished you dead there for a couple of years, but I'm over that now.

KESS: Mom . . .

EVELYN: Jo's almost fully recovered, too. From her neck, I mean. So, I guess you'd say we're all doing very well at the . . .

KESS: Mom, can I say something?

EVELYN: Of course. We're having a talk.

KESS: As I was driving down here, I was talking to myself—I was saying, "Mom's had four years. We both have. Four years of not seeing each other, not talking, not even writing. Maybe things are entirely different by now. Maybe we'll actually find that we've forgotten how we used to talk to each other. Maybe we'll invent a whole new way."

EVELYN: You talk to yourself in the car?

KESS: Why do we get into conversations like this?! Can't you just say, "Hello, Kess—it's nice to see you again"?

EVELYN: No.

KESS: Why not?

EVELYN: Because it isn't.

KESS: (*A beat.*) Why not?

EVELYN: Isn't it obvious? You left this family long ago. You never visited, you never told us anything about your life . . .

KESS: I was trying to establish something for myself.

EVELYN: And then, four years ago, out of the blue, you came down here and decided I needed medical help.

KESS: You did.

EVELYN: In your opinion.

KESS: I found you sitting on the floor behind a chair, wrapped in a blanket.

EVELYN: And you gave me a hug. I remember; it was very sweet. Then you took me out to the MHI, and . . .

KESS: What did you want me to do? Take you up to Minneapolis with me? You wouldn't go. Quit my job? Move down here?

EVELYN: That could have been a start.

KESS: I'm a professional! I have a career. It takes all my time and energy—all my love to do it well. I'm not a hack teacher somewhere. I'm extremely good at what I do.

EVELYN: I know, dear. You're a specialist.

KESS: You were only in there three months.

EVELYN: How much love would you like, Kess?

KESS: What?

EVELYN: Isn't that what we're talking about? Really? You're not here for Jo. You're here for love. You want some of my love.

KESS: That would be nice.

EVELYN: Well then, it occurs to me we may only be dickering about the amount. You're a specialist; maybe you don't need a lot of love from me. Maybe you only need a tiny bit. I think I could provide that.

KESS: Why did you try to kill Jo?

EVELYN: I didn't. I hit her.

KESS: She thinks you tried to . . .

EVELYN: You show me one mother who hasn't hit a child.

KESS: (*A beat.*) Well. I'm going to be here for a little while. I think Jo and Sherry could use whatever comfort and protection that would afford.

EVELYN: They do not need protection . . .

KESS: I think they do. I think they need that, and love.

EVELYN: You are just like Henry Briggs, you know that? Only here when you want to create new tragedies.

KESS: Mom . . .

EVELYN: You have all his false appeal and his seeming logic. But just like Henry, you become part of this family only when it suits you, and . . .

KESS: Mother . . .

EVELYN: And one day you will leave for good. Won't you? Won't you?

KESS: Why did you hit Jo?

EVELYN: I never hit Jo! (*Rising.*) I remember when a mother and daughter could converse like human beings about these things. You ask anybody in Independence about me. They'll say Evelyn Briggs is the sanest, most well-loved one among us. I am wonderful with those patients. I don't know what Jo may have told you, but it's . . .

KESS: (*Overlapping from "may."*) Jo has only been . . .

EVELYN: But it's not true! I am perfectly capable of functioning in a warm and loving universe. Which is what I try constantly to create!

JO: (*From off, in the kitchen.*) Mom! I'm back. I got your favorite! Cinnamon rolls!

EVELYN: I'd better go help Jo. Hope you like Constant Comment. (*She exits into the kitchen.* KESS *looks around the room, sighs and slumps on the arm of the couch. Lights fade to black.*)

Scene Two

Saturday morning, two days later. Lights rise to reveal JO *and* SHERRY. JO *is dressed,* SHERRY *is still in her robe.* JO *is singing from a book. She no longer wears the collar.*

JO: "It fell about the Martinmas.
When nights are lang and mirk . . ."

SHERRY: (*Yawning.*) Swing it, sister.

JO: Sherry.

KESS: (*From the kitchen.*) Don't mind her. Keep going. You're good.

JO: I am not.

KESS: (*Off.*) Yes, you are.

JO: What's "lang and mirk" mean? "When nights are lang and mirk."

KESS: Long and murky—just like it sounds. (*Entering, with two cups of tea, one of which she gives to* JO. *Like* JO, *she is dressed.*) Martinmas comes in the winter—so, naturally, long, dark nights. Go on. Your accent's great.

SHERRY: Yeah, great.

JO: "The carline wife's three sons came hame . . ."

SHERRY: Came *hame?*

KESS: Sherry. It means home. "Carline" means old, by the way.

JO: Old? Carline means old?

KESS: Yup. It's there so we know she can't have any more children. See? Everything in a ballad has a purpose. That's why they're beautiful.

SHERRY: "That's why they're beautiful." Same old Kess. (SHERRY *yawns.*)

KESS: Will you quit yawning?

SHERRY: I didn't get much sleep last night. Besides, I always yawn on Saturdays.

KESS: Go on, Jo.

JO: (*Sings.*) "The carline wife's three sons came hame
And their hats were o' the birk."

SHERRY: What the hell does that mean?

KESS: It means they're dead.

JO: What?

KESS: Her three sons are dead. They're wearing hats made of birch. "Birk" means birch.

SHERRY: Oh, that explains it.

KESS: But there isn't any birch where she lives. And the next verse indicates that while it doesn't grow there, it does grow at the gates of heaven.

JO: (*Beginning to get it.*) So . . .

KESS: So they're wearing hats made in heaven. See? They're dead. They were lost in a shipwreck three verses ago. Remember?

JO: How do you keep all this straight?

SHERRY: She doesn't. She makes it up.

KESS: The point is, we're dealing with ghosts here. This poor old woman has three sons, and she sends them all out sailing—major mistake—and word comes back they've drowned. Well, she doesn't want to believe *that* . . .

SHERRY: Why not?

KESS: So, some time later, they show up—surprisingly—and she's wild with joy. My sons are home! She doesn't notice the birch hats.

SHERRY: *I* would notice the birch hats.

KESS: She doesn't. She loves them, and she can't bear to think they're dead. So she welcomes them, and then she sits and watches over them all night long. But just before dawn she falls asleep. And they wake up before she does, and they leave her forever.

JO: That's awful. I mean it's pretty, but it's awful.

KESS: They can't help it. They have to get back to their graves.

SHERRY: Think I'll have an omelet.

JO: You always have an omelet.

SHERRY: It's all I can cook.

JO: Do you have any more songs?

KESS: Well, here's one about two crows eating a corpse . . .

JO: Oh . . . not yet. Let me work up to that.

SHERRY: Seriously—who wants an omelet?

KESS: What kind?

SHERRY: Plain or lunchmeat.

KESS: No thanks. (*As* SHERRY *exits into the kitchen.*) I'll make breakfast later. Are you taking those vitamins I gave you?

JO: Yeah.

KESS: How's the neck?

JO: (*Turning her head.*) One hundred percent.

KESS: Did you throw up today?

JO: Yup.

KESS: Good. We've got all sorts of progress in just two days. Now all we have to do is get you out exercising, instead of sitting around here all day reading drugstore novels.

JO: *Noble Incest* is not a drugstore novel. It's not a great novel . . .

KESS: We'll see if we can't find you something better.

JO: Kess? Is it fun? To be back?

KESS: Back with you? Yeah, sure it's fun.

JO: How about the town? The people?

KESS: This town? These people?

JO: Yeah.

KESS: Small-town living isn't for me.

JO: I think small towns are an important alternative to the stress of contemporary urban life.

KESS: (*Laughs.*) You do, do you?

JO: How long can you stay?

KESS: I told you. Till Monday.

JO: It's been such a relief to have you here. I really feel calm now. Mom's happier.

KESS: Not sure I believe *that*.

JO: She is. Really. Yesterday she said it's a lovely thing when a family reunites.

KESS: She didn't say it to me.

JO: But she said it. To somebody. That's progress.

KESS: You think that's progress, eh?

JO: Of course it is. It's not easy for her, you know. She has to go by little steps.

KESS: You know what I'd call progress? Real progress? If you were to decide—now that you're going to have a baby—to move up to Minneapolis with me.

JO: What?

KESS: Come and live with me.

JO: I couldn't do that.

KESS: Why not? Try and think about it rationally . . .

JO: I don't have to think about it rationally. I couldn't do that.

KESS: Why not?

JO: 'Cause I can't leave Mom. How can you even suggest it?

KESS: I'm only . . .

JO: What would happen to her? Tell me—what would happen?

KESS: She'd be all right.

JO: She would, huh? How?!

KESS: She's managed for 53 years.

JO: No, she hasn't. She's never managed alone. She's always needed someone. First there was her family, then Dad, then you after Dad left, then me. Who'd be here when I left? Not Sherry. Mom would be all alone.

KESS: (*A beat.*) So what?

JO: *So what?!*

KESS: I have a very big place in Minneapolis. There'd be room for you. My roommate wouldn't mind . . .

JO: You already asked your *roommate?* Jesus, Kess . . .

KESS: I had to know before I could . . .

JO: Is that the only reason you came down? To try and steal me away from Mom?

KESS: No, it's just that . . .

JO: If you think I'd leave Mom to move up there with you and that . . . that . . .

KESS: That what?

JO: You know.

KESS: That what? That Susan, you mean. That's her name.

JO: I think we should just drop it.

KESS: (*With control, not defensive.*) *That* roommate—Susan—is the same as me. Our life is more normal than anything that goes on in this house.

SHERRY: (*Off.*) That's the truth.

KESS: Sher, if you want to join the conversation you can come in here.

SHERRY: (*Off.*) No, thanks.

JO: (*A beat.*) I'm sorry.

KESS: That's all right.

JO: I just know I can't go up there and leave Mom, that's all.

KESS: 'Cause she needs you.

JO: That's right.

KESS: What for? What does she need you for?

JO: Everything. She needs me to listen to her. She needs me to talk to her, to be with her—to be thinking about her. What does anybody need anybody for?

KESS: Shouldn't people sometimes . . . change who they need?

JO: Mom's done that.

KESS: I don't mean Mom. I mean you.

JO: (*A beat.*) We're getting off the point.

KESS: What do you need from Mom?

JO: Nothing. I help her. She doesn't help me. OK?

KESS: Something. You get something out of it.

JO: I don't get a thing. I give. That's my life. I give to people. There's nothing wrong with it. You should try it sometime.

KESS: I wasn't saying . . .

JO: It's easy for you. You just take what you need from people. You don't care how much you change in the process. You don't care if your whole family doesn't recognize you anymore when you . . . (*She stops herself, very embarrassed.*) I'm sorry.

KESS: That's all right.

JO: It's not true—we recognize you. You're always . . . Kess. (*A beat.* KESS *sighs.*)

KESS: Well . . .

JO: Why don't you move down here?

KESS: What?

JO: Move back down. Be close to us.

KESS: I couldn't do that.

JO: Why not? You make changes. You could find a way. Bring Susan.

KESS: *Su*san. . . ? Mom'd *love* that.

JO: You could work, you could find a job . . .

KESS: Jo . . .

JO: You can do anything if you care enough.

KESS: Is that why you asked me down here? To steal me away from my life?

JO: I'm not stealing you away! I'm . . . inviting you. You could do a lot of good down here. You could really provide something for Mom . . .

KESS: I do provide. I provide a hell of a lot, as you'll recall. Who was here to put Mom in the MHI when she needed it?

JO: Who was here when she got out? You were already gone. I was the one who took her around to say hello to everybody again. I took her into each store. I shopped with her.

KESS: I'm leaving on Monday.

JO: Go ahead—leave!

KESS: I will.

JO: Fine! (*A silence.* SHERRY *enters, eating a Hostess cupcake.*)

SHERRY: How are things in here? Everybody happy?

KESS: I thought you were having an omelet. What's that?

SHERRY: Dessert. This is getting to be a lively day. What with you guys yelling, and Mom.

KESS: What about Mom?

SHERRY: You didn't hear her dawn raid this morning? It was a beaut. She caught me with a boy.

JO: She's caught you with boys before.

SHERRY: Not with two boys.

JO: *Two* boys . . . ?

SHERRY: Oh, it was just inane. I was only in bed with one of them.

JO: Well, who . . . ?

SHERRY: Ed and Red Randall. (*To* KESS.) Ed's my boyfriend.

JO: What was Red doing there?

SHERRY: He came over to ask Ed a question, that's all. I think he wanted to borrow money, I don't know. It was still dark out. Anyway—it was so stupid—Red was crawling through the window, and he slipped on my dresser and made this incredible crash, and Mom came in. And there we were: all three of us on the bed. Well, Red was kind of half on the floor.

JO: Oh, Sherry . . .

SHERRY: Mom must've been wandering around out here. She came right in, she was all dressed and everything. Anyway, she practically killed Ed and Red, thereby ruining my social life.

JO: What'd she do?

SHERRY: (*Laughs.*) She threw your picture at them. You know—your graduation picture. In the frame? (SHERRY *points to a table where* KESS *and* SHERRY*'s framed pictures sit, with a noticeable gap between them.*)

JO: Oh, no.

SHERRY: Who knows why she was carrying it around with her?

JO: Where is it now?

SHERRY: All over my room. They were both scared shitless. They were out the window in two seconds. Then she screamed, "You'll thank me someday," and ran out.

JO: Where'd she go?

SHERRY: Who knows? Maybe she went and drowned herself.

JO: I'll check her room. (JO *hurries upstairs.*)

KESS: Why didn't you tell us about this?

SHERRY: What's to tell? It's the way she always is.

KESS: Don't you care about her at all?

SHERRY: Don't you? I don't see you running upstairs. (*A moment passes.* JO *returns.*)

JO: She's . . . asleep. She's fine.

SHERRY: She's fine and Ed's terrified. (*Curling up on the couch.*) Be sure and tell me when you both finally sneak out on her for good. I don't want to be the last one out the door. (*She closes her eyes, napping. The others stare at her, then at each other. Lights fade to black.*)

Scene Three

Around noon, the same day. JO *is staring out a side window, toward the back of the house. We hear sweeping sounds from* SHERRY'S *room. After a moment,* EVELYN *emerges—a dustpan full of glass in one hand, a broom and a damaged photo in the other.*

EVELYN: That takes care of that. At least your photo wasn't too badly torn. A little scotch tape . . . (EVELYN *moves toward the kitchen with the dustpan.*)

JO: I'm sorry you had to clean it up yourself.

EVELYN: No—Sherry has every right to demand that. I was the one who lost her temper. I made the mess. (EVELYN *disappears into the kitchen.*)

JO: She wouldn't let me clean it up. I offered to, but she just . . .

EVELYN: (*Off.*) It's fine, it's fine. Your heart was in the right place. (*Reentering, sans broom and dustpan, but with the picture.*) Have to get a new frame for this. (*Sets it on the table with the other photos.*) Such a sweet picture. I'm sorry it was yours I threw. But I was looking at it right when I heard those noises, and I just . . .

JO: That's OK, Mom.

EVELYN: Well, there's a basic level of trust. In any home.

JO: I know. Did you sleep well, this morning?

EVELYN: Like a dream. Lost half the day, but I don't care. Is Sherry around? Where is everyone?

JO: Kess went out for a run. Sherry's in the backyard.

EVELYN: (*Moving to the window* JO *had been looking out.*) She is? What's she doing?

JO: Working on her sculpture.

EVELYN: Oh. Well. She should stop it.

JO: Tell her that.

EVELYN: It's so awful. And it's right next to Mrs. Anderberg's vegetable garden. She called and complained yesterday. Said if she'd only known what Sherry was going to do with those lawn ornaments, she'd never have sold them to her.

JO: Too late.

EVELYN: I said if she wanted to go ahead and sue Sherry, I'd back her up.

JO: Against your own daughter?

EVELYN: I'm not really sure Sherry is my daughter. I was so drugged up when I had her, they could've given me any baby and I wouldn't have known. (JO *laughs.* EVELYN *smiles.*) It's nice, having you all in the house again. We're never all together in the same room, it seems, but at least we're all . . . around. Do you like having her here?

JO: Who—Kess? Sure. It's wonderful.

EVELYN: (*A beat.*) It is, isn't it?

JO: Yes, it is.

EVELYN: I hope she's having a good time. I suppose she probably came down here expecting to find us locked in some sort of death struggle.

JO: She did not.

EVELYN: Lord knows what you told her.

JO: I didn't tell her anything.

EVELYN: You told her I hit you.

JO: You did hit me.

EVELYN: I did not. I struck out, that's all. I simply struck out against Fate, and there you were. It's not the same as hitting.

JO: It *felt* the . . .

EVELYN: It's not the same. (*A beat.*) There's not the same responsibility, is there?

JO: (*A beat.*) No.

EVELYN: (*Picking up a magazine.*) Kess has been talking to people in town about me. Did you know that? Mrs. Herold was angry about it. She really was. Kess walked up to her—hadn't seen her in years—and said, "How does my mother seem to you these days?" I can just hear her.

JO: I'm sure she didn't mean anything . . .

EVELYN: If I hadn't had the three of you so far apart we'd be more of a family. There'd be more of us in the room right now. Kess was nearly grown by the time Sherry was born. They must stare at each other like the Earth and the moon.

JO: Do you want some lunch . . . ? (EVELYN *puts the magazine down.*)

EVELYN: Where were you Wednesday night?

JO: What?

EVELYN: Wednesday night. The night before Kess got here. Where did you go?

JO: Nowhere important.

EVELYN: Where, though?

JO: Nowhere.

EVELYN: You must've gone somewhere.

JO: I didn't go anywhere, all right? I really didn't.

EVELYN: I'm only curious.

JO: What's it matter?

EVELYN: I guess it doesn't.

JO: That's right. It doesn't matter. It doesn't matter at all.

EVELYN: (*A beat.*) Then why can't you tell me?

JO: (*Moving toward the stairs.*) I'm going to go change. Kess and I are going out when she gets back . . .

EVELYN: Mrs. Rowley says she saw you over at Don's house Wednesday night. (JO *stops.*) Is that where you were? Don's house?

JO: Yes.

EVELYN: You went over there, and you never told me?

JO: There was nothing to tell. He wasn't home.

EVELYN: Oh. You were gone a long time.

JO: I know. I just . . . sort of sat on his step for awhile.

EVELYN: (*A beat.*) Why?

JO: I . . . thought he might come home.

EVELYN: No—I mean, why did you go see him?

JO: No reason.

EVELYN: There's always some reason. There must have been some reason.

JO: I wanted to see if he felt like going out, all right?

EVELYN: You didn't call him first?

JO: It was kind of a whim.

EVELYN: I thought you and Don were finished.

JO: We are; so what? (*A beat.*) He's dating other people. I sat for half an hour on his step. Folks walked by and said, "Hi, Jo. Don's out tonight, you know." I said, "I know." They all looked at me like I was . . . what I was. So I came home.

EVELYN: (*Moving to her, sitting close.*) I've missed you these last weeks. I'm glad we're not fighting anymore. Aren't you? (JO *nods.* EVELYN *takes her hand.*) Sometimes a man comes into your life, and you think it's the answer to your problems, but you always find out it's not. Henry was just a man. He didn't care about me. He was handsome, and he was fine while there was enough money, or there was enough whatever, but in the end he didn't care.

JO: I know.

EVELYN: I'll be glad when Sherry's gone. I shouldn't say that, but I will. Then it'll just be you and me. Won't that be fun? (JO *nods.*) We'll have Kess and Sherry visit now and then, of course. But mostly, it'll just be us. I rely on you. So few people in the world can really be relied on. Don't you think? So few things. I've lived in this house my entire life. Do you realize that?

JO: It amazes me sometimes.

EVELYN: You too. You've lived in it all yours.

JO: Yes.

EVELYN: Kess will be gone on Monday. Then Sherry will go. Just you and me. At last. (*A beat.*) I'm wearing my cameo.

JO: What?

EVELYN: I'm wearing my cameo. Did you notice?

JO: Oh . . . it's lovely. I'm sorry, I didn't notice.

EVELYN: That's because you haven't been looking at me. In the craft center they tell us to look squarely at the patients—at least at those who'll look squarely at us—and to smile, and to be encouraging. I think that's good advice for life in general, don't you? (*Of the cameo.*) It's a beautiful thing, isn't it? Family heirlooms always are.

JO: Yes.

EVELYN: Henry, your father, and I used to drive to Des Moines once a month when you were little. He went on business—allegedly—and I went to shop. After we'd done this for over a year, he suddenly looked at me on the way home one day and said, "What's that?" I said, "It's my cameo." "Where did you get it?" he asked. "I've had it for seven years," I told him. "Why haven't you ever worn it before?" "I wear it all the time," I said, "It's my dearest possession." He was just silent then, the whole way home. Never said he was sorry. (*Unpinning the cameo, examining it.*) That was the first time I ever felt sorry for him, though. Must be strange for a man, to live in a world full of only big things.

JO: You used to show it to Kess and me.

EVELYN: I did, didn't I?

JO: You let us hold it.

EVELYN: (*Starts to hand it to* JO, *then suddenly pulls it back for reexamination.*) You two fought over it. Didn't you?

JO: Some fight. Kess always won. (EVELYN *pins the cameo back on herself.*) You haven't had it on in ages. Why are you wearing it now?

EVELYN: So I don't forget to give it to Kess.

JO: You're giving it to Kess?

EVELYN: Well, I know I talked about giving it to you. But that was when I was mad at Kess, and thought she wasn't a part of us anymore.

JO: Kess is getting the . . . ?

EVELYN: You know, I thought of it just as I woke up. It's truly the perfect idea. After all, Kess has been so much calmer this trip. We need to give her something. And what better than the cameo? It's hers by rights. She is the oldest.

JO: But . . .

EVELYN: I know—I'm breaking tradition, to give it to her before I die. But I thought it might be just the message she needs to see that . . . I love her, and I'm all right. Do you think she'll like it?

JO: (*A beat.*) Of course. It's lovely.

EVELYN: It is, isn't it? I remember when your Aunt Elaine died, and I got it. Do you realize this cameo has been owned by women in our family for over 150 years? Imagine. I'm sorry I don't have one for you, too. But Kess has to live far away. We can give her this to remind her of us. You're right here. You have me. (*A beat.*) I'll tell you something else. Now that Don is . . . well, moving in another direction, I think you and I have a special opportunity—one that a mother and daughter rarely get. We have the chance to give each other something far more valuable than a cameo.

JO: What?

EVELYN: Our lives. (*A long beat.* EVELYN *kisses* JO *on the forehead.* JO *is motionless.*) Now, where can I leave this?

JO: Leave it?

EVELYN: I know! On her table upstairs. She'll find it when she goes up tonight. (*She goes for the stairs.*)

JO: Well . . . if you're going to give it to her, why don't you give it to her?

EVELYN: No, no, no. This is better. A surprise.

JO: It's ridiculous, giving her the cameo like that.

EVELYN: You don't understand—it'll be lovely. Look: I sneak in her room, leave it on her table. She walks in, wanders around, comes over to the table and . . . You see? It'll be very special.

JO: That's not special.

EVELYN: Of course it is.

JO: Putting it in her hand and looking her in the eye—that would be special. Leaving it on a table is lousy.

EVELYN: No, it's lovely. You just don't see it.

JO: I would never want to get a gift that way. Especially that gift. From my own mother . . .

EVELYN: Kess will adore getting this gift in just this way. And no amount of jealous carping . . .

JO: I'm not jealous! I'm not!

EVELYN: No one knows Kess the way I do. And I am going up this minute and leaving this cameo right on her goddamn table, is that clear?!

JO: Yes.

EVELYN: Good. Kess is my oldest. She and I communicate in ways you and Sherry would not understand.

JO: Yes, Mom. (EVELYN *starts to exit, stops.*)

EVELYN: It will be a lovely gesture. From the both of us. (EVELYN *exits upstairs.* JO *stares after her a moment, as lights fade to black.*)

Scene Four

Sunday evening, the next day. SHERRY *at a table, with a pile of slides in front of her. She looks at them one by one as she speaks, dividing them into two piles.* KESS, *wearing the cameo, sits on the couch, looking through a book.*

SHERRY: So what I'm saying is, he was fantastic, that's all.

JO: (*Off, in* SHERRY*'s room.*) He was, was he?

SHERRY: Of course he was. He's from New York. He's a biker. I met him at the bar last night.

KESS: (*Absently.*) Sounds very attractive.

SHERRY: Yeah, he's an artist.

KESS: (*Calling out.*) How about Standish?

JO: (*Off.*) What?

KESS: Standish. That might be all right.

JO: (*Off.*) Are you kidding? *Standish?*

SHERRY: I can't believe you guys are actually picking baby names.

KESS: We actually are. (*Calling.*) How about Hannibal?

JO: (*Off.*) No. Sherry, where's your black top?

SHERRY: On the closet door.

JO: (*Off.*) Oh—thanks!

SHERRY: (*To* KESS.) Don't you want to hear about this guy I met?

KESS: No. (SHERRY *suddenly steals* KESS*'s book.*)

SHERRY: Well, do—'cause he's real interesting.

KESS: Sherry . . . !

SHERRY: Come on. You can do baby names later. This guy is a grown-up.

KESS: I don't have time. I'm going home tomorrow.

SHERRY: So what? Mail it in. (KESS *grabs for the book.* SHERRY *pulls it away and sits on it. A standoff.*)

KESS: Jo, she's got the book.

JO: (*Off.*) Sherry . . .

SHERRY: Jo—try my black shoes, too. They're on the stereo. One of 'em is, anyway.

JO: (*Off.*) Oh—yeah. Thanks!

SHERRY: No problem. (*To* KESS.) So. First of all, he's very aloof. Like he's not from here, right?

KESS: (*Looking irritably at* SHERRY*'s room.*) Where's he from?

SHERRY: New York. Don't you listen? Like I said he's a biker.

KESS: Charming.

SHERRY: He's got this great big Harley that looks like it eats rabbits. And he's got leathers and chains . . . And he's got tattoos.

JO: (*Off.*) Tattoos?

SHERRY: On both arms! Plus a little one on his nose. It's like this little vine or something, curling around one nostril. Want to know what his job is?

KESS: (*Leaning in the doorway to* SHERRY*'s room, staring into it.*) No.

JO: (*Off.*) Yes!

SHERRY: He's an insect photographer.

JO: (*Off.*) A what?

SHERRY: He takes close-up shots of insects—like in Walt Disney movies and stuff. He's got this butterfly net on his bike. I saw it.

KESS: Jo, do you really think you should wear that?

JO: (*Entering wearing a showy black top.*) Why not?

KESS: You don't know what Don's coming over for, exactly.

JO: He's taking me out. He said, "Can we go someplace?" Those were his exact words. Sherry, do you like it?

SHERRY: Yeah, on me. (*A beat. They stare at* JO.)

JO: Well . . . I thought maybe he'll want to go to a restaurant or something. (*A beat.* JO*'s confidence crumbles. She goes back into* SHERRY'S *room.*)

SHERRY: Anyway, this guy's one of Disney's biggest suppliers. That's what he told me, at least. You know what insect he hates to film?

KESS: I give completely up.

SHERRY: The praying mantis.

JO: (*Off.*) What about the green?

KESS: Jo . . .

SHERRY: He says everybody does that. Every nature movie has a praying mantis in it. You ever notice that?

KESS: Sherry . . .

SHERRY: And it's always the same shot: praying mantis sits there not moving; praying mantis grabs something faster than you can see it anyway; praying mantis eats it; praying mantis sits there not moving again. It's a limited insect.

JO: (*Off.*) I'm wearing this one.

KESS: I don't think . . .

JO: (*Off.*) Forget it. My mind's made up.

SHERRY: You know what he likes better? The dung beetle. They're more inventive. They roll these little balls of dung all over hell, you know?

KESS: I know.

SHERRY: They're very creative. Anyway, like I say, this guy's an artist, and I showed him some slides of sculptures I made, and he liked 'em, *and* he's taking 'em to New York with him. To try and make me famous—you know? I'm sending him more tomorrow. Want to see 'em?

KESS: No.

JO: (*Off.*) What's his name?

SHERRY: What?

KESS: Has the Hell's Angel insect photographer art connoisseur got a name?

SHERRY: Spinner. Isn't that great? We only knew each other a couple hours. It was kind of a lightning relationship. (*Hands* KESS *her book back.*) Just thought you'd be interested. (JO *reenters in a top that's slightly more demure, but still is too dressy.*)

JO: This is it. How do I look?

SHERRY: Like Heidi Joy Duckly.

JO: Well, I don't care. It's what I'm wearing.

KESS: Jo, you don't even know where you're going.

JO: We're going somewhere. That's all that matters.

KESS: Why not stay here? You two could talk here.

JO: (*Going to the front window, looking out.*) Oh, brilliant idea.

KESS: When's he coming?

JO: A half hour. (*Moving to the couch.*) I can't believe he called. Someone must've told him I was at his house.

SHERRY: Yeah, like half of town.

JO: I don't care.

KESS: Jo, is Don really worth getting this excited about?

JO: I'm not excited.

KESS: It's just that . . . for all the trouble he's caused . . .

JO: What trouble?

KESS: Mom tonight, for one thing.

JO: Well . . . I can't help Mom. We already had one fight over it, and that's it. She's all right now.

KESS: She's out cleaning up the garage. At seven in the evening. Does that sound like she's all right?

JO: It's not my fault if she loses her temper! You should be happy I'm getting away from her.

KESS: I am, but . . .

JO: You're just mad 'cause it's your last night here, and I'm going out. I understand that. And I'm sorry, but . . .

KESS: I just wish you'd be a little less frantic about it.

JO: How do you expect me to be? Don called up. Maybe he wants to ask me to get married.

SHERRY: What if he does? You'll just say no again.

JO: I will not.

SHERRY: Will he agree to live with Mom? Will he even come in the house?

JO: I'll leave Mom.

SHERRY: Sure.

JO: I wish he'd get here.

KESS: Relax.

JO: Maybe he'll take me to a movie. We like doing that. Sher, what's on in town?

SHERRY: The new James Bond.

JO: James Bond! God. Great. Remember when we used to go to those as kids?

KESS: Yeah. Mom used to take us.

SHERRY: Sure. They were the only movies a twenty-year-old, a twelve-year-old and a six-year-old all liked.

JO: That's right. Remember, we'd all sit there eating out of those red and white striped popcorn boxes, and Mom would lean over us and say, "Watch James Bond. Watch the way he acts around women. Watch what happens to the women . . ."

KESS, JO and SHERRY. (*Together.*) "They al-l-l-l-l-l-l-l die." (*They laugh.*)

SHERRY: God, we all remember.

JO: "They al-l-l-l-l-l-l-l die." Just like that. What happened to the woman in that movie, anyway? Didn't she fall into a car-masher or something?

KESS: I think so.

JO: Yeah. (*A beat. They grow silent.*)

KESS: (*Sighs.*) OK, OK, OK. Go out with him. Have a good time. Get frantic if you want to.

JO: Thanks. So—um . . . (*Indicates the book.*) Pick more baby names.

SHERRY: Do we have to?

KESS: All right. What about, um . . . Lanier.

JO: Lanier? I don't know.

SHERRY: Could we please do anything else?

KESS: What about Banquo?

JO: Will you quit it?

SHERRY: How about Shulamith?

JO: Give me a girl's name. It's going to be a girl.

SHERRY: Shulamith is a girl's name.

KESS: Let's see: Marina.

JO: No.

KESS: Chloe.

JO: Are you ignoring all the common ones?

KESS: Who needs a book for Mary? Annabella.

SHERRY: Have we really, honestly considered Shulamith?

JO: Sherry . . .

SHERRY: Hey—how about Merlin?

JO: *Mer*lin? Why?

SHERRY: 'Cause then he could make himself disappear.

JO: He's not going to disappear! He's going to be born, and have a mother and a father!

SHERRY: Yeah, who?

JO: *Me and Don!*

SHERRY: Oh, wake up! He's probably coming over to tell you to keep off his porch!

KESS: Sherry!

SHERRY: And you—you're a bigger idiot than Jo! Picking *baby* names. I noticed you never picked one for mine.

KESS: What good would that have done?

SHERRY: It might've helped me keep it.

KESS: You were 15 years old.

SHERRY: I was old enough! You had to pry it away from me with a stick!

KESS: *I'm glad I had a stick!* (*A beat.* KESS *puts down the book.*) Let's not do this.

SHERRY: (*Quietly.*) I gave her a name myself, anyway. Shulamith. 'Course she's probably called Barbie or Cathy by now.

KESS: Wherever she is, she's in a better family than this.

SHERRY: How would you know? You only come down when you feel like it. (*Flicking* KESS*'s cameo.*) You just drop in now and then, pick up whatever you want, and leave.

KESS: Oh—I suppose you wanted it too, huh?

SHERRY: No, but Jo did.

JO: I did not.

KESS: (*To* SHERRY.) I come down here because you three can't get along without me. Eventually you always have a disaster.

SHERRY: Maybe we like disasters!

JO: You *guys* . . .

SHERRY: I can't believe it. You don't care any more about this family than I do—but everybody looks up to you. Everybody's afraid of you. And meanwhile I'm supposed to be this little *shit* . . .

KESS: Well put! (SHERRY *gives an angry yell and pushes* KESS *onto the couch. They struggle.*)

JO: Kess! Sherry! Stop it! Let go! LET GO!! (*As they fight,* EVELYN *enters via the kitchen. She is disheveled, bleeding, frightened.*)

EVELYN: Kess? Kess?

JO: (*Looking around.*) Oh, God—*Mom!* (*The others look up.*)

EVELYN: Kess, I'm hurt.

JO: (*Rushing to her, as the others rise.*) What happened?

EVELYN: (*Moving into* KESS*'s arms.*) I was cleaning the garage. I . . . found the old dishes. The old china. I think I . . . broke something. I couldn't hold onto the plates . . . (KESS *and* JO *move her to a chair.* SHERRY *runs out through the kitchen.*)

JO: I'll get a towel. (JO *exits into the kitchen.*)

EVELYN: There was just me. There was . . . I was all alone out there.

KESS: Calm down, now. Everything's all right. You're with me. (JO *reenters with a towel.*)

EVELYN: I kept seeing Jo. She wasn't . . . there, but she . . . I saw her.

JO: Are those her only cuts?

KESS: I think so.

JO: Here, let me wrap this around. (SHERRY *reenters.*)

SHERRY: Geez—I don't believe it. The garage is full of broken dishes. Everywhere you look.

EVELYN: I was completely alone. (*A car horn honks outside.*)

JO: Oh, God—Don! (*Moving toward the front door.*) Um . . . um . . . (*The horn honks again.*) Kess, I . . . that's Don . . . I . . . (*She suddenly bolts out the front door.*)

EVELYN: Where's she going?

KESS: It's all right.

EVELYN: But where's . . . ?

KESS: Why did you break the dishes?

EVELYN: What?

KESS: Why did you break the dishes?

EVELYN: They were in my hand.

SHERRY: How bad are her cuts?

KESS: Not bad. Mom, were you throwing them at someone?

EVELYN: Yes.

KESS: Who? Who were you throwing them at? (JO *reenters from the front.*)

JO: Mom? I sent him away. I told him I couldn't see him, all right? Mom? I sent Don away. He's gone. He's all gone.

EVELYN: (*Quietly.*) I threw them at Jo. (*Lights fade to black.*)

END OF ACT ONE

ACT TWO

Scene One

Lights rise on KESS *and* EVELYN, *in robes, sitting at a table. They are playing Scrabble. Late Thursday evening, four days later.*

EVELYN: I used to sit around this table with my own sisters. You know that? I remember many times we'd sit around this same room, and just talk for hours. Mostly about our friends. Well, their friends, really. I was much younger. We'd stay up whole nights. This house. My mother was born in it.

KESS: Do you allow Greek letter words?

EVELYN: Like what?

KESS: Alpha, beta, pi.

EVELYN: No. (*A beat.*) Staying up nights. I always loved that when I was young. Now I wish I could sleep.

KESS: You slept last night, didn't you?

EVELYN: Oh, yes. I'm much calmer than I was. You've been so good to me all week. I'm sorry I made you change your plans, but I'm glad you're staying longer.

KESS: I just want to make sure you're feeling better. I mean, since your . . .

EVELYN: My smash up? Oh, yes. I feel much better. Actually, that let off a lot of steam for me. I scared myself, I admit, but now I'm almost glad it happened. And I won't miss those dishes. They were terrible old things. You almost make me feel like a princess, you've paid so much attention to me since. I hope it hasn't been hard on you.

KESS: Agony.

EVELYN: Really? That bad?

KESS: (*Putting letters on the board.*) No, that's the word I'm playing. "Agony." Let's see: that's one-two-three-four-five-six-seven-eight-nine. Plus a double word score. Eighteen.

EVELYN: Who's ahead?

KESS: I am.

EVELYN: Really? By how much?

KESS: Um . . . 380 points.

EVELYN: Oh . . . (*Playing.*) "Me." (KESS *looks at her.*) That's what I'm playing.

KESS: (*Recording the score.*) Four points.

EVELYN: I think it's so sweet of you to babysit me while your sisters have a night out.

KESS: They've had three nights out.

EVELYN: Well, they need it. What with Jo having that new disappointment with Don. I think she's lost all her chances there, don't you? You can't keep telling someone to go away, and expect them to keep coming back. Has she tried to call him again?

KESS: (*Nods.*) Mm-hmm. He's never home, though.

EVELYN: Well. We're certainly home, aren't we? Just a couple old maids, home for the night. (*As* KESS *works out a move.*) How am I?

KESS: What?

EVELYN: Do you think I'm in trouble?

KESS: What do you mean?

EVELYN: In the game.

KESS: Oh—can you win? No, you can't.

EVELYN: Ah. (*A beat.*) Do you like the cameo? I've noticed you wear it a lot.

KESS: It's beautiful. Thanks again.

EVELYN: You're welcome. Is it fun having a family again? It must be wonderful to rediscover your sisters this way. I remember my own sisters. I used to have such sweet memories of them, mostly. (*Indicating the room.*) We used to sleep right in here, sometimes. All of us, together. On hot summer nights. You going to play soon?

KESS: Pretty soon.

EVELYN: We would take sheets—all of us—and we'd open all the windows and the porch door and turn on the fan, and sleep on our wonderful white heaven of bare sheets.

KESS: How about solmizations?

EVELYN: What?

KESS: Do, re, mi, fa, sol . . .

EVELYN: No, I don't allow those. Anyway, it was such an adventure for me. There I was, the baby of the family, trying to stay awake while they were all trying to go to sleep.

KESS: Uh-huh.

EVELYN: All night I would stare right along the floor, under the davenport. I don't know what I ever expected to see there. And in the morning I'd wake up, and someone would have turned off the fan, and it would be cold some mornings, if a front had gone through. And there I'd be: wrapped in a sheet, with Elaine's—she was my favorite sister—with Elaine's arms around me. That's the loveliest waking-up memory I have, and I was married for almost sixteen years.

KESS: Come back to the table.

EVELYN: Have you got a play?

KESS: Just about.

EVELYN: (*Sitting again.*) I think we go at different paces. I like to play a lot of games of Scrabble in one sitting. You make each game a work of art.

KESS: (*Playing two letters.*) Let's see . . . if I do this, it's 4 this way for "gal," 35 for "maze," and 37 for "hazel" because of the two triple-letter scores . . . which makes a grand total of . . . 76.

EVELYN: "Up."

KESS: Four points. Mom, are you enjoying this? We don't have to play if you don't want.

EVELYN: What else would we do?

KESS: Well . . . I guess we could play a little longer.

EVELYN: Why not? (*As* KESS *considers her next move.*) You know, the other night, when I was . . . throwing those dishes? I imagined Jo was there.

KESS: I know. You told me.

EVELYN: All around me, sort of. It was her I was throwing the dishes at. I knew I was imagining—I wasn't confused about that. But it was very vividly her. All those dishes.

KESS: Do you really want to go into it?

EVELYN: No. (*A beat.*) You're my quietest child. You always have been. Sherry talks with every breath, but you never tell me anything, really, about yourself. Mrs. O'Connor saw you the other day.

KESS: Mrs. O'Connor?

EVELYN: You remember her. Your fourth-grade teacher? Always smiles and wears purple? Large teeth? Anyway, she said she still remembers you from then—just the way you were: stiff as a little post, quiet as could be.

KESS: I was not stiff.

EVELYN: Oh, yes you were. She remembers it. She said it was just like you were dead, only you could move from place to place. Isn't that an odd way to put it? I can see what she means, though. Do you have a move? What are you doing?

KESS: (*Having begun to cry silently.*) Nothing.

EVELYN: Are you crying?

KESS: No, I'm fine.

EVELYN: You are. You're crying and you're not making a sound. How do you do that? Cry silently like that. You always cry that way.

KESS: I do not cry silently! I cry out loud like everyone else.

EVELYN: Such a quiet one.

KESS: I was not quiet. You just couldn't hear me.

EVELYN: You were out of the house before I even knew you were that way. "Gay," I mean. Did you know? Back then?

KESS: Of course.

EVELYN: Really? How early?

KESS: Always. There wasn't much I could do about it around here.

EVELYN: Well, of course not. I should hope not.

KESS: There were some things. The woods, for example.

EVELYN: The woods?

KESS: When you were like me, the woods were the only place you could . . . (EVELYN *suddenly rises.*)

EVELYN: I have to use the bathroom, dear. You go on talking if you want. (*She exits for the bathroom.*)

KESS: (*As she goes.*) Hey, you asked me. I'm willing to tell you. I will tell you. *Mom* . . . (*But* EVELYN *is gone.* KESS *waits a beat, then goes on in a loud voice.*) I hated the woods. I hated the birds and trees and spiders and . . . ticks. But when you're sixteen, and you want a lover—and it has to be a girl or you wouldn't be in love—you have to become a YWCA counselor and go to the woods. And just hope some other YWCA counselor is there for the same reason. And pray that people don't find out about you and fire you because they think you want to sleep with eight-year-old campers or something. I spent three summers lying terrified in a puptent for one affair that lasted two weeks, with a counselor I didn't even like. (*A beat.*) Mom? I know you can hear me.

EVELYN: (*Off.*) Go ahead and play. I'll be right out. (KESS *picks up the board and pours the letters into the box.* EVELYN *reenters.*)

KESS: Hi.

EVELYN: Did you win?

KESS: It was a tie.

EVELYN: I don't know what happened. Nature just suddenly called, loud and clear. (*A beat.*) So. What'll we do now?

KESS: Whatever you like.

EVELYN: (*Her eyes suddenly lighting up.*) Let's bake!

KESS: Bake?

EVELYN: Sure. We'll make something fun, for when the girls get home.

KESS: It's getting late . . .

EVELYN: Oh, come on. Remember when we used to do that? On nights your father was . . . when he was out? Jo'd be sleeping upstairs, and you and I would bake for hours together. Biscuits, rolls, cookies—whatever we liked. It would get so late, but you never wanted to stop. I'd say something about the time, and you'd just go, "Ssshhh," and we'd keep on baking.

KESS: Mom . . .

EVELYN: Or I'd say, "Let's wake up Jo and give her some," and you'd shake your head *no.* Very firmly. Remember how it was? Just the two of us, late at night, like the real bakers?

KESS: (*A beat.*) All right, let's bake.

EVELYN: Good! (*Moves toward the kitchen.*) I can't tell you what having you back has meant, Kess. You give me back my sense of control. (*Suddenly we hear* SHERRY *and* JO *outside the porch.*)

SHERRY: (*Off, drunkenly.*) Come on, Jo—can't you recognize your own house?

JO: (*Off, drunkenly.*) It looks different.

SHERRY: (*Helping her through the front door.*) Believe me, this is it. Hi. We're drunk.

KESS: Jo, you said you weren't going to drink.

JO: (*Collapsing on the couch.*) I didn't.

SHERRY: Relax. She only had two beers.

JO: Two and a half.

SHERRY: You shouldn't have had any. Maybe then you wouldn't've been such a social disaster.

JO: I was not a social disaster.

EVELYN: Jo, are you all right?

JO: I'm fine. Am I lying down?

EVELYN: (*To* SHERRY.) What is wrong with her?

SHERRY: Nothing. She flopped, that's all.

EVELYN: Flopped?

JO: Sherry fixed me up. Do you believe it? My little sister fixed me up. With the bartender.

KESS: Sherry, what did you . . . ?

SHERRY: He's a terrific guy. Really easy to work with. At least he was.

JO: He was so handsome. Wasn't he?

SHERRY: You blew it. You froze up every time he talked to you.

JO: I couldn't talk to a man that beautiful.

SHERRY: You wasted two hours of his time. He was really trying.

I never saw him work so hard. He liked you, stupid. (*To the others.*) She was just sitting there like Helen Keller all through it. Finally he says, "Look—I've asked you fifty questions. How about one answer?" Know what she says? "I'm pregnant." She told him she was pregnant.

JO: He asked what I did.

SHERRY: Bartenders are not looking for pregnant women. It's a well-known fact. They don't find them attractive.

JO: I thought I had a special glow.

SHERRY: Yeah, well you glowed him right out of your life. Why do you put all that on somebody when all you want is to get laid?

JO: I did not want to get laid.

SHERRY: There's nothing wrong with it. Some people even like it. (*Suddenly* EVELYN *throws the Scrabble game to the floor. The letters scatter. They look at her. She smiles sweetly, with genuine embarrassment.*)

EVELYN: I'm getting a little tired. Maybe I'd better go to bed.

KESS: Mom, no . . . you don't have to . . .

EVELYN: That's all right.

JO: I wasn't really trying to get . . . you know.

EVELYN: I know. That's all right. Good night.

KESS: We were going to bake . . .

EVELYN: Another time. (*To* SHERRY.) I'm glad you got her home alive. (EVELYN *exits to the stairs.*)

KESS: Good going.

SHERRY: I didn't throw it.

KESS: (*To* JO.) You too.

JO: I'm pregnant and I'm proud. (KESS *starts picking up the Scrabble game.*)

SHERRY: You're pregnant and you're dateless. God, look at us. It's 10:30 and we're home.

KESS: Sherry, help me with this.

SHERRY: Are you kidding? Get Mom to.

JO: (*Rolling off the couch, onto the floor.*) I'll help.

SHERRY: (*Watching them.*) I can't believe it. This is what I get? After three nights of intense therapy?

KESS: Therapy? You've been taking her out to bars.

SHERRY: I've been introducing her to alternative lifestyles. She's the one who wanted to go.

JO: I just want to forget about Don.

KESS: There are better ways.

SHERRY: No, there aren't. Meet new guys. It's the code I live by.

KESS: Yeah, right.

JO: He really was good-looking.

KESS: Wonderful.

SHERRY: What are you mad about? Jo enjoyed herself tonight. She didn't walk around all mopey like she does here.

KESS: How does it feel to be eternally thirteen?

SHERRY: Great. And I'll tell you what else feels great. Getting Jo out of this house and away from a crazy woman.

KESS: *Mom is not a crazy woman.*

SHERRY: She isn't? You don't think it's crazy, trying to kill yourself with a dinner set?

KESS: You heard Dr. Hanson the same as I did. The same as all of us did.

SHERRY: You think I believe a man who's only seen her once?

KESS: He works with her out there.

SHERRY: But he only looked at her once! Yesterday. And I'm supposed to believe him when he says, "Oh, her behavior's just a little extreme—she's not really deeply emotionally disturbed?"

KESS: Yes!

SHERRY: Well, I think it's bullshit. He just doesn't want to be near her, either.

KESS: (*A beat.*) He said, if you'll recall, that she doesn't need to be committed. She just needs to work out some problems here, with us. I think that could happen a lot faster if you guys would stop going out every night.

SHERRY: What do you think we should do? Sit around and have tea all day?

KESS: It might help.

SHERRY: Wonderful. We have tea for a week, and then you leave for Minnesota again.

KESS: Who says I'm leaving in a week?

SHERRY: You have to go back sometime. Face it, Kess, you can't do her any good.

KESS: What good are you doing her?

SHERRY: *I'm* ignoring her. (*A beat.*) Who did you come down here for, anyway? I thought it was Jo.

KESS: (*Tiredly.*) Everybody. I came down for everybody.

SHERRY: I think you came down for you. (*A beat.*) To hell with this, I'm going to dance. (SHERRY *moves toward her room.*)

JO: Oh . . . Sherry, *no* . . .

SHERRY: (*Disappearing into her room.*) Why not? Time for music!

JO: You always play it too loud . . .

SHERRY: (*Off.*) Too loud! You're crazy! (*Loud rock music suddenly issues forth.* SHERRY *reenters, as* KESS *exits into the kitchen.*)

JO: This is not considerate!

SHERRY: (*Dancing.*) Why? 'Cause it's what I like?

JO: You do this all the time! (*As they speak,* KESS *reenters, carrying a pair of scissors, such that* SHERRY *doesn't see them.* KESS *goes into* SHERRY*'s room. The music stops.*)

SHERRY: Hey! Turn that back on! (KESS *returns, with the scissors.*) What are you doing?

KESS: (*Working the scissors.*) You need new speaker wires.

SHERRY: *What?!* (*She hurries into her room.* KESS *looks at* JO *on her way upstairs.*)

KESS: I'll expect everybody for tea at five tomorrow.

JO: Kess . . . (*But* KESS *disappears upstairs.*)

SHERRY: (*Off.*) You're a *barbarian!* (*Reentering.*) Where is she?

JO: She went up . . .

SHERRY: (*Starting for the stairs.*) I'll kill her!

JO: (*Grabbing her.*) Sherry, stop . . . !

SHERRY: You screwed-up, over-achieving dyke!

JO: (*Holding her.*) Sherry . . .

SHERRY: *I'm gonna rip up all your books!*

JO: Sherry, let's do something fun, ok?

SHERRY: *I'm gonna blow up your car!*

JO: Sherry . . . !

SHERRY: *You hear me?*

JO: Let's do something fun! Please? Let's just do something fun! (*Lights fade quickly to black.*)

Scene Two

Friday afternoon, the next day. KESS *and* EVELYN *enter from the kitchen.* KESS *carries tea for four on a tray, which she sets on a low table near the couch.*

KESS: (*In a loud voice, as she enters.*) Come on, everybody. This is going to be fun.

EVELYN: Where should I sit?

KESS: Anywhere. Wherever you're comfortable. (EVELYN *looks dubiously at all potential seats.* KESS *points out a chair.*) How about there?

EVELYN: (*Sitting.*) All right.

KESS: Sherry? Jo? You coming?

SHERRY: (*Off, in the kitchen.*) We're thinking about it.

KESS: Come on, come on—the tea'll get cold. (*To* EVELYN.) You want cream, right?

EVELYN: Thanks.

KESS: (*Sing-song.*) Sher-ry, Jo-o . . .

SHERRY: (*Entering in a dirty shirt and jeans, mimicking* KESS'S *tone.*) All ri-ight, we're com-ing.

JO: (*Entering, neatly dressed.*) Where do you want us to sit?

KESS: Wherever you like. (SHERRY *and* JO *look around dubiously.*

KESS *points out two places.*) Ok, you: there. You: there. (*They sit.*) Everyone comfortable? How do you want your tea?

SHERRY: In my room.

KESS: Jo?

JO: Just plain.

KESS: (*Handing a cup to* JO, *then* SHERRY.) Fine. Sherry? (SHERRY *pauses, then takes a cup.*) Good. Now. Here we are—just as Dr. Hanson suggested—all four of us, sitting down together. First, I want to thank you all for agreeing to try.

SHERRY: I'm only doing it to show I can. Besides, I'm tired of working on my sculpture.

KESS: That's OK. Dr. Hanson said it's more important to go through the motions of being a happy family than it is to actually feel like one—at least, at this point. The more we act like a normal, happy family, the better the chance we'll become one someday. The new way of behaving will become as natural and unavoidable as the old, bad way.

SHERRY: I like the old bad way.

KESS: I know. But for now, let's act nice. OK? As an experiment. So—who'd like to be the first to say something nice? (*A long silence.*)

EVELYN: The tea is very good.

KESS: Thank you. That's a good start. Would anyone else like to offer something positive? (*Another awkward silence.*)

JO: I like my cup. I mean, I've always liked these cups, ever since you got them.

EVELYN: Thank you.

KESS: Good. Anyone else? (*A beat.*) Sherry, I think I'm getting to like your sculpture.

SHERRY: Fuck you.

JO: *Sherry . . .*

SHERRY: I didn't raise my voice.

KESS: That's not the point.

SHERRY: Well, you're only saying that. You don't like my stuff any more than anyone else.

KESS: I know, but I'm pretending to.

SHERRY: Then you're just lying.

KESS: That's right.

SHERRY: Why?

KESS: *To be nice!! (With more control.)* Sorry. Please—just say thank you, OK? You don't have to know what it means; you don't have to feel it. Just say it. (*A beat.* SHERRY *rises.*)

SHERRY: No way.

JO: Why not?

SHERRY: (*Moving toward her room.*) This is stupid. I don't want to do this.

KESS: You mean, you can't do it.

SHERRY: (*Stopping by her door.*) I can do it.

KESS: No, you can't.

SHERRY: I can.

KESS: Prove it.

SHERRY: (*A beat. With extreme unpleasantness.*) Thank you, Kess. That was a lovely compliment about my sculpture.

KESS: You're welcome. Wouldn't you like to come sit down again?

SHERRY: I'll stand.

KESS: That's fine with me—everybody else?

JO: Sure.

EVELYN: Sherry can do what she likes. She always does.

SHERRY: You call that positive?!

KESS: Mom, I thought we agreed to try this.

EVELYN: Aren't I doing it right?

KESS: Let's start over. How about if each of us talks about something she's doing, and then the rest of us find a positive comment to make about it? How would that be?

SHERRY: Stupid.

KESS: Sherry, why don't you tell about your sculpture? What do you like about it most?

SHERRY: It's grotesque.

KESS: (*Forging ahead.*) OK. Grotesque. Good. Why do you like that?

SHERRY: It scares Mrs. Anderberg. Ever since I put the little fawn and the stable boy together in an unnatural act. Makes her weed her garden a lot faster.

KESS: Does anyone have anything . . . positive to say about that?

JO: Well . . . weeding faster is probably good exercise.

KESS: Good, Jo. That's a positive comment. So, fine. So. We have one . . . sort of . . . civil exchange. Let's try for more. Mom? Tell us what you've been doing.

EVELYN: Me? Oh—nothing. You know me.

KESS: What'd you do this morning?

EVELYN: Went out for a walk.

KESS: And?

EVELYN: I walked.

KESS: Did you see anybody?

EVELYN: Certainly.

KESS: (*A beat.*) Who?

EVELYN: Who? Um . . . Mrs. Matthews.

KESS: How was she?

EVELYN: Fine. I didn't really have a very eventful morning. Why don't we go to Jo?

KESS: Did you and Mrs. Matthews talk?

EVELYN: Yes, but . . .

KESS: What about?

EVELYN: Oh, nothing much.

KESS: What?

EVELYN: Just . . . Jo.

KESS: Jo. Fine. Did she have anything nice to say about Jo?

EVELYN: Of course. She's always liked Jo. Why don't we talk about . . . ?

KESS: What exactly did she say about Jo?

EVELYN: Nothing. Just that Jo's a very strong girl in some ways.

KESS: Did you hear that, Jo? Now, that's exactly what I mean, Mom. Why should you be slow to tell us a thing like that?

EVELYN: Well . . .

KESS: What's strong about her? How did it come up?

EVELYN: Oh, I don't know . . .

KESS: It must've come from something.

EVELYN: Not really.

KESS: Mom, what aren't you telling us?

EVELYN: Nothing.

JO: Mom? What is it?

EVELYN: Oh, Jo—I'll tell you later, all right? When we're alone.

JO: Is it private?

EVELYN: Well . . .

SHERRY: So what is it? Don getting married or something?

EVELYN: Who told you?

SHERRY: You're kidding. That was a joke.

JO: Don's getting married?

KESS: Mom, what are you . . . ?

JO: Who to?

EVELYN: I was going to tell you later . . .

JO: *Who to?!*

EVELYN: Heidi Joy Duckly. Mrs. Matthews heard it this morning from Heidi's mother.

JO: Oh, God . . .

KESS: Jo . . .

JO: Oh, *God.*

KESS: Jo, listen—there are two ways to handle this.

SHERRY: Yeah? Suicide and what?

KESS: Shut up!

SHERRY: Very positive.

KESS: Jo, we can fly off the handle here, or we can be calm about it. We can find something useful in it.

JO: *Useful?!*

KESS: Yes. Something. That's the problem with us. Trouble comes, and we break down. Let's not do that.

SHERRY: Heidi's folks must feel great to get rid of her. The wedding oughta be a prize pork show.

KESS: *Sherry.*

SHERRY: She's only losing a Subaru.

EVELYN: I think you're lucky to be rid of him.

JO: I'm not *lucky!* (*She rises, moves toward the stairs.*)

KESS: Where are you going?

JO: My room! (*But she stops suddenly, slumps against the archway.*)

SHERRY: What are you stopping for?

JO: We used to make love up there.

EVELYN: That's the trouble with an old house. It always fills up with ghosts. Good memories turn into bad ones. I know I see your father in every room. Not literally, of course. Speaking of memories, Jo—do you know what I've been doing in the attic?

JO: What?

EVELYN: I've been painting. Just a little, every day. Guess what I've been painting.

JO: What?

EVELYN: The baby furniture. All the baby furniture—yours and Kess's and Sherry's. I've been making it new for your new baby. I was going to keep it a secret, but I think you can use a little good news right now. Would you like to come up and see?

JO: Well . . .

EVELYN: Oh, come on. It's turning out so nice. Your baby is going to live right here with us—with her mother and her grandma. Just the way I did when I was a little girl. And she's going to be every bit as happy and well-cared-for and loved as I was. Doesn't that sound nice? Wouldn't you like to come up and see?

JO: All right.

KESS: Jo . . .

EVELYN: (*Rising.*) Good.

KESS: *Jo*—don't you think it would be better to keep trying this? You can see the furniture later.

JO: (*A beat.*) I'm going up. (JO *turns and hurries upstairs.*)

KESS: Jo . . . !

EVELYN: Kess, I'm sorry this game didn't work out. Maybe we'll do better another time. (EVELYN *exits upstairs.*)

KESS: (*A beat.*) You see what I'm trying to do, don't you?

SHERRY: Sure. You're trying to make a family where there isn't one. (*A beat.*) Jo and I are going to see the new James Bond tonight. Want to come? (*A beat.*) Be a chance to get away from Mom.

KESS: (*A beat.*) All right.

SHERRY: Good. (SHERRY *exits into her room.* KESS *sighs, leans her head back on the couch. Her hand moves up to touch the cameo. Lights slowly fade to black.*)

Scene Three

Late that same night. The room is empty, the tea set is gone. After a moment, we hear the giggling of KESS, JO, *and* SHERRY *outside the porch.*

SHERRY: (*Off.*) I'm not going in first. Jo, you go.

JO: (*Off.*) Why don't you?

SHERRY: (*Off.*) Kess?

KESS: (*Off.*) You're standing next to the door. Go on in.

SHERRY: (*Off.*) What if Mom's in there?

KESS: (*Off.*) Of course she's in there . . .

SHERRY: (*Off.*) But what if she's waiting for us? With a plate?

KESS and JO: (*Off, disapprovingly.*) *Sherry* . . .

SHERRY: (*Entering.*) OK, OK. Lousy joke.

JO: (*Entering with* KESS.) Very lousy.

KESS: Mom? We're back. Mom? (*Looking into the kitchen.*) Where are you?

JO: I'll go look in her room. (JO *exits upstairs.*)

KESS: You think we made enough noise walking home?

SHERRY: I still say we should've hit Popeye's for a beer.

KESS: Jo's pregnant.

SHERRY: *I'm* not.

KESS: It's been a long time since I actually enjoyed walking around this town. Maybe I should make some coffee.

SHERRY: What is this thing between you and caffeine? (JO *reenters.*)

JO: She's OK.

SHERRY: She's OK and I'm sober. (*Flops into a chair.*)

KESS: I'm glad we did this tonight. We saw a good movie.

JO: You think so? I didn't like it.

SHERRY: You're just mad 'cause the woman didn't die.

JO: I think that really changes things . . .

SHERRY: Sure. Dead, you don't mind. What you hate is when they sail off into the sunset for a lifetime of meaningless sex.

JO: Well, yes, as a matter of fact.

SHERRY: Believe me, big sister—it's the best way to get out of this house. Dedicate yourself to meaningless sex.

JO: Don't be ridiculous.

SHERRY: I mean it. You should go out and do it with whoever you want, whenever you feel like it, and not think about it afterward. Puts you in a very different state of mind.

JO: I can't do that.

SHERRY: Sure you can. Want me to set up? I know a bunch of guys—we'll toss their names in a hat. It's what I do myself.

KESS: How many lovers have you had?

SHERRY: My share. And all meaningless, too. I'm the first lady of meaningless sex. You guys screw up 'cause you think it's supposed to mean something.

JO: It does.

SHERRY: No, it doesn't. I slept with a guy once 'cause I liked his socks. What'd that mean?

KESS: Not much, I guess.

SHERRY: Damn right. I've slept with guys who would make you vomit. This one I knew was really sloppy. A total pig. But I wondered if maybe he was just profound and didn't have time for cleaning. So I went home with him.

KESS: Naturally.

SHERRY: His place was incredible. It looked like he cooked in the bedroom and slept in the kitchen. So anyway—we did it on this bare mattress on the floor. And when we got done, he rolled over, reached under the dresser, among all the hairballs and shit, and pulled out a spoon.

JO: Oh, God! God! Stop it!

SHERRY: And he said, "Want some chili?"

JO: Sherry, stop it! Ew!

SHERRY: Hey—truth is gross.

JO: Well, I've never had any meaningless sex.

SHERRY: Ever faked an orgasm?

KESS: I faked an orgasm with a woman. (*They look at her.*) I mean, if you want to talk meaningless.

SHERRY: You're kidding.

KESS: If you want to talk true meaningless, I've had sex with a man, just so I could meet his sister. Top that.

SHERRY: You really did that?

KESS: Yes, when I was young and stupid.

SHERRY: I had sex with a guy at a concert and never even knew his name. Top that.

JO: You guys . . .

KESS: I had sex with a woman in a dorm laundry, and never even saw her face.

SHERRY: Yeah, but did you talk to her? I never talked to my guy at the concert.

JO: You guys! Is this all we can talk about? I don't care what either of you did. I think it's more disgusting to talk about that kind of sex than to have it.

SHERRY: I'd rather be disgusting than pitiful. You've got the most screwed-up sex life I ever . . .

JO: *I'm* screwed? You're the one who always forgets who she had the night before.

SHERRY: At least I have someone to forget.

JO: I had someone.

SHERRY: Yeah, and now he's marrying Heidi. Hope you and Mom'll be very happy together.

JO: (*A beat. Quietly.*) Well, at least with Don it wasn't meaningless.

SHERRY: Oh, yes it was.

KESS: Why don't we talk about the movie?

SHERRY: It was. Simpleton thinks Don was faithful the whole time they were together.

JO: He was faithful.

SHERRY: Don slept with at least six girls while you were dating. Including Heidi.

JO: How do you know that?

SHERRY: They told me.

JO: You're lying! That's just a complete lie.

SHERRY: Wake up. Don sleeps with everybody in town.

KESS: You guys . . .

JO: He does not!

SHERRY: Oh yeah? He slept with me! (*A beat. They are all perfectly still.*) Once.

JO: When? (*A beat.*) When?!

SHERRY: After you dropped him. What do you care? It's all meaningless.

JO: Not to me!

SHERRY: For God's sake, Heidi's the one who should be mad, not you. I wouldn't've told you, but you just keep being so pitiful about it all. You want him and then you don't want him . . . (*She trails off, in deep embarrassment.*) I'm sorry.

JO: It's so easy for us to criticize Mom. To say she made us like we are. But she never did anything just for the cruelty of it. If she hurts us, it's because she's afraid, and disappointed and doesn't want to be left alone. But we do it just for the fun.

KESS: Jo . . .

JO: We're supposed to be the healthy ones. Aren't we? Aren't we? (*She rises.*) Good night. (JO *exits in silence.* KESS *looks at* SHERRY.)

SHERRY: I'm sorry. It slipped out. (*A beat.*) Maybe we should have some coffee.

KESS: As long as you make it on your knees.

SHERRY: (*Exiting into the kitchen.*) I said I was sorry. (KESS *starts for the stairs, stops.* SHERRY *calls from the kitchen.*) Hey, what are these letters on the counter?

KESS: The mail. I brought it in today.

SHERRY: (*Off.*) No wonder I can never find it. (*A beat.*) Hey! Hey, Kess! I got a letter! From Spinner!

KESS: Spinner?

SHERRY: (*Off.*) My biker!

KESS: Oh. Wonderful.

SHERRY: (*Reentering with the letter.*) No, Kess—wait! It's from a *gallery!!* He enclosed a letter from a gallery! It's the . . . um, the Raoul Gallery in . . . um, *BROOKLYN!!* They want to talk to *me!*

KESS: About what?

SHERRY: About me, about my work! Don't you see? Spinner really took my stuff to New York! I didn't think he would, but he did! And they love my slides! They're calling my stuff a whole new school of art! It's . . . it's . . . um, Post-Post-Modern Infantilist! Isn't that great!? I'm knocking 'em dead back there!

KESS: Sherry . . .

SHERRY: Kess! They want to do a show! They want me there right now! Just when I was starting to think he didn't really work for Walt Disney!

KESS: They want you where?

SHERRY: New York! For the show. They want to fly me in. Do you know how they live in New York? They are total animals! I can't *wait!* I'm flying tomorrow.

KESS: Who pays?

SHERRY: What?

KESS: Who buys the plane ticket?

SHERRY: I do. Why not? The whole point is getting the chance.

KESS: What's the name of the gallery?

SHERRY: The Raoul Gallery.

KESS: Sherry.

SHERRY: What?

KESS: The *Raoul* Gallery? In Brooklyn?

SHERRY: What's wrong with that?

KESS: It's ridiculous. It's a joke.

SHERRY: You think they're not real?

KESS: Sherry . . .

SHERRY: (*Defensively.*) They're real. They've got a letterhead. They're real.

KESS: Sure.

SHERRY: They're real!

KESS: Can't you see that Spinner is just doing this to you? God knows why, but . . .

SHERRY: Spinner is a professional!

KESS: A professional what—that's the question.

SHERRY: Spinner and I had the one honest exchange of my whole senior year.

KESS: How much did you exchange?

SHERRY: Damn it, if he says it's real, then it's real!

KESS: Sherry, look at me. Come on, look in my face. Do you really believe there is a Post-Post-Modern Infantilist school of art?

SHERRY: (*Exploding.*) *Yes!!* God damn it! I believe more in that than in this goddamn, stupid fucking family! There *is* a Raoul Gallery!

KESS: Sherry . . .

SHERRY: There is!

KESS: Sherry, take it easy . . .

SHERRY: I'm having a show! And I'm going!

KESS: (*Touching her.*) Shh—I know you are.

SHERRY: I am!

KESS: I know, it's all right.

SHERRY: It's in Brooklyn! (*She is near tears.*)

KESS: (*Taking hold of her.*) I know. I know it is.

SHERRY: Brooklyn, New York. And I'm going, I'm . . .

KESS: Shh. I know. You're going to New York. I know. You're going to New York. (*They are silent.* KESS *holds her and rocks her.*)

SHERRY: (*Quietly.*) How did Mom live a whole life here?

KESS: She had us. (*Lights slowly fade to black.*)

Scene Four

Afternoon, the next day. No one is onstage. JO *rushes in the front door.*

JO: Kess? Kess!?

KESS: (*Off.*) I'm upstairs!

JO: Can you come down?

KESS: (*Off.*) In a minute. (JO *looks around the room, goes to* SHERRY*'s door, looks in.*)

JO: Sherry? You home? (*No response.* JO *stands nervously.*) Kess!

KESS: (*Off.*) I'm coming, I'm coming! (KESS *enters from upstairs.*) What's wrong?

JO: Where were you?

KESS: Upstairs.

JO: Nobody seemed to be here.

KESS: What's wrong?

JO: Where's Mom?

KESS: She's at the store.

JO: Where's Sherry?

KESS: With Mom. Jo, what are you . . . ?

JO: So, they're not here.

KESS: (*A beat.*) Jo, where have you been all morning?

JO: On an errand.

KESS: A four-hour errand?

JO: I had to go over to Waterloo. (*A beat.*) Kess, do you remember when you asked me to come up and stay with you?

KESS: Yes.

JO: Did you mean that?

KESS: Well . . . yes, at the time . . .

JO: I want to come up. I want to come up right now.

KESS: Now?

JO: Yes. And I want to stay. I want to stay for the summer at least, maybe a lot longer.

KESS: Jo, what are you talking about?

JO: I want to come up. You said I could come up. You said that roommate of yours, that . . .

KESS: Susan.

JO: You said Susan thinks it's OK.

KESS: Well, yes, but . . . why now?

JO: I have to get away from Mom.

KESS: What'd she do?

JO: Nothing.

KESS: (*A beat.*) Yesterday you and Mom were planning which room to use for the nursery. What happened? Why are you so scared?

JO: I just did a . . . very odd thing. I went over to Heidi's house. I thought I was only going over to talk with her. Just to . . . look her in the eye once, and ask her if she really slept with Don while he and I were . . . you know, like Sherry said . . .

KESS: I know.

JO: But as I turned the corner I saw her pull out and drive away. So I followed her.

KESS: To Waterloo? (JO *nods.*) What did you do there?

JO: I watched. I watched the way she drove. I watched the way she shopped. She hit all the bridal shops, plus a few others. She's a good shopper.

KESS: Did she see you?

JO: No. I hid. I stayed two cars behind her, like on TV, and I hid behind pillars in the stores. I never lost her. I stared at her and stared at her for four hours, and she never saw me and I never lost her. I didn't want to talk with her anymore. I just wanted to watch her. On the way home, I thought, "My God, why am I doing this!?" But I just kept following, I thought, "*Mom* should be driving this car. I should be Mom doing this." Then I thought, "I am." Kess, I love Mom.

KESS: I know that.

JO: I thought of how I'll be in ten years, if I stay with Mom. Kess, I can't be Mom. How can I help her if I'm just like her?

KESS: Jo . . .

JO: I want to leave tomorrow. And I want to stay with you. Is that all right?

KESS: Well . . . I'm not sure that's the best idea anymore.

JO: *Kess . . .*

KESS: Jo, we can't leave Mom the way she is. I thought we could, but that was before I saw how lonely she was . . .

JO: I don't care . . .

KESS: Besides, she could hurt herself. That's why I've stayed down here so long—to make sure she's all right.

JO: She's all right; let's go.

KESS: She's not all right.

JO: She never will be!

KESS: Jo, what if I stay down here another few days, and then come back on regular visits, once a month, for as long as . . . for as long as it takes? Could you stay here then?

JO: No! I'm coming up north, and I'm living with you. You offered it. And I need it.

KESS: Jo . . .

JO: You owe me! (*A beat.*) I don't care how guilty you feel, Kess. I don't. We can't save Mom. Save me. (*We suddenly hear* SHERRY *and* EVELYN *at the front door.*)

SHERRY: Here we are—Shoppers Anonymous. (*Entering.*) Hi, everybody. It's everybody else. Where'd you go this morning, Jo? Somewhere fun?

JO: No.

SHERRY: (*Carrying the bag into the kitchen.*) Should've come with us. The store was full of living sculptures.

EVELYN: (*At the screen door, with a bag of groceries.*) Can someone help me with the door?

KESS: (*Hurrying to open it.*) Oh—sorry.

EVELYN: Thank you. Hi, Jo. Did you have a good morning? Oh, let me set these *down.* (*Doing so, on the couch.*) There. Why is modern food so heavy? Sherry and I decided to have a big dinner tonight, for Kess. We haven't really done that yet, and Kess is starting to fit in so well.

SHERRY: (*Reentering, to* KESS.) Yeah. Are you sure you're not crazy?

EVELYN: Jo, do you want to help me cook it?

JO: No.

EVELYN: Oh? Are you busy tonight?

JO: No.

EVELYN: (*A beat.*) Oh. Well, maybe you can, Kess.

JO: She can't either.

EVELYN: Why not?

KESS: Jo, this isn't the right time . . .

JO: She'll be packing. So will I.

EVELYN: Packing? What for?

JO: I'm going to Minneapolis with her.

EVELYN: (*A beat.*) Really?

JO: Yes.

EVELYN: I don't understand. You mean for a visit?

JO: No.

EVELYN: For longer?

JO: Forever.

EVELYN: (*A beat.*) You're pregnant. You can't travel.

JO: Two and a half months. We're not going by covered wagon.

KESS: Jo . . .

EVELYN: Oh, this is a joke. Isn't it? You and Kess have created a joke. Oh, I see now. Well, it's very funny. (*She takes an orange out of the bag.*) Isn't this a joke, Kess?

KESS: No, not exactly . . .

JO: Mom, I've been following Heidi around.

EVELYN: Following Heidi? What for?

JO: Just to watch her. Just to watch what she does all day.

SHERRY: That must be a thrill.

JO: I couldn't help myself. I just followed her.

EVELYN: We all have impulses that are hard to control. (*She tosses the orange casually onto the couch.*)

JO: I'm afraid I'll go crazy.

EVELYN: (*Flaring.*) What in hell do you know about it?! I've *been* in mental hospitals!

JO: I was only . . .

EVELYN: You were only trying to sneak out of here! In the dust of everybody else galloping away! (*She tosses another orange onto the couch.*)

SHERRY: Mom, what are you doing?

EVELYN: What?

SHERRY: You're putting oranges on the couch.

EVELYN: Well, of course I'm putting oranges on the couch! This is my house. People used to live in it. (*A beat.*) Who's going to stay here?

JO: Well . . . Sherry . . .

EVELYN: She'll be out the door twenty seconds after commencement.

JO: Kess says she'll visit . . .

EVELYN: Who'll *live* here?

JO: When I followed Heidi, I even followed her home. I did. I sat in my car and watched her mother come out and help her bring in the things she'd bought. They were laughing. They looked like sisters.

EVELYN: Jo . . .

JO: You're crazy! And when you're not crazy, you're angry. When you're not angry, you're demanding. It can be months between times we have any pleasure!

EVELYN: Jo . . .

JO: I'm the only person who has ever put up with you!

EVELYN: (*Reaching to embrace her.*) Jo . . .

JO: (*Retreating.*) No! I'm living with Kess. I have to. I have to.

EVELYN: (*A beat.*) You can't. You can't, and that's all there is to it. It's a ridiculous idea. Kess, was this your idea?

KESS: No . . .

EVELYN: Jo could never live with you. She's going to have a baby.

KESS: What are you talking about?

EVELYN: You could never live with a baby.

KESS: Of course I could live with a baby.

EVELYN: You don't know the first thing. You'd panic in a minute.

KESS: I can live with a baby!

EVELYN: *You don't know what they want!*

JO: It's my baby!

EVELYN: You shut up! I'm talking to Kess.

KESS: Mom, what if Jo just comes up for a little while? Just to see how it goes?

JO: *No.*

KESS: We could come down on visits.

JO: *No!*

EVELYN: Do you really want to take her from me?

JO: I'm going!

KESS: I don't want to take anybody from anybody . . .

EVELYN: Well, that's what you're doing. You girls would like a world full of strangers, wouldn't you? You'd like it if there was no connection between people at all. (*Focusing on* JO.) Well, there isn't. Not unless you make one. Kess and Henry taught me that. They were the two most silent people I ever knew. For eight years they were my whole family. Henry and Kess. Can you imagine what dinners were like? I had to beg Henry for you. You were all I ever got out of my whole family. You're the only one I can look at and not see Henry.

JO: (*Backing away.*) I can't help you.

EVELYN: Then who can?

JO: I can't help you.

EVELYN: I just need you to be here a little more. Just a few days.

JO: I can't! I can't help you, I can't be with you, I can't look at you, I can't think about you, I can't talk to you, I can't hope for you . . .

EVELYN: Can you love me?

JO: *It's not a matter of love!!*

EVELYN: Can you?

JO: Kess!

EVELYN: What do you think families are for? Do you think parents die when you turn twenty-one? I might as well have, if all you're leaving me is the Mental Health Institute and a townful of people saying, "Poor Evelyn Briggs. First her husband walks off, then every one of her daughters abandons her."

KESS: We're not abandoning you. We'll be back. We'll visit.

EVELYN: When? How often?

KESS: Once a month.

EVELYN: Once a month?

KESS: Twice, then. Twice a month.

JO: No . . . !

KESS: *Jo!* Mom? What do you say?

EVELYN: I have wasted my life raising three *animals!!*

JO: (*To* KESS.) I won't come down!

EVELYN: I lived my life for you! My mother lived her life for me. That's what family means—each generation destroying itself willingly, for what comes after. Even if it's you! (*A silence.* KESS *slowly unpins the cameo from her dress.*)

KESS: (*Quietly.*) Jo and I are going to go upstairs and pack. We'll talk about visits later. (*Placing the cameo on a table next to* EVELYN.) I think you should keep this for awhile. (*A beat.* KESS *starts for the stairs.*) Come on, Jo. (*As* JO *starts after her,* EVELYN *reaches into the grocery bag and pulls out a can. She raises it high in the air.*)

SHERRY: Mom! (EVELYN *smashes the can down on the cameo.*)

JO: *NO!*

KESS: Mom!

SHERRY: Jesus! (*A beat. The heirloom is in pieces.*)

JO: How could you do that? How could you do that?!

EVELYN: Because it was mine. (*Lights fade to black.*)

Scene Five

Morning, the next day. Before lights rise we hear SHERRY*'s voice in the darkness. Lights slowly fade up midway through her song to reveal her sitting with* KESS*'s ballad book open in her lap.*

SHERRY: "Tis down in yonder garden green,
Love where we used to walk,
The finest flower that e'er was seen
Is withered to a stalk.

(*She shifts from the traditional tune to a punk version.*)

The stalk is withered dry, my love
So will our hearts decay . . ."

(KESS *enters through the porch, and* SHERRY *immediately snaps the book shut.*)

KESS: Is Jo ready? I've got all my stuff in the car.

SHERRY: (*Holding the book up.*) You don't have this.

KESS: (*Taking it.*) Oh—thanks. Jo upstairs?

SHERRY: Guess so.

KESS: What'll you do? When we're gone?

SHERRY: Graduate. Move out.

KESS: (*A beat.*) You're welcome to come and see us, if you ever . . .

SHERRY: (*Suddenly rising.*) Look, I'm going to go over to Ed Randall's for awhile. If Mom asks, tell her I'm there, OK?

KESS: Sure . . . Don't you want to say goodby to Jo?

SHERRY: No, that's OK.

KESS: Sherry?

SHERRY: What?

KESS: Glad I got to know you again.

SHERRY: Yeah, well . . . see you in four years. (SHERRY *exits out the front.* KESS *looks around the room a little nervously, then calls.*)

KESS: Jo-o! I'm all set! (JO *enters from upstairs with a pair of bags.*)

JO: Here I am.

KESS: Is that all your stuff?

JO: The rest is in the car.

KESS: Well . . . then, um . . . let's go, I guess.

JO: Could you take these out? I'd like to say goodbye to Mom.

KESS: I already tried. It's not much use.

JO: Could you anyway? (KESS *shrugs, takes the bags.*)

KESS: I'll be in the car. (KESS *exits out the front.*)

JO: (*Calling upstairs.*) Mom?! I'm leaving! Mom? Could you come down? (JO *waits uncomfortably for a moment.*) Mom?! (*She waits again. Finally she shakes her head and starts for the front door.* EVELYN *appears from upstairs.*) Oh—um, we're leaving now.

EVELYN: I know.

JO: I'm sorry I took so long to pack. (*A beat.*) I'm going to write, you know. Whether or not you write back. (*A beat.*) And . . . I will visit, after awhile. If you'd like me to. (*A beat.*) I talked to Mrs. Anderberg. She said she'll be glad to come over, as much as you need.

EVELYN: That's nice. She wasn't really born here, you know. She's from Michigan.

JO: I called Dr. Hanson. He'd like to talk with you sometime. Just talk. Whenever you'd like to.

EVELYN: (*A beat.*) Is there anything else?

JO: I want to hug you.

EVELYN: (*A beat.*) Go ahead. Hug me. (JO *hesitates, then does so.* EVELYN *doesn't resist, but neither does she raise her arms to hug back.* JO *steps back and stares at her.*)

JO: I could call when we get up there. This afternoon, I mean. (*A beat.*) I think I will. (*A beat.* JO *starts to leave, stops.*) Should I? (*A beat.* JO *leaves. Lights slowly fade to black as* EVELYN *remains still.*)

THE END

BEAUTIFUL BODIES

Laura Cunningham

BEAUTIFUL BODIES premiered at The Whole Theatre (Olympia Dukakis, Artistic Director) in October 1987. It was directed by Vivian Matalon; the set design was by Michael Miller; the costume design was by Sam Flemming; the lighting design was by Richard Nelson; and the production stage manager was Kathleen Cunneen. The cast was as follows:

JESSIE	Karen Allen
NINA	Maria Cellario
LISBETH	Ellen Foley
MARTHA	Caroline Aaron
SUE CAROL	Mia Dillon
CLAIRE	Amy Van Nostrand

CAST: Six women, all in their thirties

SET: Non-realistic NoHo loft

ACT I

The stage is dark. A sudden, single beam of light illuminates the figure of a young woman (JESSIE). *The momentary vision*—A WOMAN, *kneeling in profile. Then: darkness. Next: A backdrop of lower Manhattan flickers into view. The effect accelerates as if dusk has fallen on the city and the downtown buildings have begun to light up the night sky. The view is that of a second floor loft in NoHo. We see the sparkle of the twin towers, the giant clock face. The night cityscape is close, dominating. Now, interior lamps begin to illuminate the loft itself. We now see that* JESSIE *is kneeling center-stage in her living room. The loft has been created from a factory space, and throughout,* JESSIE*'s warm, beautiful touch does battle with the industrial design. The set should not be strictly "real" but can be stylized: seating platforms instead of sofas, a token Deco floor lamp: artifacts of more gracious times. The loft is not slick, but still raw. Only as* JESSIE*'s rose-colored lampshades light do we enter her softer world. We see a kitchen area, stage left, with a meal in progress being cooked. Also stage left: a bathroom door. Down stage right: a freight-style elevator door. The loft has been prepared for an informal gathering: odd chairs or floor pillows form a semicircle. In the center, an antique bassinet.* JESSIE *kneels to arrange this bassinet, then moves with increased speed to finish her preparations for the party. She tries to "hide" cooking mess, stashing pots, shoving trash bag aside. She turns on her CD player—a fugue sounds. Instantly, she switches to something lighter. She runs around, applying last minute touches. As she places a toy—a baby lamb—in the basket, it begins to* baaaah.

JESSIE: (*Ironic*) Jesus.

(*She is trying to silence the* baah-*ing lamb, when the door buzzer shrills.*)

JESSIE: (*Continued.*) (*As she runs to answer the door.*) Who is it?

NINA'S VOICE: Me.

(NINA *enters.* NINA *is also thirty-three, but is an altogether bigger woman: bigger voice, bigger breasts. She even wears bigger rings. She enters, bundled for winter weather, shivery as if she was caught in a bitter wind. As she removes her heavy coat, we see she is faddishly dressed in a designer outfit that is almost too small.* NINA *and* JESSIE *kiss, ritually, missing each others' cheeks. They trade pleasantries in unison.*)

JESSIE, NINA: You look terrific.

(*They inspect one another.*)

I mean it. You look terrific.

JESSIE: You've done something. Your hair. Your hair was never red.

NINA: It oxidized.

JESSIE: It suits you. It is you. You look great.

NINA: I guess. Nine guys molested me on my way over . . .

JESSIE: Nine? Really? No one molests *me* anymore . . .

NINA: Oh, they don't really molest me . . . They just make noises . . .

(*She imitates lip-smacking, kissing sounds.*)

JESSIE: They used to do that when I walked by. Now, they offer me drugs.

NINA: (*Handing her a box.*) Here. It's a chocolate mousse cake.

JESSIE: Oh, a mousse cake!

NINA: Don't let me eat any of it. It's for all of you.

(*Pause*)

I'll just watch.

(*Pause.*)

I can't eat till Thursday.

(*She waves a Diet Center packet.*)

I'll just mix up my little packet when you all eat. I haven't had solid food since July.

JESSIE: No! You *have* to eat! I've stuffed five Cornish hens.

(*She gestures toward kitchen.*)

It looks like a Cornish hen mass murder in there.

NINA: It's okay . . . I still take pleasure in watching others eat. It's become a kind of spectator sport for me.

(NINA *circles the bassinet, inspects baby shower decorations, preparations.*)

God, Jessie. You don't kid around.

JESSIE: I want Claire to have the whole thing!

(NINA *sets her gift boxes on the table. She looks askance at the display.*)

NINA: Am I going to have to "ooh" and "aah"?

JESSIE: Over every little bootie.

NINA: Omigod. You'll have to help me. I don't know if I can get through this. I haven't been to a baby shower since Kew Gardens.

JESSIE: They had a lot of them?

NINA: Are you kidding? That's what Kew Gardens is *for* . . . God, it's fertile out there . . . Everybody reproducing. Half my high school *had* to get married. We didn't use birth control. We just denied sex took place.

(*Pause.*)

Cynthia Greenspan didn't even make it to graduation. Her water broke in Social Studies.

(*Pause.*)

Christ. Her kid must be fifteen. I could go out with him.

(*She shivers.*)

Almost.

(*She moves away from the table.*)

So who else is coming?

JESSIE: The usuals. Lisbeth. Sue Carol. Martha. Martha might be late. She had a closing uptown. And Claire of course.

NINA: I guess we had to invite Martha.

JESSIE: She would have been hurt.

NINA: She'll ruin everything . . .

JESSIE: No! I planned it perfectly . . . Martha's coming, but she can't stay . . .

NINA: Martha can always *stay* . . .

JESSIE: (*Laughing self-congratulation.*) Un-unh. Not tonight. It's Donald's birthday. Martha's taking him to dinner at Bouley . . . She's had the reservation for eleven months! She has to leave here by eight forty-five, or she'll lose it!

(*Exalted.*)

So if Claire's late, they may miss each other completely!

NINA: (*Impressed.*) God, you're some hostess. You're *sure* . . . she can't stay?

JESSIE: That's why I picked tonight. To avoid a disaster.

(*Amending.*)

Oh, I feel guilty talking about Martha . . .

NINA, JESSIE: (*Ritually, with humor.*) She's basically a good person.

(*They laugh.*)

JESSIE: Here . . . have some wine before everyone gets here. Why don't you sit down?

NINA: I look thinner standing up.

JESSIE: Are you okay?

NINA: You want the truth or something we can both live with?

JESSIE: Nina!

NINA: Oh, it's nothing. I saw a guy this afternoon. You know the guy in my building? He's a Zen Buddhist but he's Jewish. He's invited me in for herbal tea a couple of times.

JESSIE: (*Knowing, dry.*) One of the Celestial Seasonings guys.

NINA: "Red Zinger." I thought maybe he was some kind of monk. Or asexual. I put him in the "friend" category. You know—"nothing doing." Then, Sunday, I ran into him in the laundry room, and he said out of the blue—he had had a vision. He's been celibate for five years . . . so I thought—"I better *go* for it!"

JESSIE: He sounds like a good possibility . . .

NINA: Oh, he's unique! He had it all planned. We had to fast for three days first—that was easy for me—I was almost *there* . . . Then I could come to him—today—dressed only in pure non-synthetic fibers, and we'd be able to do it . . . It was such a cuckoo offer, I said "yes." So I went up there . . .

JESSIE: What happened?

NINA: Don't ask, and I won't tell you . . .

(*Buzzer shrills, interrupting what could be a confidence.* JESSIE *runs to the door.*)

JESSIE: I better get this. Pour yourself some wine . . .

(NINA *goes to kitchen area, pours from a giant jug of Gallo Hearty Burgundy.*)

JESSIE: Who is it?

LISBETH'S VOICE: It's just me. (*Wispy.*) Lisbeth.

(*Door opens.* JESSIE *admits* LISBETH, *a malnourished, professional beauty.* LISBETH *floats in, carrying a large, fancy gift, and a bouquet of lilies. She wears an antique blouse, tight pants, and cape.* JESSIE *and* LISBETH *hug and sway in a ritual dance of greeting: a softer, more heartfelt embrace than the one shared by* JESSIE *and* NINA.)

JESSIE: (*Voice adapting to* LISBETH*'s breathiness.*) Oh, you look beautiful.

LISBETH: *You* do.

JESSIE: Oh, Lisbeth.

LISBETH: Oh, Jessie.

JESSIE: I love your blouse.

LISBETH: It's old.

(*From her station near the food,* NINA *acknowledges* LISBETH.)

Nina!

NINA: Lisbeth!

LISBETH: (*Excited whisper: a news bulletin.*) I saw him. I just saw him.

JESSIE: . . . Steve?

LISBETH: He was on my train.

NINA: That shit.

LISBETH: Please don't call him that . . . I love Steve!

(*She takes in* NINA*'s outfit.*)

You look great. Is that new?

NINA: It was.

LISBETH: Your hair! Your hair! It's red!

NINA: It oxidized . . . So what's Steve up to? I thought that was over.

(JESSIE *cautions* NINA *with a warning look.*)

LISBETH: Over? Oh, no! We're just . . . (*She fumbles.*) . . . in transition. He's going through something. When he's ready, he'll call and we'll get back together.

(*She lights up.*)

It was just so great to see him!

JESSIE: How did he look?

LISBETH: Well . . .

(*Halting.*)

. . . He was all the way at the other end of the car.

(*Faster.*)

Thin.

(*Upset.*)

He doesn't look that well. His eyes . . . God, his eyes.

(*She bulges her own eyes.*)

They looked so . . . vacant.

NINA: Coked up.

LISBETH: (*More reportorial style.*) He's grown a moustache . . . and a beard. A weak, wispy beard.

JESSIE: I can't picture Steve with a beard.

NINA: Are you sure it was Steve?

JESSIE: I can't picture Steve with a beard.

LISBETH: It was his raincoat! I'd know that raincoat anywhere. With the torn epaulets . . .

(*She smiles.*)

The pockets are torn, too. I used to put my hand in his pocket when we went for walks . . .

(*Reverential.*)

I could feel his thigh.

(*Becoming uncertain.*)

I *think* it was Steve. I tried to get to him, but the train was so crowded . . .

(*Halting.*)

And then he got off. Well, it was nice just to see him.

(*Shrugging off the spell.*)

Well, here . . . Jessie . . . I got you some flowers.

JESSIE: Oh, lilies! You shouldn't have! I better put them in water.

(JESSIE *puts flowers in a vase.* LISBETH *moves to the baby gift display, sets down her present.*)

LISBETH: I got Claire a christening dress. Hand-tatted. With a matching little cap.

NINA: Uh-oh. The first "little" of the evening. One "precious" or "darling" and I'll puke.

(*She offers* LISBETH *a canape.*)

Here, eat something. Put some flab on your bones. How much do you weigh now? Eighty pounds?

(*She picks up* LISBETH*'s arm. Mock shriek of alarm as she measures the bicep.*)

Huhh! Look at this! Look at this arm! Jessie! Look at Lisbeth's arm!

JESSIE: (*Sadly.*) I've seen it.

NINA: Is this an arm? This isn't an arm! It's a pipe cleaner!

(*She inspects* LISBETH*'s body.*)

Your breasts have shriveled. You have no ass.

LISBETH: I have an ass!

NINA: Not in the true sense.

(*She pokes out her own rump.*)

This is an ass. What makes me sick, is that I can remember when we wore the same size. Now you could fit in my pant leg.

(JESSIE *pours wine, gives* LISBETH *a glass, offers her a plate of canapes.*)

JESSIE: (*To* LISBETH.) I'd love to know the last time you had a real meal . . . Try some of this cheese; it's triple creme.

LISBETH: (*Dreamy.*) It was with Steve. We went to Manana. We started with nachos and chalupas . . . and then had the combanacion platters.

(*Wistful.*)

Burritos.

(*Sigh.*)

We ate from each other's plates.

NINA: You can eat with him, you know.

LISBETH: He always ordered for me.

NINA: So now you're going to starve yourself to death?

LISBETH: I eat!

JESSIE: What?

LISBETH: Triscuits.

NINA: I'm surprised you still get work. I never thought I'd say this, but you're too thin for *Vogue* . . .

JESSIE: No one's too thin for *Vogue.*

NINA: Well, too *limp.* Their thinness has some oomph. They're always leaping around, extending their legs on boulders.

LISBETH: Oh, I haven't done fashion or editorial in months. I haven't been in *Vogue* since the April issue. I'm mostly in *JAMA* now . . .

JESSIE: *JAMA?*

LISBETH: *Journal of the American Medical Association.*

NINA: As a case history?

LISBETH: I'm a Prozac model.

(*She slumps into dejected pose, ragdoll-limp, hands trailing.*)

"Feel walled in by loneliness? Trapped and helpless?—When life's simplest problems seem unmanageable . . . Give her Prozac."

JESSIE: You're good!

LISBETH: Working my way up to Thorazine.

(*More animated.*)

The work is easy, and I'm making a fortune!

(*She kids.*)

Somedays, it's even hard to look depressed.

(*Feigning higher spirits,* LISBETH *arranges her gift on the display.*)

I hope Claire likes this. I got her a beautiful antique nightgown. It sort of matches the baby's dress. I picture her holding the baby . . . both of them, all in lace.

NINA: I can't picture Claire in lace.

LISBETH: Well, this will bring it out in her . . . Don't you think?

(*A bit concerned.*)

God, maybe I should have gotten her something else . . .

JESSIE: I'm sure she'll love it!

(*Relieved.*)

I'm just glad Claire's *coming.* It's not like her not to see any of us for this long . . .

NINA: . . . Something's wrong. We've never gone six months without getting together . . . I finally got her on the phone. Yesterday.

LISBETH: Well, how did she sound?

NINA: All right. But she might have been faking. She said she was "grotesquely fat."

JESSIE: Oh, Claire could never get fat! I'm sure she looks beautiful.

NINA: No! . . . Didn't Martha tell you?

(*They respond "no."*)

Martha saw her on 57th Street last week, and she said—she's unrecognizable! She was wearing old clothes and no makeup and her body was completely misshapen and her hair had turned totally gray!

JESSIE: That's impossible. Not in a few months!

LISBETH: It can happen. "Trauma."

NINA: And she was so obviously depressed that she didn't even hear Martha screaming to her from across the street. She got on a bus, but Martha got a really good look at her, and she says her face is *gone.* She's all striated with a ropey neck, and enormous bags under her eyes.

JESSIE: That's ridiculous! If she was that unrecognizable, I'm sure it wasn't Claire!

LISBETH: It's weird no one's seen her. She dropped out of ballet . . .

JESSIE: Well, she's in her seventh month, for God's sake . . . What do you expect: a grand jeté?

NINA: She could still plié.

LISBETH: Half the class is about to deliver. It's starting to look like a Lamaze group.

(*To* JESSIE.)

Well, how did you talk her into *this?*

JESSIE: I insisted! When I finally got through to her on the phone, I told her everything had been done.

(SHE *gestures toward the food, the bassinet. Lighter.*)

I'm sure she's fine.

NINA: No! She's avoiding us. It's peculiar. The last time I saw her, she had just met this man, and then, suddenly, she goes into hiding . . .

LISBETH: (*Wistfully.*) . . . You know how it is when you're really in love. You can stay in bed for a year.

NINA: No. She won't even talk about him on the phone. It must be too awful.

JESSIE: I had the impression it was too wonderful. She was "saving it" for "in person." She *did* say she's grotesquely fat. Oh well, even if she is, I'm sure she'll lose the weight, after she has the baby . . .

NINA: Oh, they all say that. I haven't lost the weight, and I haven't even had a baby. I can't get my figure back after a meal.

(*Doorbell buzzes:* JESSIE *runs for it.*)

JESSIE: Who is it?

MARTHA'S VOICE: Martha.

(JESSIE *opens the door to admit* MARTHA, *whose stolid form matches her flat voice. The most conservative of the group,* MARTHA *is dressed for success in a suit with shoulder pads and designer shoes. She enters hopping on one foot, and deposits a large gift carton inside the door. With a gesture she indicates more gifts in the hall.*)

MARTHA: A wino pissed on my shoe! Right downstairs!

(MARTHA *hops to the sink. The others fetch the remaining gifts: a massive assortment of boxes.*)

MARTHA: (*Authoritative, fast.*) Get those gifts.

(*In greeting.*)

You all look great.

(*Re her wet shoe.*)

Isn't this terrific? I don't want to touch it! Get me a paper towel.

(JESSIE *rips paper towel, gives it to* MARTHA.)

MARTHA: Does piss tarnish brass?

NINA: Yes.

JESSIE: That must have been Old Howard.

MARTHA: "Old Howard?" You *know* him? I just assumed he was just some disgusting old wino who wandered in to piss.

JESSIE: Oh, no, he pisses there on a regular schedule. Everyone in the building encourages it . . . keeps the burglars and muggers away . . .

(NINA, LISBETH *laugh.*)

MARTHA: Go ahead: laugh. You wouldn't think it was so funny if he pissed on *your* shoe.

(*Frowning at shoe.*)

This was new.

JESSIE: Well, I am surprised. He's usually so careful to aim it at the corner of the vestibule. It just puddles there.

MARTHA: (*She reenacts the pissing.*) Well, I was coming in just as he was pissing . . . He heard me and turned around . . .

(*She mimics a hose motion with her hand.*)

. . . and that's when he got me.

JESSIE: So it wasn't deliberate on his part. I'm glad.

MARTHA: (*Completing her wipe-up.*) I can't stand other people's piss on me. It's bad enough going into ladies' rooms and finding all those splatters on the seats.

JESSIE: Those are bad. I always wonder: How do they get here? *I* never leave splatters.

NINA: It's all the women who've been taught not to lower their asses to public surfaces. They're afraid of contamination. So they crouch over the seat . . .

LISBETH: . . . ruining it for everybody else.

NINA: If everybody would just sit down, it'd be great.

MARTHA: Can we stop talking about urine?

(*To* JESSIE.)

I need a drink.

(*To* NINA.)

Well, you're looking more fit.

NINA: Thank you. *You* never change.

MARTHA: Thank you, Sweetie. Your hair's oxidized.

(*Before* NINA *can respond,* MARTHA *moves on to* LISBETH.)

MARTHA: (*Continued.*) (*With false concern.*)

You look so pretty sitting over there . . . so itsy-bitsy, like a miniature of your former self. Well, I guess it's all the style.

(LISBETH *quivers, but before she can respond,* MARTHA *confronts* JESSIE, *who hands her a drink.*)

MARTHA: (*Continued.*) Thank you. You're an angel.

(*Eyeing the loft: a practiced realtor.*)

Oooooh! Let me see what you've done. The floors weren't this color!

JESSIE: I sanded them myself. It took all summer.

MARTHA: They look fantastic! The place is really getting there.

(*New tone.*)

How are you finding the neighborhood? Are you getting used to it? It still doesn't bother you? Coming in late at night . . . *alone.*

JESSIE: No. I love coming up here, late at night, *alone.*

MARTHA: You're so brave. The view is sensational. It's just the right aesthetic distance. You don't miss uptown?

JESSIE: I love it here. I just spent a year fixing the place up.

MARTHA: That's the ideal time to unload it.

(*Sweet.*)

I can't help being concerned about you.

(*Looking at her shoe.*)

Look what goes on down there. The neighborhood's

literally a toilet. Of course, you've made it charming. Your magic touch.

(*Shrewdly.*)

You have a wraparound mortgage—I could work with that. And people will pay to live in these surreal surroundings . . .

(*Cajoling again.*)

Wouldn't you really rather live in my neighborhood?

(*For emphasis.*)

Near me.

(*Musical sales pitch voice, sing-song.*)

I'm condo-ing a townhouse on 65th between Madison and Park . . .

JESSIE: "Condoing" is not a verb.

MARTHA: It is now. I just *condo*-ed a thirty-five-story apartment tower with an indoor shopping palazzo and an underground garage.

(*Reverent.*)

Mondo Condo.

(*Proudest.*)

I just sold a parking place for eighty thousand dollars.

LISBETH: Is it pretty?

MARTHA: It's a parking place.

(*Resuming a habitual sales pitch.*)

Well, it's attractive. It'll appreciate two hundred percent in two years.

LISBETH: If the city's still here in two years. Did you read today's *Times?* About the neutrinos?

JESSIE: I skimmed it. What are neutrinos?

LISBETH: (*Airy.*) For years and years, everybody thought they were particles without mass.

NINA: (*Grim.*) And now they have mass?

LISBETH: They think so!

(*She waves her hands—a graceful dance move.*)

They're in the air.

(*A hula wave above her head.*)

All around us. Like an invisible sea.

(*They gaze around the room, as if expecting to see the neutrinos.*)

LISBETH: (*Continued.*) . . . and their presence means that someday the universe will stop expanding and collapse upon itself.

MARTHA: Not midtown. I'll keep you in mind if I run into something irresistible . . .

JESSIE: I'm sorry. I'm staying here.

MARTHA: An estate sale?

(JESSIE *laughs, then to distract* MARTHA, JESSIE *goes to the door, to eye the massive carton and other Martha gifts.*)

JESSIE: Martha, you're incredible. What have you got in all those boxes?

(MARTHA *brightens, heaving her massive carton, boxes, toward the table, where they dwarf the other gifts.*)

MARTHA: We'll have to rearrange all these gifts. Whatever you all have gotten will be extra. *I* got the complete layette.

(*They look offended.*)

MARTHA: (*Misreading their response.*) Well? I have the money. Why not? I've never been cheap!

JESSIE: (*Soft, diplomatic.*) I know. But I'm sure that among the five of us, we'll be giving her everything she needs.

MARTHA: (*Snapping.*) What she needs is a husband.

LISBETH: She says she doesn't have room for one in her apartment.

(JESSIE *laughs,* MARTHA *doesn't.* NINA *snorts.*)

MARTHA: (*To* JESSIE.) Be a sweetie. Get me a knife. I want to erect the crib before she gets here. God, I wish I could *stay.* This is the one night of the year that I just have to go . . . Jessie: I don't know how you could have done this . . . You *know* I've been planning Donald's birthday all year . . .

JESSIE: (*Abashed.*) I didn't think.

(JESSIE, LISBETH, NINA *exchange a secret, unseen look.*)

MARTHA: (*Arranging her boxes.*) Well, I have to work fast. Now: Promise. Don't let me *stay* . . . I have to leave almost immediately. Kick me out in five minutes . . . I mean it . . .

GROUP: We will.

(MARTHA *starts to open her large carton.* JESSIE *moves to stop her.*)

JESSIE: Don't do that! . . . We're going to let Claire open everything at the same time. Then pass them around . . .

MARTHA: Well, mine is too large. I want to erect it and fill it with my smaller gifts.

(*Pleased.*)

It will make a better display.

(JESSIE *sighs, signals others: be cool, she's going soon, and gets her the knife.* MARTHA *hacks open the carton, lifts the crib menacingly in the air.*)

LISBETH: (*Whisper to* JESSIE.) Omigod . . . She's going to make Claire feel awful . . .

JESSIE: (*Whisper.*) Don't worry. She's leaving any minute . . .

NINA: (*Whisper.*) Don't bet on it.

MARTHA: (*Raising the assembled crib.*) Oh, feel this frame! It's solid. It cost three hundred dollars! Don't tell Claire . . . I don't want her to feel . . . indebted.

(*Thinking.*)

Do you all *know?* Claire isn't even *covered!*

LISBETH: Covered with what?

MARTHA: Blue Cross, Blue Shield.

JESSIE: Martha, please don't bring it up.

MARTHA: (*Unheeding holding crib.*) You can keep the child in this for years!

NINA: Till it's an adult?

JESSIE: Listen. Before Claire gets here. I think we should . . . be careful. Careful of what we say. We don't want to strike the wrong notes . . .

LISBETH: Oh, I think Claire can carry this off. I think she'll be just fantastic . . .

NINA: I never thought Claire would be the one to go first . . .

MARTHA: It should be me. Donald and I already have a room prepared with giraffes. We're as good as married. Or, if one of you had to have one of her own . . . It should be you [NINA] or you [LISBETH] or you [JESSIE]. You [the GROUP] can afford one.

NINA: I'm waiting for the freeze-dried zygotes.

MARTHA: (*Bearing down on* LISBETH.) Well *you* . . .

(LISBETH *turns, avoids* MARTHA*'s gaze.*)

LISBETH: When Steve and I get back . . .

(*Whisper.*)

Not now.

MARTHA: (*To* JESSIE.) Well, Jessie. *You* have no excuse.

JESSIE: Oh, where would I put it?

(MARTHA *surveys the loft, points to a corner.*)

MARTHA: Over there!

(JESSIE *walks to the empty space, studies it.*)

JESSIE: But it's so dark.

NINA: Hang a lamp over its head.

JESSIE: (*With a small shiver.*) There's a draft.

(*Shrugging off the feeling.*)

Oh, I'm not nearly ready. I know it's ridiculous but I keep thinking, "I'm too young" . . . early thirties.

MARTHA: There's nothing early in your thirties. Our eggs are rotting as we speak.

NINA: So now you can use donor eggs. Women are having babies in their sixties.

JESSIE: (*Mock relief.*) *Whew* . . . the heat is off. What's the rush?

MARTHA: The rush is—not to mix obstetrics with geriatrics! Do you both want to be in diapers at the same time?

(*Telephone shrills.* JESSIE *answers.*)

JESSIE: Hello? (*Into phone.*) Stay on the IRT. Just don't let it take you to Brooklyn . . . Are you sure you're all right? One of us can come get you. (*To* GROUP.) It's Sue Carol.

MARTHA: I bet she forgot to buy a baby gift.

JESSIE: You sound good, you're in control.

(*She hangs up, faces* GROUP.)

She sounds awful.

NINA: Don't tell me . . .

JESSIE, NINA, LISBETH, MARTHA: She's divorcing Bob.

JESSIE: She says this is the real divorce. She's *had* it.

NINA: She has. She just keeps on having it.

LISBETH: Oh, she won't go through with it! She's madly in love with Bob!

NINA: Bob is a shit.

JESSIE: I think when they're attractive, they should be called something else.

LISBETH: He's a cute one. Did you see him as Laertes?

NINA: (*Begrudging.*) He's cute in tights.

JESSIE: And he can act, too.

LISBETH: Sue Carol will never leave Bob. I'd have never have left Steve. I'd have been happy to die with him.

NINA: Oh, *dee*-lighted.

MARTHA: You might still get the chance.

LISBETH: You know what they say: "Find someone to die with, and you've found someone to *live* with . . ."

MARTHA: If I were you, I'd start thinking of someone to eat out with . . .

JESSIE: Who said that?

LISBETH: Someone dead I think. But isn't it a beautiful idea?

MARTHA: It's marvelous.

JESSIE: (*To* MARTHA.) Oh, don't make fun of that. There's something there. You know when I was married to Hank . . . it used to haunt me. I just couldn't imagine myself dying with him there, holding my hand.

(*Pause.*)

I was afraid he'd say the same thing he did when I stayed too long in the bathtub or took too long in bed . . . "Are you *done* yet?"

LISBETH: You never told us that!

JESSIE: Well, officially, I left over his burping. He refused to say "excuse me" . . . But I'm not sure that was the real issue.

(*Thinking.*)

Although it was relevant. What if he burped while I was dying?

LISBETH: (*Hushed.*) It would negate your entire life.

NINA: Oh, they all burp. They just wait till you're used to having them around.

MARTHA: Men have more gas. They are just full of gas. It builds up.

LISBETH: (*With surprising vehemence.*) Well, let them swallow it! A sensitive man doesn't burp while you're dying!

NINA: (*Nibbling cheese.*) You're dead, you're dead. What difference does it make, who's there, what they're doing.

LISBETH: You want to look into a great pair of eyes!

JESSIE: I want the eyes, too!

NINA: I'd rather see a medic with cardiac equipment.

MARTHA: Then you're not dead.

(*She makes a face.*)

This cheese tastes ammoniated. I shouldn't eat it anyway—I'll spoil my appetite.

JESSIE: That's its taste. Try something else. We have enough for an army.

(*Distracted.*)

I just hope Sue Carol can get here. She was completely disoriented. She didn't know whether she was on the East Side or the West Side. All she knew was she was heading downtown.

NINA: She ought to dump that shit.

LISBETH: We were at their wedding.

MARTHA: God, ten years.

LISBETH: In May.

NINA: We were all still living at the Beaux Arts . . .

MARTHA: I wish I could have bought my room.

LISBETH: We walked to the Little Church Around the Corner . . . there were daffodils.

NINA: And Bob was an hour and forty-two minutes late. I would have told him to can it then.

JESSIE: I can't believe we all wore turquoise chiffon.

NINA: And those repulsive bonnets.

LISBETH: We glued false eyelashes on up and down . . . we must have looked like clowns.

NINA: And now they're getting divorced. Finally!

JESSIE: (*Gently admonishing* NINA.) Nina! You don't know what the marriage is about . . . Only those two people know what that marriage is about . . .

MARTHA: Is that from one of your little self-help books?

JESSIE: (*Embarrassed.*) I'm doing another one for Simon and Schuster. *How To Be Your Own Lover.*

NINA: What a vomiter.

JESSIE: (*Laughing.*) I know. I became slightly nauseous when I thought of it. But you can't sell satire anymore. People take it seriously. The big irony is that there is none.

LISBETH: I remember when you won the Yale prize for Poetry. You did such beautiful work in school . . .

MARTHA: We all did beautiful work in school. Now, we have to make a living. It makes me so nervous that you're all self-employed. You should have IRAs. Have you incorporated yourselves?

JESSIE: (*Ironic.*) I have.

NINA: (*Proud.*) I'm Nina Markowitz Inc.!

MARTHA: No more "Nails by Nina"?

(*She dangles her nails.*)

NINA: (*Defensive rush.*) It just says that on the window!

MARTHA: I know. I pass it.

NINA: I don't even have to be there anymore! I have fifteen of the best manicurists in the Western hemisphere. They make house calls.

LISBETH: God, I have no nails.

NINA: (*Raising her voice.*) I have no regrets! It's very good money! I bought my apartment!

MARTHA: Well, I know. And that's good.

(*Sweetly.*)

Why are you raising your voice? Did I say something? There's no need for you to be . . . defensive.

(*Sighs.*)

I was just remembering when you wanted to be a neurosurgeon.

NINA: I wasn't sure! It was an interest! I loved reading about brain tumors. When I was in ninth grade, I read this great book about the ancient Egyptians. They invented brain surgery. They drilled straight into people's heads.

(*Doorbell shrills.* JESSIE *runs to the door.*)

JESSIE: Who is it?

SUE CAROL'S VOICE: Sue Carol.

(JESSIE *opens the door to admit* SUE CAROL, *a very pretty but disheveled woman of thirty-six. She speaks with a Kentucky accent and is somewhat dramatically dressed in a black turtleneck sweater, baggy black trousers, boots. She wears sunglasses atop her head and has the exhilarated despair of the actress that she is. She carries a suitcase and a large paper bag, plus one smaller, plastic grocery sack.*)

SUE CAROL: (*Fast, breathless, high insecurity.*) Don't say a kind word to me. If you do, I'll go all to pieces. I can take anything but kindness.

JESSIE: You look beautiful.

SUE CAROL: Do I?

EVERYONE: You do! You look wonderful . . . terrific . . .

SUE CAROL: (*On verge of tears.*) Oh,

(*Greeting wails.*)

Nina! Lisbeth!

(*Flatter tone.*)

Martha.

(*To* JESSIE.)

Oh, Jessie! I meant to bring you something. I wasn't thinking.

(*Slightly lower voice.*)

Is it okay if I sleep over? I just can't go back to that apartment.

JESSIE: Of course. Here let me take these . . .

(*She stows the suitcase on the side.*)

We'll get you squared away later . . . Here, let me put your present with the others . . .

MARTHA: (*Eyeing the large bag.*) I hope that's not a strombolla. I got her the strombolla.

SUE CAROL: (*Closer to crying.*) It's not a strombolla . . . It's . . . just some stuff I couldn't leave behind.

(*She hands the grocery sack to* JESSIE.)

I feel awful, with all this going on, I didn't get a chance to get a baby gift. And I was going to go to FAO Schwarz and everything . . . or go to my grandma's house and get the old family cradle . . . but I didn't have time to do that either . . . so . . .

(*Breathless.*)

I stopped at the Korean market and got some incredible vegetables . . .

(EVERYONE *looks stunned at the puny nature of this gift.*)

SUE CAROL: (*Continued.*) . . . well, they're all little *baby* vegetables, and I just saw them as I was running by, and I thought what darling little carrots and what sweet little tiny eggplant . . .

and there's even a little mini watermelon . . . That's good for a baby shower, isn't it?

NINA: (*Whispering to* LISBETH.) She's lost her mind.

MARTHA: (*Hissing to* LISBETH, NINA.) She must have spent three ninety-nine.

JESSIE: You brought yourself, that's the main thing. I'm sure Claire will be thrilled.

(*A bit desperate.*)

Where is she?

(*To* MARTHA.)

You know, Martha, you made me promise: You don't want Donald to arrive at the restaurant alone, on his birthday . . . We can tell Claire you were here . . .

MARTHA: I'll just wait a bit longer. The second she gets here, I'll grab a cab. I have to *see* her . . .

JESSIE: (*Under her breath.*) Shit.

SUE CAROL: Now, if I start to cry, you all just tell me to shut up and sit in a corner. If I spoil tonight, I'll hate myself forever. We're all going to have the *best* time.

NINA: We are?

(JESSIE *carts* SUE CAROL*'s suitcase toward the Stage Left hallway.*)

JESSIE: (*Starting to unravel.*) I can't imagine what's keeping Claire . . . she should be here by now. Martha, I wouldn't give this more than another minute. You know Claire: Sometimes, she runs very late . . .

(MARTHA *signals her: No, not yet, keeps fussing with gifts.*)

MARTHA: She'll get here.

SUE CAROL: Claire's so good, she's being so good. She's so strong, I could cry . . .

(*Her voice breaks.*)

JESSIE: Bite your lower lip. Hard.

(SUE CAROL *bites her lower lip, hard.*)

SUE CAROL: (*Regaining control, smiling brightly.*) Thank you! I'm fine! I'm going to be all right. This is the best thing that could have happened . . . it's really a relief. I've cried myself out and now I can look ahead. I can see clearer now . . .

(*She squints.*)

. . . except I can't see nothing out of my left eye. I cried so hard, my tear duct dried up, and my contact lens dried out . . .

(*She digs in her pocket.*)

Now it's turned all hard and funny. It looks like a fingernail. I can't put this in my eye.

(*She pockets the dried contact lens.*)

I feel so wonderful now that the decision is made.

LISBETH: You look wonderful.

SUE CAROL: Do I? You know, people keep telling me that. I don't know if I really look that good, but I must look younger than I am. People keep saying things that *prove* I look younger . . .

NINA: Like what?

SUE CAROL: (*Straining to come up with examples.*) Well . . . I was in the bank yesterday and a man said to the teller—"This *girl* was here first." And everybody still calls me "Miss!" Just now, on the subway, a man bumped into me, and said, "Excuse me, *Miss.*"

JESSIE: They started calling me "Ma'am" last week.

LISBETH: Really? I don't think you look like a Ma'am at all.

MARTHA: I've been Ma'am all my life.

(SUE CAROL *squints, covering her left eye, and refocuses on the group with her right eye.*)

SUE CAROL: You all look so gorgeous.

JESSIE: It's the lighting. *You*'re the one who looks gorgeous.

SUE CAROL: Do I? I guess I do, if people keep telling me I do. I don't know how I get away with it, but I'm getting callbacks on ingenue parts . . . If I comb my bangs so the wrinkles don't show.

JESSIE: You don't have wrinkles.

SUE CAROL: Count 'em.

(*She pushes back her bangs.*)

Three. And I'm wearing turtlenecks to hide my neck and sunglasses when I'm outside—for the crow's feet.

(*She lowers her glasses.*)

LISBETH: You really don't look your age . . .

SUE CAROL: . . . there ain't that much of me showin'.

(*Pause.*)

But I know I'm lucky. This is the perfect time for me to get divorced, if I have to get divorced, which I do or

(*Lightly.*)

I could just shoot myself. I'm in shape. I've got some savings. I've had two callbacks to play a fifteen-year-old in a great play at the WPA. And I have great friends. You're all so wonderful. God, I'm so lucky!

(*Too abruptly, to* JESSIE.)

Watch you got to drink? Here, don't fuss. I'll get it.

(*She moves swiftly to the bar.*)

Can I get anyone else something?

(*Professional waitress voice.*)

"Would anyone care for something from the bar?"

JESSIE: You do that so well.

SUE CAROL: Come down and see me at Neptune's Garden . . . Mondays, Tuesdays, and Wednesdays. It's really kind of fun. It's like an acting job the way I do it. I play at being a waitress. God knows what would happen to me if I thought I really was one.

(*She shrugs off oncoming mood.*)

Come down any time. I'll sneak you something extra.

(*She roots through liquor supply.*)

Watcha got down here? Something that goes good with valium?

MARTHA: Nothing goes good . . . goes well . . .

(*Correcting the grammar.*)

. . . with valium. Are you crazy? That combination can kill.

JESSIE: It isn't a good idea to mix . . .

NINA: Just drink more . . .

SUE CAROL: Oh, don't you go bein' ole worry warts: I haven't even taken the valium yet. And I'm feeling so good, I probably won't . . . I'm just saving them, in case . . .

(SUE CAROL *touches her hip pocket.*)

NINA: I wouldn't give Bob the satisfaction.

SUE CAROL: He won't know.

JESSIE: He'll intuit it.

LISBETH: That's true. These things are in the air.

MARTHA: With the neutrinos?

LISBETH: Maybe. Do you think thoughts have mass? I could swear I've felt Steve's thoughts. And I keep beaming mine out to him.

SUE CAROL: I used to do that with Bob. When he was on the road.

(*Reflective.*)

It really cut down on our phone bills. He always got the message. Bob used to say . . .

(*Her voice catches.*)

JESSIE: (*Resigned.*) All right. What's he done?

SUE CAROL: Nope! I'm not even getting started . . .

(*To* JESSIE.)

I'm going to start looking for an apartment in the morning.

NINA: Now you're talking!

SUE CAROL: I sure am. This is it. I'm leaving him. I've left him.

JESSIE: (*Soft.*) You may change your mind.

SUE CAROL: Not this time. It's now or never and it's now. There's some crap even I won't take!

NINA: I'm glad to hear it!

LISBETH: What crap?

MARTHA: Don't give up a rent controlled apartment . . . !

LISBETH: He's so good looking.

SUE CAROL: (*Flagging.*) I know. And the minute I leave him, he gets even better . . . Something with his mouth and chin; they tighten up. He even seems to get a little taller.

NINA: They all do that.

(JESSIE *notices that* SUE CAROL *has lost her momentum as far as getting her drink, so* JESSIE *goes to assist, and hauls out a jug of Gallo Hearty Burgundy. She starts to pour into* SUE CAROL*'s glass.*)

JESSIE: Say when.

(SUE CAROL, *too dazed to signal when the wine should be stopped, simply stares as the glass fills to the brim. Silence is broken by a loud door buzz.*)

JESSIE: This has got to be Claire!

(CLAIRE, *pregnant but buoyant, enters: wearing racing bike gear. She wears electric colored tights, biking shorts, scarves, jewelry. An overblouse is the single accommodation to her condition. She is a pretty and youthful thirty-six, but her appeal may depend as much on her ebullient mood as upon any physical trait. She wears a bike rear-view mirror on her head. She is instantly besieged by the* GROUP.)

EVERYONE: You look terrific!

(GROUP *screaming.*)

CLAIRE: (*In apology for not "calling."*) I know! I know! I've been bad. I kept meaning to call, and then I . . . didn't . . . and then it seemed too much time had gone by . . . Oh, I'm sorry!

EVERYONE: It doesn't matter! It's okay! You're *here!*

(*Mass confusion of greeting kisses, hugs.*)

CLAIRE: Jessie! Nina! Lisbeth! Sue Carol!

(*Beat.*)

Martha.

(*She sees display of food, gifts.*)

Oh my God! All these presents!

(*Shrieking with delight.*)

Oh, Jessie . . . you didn't do all this for *me?*

MARTHA: It's from all of us. I bought the complete layette and the crib . . .

(*Behind* CLAIRE, JESSIE *signals* MARTHA: "*It's* time," *pointing to her wristwatch.* MARTHA *caught up, signals: In a minute.*)

CLAIRE: I don't know what to say! I'm speechless. Thank you! God, this is . . . overwhelming!

(*New tone.*)

Oh, here, Jessie . . . this is for you, before I forget. I've been meaning to give you this for months . . . I hope you like it . . .

(*To* OTHERS.)

I have things for all of you, I just keep forgetting to give them to you.

(JESSIE *opens her present, produces a small hunk of plaster.*)

JESSIE: Oh, I love it! What is it?

MARTHA: It looks like mortar.

NINA: Is it cocaine?

CLAIRE: It's a piece of the Wailing Wall! I picked it up last year when I was in Israel.

(*Pause.*)

It fell off the Wailing Wall. It really was just lying there.

(*Pause.*)

I wouldn't hack it off.

JESSIE: I know you wouldn't . . . It feels nice . . . kind of . . . soapy.

CLAIRE: I know . . . the whole wall is like that. I guess it's from all the millions of people rubbing their hands on the stone. It gets soapy.

(*She instructs the others.*)

Touch it.

(*They pass the stone hand to hand.*)

CLAIRE: (*Continued.*) See? Can you feel all that concentrated prayer?

LISBETH: Oh I do!

CLAIRE: People leave written prayers in the wall . . . they stuff them in the cracks.

(*Musing.*)

Actually, they look like millions of spitballs.

MARTHA: Did you leave one there?

CLAIRE: You bet.

(*Trying to be more casual.*)

Oh, I forgot.

(*She dodges* MARTHA, *going to the table.*)

I can't get over this spread! All these gifts! And food! You're spoiling me!

MARTHA: Should you be riding a bike?

CLAIRE: It's easier than walking!

MARTHA: I don't think you should be bicycling. Your center of gravity is supposed to be way off . . .

CLAIRE: I don't have a center of gravity. Maybe this . . .

(*Her belly.*)

is correcting my balance. I'm doing thirty miles a day . . . I'm faster against a headwind than I ever was before . . .

MARTHA: What if you go into labor on the bicycle?

(OTHERS *glare at* MARTHA. JESSIE *futilely signals* MARTHA, *again, to leave.*)

CLAIRE: Well, it might be wonderful! I just heard this fantastic story of this woman racer out in Missouri or someplace: She did go into labor, and it was during a hurricane, and her husband was not around, so she just rode all the way to the hospital herself . . . fifty miles through heavy rain, and when she got there, she had a really *fast* easy delivery. And she left the hospital the next day . . .

LISBETH: On the bike?

CLAIRE: Uh-huh! She had a baby seat on the back! So you see, there's nothing to worry about!

MARTHA: That woman has nothing to do with you.

(JESSIE *grabs* MARTHA *by the elbow, squeezes.*)

MARTHA: (*Continued.*) (*Unstoppable.*) That woman was married.

CLAIRE: (*Ignoring* MARTHA.) I've never felt better! It's a kick! And it clears up your skin. And look at this . . .

(*She flexes.*)

Cleavage!

(CLAIRE *starts munching hors d'oeuvres.*)

MARTHA: Aren't you nauseous in the morning?

CLAIRE: I'm never up in the morning. I slept through the first three months.

MARTHA: The First Trimester.

CLAIRE: Is that what it's called? I missed it then. The First Trimester.

MARTHA: When the brain is formed.

CLAIRE: Is that when it happens?

(*She devours the whole platter of canapes.*)

Ummm . . . these little caviar things are delicious. Don't let me eat all of them. I have no control. I'm so hungry all the time. I just can't stop myself. This afternoon, I bit into a chunk of styrofoam.

MARTHA: The demented appetite.

JESSIE: (*To* MARTHA.) Your dinner.

MARTHA: In a second.

(*To* CLAIRE.)

It's Donald's birthday . . . I'm taking him to Bouley . . . I wish I could *stay* . . .

CLAIRE: That's all right. I understand.

JESSIE: It was wonderful you could be here at all.

NINA: Yes, it was great to see you.

(THEY *are trying to get* MARTHA *toward door.* JESSIE *sees* CLAIRE *has eaten everything, looking for more food. She is distracted by her split hostessing tasks: she turns to* CLAIRE.)

JESSIE: Oh, here, let me get you some more . . .

CLAIRE: I'm dying for a drink!

JESSIE: It's just Gallo Hearty Burgundy . . .

NINA, SUE CAROL: But it'll dull the pain.

MARTHA: It'll destroy your DNA, that's what it'll do.

JESSIE: Martha . . . *please.* You don't want to be late . . . for Donald.

MARTHA: (*Rapid-fire.*) I'm meeting him at the restaurant.

(*To* CLAIRE.)

You haven't seen the reports? On fetal alcohol syndrome? The furry babies. It's terrible for the fetus.

CLAIRE: Oh, come on, a little red wine . . .

SUE CAROL: (*Drinking deeply.*) Don't hurt, don't hurt a bit.

MARTHA: Seriously, your chromosomes . . .

(JESSIE *fetches* MARTHA*'s coat, stands behind her, hoping to get* MARTHA *moving out.*)

CLAIRE: . . . are already wrecked.

(*She loops her arm around* JESSIE *who indecisively holds the wine jug.*)

Martha thinks I'm bad to have a baby without a husband.

JESSIE: (*Seeing the disaster coming.*) Martha, maybe I can call you a cab?

MARTHA: I'll find one.

(*To* CLAIRE.)

I didn't say that. Are you . . . engaged?

CLAIRE: No, I'm pregnant.

(*She giggles.*)

I don't want a husband. I don't have room for one in my apartment.

MARTHA: But you're still seeing him?

LISBETH: Oh, you promised you'd tell us all about him when we were all together.

CLAIRE: When I've had something to drink.

(*She leans forward, takes a glass from* JESSIE, *and holds the empty glass under* JESSIE*'s jug.*)

Go on, I'll just inhale it . . .

(*She sniffs the wine.*)

MARTHA: There go the arms and legs.

NINA: No. I think those are all set. I think it's just intelligence at this stage.

(*Confused.*)

Or is it sex differentiation?

CLAIRE: I wouldn't mind a little hermaphrodite.

(*Munching.*)

Ummm . . . Jessie! I've eaten an entire cheese! I'm sorry!

JESSIE: Don't apologize. It's for you! There's more . . .

(*Meanwhile,* CLAIRE *is rummaging through the gifts.*)

CLAIRE: Can I open the presents now?

JESSIE: Sure. They're for you.

(CLAIRE *rips open* LISBETH*'s package, produces a baby cap, puts it on her own head.*)

MARTHA: That's for the child.

LISBETH: That's all right. It's nice on Claire. There's something in there for you, too . . .

(CLAIRE *produces the second gift: the lace nightgown that matches the christening set.*)

NINA: (*In spite of herself.*) Oh, how precious!

JESSIE: (*Catching* NINA*'s lapse.*) "Darling . . ."

NINA: (*Thrusting her package at* CLAIRE.) This is from me, and partly from my mother. You remember her.

CLAIRE: (*Still reacting to* LISBETH.) Thank you . . . All this lace . . . I hope it's a girl.

(*Simultaneously,* CLAIRE *rips open* NINA*'s gift box, and pulls out a naked baby boy doll.*)

NINA: It's anatomically correct.

CLAIRE: (*Eyeing the doll.*) You're not kidding.

NINA: When I say "correct," I mean "correct."

(MARTHA *examines the doll over* CLAIRE*'s shoulder.*)

MARTHA: I would say "exaggerated."

(*Pause.*)

Does it simulate natural functions?

NINA: Almost all of them.

CLAIRE: (*Delighted.*) Oh! This is so uncanny. This actually looks like the father.

(CLAIRE *holds up the little doll, which has shaggy blond acrylic hair.*)

LISBETH: (*Intent on hearing about the man.*) So come on. You *promised.*

(SUE CAROL *returns to the table, bearing prepared plates.*)

SUE CAROL: (*Eyeing the baby doll.*) Is he this blond?

(MARTHA *takes the baby doll, examines it, squeezing: It squirts on her lap.*)

MARTHA: (*Reacting.*) Oh, no! Not again!

NINA: I filled it with cologne.

MARTHA: Well, it's leaving a stain.

(MARTHA *wipes her lap, sets the baby doll on the table, where he stares wide-eyed at the* GROUP, *with sightless blue eyes.*)

LISBETH: (*Re the man.*) So. . . ?

MARTHA: Where is he?

CLAIRE: He went back to Athens.

NINA: Athens?

SUE CAROL: Georgia?

CLAIRE: Greece.

JESSIE: Is he Greek?

CLAIRE: No, he just works there. He's an architectural engineer.

MARTHA: Really? I love architectural engineers. And that's a good sign. He must be intelligent, and the general rule is that the child will favor the *higher* intelligence.

CLAIRE: He's restoring the Acropolis.

JESSIE: I love him already.

SUE CAROL: Me too!

LISBETH: Um. An artist. Steve's an artist.

NINA: (*Cutting in.*) They're all artists.

CLAIRE: He restores antiquities . . . He works for hours, days, weeks, even years sometimes, just to lift some delicate object out of the rubble.

MARTHA: Well, when will he be done?

CLAIRE: Done?

MARTHA: With the Acropolis? When will it be done?

JESSIE: I don't think the Acropolis is ever *done.*

MARTHA: (*Misunderstanding, confirming her suspicion.*) He drags the job out.

(*Flinty to* CLAIRE.)

So he won't be back in time for the baby?

CLAIRE: Well, I don't know . . .

(*Dreamily.*)

I don't know if we should see each other again. It might not be the same. These things are pretty mysterious. We had a great night . . .

MARTHA: Just *one?*

CLAIRE: Not *just* one. *The* one.

(*Sigh, smile.*)

But in the morning, we both had rug burn on our thighs . . .

MARTHA: Rug burn?!

NINA: (*Translating.*) From friction against the carpet.

CLAIRE: (*Giggling.*) We had this rug burn . . . and I don't know . . . we sort of wanted to escape from each other . . .

LISBETH: (*Trying to comprehend.*) It was so intense.

CLAIRE: He had to catch a plane, and I had to go to a rehearsal. We said goodbye on the First Avenue bus.

SUE CAROL: Hey! You're skipping the good parts!

NINA: Was he worth the trouble?

LISBETH: You were in love, weren't you? You wouldn't have the baby if you weren't in love.

CLAIRE: Oh, I was in it. That's why I decided to go ahead and have the baby. Who knows when I'll fall in love again? It could be *years.*

MARTHA: And by then you'd be infertile. It takes four years to have a baby.

JESSIE: I thought it was nine months.

MARTHA: At *least* four years. Two years to seek out the perfect partner. One year to see if you can stand living with him. And one year for the pregnancy plus a few months of "trying."

NINA: *You*'re halfway there, aren't you?

MARTHA: I expect a baby in [*two years from current date*]. I've already stopped using birth control.

SUE CAROL: What were you using? The Pill?

MARTHA: Diaphragm and jelly . . .

(*Pause.*)

and an I.U.D. I thought: Why not be sure?

(*Frown.*)

Though sometimes I worried that the I.U.D. would rip the diaphragm.

(*Shrug.*)

Well, it's all out now.

(*To* CLAIRE.)

What were you using?

CLAIRE: My imagination. I just willed it not to happen until I was ready.

MARTHA: You consider yourself ready?

(*The* OTHERS *admonish* MARTHA *with their eyes.*)

MARTHA: (*Continued.*) (*To* GROUP.) Look! I did her tax returns last year! I know her situation better than she does!

(*To* CLAIRE.)

Tell them . . . tell them . . . Tell them what you make.

JESSIE: Martha . . . that's very personal. And you're going to be *late* . . .

MARTHA: Her income is less than her phone bill!

SUE CAROL: Hey, that's okay! That's the life force!

JESSIE: I'm sure Claire can make a good living:

(*To* CLAIRE.)

You're a wonderful musician.

CLAIRE: I get away with it.

LISBETH: You play beautifully.

CLAIRE: I get away with it.

MARTHA: You just have no idea what's involved. Sitters. Pediatricians. Orthodontists.

LISBETH: It may not need orthodontists.

JESSIE: Claire has perfect teeth.

SUE CAROL: Look at her smile.

(CLAIRE *smiles.*)

MARTHA: They can't hurt.

(*In a dither.*)

There's preventive orthodontia.

(*Suspicious.*)

We've never seen *his* teeth.

CLAIRE: (*Teasing* MARTHA.) He had quite an overbite.

MARTHA: That will cost you. You should have savings, IRAs, Blue Cross, Blue Shield, own your own home, have live-in help, before you even conceive of conception.

CLAIRE: Those things don't make you ready!

NINA: What does?

LISBETH: Just being in love and wanting a baby?

CLAIRE: No, not that. It's having had good times . . . so there's no resentment, no regrets. And now I have something to tell a child. God, I've had fun . . . haven't I? I've done almost everything I wanted to . . . I went to Red China and rode on the uncomfortable trains . . . I worked a riverboat cruise down the Nile. I played my bassoon on the beach at Maui. I climbed the Matterhorn in zero visibility.

MARTHA: Zero visibility!

CLAIRE: It looked great!

(*Building.*)

That's why I can see clearly now: I'm ready! And I knew it . . .

(SHE *gets into a dither, too.*)

the second I conceived of conception.

LISBETH: Did you feel something different? At the exact second?

MARTHA: Some women feel a piercing pain.

CLAIRE: I didn't. But it was . . . different. Special!

(*Shy.*)

I felt this sort of cold sweep up my spine. Have you ever felt that?

NINA: Uh-huh.

CLAIRE: And you'll think this is silly . . .

LISBETH, JESSIE: No we won't . . .

MARTHA: What?

CLAIRE: But the cold sweep went straight through me . . . in a way nothing ever went through me before . . . It was as if I could feel my soul . . . shiver.

NINA: You had a great orgasm.

CLAIRE: (*Grinning.*) Which should produce a great baby.

MARTHA: There's no correlation!

CLAIRE: Hah! Most people are conceived in boredom, and just look at them!

(CLAIRE *looks at* MARTHA.)

JESSIE: I hope this man shares your . . . uh . . . philosophy.

NINA: Did he have a nice shlong?

CLAIRE: He did share my philosophy . . .

(*She builds, telling the story.*)

We just knew it the second we met. We took one look at each other and we started grinning. I didn't know it could start that way. With grinning. It was just so easy. We both knew . . . instantly that we'd be together and it'd be great.

MARTHA: Where? Where did you meet?

CLAIRE: At the fruit store.

(*There is a moment's silence as this information is absorbed.*)

MARTHA: You're not saying you met him on the street? You conceived a child with someone from the street?

CLAIRE: It didn't happen on the street.

LISBETH: She said at the fruit store.

MARTHA: Anything not at a party, through work, or through friends, is "on the street."

CLAIRE: What difference does it make? They're the same people they are at parties or at work . . .

MARTHA: No they're not! No matter what happens next, he'll always be privately thinking "the corner of 78th and Third". . . And then the contempt and abuse will start. Because you were something he found on the street.

NINA: Oh, you can meet good ones on the street.

(*Thinking.*)

Didn't you meet Donald on the beach? What difference does it make? So there was sand.

MARTHA: It wasn't the beach! It was the Vineyard! And we were introduced.

(*Vehement.*)

We had the same dentist.

JESSIE: (*Laughing.*) Well, *you*'re in the clear.

MARTHA: I'm sorry, but I have to say something. I can't just sit here, silently by. . .

JESSIE: Please don't . . .

(*Lowest whisper to* MARTHA.)

Try not to be judgmental.

MARTHA: (*Hissing whisper to* JESSIE.) I can't listen to another word about this Greek creep she met on the street. At the height of a sexual epidemic!

JESSIE: *Sssssh* . . . please . . . you'll spoil everything.

NINA: (*Whisper to* MARTHA.) He obviously wasn't in a risk group.

MARTHA: They're all in a risk group. They're out there dealing death with their doo-hickeys . . .

SUE CAROL: Why do you seem so *glad?*

MARTHA: I'm not glad! I'm sad. Sad to be proven right, again! I was right all along. I always said it was unhygienic. I was right to shine high intensity flashlights on men's genitals as early as 1968! Then I was only looking for herpes . . .

NINA: Hoping to find some.

LISBETH: Did you?

MARTHA: I saw enough to think twice.

JESSIE: You were a Tory, during the Sexual Revolution.

MARTHA: That's better than being a fatality!

(CLAIRE *and* MARTHA *glare at one another.*)

CLAIRE: Well, I was tested! And I'm fine!

MARTHA: Well, I'm relieved. But you *could* have gotten it . . . You knew nothing about this man . . .

JESSIE: I'm sure he's a lovely man.

(*Trying to retrieve the original polite tone.*)

(*To* CLAIRE.) So how did you actually start talking to him?

CLAIRE: Well, I was going through the bananas, trying to find the ripe ones.

MARTHA: I'm not surprised.

CLAIRE: . . . and all I could find was green ones.

LISBETH: This is like a dream I had.

CLAIRE: I had been aware of him, in my peripheral vision. He was over by the tangelos. He came over to the bananas, and said, "The good ones are in the bin outside."

MARTHA: On the street.

CLAIRE: On the street! So we went outside together and had this funny conversation about the difference between the fruit outside and the fruit inside and how come it often looks pretty much the same, but it's always cheaper outside. How do the people who run the fruit store make these decisions? I mean, is it completely arbitrary on their part?

MARTHA: They're trying to move the rotten fruit.

CLAIRE: Well, he pulled out this other bunch of bananas and they were sort of speckly but he said, "These are the ones. I get them this way all the time. They look bad, but they taste good." So I got them.

NINA: Did he pay?

CLAIRE: I did. He bought some Hawaiian pineapple . . .

MARTHA: Big spender.

CLAIRE: It was just understood—that we were going to eat all the fruit together. He even got some yogurt, the 16-ounce size. And he said he was going to show me how he makes this really great fruit salad. We just naturally started walking back to my apartment—it was as if we had known each other a long time. And when we got up there, he really liked my having the bed in the center of the room . . .

SUE CAROL: Well why not?

CLAIRE: Well, not everyone has liked it there. Then he mixed up the bowl of yogurt and fruit . . .

NINA: Before you did anything?

CLAIRE: Uh-huh. He said, "It's really better if it sits for fifteen minutes. The juices flow."

LISBETH: Oh, I like him!

JESSIE: He's winning me over.

MARTHA: At least he mixed the salad. That's something.

CLAIRE: Then he sort of prowled around my apartment. It's funny, isn't it? How men always prowl around the first time they're in your apartment? As if they're looking for something.

SUE CAROL: They're looking for signs of other men.

CLAIRE: Well, he looked around . . . and he examined my instruments. And you know? He knew what they were before I told him! The first man who could identify a krummhorn! I didn't have to tell him—"the krummhorn is an early predecessor of the oboe . . ." And he really went wild over my bassoon.

NINA: When did you take your clothes off?

CLAIRE: Oh, that was funny! He just said, out of the blue, "Let's take a bath first." And I said, "Okay." Fortunately, I'd cleaned the tub, and I had some bubble bath and a scented candle . . .

MARTHA: That certainly was fortunate.

SUE CAROL: Who went in first?

CLAIRE: He did.

LISBETH: I'm trying to picture it. What was he wearing?

CLAIRE: Jeans. A shirt. Plain white underpants. Gray socks. He had a really nice body underneath. He looked beautiful.

MARTHA: Men aren't beautiful.

CLAIRE: This one was. He has this great mouth . . .

MARTHA: God knows where that mouth has been . . .

CLAIRE: . . . with the full lips, really good for kissing.

MARTHA: I don't like them *too* full. It can get sloppy.

CLAIRE: He didn't slobber . . .

JESSIE: I can't kiss a man without lips.

SUE CAROL: Well, Bob's are famous.

MARTHA: Donald's lips have a lovely, dry texture.

NINA: Did he have a big shlong?

JESSIE: Nina! You don't ask questions like that.

MARTHA: That's gross.

LISBETH: I miss Steve.

JESSIE: You always miss Steve.

LISBETH: This is making me miss him more.

NINA: So how big was it?

MARTHA: There are other considerations than how long a man's member is . . .

NINA: I wasn't thinking so much of length as width . . .

JESSIE: Member? It sounds like it belongs to a club.

NINA: It does.

JESSIE: Go on . . . the candle was lit, he took off his jeans and got in the bathtub . . .

CLAIRE: Then I got in, too, displacing some of the water.

NINA: Did he say you had a beautiful body?

CLAIRE: He didn't comment. We just greeted each other like old friends.

MARTHA: . . . who happened to meet in the bathtub.

CLAIRE: The candle burned low . . . We smoked a little grass . . .

(MARTHA *winces.*)

CLAIRE: (*Continued.*) . . . and the room seemed all sparkly. The bubbles were iridescent; we played with them . . . Then we dried each other off . . . I have these big, rough towels that feel so good. I heat them on top of the radiator.

JESSIE: I'm gaining fresh insight into your life, Claire.

LISBETH: I'm going to kill myself.

NINA: I'm into it.

CLAIRE: Then we went into the other room . . .

(CLAIRE *rises, moves away from the* GROUP, *reenacting the memory. Soft to* GROUP.)

I can't look at you and tell you this . . .

NINA: (*Wild.*) Don't stop!

CLAIRE: Well, I'll try.

(*Softer.*)

Oh I don't know what happened next . . . it gets fuzzy . . . I guess he turned on the radio. And I remember saying, "Would you like to dance?" And he said . . . in this really low voice . . . It was different from his usual one . . . "Yes, I'd like to . . ."

(SHE *looks down, caught in the spell of memory and the confidence. The* OTHERS *lean toward her.*)

CLAIRE: (*Continued.*) We never did dance. I think we took maybe one step. And that was it. We just stood there. It was as if we couldn't wait to start . . . kissing. I don't know . . . it seemed . . . momentous . . . but I think we could still laugh. My knees just went. I started to sink to the floor and then . . . he whispered it into my hair . . . so low, I couldn't understand a word except that he had asked a question . . . "Do you like . . . something or other?" And I said, "Yes". . .

(*Soft laugh.*)

Apparently I was ready to agree to anything. Maybe he just said . . . "Do you like me?"

(*She shakes her head.*)

I don't know . . . Anyway, I remember we were kissing . . . and I could feel the bristle on his upper lip . . . the feel of his cheek against mine . . . And then, well, it seemed accidental. Sometimes, it seemed as if we weren't moving at all . . . except for the tremble in our arms and then the tremble was inside, too, and . . .

(*Her voice drops, she breaks off. Smile.*)

CLAIRE: (*Continued.*) We fell asleep on the floor and woke up later. It was very dark. I woke up first and watched him sleep. He must have somehow felt me watching—he opened his eyes right away.

(*Softest.*)

And I'll never forget how he smiled.

(*The* OTHERS *are fixed in poses of total attention.* CLAIRE *stands apart, under the spell of memory. Then she snaps back to the moment, tries to make light of her confession.*)

CLAIRE: (*Continued.*) Hey, don't quote me.

(*She returns to the table, retrieves her wine glass.*)

SUE CAROL: I'll drink to that!

(JESSIE *trails* MARTHA, *helping her into her coat. She is almost out the door when the phone rings.*)

JESSIE: (*Almost screaming.*) I'll get it!

(*She picks it up.*)

Hello . . . yes . . . she is . . .

(*To* MARTHA.)

It's Donald . . . He's at the restaurant.

(*To* DONALD.)

She's on her way out . . . She'll be there as fast as she can . . .

(MARTHA *seizes the receiver.* JESSIE *looks stricken.*)

MARTHA: (*Into the phone.*) Sweetie? Listen, this is very important. I can't talk.

(*Covers her mouth, sotto voce.*)

I can't talk . . . they're all around me . . .

(*More normal tone.*)

I know you'll understand. I'll tell you everything later . . . It's absolutely essential that I . . .

(*She eyes the* GROUP.)

stay.

(MARTHA *begins to set down receiver, as* JESSIE *speaks.*)

JESSIE: Oh, don't make that sacrifice . . . Donald! his *birth*day!

(MARTHA *hangs up. A moment of realization spreads, like an odor through the room.* JESSIE, *to recover the etiquette of the situation, stages an impromptu toast.*)

JESSIE: (*Distributing wineglasses where needed, and lifting her own.*) A toast! A toast to Claire!

(*The* OTHERS *lift their glasses.*)

MARTHA: (*Lunging near* CLAIRE.) Don't you dare drink that!

(*As* EVERYONE *attempts to clink glasses,* MARTHA *makes her definitive lunge for* CLAIRE*'s glass. The red wine spills: A stain as if from a fatal wound spreads across* MARTHA*'s chest. A moment of chaos as the toast proceeds on its verbal momentum.*)

NINA: (*Dry, foreseeing trouble.*) Le Chaim!

MARTHA: (*Flat, war-like.*) Skol!

(BLACKOUT)

ACT II

A short time later. MARTHA *is offstage, rinsing her wine-stained blouse in the bathroom sink.* JESSIE *is handing her a container of salt through the door. The* OTHERS *are gathered around the couches, buzzing about* MARTHA. *They are temporarily ignoring the gifts, or paying only pro forma attention to them. They are primarily engaged by the crisis at hand: They will have to deal with* MARTHA *all night.*

JESSIE: Here. Try this salt . . . it's supposed to take out any stain . . . (*She hands in the salt.*)

NINA: Well I called it. I knew she'd never leave.

LISBETH: (*Whisper to* CLAIRE.) She's tactless . . .

JESSIE: Oh, God . . Promise you won't let her upset you. No matter what she says?

CLAIRE: (*Gay, defiant.*) I thrive on disapproval. It reminds me of home.

JESSIE: *Seriously,* if she gets really crazed, I'll ask her to leave . . .

SUE CAROL: Ha! You wouldn't ask Ivan the Terrible to leave . . . you're relentlessly polite . . .

JESSIE: Oh, just watch me. I have a threshold. If she crosses it, she's *going* . . . (*Panicky.*) Oh, I have to put the hens back in! Oh, no. I only have five.

NINA: You can give her mine.

MARTHA: (*Reentering.*) Well, now I have a wet, salty stain. This was new. From Bendel's.

CLAIRE: (*Opening gift—a baby kangaroo.*) Oh, isn't this adorable? Thank you, Jessie! I'm going to play with this myself!

(*Baby kangaroo goes into circulation, reaches* LISBETH.)

LISBETH: He was one of the New Men. The new, sensitive, caring ones . . .

NINA: (*Receiving another gift on the examination circle-route—the toy lamb.*) . . . the kind who know how to find a clitoris.

CLAIRE: Well, it's not that hard to locate.

(*Unwrapping a bunting.*)

Oh, Jessie! You're giving me way too much!

NINA: (*Still obsessed by clitoris topic.*) . . . You wouldn't know it by me. I'm thinking of drawing a map with an arrow down my stomach. This way: Guys.

SUE CAROL: You could put in directional signals.

JESSIE: Oh, they usually know where it is.

NINA: The older ones have trouble finding it.

SUE CAROL: Then they aren't looking.

(*She passes a pair of booties.*)

Have you ever seen anything so tiny?

LISBETH: Maybe they can't see it. A lot of older men are farsighted . . .

CLAIRE: (*Unwrapping baby blanket.*) Oh, I love this! You're spoiling me!

(*She returns to other topic.*)

You know the younger generation all seem to know where it is. Anyone born after 1955. That seems to be the dividing line.

JESSIE: The Korean War.

(CLAIRE *jumps up, rips into* MARTHA*'s bigger box, whips out the Jolly Jumper. As* CLAIRE *tries to assemble this, the conversation continues.*)

NINA: Let's face it, a lot of men still don't want to deal with it.

CLAIRE, SUE CAROL, LISBETH: They have to want to!

MARTHA: Well, m'dears, have you ever considered how boring, how *tedious* it may be for them? How would you like to rotate your finger in concentric circles on some little nub of flesh no longer than the average pencil eraser for anywhere from ten minutes to over half an hour? They have to be . . . motivated . . . I don't know that I could tackle it.

(*Now distracted by the assembled Jolly Jumper.*)

Oh, I hope you like this!

CLAIRE: It's fantastic? What is it? A strait-jacket?

MARTHA: It's a Jolly Jumper! You hang it in the doorway, and the baby can swing in it . . .

(*She sets the Jumper in place, hooking it over an exposed beam or pipe, or in doorframe. It dangles: An empty reminder.*)

It's great in small apartments, where the child is . . . confined.

(CLAIRE *rises, gives the Jolly Jumper a tentative shove: Her eyes widen with minor alarm.*)

MARTHA: (*Continued.*) Oh, open more from me!

CLAIRE: Martha! You're too much!

MARTHA: I know. I tried to think of everything, and I have! Oh, open my others . . . *Here* . . .

(*She shoves another box at* CLAIRE, *who pulls out a milk-expressing kit.*)

CLAIRE: Oh, Martha! You shouldn't have . . .

(*She throws a wink at the* OTHERS.)

What is it?

MARTHA: It's a breast pump! For when you're not lactating properly.

CLAIRE: I'm going to be lactating?

(*She playfully works the breast pump.*)

MARTHA: (*Nodding vigorously.*) And here are your nipple shields. And a container to store your extra milk.

(*Warning.*)

Don't try to keep it in the freezer for more than two weeks. And *never* pour your fresh hot milk onto the frozen milk. It will thaw.

CLAIRE: I don't even have milk and now it's *thawing* . . .

MARTHA: Don't worry! If you run out, call La Leche League—they'll rush some fresh-squeezed over to you.

(CLAIRE *rather hastily passes the breast pump down the line.*)

MARTHA: (*Continued.*) Oh, I hope I got you the right one. They have *power* pumps: You can plug into an outlet . . . they really drain you. But this is more portable.

(NINA *offers* CLAIRE *one of her gifts.*)

MARTHA: (*Continued.*) (*Sniping at* NINA.) I have more.

NINA: This kind of goes with what *you* gave her . . .

(CLAIRE *unwraps the gift, holds up a nursing bra.*)

CLAIRE: A bra with holes!

(*She pokes her fingers through the nipples: then, laughing, puts it on over her clothes.*)

NINA: I bought it for myself, by mistake . . .

MARTHA: That's a really nice one.

SUE CAROL: That's so you can nurse in public while still being discreet.

CLAIRE: Hey! Do I have to do it in public?

(*She clowns, miming herself nursing a baby in public.*)

MARTHA: You'll want to . . . In waiting rooms, airports, train stations . . .

(MARTHA *digs into her gift supply, extracts a stack of paperbacks.*)

And I want you to read these books.

(*Reading.*)

"Your newborn will be no beauty. He will be covered with a thick white substance called vernix, and his body will be matted with fine dark hair known as 'lanugo.'"

NINA: Hey! Wait a minute! I've seen kids! My sister had a baby, and it wasn't covered with lanugo!

CLAIRE: (*To* NINA, *while accepting the first book.*) It's okay. I can groom it.

MARTHA: And you must read this! "Toilet training in less than a day!"

CLAIRE: (*Accepting this book, too, reading aloud.*) "Mrs. James potty-trains Mickey . . . She had required Mickey to clean up his puddle ten times . . . 'Now sit on the floor, and pull off your pants. Your loved ones do not like wet pants'. . ."

NINA: Kink-*y*.

LISBETH: God, what power.

SUE CAROL: No wonder they grow up and hate us.

(CLAIRE *tosses the book aside.*)

CLAIRE: Hey, I don't want to order the poor little kid around. In China, the babies just wear bottomless pants . . . and it hits the floor . . .

(MARTHA *pushes another book at her.*)

MARTHA: You have to train him! You have to train yourself! Do you think motherhood comes *naturally?* Nothing is natural.

(*Pause.*)

Here! Read *Painless Childbirth!* Even natural childbirth isn't natural. You have to study it. You should be learning your exercises already.

(*Squint.*)

I'll bet you haven't even tried the breathing.

(MARTHA *looms over* CLAIRE, *exhaling mightily in her face.*)

"Pant! Pant! Pant like a dog!"

(CLAIRE, *eyes widening in true alarm, takes a sharp intake of breath: her first visible panic. For an instant, she seems on the verge of hyperventilating.*)

CLAIRE: (*Gasping, recovering her wits.*) Hey, I'll breathe later!

JESSIE: (*Whisper to* MARTHA.) Martha . . . take it easy.

(MARTHA, *offended, whips out another collapsed gift: a baby gate. She blocks the exit, snapping the pressure gate into the door frame.*)

MARTHA: Okay! Look at this baby gate. You'll need this to seal off areas. Allow yourself some freedom of motion in your apartment . . .

(CLAIRE *playfully hops over the gate.*)

CLAIRE: If my baby's anything like me, she'll jump over it.

MARTHA: Not for two years, she won't. You'll have to block her every move so you can do simple things such as vacuum . . .

(Now, MARTHA *tears through her largest box, exposing her full arsenal of baby gear: a sight gag of excess equipment: Strombolla, another bassinet, changing stands, tubs, car seats, etc.)*

CLAIRE: I didn't realize there was so much equipment . . .

(SUE CAROL *seeing* CLAIRE*'s moment of distress, roots through the pile to produce her own gift—the grocery sack.)*

SUE CAROL: Here. This is from me.

CLAIRE: (*Relieved to see the baby vegetables, as she produces the tiny watermelon.*) Oh, this is wonderful. A baby watermelon . . .

SUE CAROL: I didn't have time to get anything else . . . but I thought, honestly, *you* would like it . . .

CLAIRE: I do! I know I'll use this!

SUE CAROL: And there are miniature carrots and a miniature eggplant in there, too . . .

MARTHA: (*Hissing to* OTHERS.) I can't believe it: She's so cheap.

SUE CAROL: (*Angry, overhearing.*) Well, I knew Claire would enjoy them. Besides, when I get a chance to go to my grandma's, I'm going to come back with a hand-carved cradle, that's been in our family . . .

(*Furious to* MARTHA.)

for *three hundred years!*

CLAIRE: Oh, God! Sue Carol . . . you have to keep that for yourself.

SUE CAROL: No . . .

(*A beat.*)

I'll give it to you.

CLAIRE: But you'll want it for yourself some . . . day . . .

(*Caught, realizing this is delicate territory.*)

SUE CAROL: No need.

MARTHA: (*Onto* SUE CAROL.) What do you mean . . . no need?

CLAIRE: (*Cutting her off.*) Honest! I love the idea of the vegetables . . . I'll take this

(*Holds up baby eggplant.*)

and make a spoonful of ratatouille!

SUE CAROL: (*Laughing, to recover her equilibrium. She removes empty wine jug.*) Here . . . let me get us a fresh jug.

(*Professional tone.*)

"Would anyone else care for anything from the bar?"

JESSIE: Sit down, Sue Carol, let me do that.

SUE CAROL: No I want to . . .

NINA: Maybe I will have some more wine.

(*They check the wine cabinet under sink.*)

JESSIE: Let me check the wine cellar. I think we may have another bottle of that excellent Chilean red . . .

LISBETH: Oh, could it match the one we just had?

JESSIE: I don't know if it's the same year.

NINA: Any year but this one.

(JESSIE, SUE CAROL *crash into each other*—LISBETH *rises unsteadily to assist. They play a game, to distract themselves from more serious undercurrents.*)

SUE CAROL: (*Greeting* LISBETH *on the floor.*) Sommelier! We have the sommelier here! Tell me. Does a jug wine have to be opened ahead of time, to breathe?

LISBETH: Oh, yes, they're very heavy breathers. They need an extra hour.

(LISBETH *weaves, lifting giant jug which she carries to the table.*)

SUE CAROL: Ask her if she'd like to sniff the screw-on cap. You want to sniff it, don't you?

NINA: Oh, yeah. I want to sniff it.

(LISBETH *unscrews cap, proffers to* NINA. *Meanwhile,* SUE CAROL *haphazardly serves the appetizers. She also passes a stick of marijuana to* MARTHA. MARTHA *sniffs the joint, screws her features into an expression of disgust.*)

MARTHA: I thought I smelled burning socks.

SUE CAROL: Oh, try some. It'll loosen you up.

MARTHA: I don't want to be loosened.

CLAIRE: You'll get a contact high, anyway.

(MARTHA *sucks up the marijuana, holding the smoke for two long telltale moments.*)

MARTHA: I do this socially, sometimes, to be polite.

(NINA *sniffs the screw-on cap.*)

NINA: (*Exaggerated polite tone, kidding.*) I'm sorry. The Chilean is usually so . . . full-bodied . . . but I'm afraid this jug has gone off a bit.

JESSIE: Pard*one.* Would you rather a Paul Masson? Or the Almaden . . . I believe I have an excellent Mountain Red.

NINA: Perhaps the Almaden . . .

(SUE CAROL *totters off, fetches a second jug.*)

SUE CAROL: Here . . . allow me . . . I think you'll find this more satisfactory.

NINA: But this is the Paul Masson.

SUE CAROL: (*Too truly frustrated.*) Oh, no. *Shit.* I can't keep nothing straight. This *is* like work.

NINA: (*Really trying to console.*) Oh, please . . . I like the Paul Masson . . . better. It's all right . . .

SUE CAROL: No it ain't. I'll get you the right one.

(SUE CAROL *tries to turn, but is blocked by* JESSIE.)

JESSIE: Sit down. I'll get it.

(JESSIE *produces the Almaden jug, sets the bottle down with a clunk.* SUE CAROL *collapses on couch, pours herself some wine, takes a deep toke.*)

SUE CAROL: Shit.

CLAIRE: It doesn't matter. You're not working tonight . . .

SUE CAROL: Might was well be . . . I can remember all of Ophelia, and none of the Specials of the Day. Shit. I always say "It's Tuna Melt." Tuna Melt! This shit's been going on for ten years, it could keep up. You know how old I am?

MARTHA: Thirty-six and a half.

SUE CAROL: (SHE *laughs at herself and at* MARTHA.) I am a thirty-six-year-old waitress . . . Well . . . now, maybe a bit more—a hybrid cross between a waitress and an actress . . . A professional wacktress. Something tells me there's a statute of limitations even on that . . . And if I don't get a part in X numbers a years, I'm just a plain old waitress, who goes to auditions, but whose real business is knowing the house dressing.

(*Sniff.*)

"Creamy Vinaigrette."

CLAIRE: Come on, you just did *Oklahoma!*

SUE CAROL: O.K.L.A . . . Oh, *shit!*

JESSIE: You were terrific.

SUE CAROL: You were terrific to come see it.

(*Sniff.*)

That was three years ago! At a dinner theatre.

(*Musing.*)

I can't get away from food no matter what I do.

MARTHA: Well . . . Can't you regard *that* as the height of your career, and go on and have a baby?

SUE CAROL: I can't do much, but I don't kid myself. I'm not going to reproduce because I'm giving up on the rest of my life.

(SHE *laughs, bitter.*)

When I broke up with Bob this morning, I said, "Well, at least I still have my career . . ."

(*Laugh.*)

"My career!"

MARTHA: So now you have nothing.

SUE CAROL: (*Sharp, to* MARTHA.) Would you like to see a menu?

(OTHERS *glare at* MARTHA.)

MARTHA: Well, I told you to study computer programming.

JESSIE: Jesus. Martha.

(*To herself.*)

God, I better serve the dinner.

(*To* SUE CAROL.)

You'll be all right! You'll get something!

SUE CAROL: I'd rather die! It's just all over for me, all over . . .

(CLAIRE *walks over to* SUE CAROL *and hoists her from behind, pulls her to a full-length mirror.*)

CLAIRE: Look at yourself. Look at the face. Look at that hair. Gorgeous! Look at that body: Great!

SUE CAROL: (*Inchoate wailing.*) Waaaaaw!

(*She looks in mirror, plays tragic heroine, eyeing herself. A pause, then she blurts out the news.*)

Bob slept with someone else last night!

MARTHA: Is there evidence?

SUE CAROL: Yes!

JESSIE: I'm sure you're worrying for nothing. Come on, let's have the Cornish hens now . . .

(*Knowing it's futile,* THEY *ignore* JESSIE*'s attempt to serve dinner.*)

SUE CAROL: (*Fast, breathless.*) Well, at first I wasn't. Two weeks ago, somebody started calling our apartment and hanging up when I answered. At the same time, Bob started working out with weights.

NINA: Fits.

CLAIRE: I don't see why.

SUE CAROL: She called again yesterday.

JESSIE: How do you know it's the one who hung up?

SUE CAROL: Oh, I know! It's the same kind of ring.

(*She shrills.*)

Sides, she only hung up the first few times. Now, she's getting bolder. She talks.

LISBETH: What does she say?

SUE CAROL: She says, "Is Bob there?"

NINA: He's screwing her.

SUE CAROL: I said, "No, he's not home. Would you care to leave a message?" Then there was a really long pause.

LISBETH: Maybe he is screwing her.

JESSIE: Lisbeth! Come on, let's not get into this. Let's eat . . .

CLAIRE: How does she sound?

SUE CAROL: (*Poisonous.*) Sweet.

MARTHA: It's not conclusive.

(SUE CAROL *digs in her pocket, produces a folded tissue, holds up a long black hair. Meanwhile,* JESSIE *turns around with a platter of five roast Cornish hens: No one notices. She's fraying: fast.*)

SUE CAROL: I found this in our bed. It's her hair.

MARTHA: He's screwing her.

LISBETH: (*Hushed.*) In your own bed.

SUE CAROL: While I was working my butt off at the restaurant.

NINA: Let me see it.

(*She examines the hair.*)

Oriental.

JESSIE: *Asian.*

NINA: Possibly American Indian.

JESSIE: *Native American . . .*

SUE CAROL: You want to hear the worst part?

MARTHA: Yes.

SUE CAROL: He looked me straight in the eye and said—"As long as I'm going to be late, maybe *you* could work another shift?" I came home at three A.M. He was in bed, asleep. I had brought him a baggie full of Alaskan King Crab legs. He woke up. I guess he smelled them. I said, "Honey! Treats!" And he was going for a crab leg when he kind of sat up in bed and that's when I found it. The hair.

JESSIE: And you brought him crab legs. You're so sweet! I love you!

(JESSIE *sets down food, kisses* SUE CAROL. LISBETH, CLAIRE *come in closer.*)

LISBETH, CLAIRE: Oh, Sue Carol . . .

SUE CAROL: (*Teary, to* GROUP.) Oh, I love you all. I hate him.

NINA: He's typical.

(MARTHA *stands, seizes the hair.*)

MARTHA: Listen to me! It's not too late! You never saw this hair!

SUE CAROL: I already told him.

MARTHA: Take it back! You were mistaken! This is . . . nothing! All men are unfaithful. They're not like us. But it means less when they do it. It's just a diversion. Like going to the fight. He might as well have gone to the Knicks game! It's the same thing!

(SUE CAROL *tries to grab back the hair.*)

SUE CAROL: Hey, let me have that hair! That's my property!

MARTHA: I'll keep custody of the hair. You listen to me. Thank

God, you told me before it was too late. You almost lost everything. You can still recoup. You do not acknowledge that this American Indian was in your bed. Let me tell you something.

NINA: Maybe she's heard enough . . .

MARTHA: I never talk about it, it could be construed as disgusting, but my father was unfaithful to my mother twice a week . . . always with chunky redheads. And do you know how my mother handled it?

JESSIE: How?

MARTHA: (*With delight.*) Everytime he slept with another chunky redhead, my mother went shopping and bought herself a nice new dress.

(*Pause.*)

They were married for forty-two years . . .

(*Pleased.*)

till he died.

(*The ultimate.*)

She had an incredible wardrobe.

(*Silence as impact hits* EVERYONE.)

JESSIE: Martha. That is not . . . a marriage to . . . uh . . . brag about.

MARTHA: She had twelve fur coats. They were both happy!

SUE CAROL: Oh, it's not that he's been unfaithful. I could understand something casual and meaningless taking place in a Howard Johnson's in another state. But in our bed, while I was working . . . for us. It's kind of the low water mark, I guess. I mean, he knows how I've been thinking lately. That what I want will . . .

(*Her voice catches, goes low.*)

. . . just never be.

(SUE CAROL *sinks to the sofa, cries.*)

NINA: Dump him.

MARTHA: Reconcile.

(MARTHA *ignites a cigarette lighter, and torches "the hair."*)

SUE CAROL: The hair!

JESSIE: You're better off without it . . .

CLAIRE: You'll meet someone you'll have more fun with . . .

LISBETH: Someone sweeter . . .

JESSIE: Who appreciates you . . . Now, let's have these Cornish hens before they get cold . . .

SUE CAROL: Easy for you to say! You have Michael and Paul.

NINA: Two hunks.

JESSIE: I don't *have* them. I *know* them. And I want to show you something.

(JESSIE *escorts* SUE CAROL *to a free-standing antique terrestrial globe. She spins the globe.*)

Michael's in Micronesia and Paul's in Antarctica. And I'm here.

(*She points to New York.*)

They're both marine biologists . . . I keep falling in love with men who are underwater . . .

(SUE CAROL *squints at the globe.*)

SUE CAROL: Michael's closer.

NINA: They're both in different time zones.

JESSIE: Most of the time, I stay by myself.

SUE CAROL: You don't mind?

JESSIE: I love it! I get more done.

SUE CAROL: More what?

JESSIE: Work. You know, with men, or without them—we make our own lives.

SUE CAROL: And you don't have to sleep with one? I mean *sleep?*

JESSIE: I sleep better without them.

(SUE CAROL *heads for the door.*)

SUE CAROL: Uh-oh, not me. I need to feel a man's body heat . . . I need to hear his heart beat.

CLAIRE: We all like that . . . but sometimes it's better to do without for awhile.

JESSIE: I take long intermissions. Two years. Sometimes three.

SUE CAROL: I can't even eat without Bob.

LISBETH: Look at Jessie!

(EVERYONE *swivels: stares at* JESSIE.)

LISBETH: (*Continued.*) I came over one time, without calling, and you know what she was doing? Cooking bouillabaise. For herself.

MARTHA: That is impressive. What do you do with all the fish heads?

JESSIE: I freeze them.

SUE CAROL: That's great, but it ain't for me. It ain't in me. Maybe I should just go home and see if Bob's back. Maybe I should forgive him . . .

(*Thinking.*)

then punish him.

JESSIE: No! Don't blame him. Leave him.

(*More confidential.*)

Listen, I never told you why I left Hank.

LISBETH: He burped and didn't say "excuse me" . . .

JESSIE: That too. But I was used to him. It was . . . bearable. In a way, being married to him gave a focus to my discontent. I was vaguely unhappy and when I looked over at him, I knew why.

MARTHA: So it could've worked out.

(*Pause.*)

Did you consider having kids with him?

JESSIE: His eyes were too close together. Finally, I didn't even want to resent him anymore. I wanted to be more than some catalogue of injustices, a record of hurts . . . Of what he'd done, what I'd done.

SUE CAROL: Catalogue? Well, if you were a catalogue, I'm the Sears Roebuck. Oh, he's hit every base. He's good at this. He's the best.

JESSIE: Superlatives? Oh Sue Carol—You're too impressed.

SUE CAROL: (*Catching on a bit.*) I guess.

(*Backsliding.*)

Why is he sleeping with someone else? Maybe there *is* something wrong with *me.*

NINA: You're perfect.

LISBETH, CLAIRE: You are!

SUE CAROL: You ain't slept with me. He once told me other

women are more passionate. They get so carried away, they actually *flip* him out of the bed.

MARTHA: Oh, they all say that.

SUE CAROL: Are you all flippers?

(THEY *contemplate each other.*)

SUE CAROL: (*Continued.*) Come on. We've known each other all these years, have had all this wine and cheese, and heart-to-heart talks, none of us really knows what we're like when we're alone with them. Are you? Are you all flippers?

MARTHA: I get the job done.

(*Pause.*)

I flip Donald . . . occasionally—to be polite.

LISBETH: I never flipped Steve.

(*Wide-eyed.*)

I thought of it.

CLAIRE: Oh . . . sporadically.

NINA: Well I never have.

JESSIE: (*Giggling.*) I'm a flipper.

(*They stare at* JESSIE.)

JESSIE: (*Continued.*) Every time. I once tossed Paul against that wall.

(*The* OTHERS *regard the wall.*)

JESSIE: (*Continued.*) Well, it's those long intermissions.

SUE CAROL: Oh my God. Then it might be *me.* Now I don't know what to do.

(*She goes to the door, sways.*)

Oh, the room's spinning . . .

JESSIE: Too much wine.

SUE CAROL: Did I drink half a jug?

(*She holds her head.*)

My blood is running. The walls are undulating.

JESSIE: Better sit down. Here, you haven't touched your hen—don't let it have died in vain . . .

SUE CAROL: Oh, don't let me close my eyes. If I close my eyes, there's no hope. I'll be sucked down into it . . .

(*She stares, reeling drunk.*)

I don't know what to do . . . I could give it another shot. I could have new pictures taken. I could try . . . one more time . . . for some real good part. Medea! I could do Medea! Or I could go home.

CLAIRE: See! You have so many alternatives!

JESSIE: Just relax. You don't have to solve all your problems tonight.

SUE CAROL: I do!

CLAIRE: Later . . .

SUE CAROL: There is no later.

(CLAIRE *reacts: her own apprehensions becoming more visible.*)

JESSIE: No one's eating!

MARTHA: Jessie—don't get mad at me but you know what I'm really in the mood for? Didn't you say there was dessert?

NINA: Chocolate mousse cake. Don't let me have any. I'll just have my packet . . .

(*She mixes up the diet drink: dumping it in her wine.*)

MARTHA: We won't. I like the progress you're making. Your hips are almost normal now.

SUE CAROL: Don't let me close my eyes.

MARTHA: We won't.

(*Pause.*)

I must say—I feel better now that that hair is out of here: You have to go back to Bob. You can force him to be faithful. Tell him more medical horror stories.

(JESSIE *goes to fridge, produces the mousse cake.*)

JESSIE: Everybody but Nina in on this?

MARTHA: Claire shouldn't. Sweets are no good for her now.

CLAIRE: Come on. I'm starving. Chocolate mousse cake doesn't cause birth defects.

MARTHA: I'm thinking of you. You'll get sugar-crazed.

JESSIE: Oh, you can have some. We have to slice it with a wet knife. I don't know why.

NINA: It would be a tragedy if we did it wrong.

(JESSIE *serves the cake. She waves a piece in front of* SUE CAROL, *who comically bites a hunk in her glazed state.* NINA *passes.*)

LISBETH: This must be 3,000 calories.

(MARTHA *tears into her slice.*)

MARTHA: I shouldn't. You know the rate our metabolisms slow down? After twenty-five, we gain two pounds a year.

CLAIRE: So what?

MARTHA: When I'm seventy, I'll weigh 180 pounds.

JESSIE: You mean life is a long depression ending in overweight?

CLAIRE: It can be more than that.

(CLAIRE *tastes the cake, a bit too hungrily—a growing anxiety.*)

LISBETH: Or less.

CLAIRE: Good men will love us as we are . . .

MARTHA: Oh no. It's all over at forty. New men don't want you then . . . That's why you have to have an old one of your own.

JESSIE: If it's like that I'd just as soon skip it.

MARTHA: Maybe you will.

(*Beat.*)

Brigitte Bardot has given up on men. She's turned to animals. They give her a more sincere kind of love.

NINA: I buy that.

LISBETH: Brigitte Bardot . . . BeBe.

MARTHA: Now, she's living with thirty-five canaries.

(*Pause.*)

A lot of women are already living alone with dogs.

LISBETH: I like dogs.

MARTHA: Well, *good*.

(*Pause. Warning.*)

I have an aunt who makes complete outfits for a chihuahua. Hats. Little coats. Even tiny boots.

JESSIE: (*Fighting back.*) I bet they match her own outfits.

MARTHA: (*A retort.*) Actually, they're a little more elaborate.

(*Building steam.*)

I wish you'd gone out to dinner with Donald and I last week. We went to Lutece. You would have learned something.

NINA: What?

MARTHA: The couple at the next table . . . They had brought . . .

(*Pause.*)

a stuffed animal with them.

(*She makes a pained expression.*)

A kind of teddy bear. It sat on the chair between them. And . . .

(*The ultimate.*)

They ordered for it.

JESSIE: A la carte?

MARTHA: Go ahead, laugh. Don't you think you could go that way?

JESSIE: Give us a break.

MARTHA: After a certain point, there are no men, no sex. You just get rashes.

(*Sigh.*)

So you end up wearing the funny hats, talking to yourselves on escalators. Wearing too much rouge. Applying lipstick above your mouth . . .

SUE CAROL: (*Drunken singing.*) "Eleanor Rigby . . . her face in a jar by the door . . . Oh, where do they all come from . . ."

(*Switching songs.*)

"Delta Dawn, what's that flower you have on? Could it be a faded rose from days gone by . . . ? Oh, would you . . ."

(*The* WOMEN *give a collective shiver. To break the mood,* MARTHA *interrupts* SUE CAROL*'s dazed singing.* MARTHA *leans forward, displaying her new earrings. She holds her index fingers behind each lobe, and wiggles them.*)

MARTHA: No one's said anything about my earrings.

EVERYONE: (*Dispirited murmurs.*) They're beautiful. Exquisite. Very nice.

MARTHA: Donald gave them to me! My pre-engagement present. We'll be married on Valentine's Day. Then I thought we'd take the QE II . . . maybe wind up in Laggio Maggiore.

(*She smiles.*)

You'll all be in my wedding.

NINA: Will we have to wear turquoise?

MARTHA: Puce.

(*To* LISBETH.)

I want you to be my maid of honor.

LISBETH: (*Appalled at the tactlessness of this suggestion in front of the* OTHERS.) Oh, no! Anyone would be better!

MARTHA: (*To the* OTHERS.) Nothing personal. She's the most photogenic.

(*Benign.*)

Of course, you'll *all* be in some of the pictures.

(*Gaining momentum.*)

And I thought perhaps Jessie—You would recite a little poem? About Donald and I—our love.

JESSIE: I uh don't know.

MARTHA: You'll think of something clever.

(*To* NINA.)

And I thought you could do my nails.

NINA: I can't wait.

MARTHA: Claire . . . of course, you'll bring your instruments. You'll play something for us.

(CLAIRE *looks shaken.*)

CLAIRE: I don't know. I think I may be too . . . large.

MARTHA: We can put you in a muumuu.

(*Thinking.*)

Or you can stand behind a partition.

(*Gladdest tone.*)

And I want Sue Carol to sing!

SUE CAROL: (*Roaring.*) "Delta Dawn . . . What's that flower you have on?"

MARTHA: Not that.

(EVERYONE *appears displeased with the nuptial plans.* LISBETH *has wandered to the Jolly Jumper and climbed in. She dangles in place.*)

LISBETH: Listen, Martha. I don't know.

(*Whimper.*)

I don't think I can come to the wedding. I don't feel well.

MARTHA: It's two months off!

LISBETH: I just don't want you to count on me . . . as maid of honor. I've been feeling kind of woozy.

(*Throughout the following conversation, the scrim behind the window reveals a cityscape glaring brighter, dominating the interior, the* WOMEN. LISBETH *continues to dangle in place in the Jolly Jumper.*)

LISBETH: (*Continued.*) I've felt so funny since Steve.

(*Dreamy.*)

It was strange seeing him on the subway tonight. Maybe it's an omen! That we're getting closer.

NINA: I think Steve is finito, kid.

LISBETH: Oh, no . . . never . . . This is forever. You know, even though we never talked about getting married, it was understood. We talked about . . . our children.

(*To* CLAIRE.)

I made the christening dress for . . .

CLAIRE: Oh no! Please take it back!

LISBETH: I want you to have it. I can crochet another one when . . .

MARTHA: So he is coming back?

NINA: (*Sotto voce to* MARTHA.) Don't encourage this. He's gone.

LISBETH: (*Overhearing.*) Oh, no! You don't understand. It wasn't like that, at all. We never broke up, or anything . . . The last night we were together was the best . . .

NINA: That's always a bad sign.

LISBETH: It was the happiest night of my life. His, too. I know it was. We were at my apartment. It was snowing outside. We lay in bed together, just watching the snow. There was a kind of violet light . . . We fell asleep on and off. And I had the most wonderful dreams. You won't believe this, but we were having the same dream, something about floating together in a turquoise sea; the sun on us. The dream went from his head to mine. These things happen when you're very close . . .

(*She breaks off.*)

He said he had to go back to his apartment to get some extra clothes and books so he could stay with me without having to leave again for a long time . . . He said, "Don't get out of bed, I'll be right back." He kissed me on the forehead and said, "We're going to have a wonderful life, Boo."

MARTHA: "Boo?"

LISBETH: We called each other "Boo."

NINA, MARTHA: *Ooooo.*

CLAIRE, JESSIE: *Sssssssh.*

NINA: That was it?

LISBETH: He just didn't come back.

JESSIE: You never called or anything?

(LISBETH *swings, affirming.*)

CLAIRE: Why didn't you call him? I would have called him.

MARTHA: (*To* CLAIRE.) Why don't you call Greece?

CLAIRE: That's different. *Ssssssh* . . .

LISBETH: Oh, I couldn't. I wanted to talk to him too much.

(LISBETH *swings, harder, in the Jolly Jumper: rising almost precariously high.*)

JESSIE: So you've just been waiting?

LISBETH: It'll be a year in January. It's a pretty full time job. When the phone rings, I know it's silly, but I think—"It's him." The first day . . . I was so sure he was coming right back . . .

(*She laughs weakly.*)

I stayed in bed for hours. I felt so warm and snug, as if I had an extra blanket. Then I don't know when exactly but I started to feel sick: hot and cold, and my bones felt heavy. I didn't wake up until the next day. "Okay," I told myself, "he backed away. But I'm still here. The worst is over." But then I had . . . a relapse. I felt as if I had no marrow in my bones. I walked around New York as if I was on Mars. Then I started to read his letters and listen to the songs he liked. And, I can't explain it, but I felt better! I felt great! It was as if he hadn't gone at all. He was with me, there, somewhere to the right. I could smile at him, if I felt like . . .

(*She smiles.*)

Oh I didn't actually *see* him or anything.

(*She laughs.*)

It wasn't like *Topper.*

(*The* OTHERS *laugh to release tension.*)

LISBETH: (*Continued.*) . . . but if I leaned against the wall and pressed my cheek against it, the wall became Steve, and the plaster was cool, like his skin . . . When I go to bed, he's there with me, in the dark over on his side. The bedding becomes his body, the pillow is his chest: Everything can become Steve . . . my *jeans,* even the sofa. I fall into the sofa and into his lap. We laugh and tell stories . . . of where we've been and what we do . . . We're always together now . . . Actually, it's working out perfectly: We're very happy. We never fight . . .

(NINA *goes to* LISBETH, *helps her from the Jolly Jumper.*)

MARTHA: I don't get this . . . What's going on? She rubs herself against the wall?

NINA: (*To comfort* LISBETH.) Listen, you have to cut down your reaction time: A year is too long. I've got my time down to an hour and five minutes. You have to snap out of it.

LISBETH: I don't know.

NINA: I do! I've been left by millions of men. I've been rejected by men I didn't even want. But you see—I'm still here! And I'm fine about it really . . . You get used to it.

LISBETH: Really?

NINA: Absolutely! Cut your losses, and you can even enjoy yourself. You know, in a funny way—I fall in love every time. It's that lost, blind thing they do at the very end . . . They seem so helpless. For a few seconds, they all belong to me. I feel like I can carry men in my arms forever. I feel I should nurse them back to health . . .

(*Musing.*)

I wonder if that's why I bought that nursing bra . . . by mistake. I even have this dream—Oh, this is really dumb—that I'm breastfeeding grown men—long lines of them. We seem to be in a kind of barracks. Well, it's military. I think a naval hospital . . .

LISBETH: I once dreamt I was a cook on a submarine!

NINA: Well, you see—it's . . .

MARTHA: . . . Similar!

CLAIRE: Do you have this dream often?

NINA: About once a week. Then I got out with one, and that seems to cure me. They don't want my solace. The second I start to offer them something, they start for the door, pulling their pants up as they go . . . Is there any sound as loud as a zipper on its way up?

SUE CAROL: No.

NINA: They slide down silently enough, but what a racket on the return trip.

(*Outside the window, the sound of hurtling garbage can lids, the clatter of tin cans, and the city wind increase in volume.*)

NINA: (*Continued.*) When I was younger, it used to bother me, the way it's bothering you, but now I find I can even take a kind of *nourishment* . . .

(NINA *unconsciously seizes a piece of chocolate cake, devours it in compulsive need.*)

I just smack them on the tushy and say "so long." I guess I like my babies six feet tall. Ah, they don't mean me any harm: They're just gone. In a way, they make me feel strong . . .

CLAIRE: You are strong.

NINA: (*Noticing her empty cake plate, in alarm.*) In some ways. Oh, why does something always have to spoil it? Some flat remark, a too hasty exit? Like this afternoon . . . I got over it in less than an hour but . . .

JESSIE: You started to tell me·

(*To* OTHERS.)

Nina finally saw that guy in her building . . .

GROUP: The Zen Buddhist . .

LISBETH: —but-he's-Jewish.

SUE CAROL: Oh, yeah, the Celestial Seasonings Guy.

JESSIE: He finally made his move! You have to hear this—it's one for the books! He ran into her . . .

NINA: . . . in the laundry room!

JESSIE: And said he'd had a "religious vision". . .

NINA: Of our "union."

JESSIE: He said they had to *fast* for three days first and she had to wear white non-synthetic fibers . . .

NINA: I went up there this afternoon . . . He's in 14J.

MARTHA: How was it? Spacious?

NINA: A studio. He had it all fixed up. Rice paper. Futons. He was wearing what looked like a white diaper. He said we weren't supposed to talk, so we kind of *nodded* at each other. Then, Stan—that's his name—led me over to a futon. We were just about to start when the doorbell rang. Stan asked—"Who's there?" and a guy yelled, "Exterminator!" And Stan turned to me and said, "Would you mind? I've been waiting a month." So the exterminator came in and we made love—in a cloud of roach spray.

SUE CAROL: How was it?

NINA: (*Pantomiming a dead roach: hands curled on chest, she falls to floor.*) I died!

(*They laugh:* NINA *pops up. The wind howls louder: tin cans hurtling, human shouts. The cityscape hardens, grows icier, more dangerously brilliant.*)

JESSIE: What's going on out there?

(CLAIRE, *anxious for motion, tries to go to window:* MARTHA *blocks her.*)

MARTHA: Sit down. You'll get phlebitis.

NINA: Is that rain or hail?

MARTHA: It's a garbage storm. The wind is blowing the crud all over the place . . .

(JESSIE *goes toward her window, pulling on an afghan as she nears the drafty places.*)

JESSIE: You can feel the wind in here . . . You know, on winter nights like this, when I was little, my father would build a fire and lie down on the floor in front of it. My mother would lie down on his back . . .

(*Small laugh.*)

and I'd lie on her back. We were a family pyramid. We spent whole nights like that . . . It was quiet.

MARTHA: Well, you lived in an isolated place. There was nowhere to go. I love Vermont, but it's bleak.

JESSIE: No, it was wonderful! I always thought I'd live like that . . .

MARTHA: On a husband's back? With a little kiddie?

JESSIE: (*Laughing.*) Oh, yes, I was so sure. I had ten dolls and no doubts. When I was seven, I remember thinking, "I can get married and have children when I'm eighteen, only eleven years to go!"

MARTHA: So?

JESSIE: So . . . I haven't found what my parents had, and if it's not like that, I don't want it! I need that . . . sacred silence.

(*A piece of garbage strikes the windowpane.*)

JESSIE: (*Continued.*) Maybe it was a mistake to get a place with a big view. It makes me feel small.

MARTHA: You are small.

(*With professional alacrity.*)

So will you sell?

JESSIE: I don't know. When the wind blows, the window seems to bend and I see the whole city's on a warp, bearing down on me . . .

(*She shivers.*)

Oh, God, why do I fight it? Maybe I should just run out there and grab the first person I can stand? As if sensible decisions were being made. Sensible decisions on freezing nights in NoHo. Who has a choice? Who can stay out in the weather?

(*To* CLAIRE.)

I think you're going about this the right away. Grow your own.

(JESSIE *embraces* CLAIRE.)

CLAIRE: She generates a lot of heat. This is the first winter I haven't felt the cold . . .

JESSIE: And I've never felt such a chill. It's a cold spot here . . . in the center of me. Sometimes, I have to ask myself, "Why am I here? Why am I here at all?"

MARTHA: You mean in New York? Or downtown?

JESSIE: I meant on earth.

MARTHA: Well, I can see how you'd feel hopeless . . .

JESSIE: Hopeless!

MARTHA: Sweetie, I'm not an insensitive person: I see you're all running on empty. Believe me, I feel sorry for all of you . . .

GROUP: Sorry!!!?

(CLAIRE *flinches.*)

JESSIE: Sorry! *You* feel sorry for *us?* Martha, I wouldn't pursue this line of thought . . .

(MARTHA*'s mouth opens wider.*)

JESSIE: (*Continued.*) (*In vehement attempt to salvage the night.*)

This is a festive occasion.

MARTHA: This is a disaster! I can't believe what I'm seeing and hearing in here! Somebody has to talk sense around here. There are certain verities, and you cannot break the verities and get away with it. You must make a living, get married, and have children . . .

(*She stalks the room, moving among the* WOMEN, *who lie, as though wounded, on the couches and the floor.*)

MARTHA: (*Continued.*) What kills me is that this was all unnecessary . . .

(*She pauses to pat* JESSIE*'s hand.*)

Here you are . . .

(*Not unkindly.*)

practically middle-aged.

(EVERYONE *makes a face.*)

OTHERS: Middle-aged!

MARTHA: (*Matter-of-fact.*) Middle-aged. And still as confused and goopy as you all were twenty years ago.

JESSIE: Maybe that's good! Maybe some of us are still looking for . . . *whatever it is you look for* . . . when you don't like what you're *looking at!*

MARTHA: It's unnecessary.

SUE CAROL: We're doing the best we can. What were we supposed to do?

MARTHA: (*The ultimate.*) I would have introduced you to my male cousins.

(OTHERS *laugh in surprise.*)

CLAIRE: Pass.

LISBETH: No thanks.

SUE CAROL: Her *cousins?*

NINA: (*Dissolving in laughter.*) I've seen them.

MARTHA: (*Stiffening.*) Go ahead. Laugh at me.

(*They do.*)

MARTHA: (*Bearing down on* NINA.) *You*'re laughing? You, who come down here, straight from this sordid situation with a man in diapers? Still reeking from his roach spray!

NINA: Hey, is that my fault?

MARTHA: Yes! You sleep with them too soon!

NINA: You mean, if I *waited,* he wouldn't have let in the exterminator?

MARTHA: Absolutely not! You set yourself up. A) I would not have gone to his apartment. B) I would have insisted he take me to a good restaurant. Roach spray would never have entered into it . . .

LISBETH: No, it wasn't her fault!

MARTHA: And you'd know—you're home, mooning around, talking to the sofa.

SUE CAROL: Good Lord!

MARTHA: And you waltz in here with a baggie full of cheap vegetables—what did you spend? $3.99!? And another woman's hair! You're a big help!

JESSIE: Cut it out!

MARTHA: Why? So you can sit around waiting for a sacred silence? It's going to get *real quiet* for you, up ahead. You'll be alone in here with a frozen fish head!

CLAIRE: I can't take this . . .

MARTHA: And *you,* whom I'm so crazy about, you disappoint me by coming down here on a bicycle, totally unprepared to be a mother . . .

JESSIE: (*Interrupting.*) No, she's not!

MARTHA: . . . drinking this rotgut wine that will cause a furry baby. And *I* try to be sympathetic and helpful . . . I won't even mention how much money I spent! And to add insult to injury, *you* all treat me as if I'm a fool!

JESSIE: Martha, you are over the line.

MARTHA: No, let's clear the air! All night long, you've all been talking about me behind my back!

SUE CAROL: Uh-oh. The grass. Some people get paranoid.

(MARTHA *strikes, moving on the tippy-toes of paranoia: fast and furious.*)

MARTHA: Some people! Not me! What're you trying to pull? Talking and giggling about me behind my back? I've felt it underneath for years. Through all the phonecalls and the lunches, the dinners, and the movies. You only see me because it would be harder to stop seeing me than just see me once in awhile . . .

JESSIE: It's not like that!

MARTHA: It is so! So! Fine! Fine! It's been making me sick for years, but I know what's behind it . . .

NINA: What?

MARTHA: My mother told me not to even bother to come tonight. She said—"They're all jealous of you. Because of your obvious advantages." And I told her, "No, Mommy, you're *wrong* . . . They don't begrudge me the apartment, Donald, my success." But you *do!*

JESSIE: We don't want what you have!

MARTHA: Hahahahahahaha. I'm not stupid. Even I knew enough to downplay my achievements. Last year, I didn't even tell you, because I worried how it would affect you . . . that's only human . . . that I reached the top: I was voted *"Realtor of the Year!"*

(*The* OTHERS *collapse, laughing in shock.*)

MARTHA: (*Continued.*) See! You can't stand it! Can you? You want to vomit when you see me in my apartment, don't you?

NINA, SUE CAROL: (*Cracking up.*) Yes!

MARTHA: Does anyone ever say anything about *my* clothes? And I'm so careful to compliment you all, no matter what you have on. And does anyone ever have a nice word for Donald? No, you treat him like furniture. You should have seen your faces when I talked about my wedding, the honeymoon trip. When I said "Lago Maggiore," you all looked like you wanted to throw me in it!

LISBETH: That's not true!

MARTHA: Oh, you're so sick with jealousy you won't even be maid of honor, you won't wear a dress and . . . a bonnet! Huh? What's that?

NINA: Martha: Cool it.

MARTHA: Oh, I should cool it? How long do you think you can go your hotsy-totsy way? In a couple of years, men won't even be interested enough to abuse you. You'll be lucky if you can make love with the exterminator.

JESSIE: Martha! That's enough!

SUE CAROL: You got a mean streak in you, Martha!

MARTHA: (*To* JESSIE.) And you won't have anyone to take care of you in your old age, you'll just get weirder and weirder and weirder!

JESSIE: I'd rather be weird than what you are!

MARTHA: Oh, go on. Get it over with . . . Buy the chihuahua! Knit dog booties! You'll need something. I'll have a family. I'll be happy, and none of you want to see it!

SUE CAROL: It would make anyone want to puke!

MARTHA: Woooo! Finally! It's coming out! Admit it. Admit it—*You're sorry you invited me!*

(GROUP *profound silence: an admission.*)

MARTHA: (*Continued.*) (*Marching to her gift pile.*) Look at these gifts! You all talk a good game. But who actually does the most?

(CLAIRE *is now in a silent panic, noticeably shaken.*)

MARTHA: (*Continued.*) Who does the most for Claire! I put my money where my mouth is!

(MARTHA*'s mouth opens wider, as* CLAIRE *bolts for the door.*)

CLAIRE: (*To* JESSIE.) I can't stay. I'm sorry. I have to go.

OTHERS: No!

(*They pursue* CLAIRE *toward the door.*)

SUE CAROL: Don't let Martha push you out!

NINA: This party is for you!

(CLAIRE *squeezes eyes shut, bites her fist against the tears. She picks up her detached front bike wheel, flees.*)

CLAIRE: I want to go home! I just want to go home!

MARTHA: Don't you dare go!

(CLAIRE *exits through elevator door, door slams shut.*)

MARTHA: (*Continued.*) . . . It's too late.

(GROUP *shock.* OTHERS *stare at the door, then turn on* MARTHA *and one another.*)

JESSIE: How could you?

SUE CAROL: I've never seen a mouth go meaner . . .

(*To* JESSIE.)

Why'd you invite her?

LISBETH: You gave her such ugly gifts . . . You didn't consider . . . the aesthetic effect. I thought and thought about what to give Claire . . . something beautiful, permanent . . . with emotional meaning . . . You wanted to depress her!

NINA: At least the doll I gave her was *cute!*

JESSIE: I'm really glad I had this in my house . . . I'm so thrilled I spent over three hundred dollars at Dean and DeLuca . . .

MARTHA: I would never have had that rotgut wine if it was at my place. It should have been at my place.

SUE CAROL: Your place looks like the lobby of a Ramada Inn!

MARTHA: A Ramada! That shows what *you* know . . . It should have been at my place . . . It's bigger and more conveniently located . . . I would have had it catered . . .

JESSIE: (*Whisper to* LISBETH.) I want to kill her.

(LISBETH, JESSIE *huddle, conspiring, and* NINA *and* SUE CAROL *join them—a team is forming, with* MARTHA *on the "other side."*)

LISBETH: (*Whisper to* JESSIE.) Tell her off, tell her off . . .

NINA: (*Also to* JESSIE, *whisper.*) Let her have it . . .

SUE CAROL: When I think how I rushed to get here . . . On a night when my own life was falling apart all around me . . . But I thought "Oh, we'll have a good time, we'll be happy, we'll forget . . ."

MARTHA: That your lives are shit.

(JESSIE *has been building, trying to get a word in edgewise.*)

JESSIE: Stop it . . . Stop it . . . Stop it . . . All of you . . .

(THEY *ignore her, overlapping accusations to one another.*)

MARTHA: (*To* SUE CAROL.) All you ever think about is yourself . . . You're so cheap . . . When was the last time you picked up a check?

SUE CAROL: I'd rather pick up a check than eat with you . . .

MARTHA: You'd split the tax . . .

NINA: (*To* MARTHA.) Don't ever call me . . . Next Tuesday is off . . .

LISBETH: The whole world is disintegrating . . . I want to die, I want to die.

(*To* JESSIE.)

When I came in here tonight and saw all the decorations I wanted to take an overdose of something . . . anything . . .

NINA: I could have stayed in bed with Stan . . . I didn't need this . . .

(JESSIE *grabs the dinner platter, bangs it down.*)

JESSIE: (*Peak.*) Look at me! I'm exhausted! I was up at dawn to peel radishes into rosebuds! I was on line for groceries for three hours! I couldn't wait for delivery so I *pushed* a cart for ten blocks, and rode up in the elevator . . . I carried those wine jugs! Do you know how much they weigh? My cleaning lady didn't show up, and I had to vacuum . . . and my vacuum broke . . . I breathed in dust! I didn't have time to take a shower! I didn't have time to pee!

NINA: (*Nodding to the war drum beat.*) She busted her hump . . .

JESSIE: And I'm sorry! I'm sorry! I'm sorry I bothered! I feel like a real jerk for even . . . making *the effort!* I wanted tonight . . .

(*She trashes the rest of her party display.*)

to be *perfect!* And nobody has showed the least bit of consideration *for me!* I was the hostess here! I'm always the hostess! And nobody cares about me! I shouldn't have bothered!

NINA: I brought the cake.

MARTHA: And you ate it.

NINA: (*To* MARTHA.) Oh why don't you shut your trap and get out of here?

SUE CAROL: I brought all those vegetables . . .

MARTHA: That was a new low, even for you . . .

SUE CAROL: I hate you, I hate you . . . When you call me and I'm home . . . I leave my machine on . . .

LISBETH: I do too . . .

SUE CAROL: Just get the hell out!

MARTHA: It's Jessie's house!

JESSIE: Oh, you can all go: I'm going to bed . . .

LISBETH: (*To* MARTHA.) And take all your presents with you!

(*She roots through pile, selects her own christening dress.*)

(*Low, to herself.*)

I might as well take this . . .

NINA: (*Picking up baby boy doll.*) (*To* JESSIE.) I sensed you resented having this at your place.

JESSIE: I do *now!*

(EVERYONE *scrambles, selecting their gifts, coats, heading for the door. They are giving up, leaving:* MARTHA, *as usual, leads. She is almost at the door.* JESSIE *is on the verge of tears.*)

JESSIE: (*A near sob: choking grief.*) Tonight was about kindness!

(*Simultaneously, the door swings open:* CLAIRE *reappears, holding a vandalized parking meter pole, like a spear, her bike lock dangling from it. She stamps the meter pole: She looks fiery, determined.)*

EVERYONE: Claire!

(CLAIRE *confronts* MARTHA.)

NINA: Don't even talk to her. I wouldn't even talk to her . . .

CLAIRE: No! I'm not taking this! You have a lot of nerve coming down here . . . like a SAC missile: You hit every weak spot! You're unerring!

MARTHA: I just want you to face reality!

CLAIRE: No! Reality will have to face me! I haven't been so mad since my folks told me to forget medieval music and teach math! Well, I fought them, and I *fight* you . . .

MARTHA: What's wrong with being a math teacher? At certain points in life, you must make certain compromises . . .

CLAIRE: Well, I don't intend to end up looking mine in the eye! Keep it up Martha . . . Keep droning on about orthodontia and IRAs! You only make me fight harder! I sense a miracle upon me, and I refuse to let you make it . . . *mundane.* Don't infect me with your fear . . . I have my own!

MARTHA: It's not enough!

CLAIRE: Oh, yes it is! I'm the one who has to go through with this! I'm the one who wakes up at four A.M. . . . I hear *two* pounding hearts! I sleep all day, and lie awake all night! I go grocery shopping at four A.M. . . .

MARTHA: That's foolish . . .

CLAIRE: No! This is the way it is now . . . It's getting stranger and stranger out there . . . A trip to the Safeway is like a visit to Mars . . . It's crazy and new, and it's not going to defeat me . . . I don't care if you think I'm unfit; I don't care if I'm broke . . . I have new life in me! And only a child can lead any of us, out of this . . . Children are our guides to this future . . . This is a world they will explain to us! They know how to play, to bring joy to this terrible place . . . I saw a little boy, in a subway arcade . . . and he was laughing, and winning a war at a machine that led him into outer space . . .

MARTHA: You're having a baby so you can know how to play video games!

CLAIRE: (*Thrown for a moment, then regaining her momentum.*) Yes! Yes! In a sense! Because, otherwise, it will get worse! There's a bad wind blowing . . . and a new cold is creeping toward us . . . Each day, something new and awful happens . . . (*Rattling the meter.*) We have worse enemies than ourselves . . .

MARTHA: Your bike was stolen . . . I'll buy you a new one.

NINA: That's the least you can do . . .

CLAIRE: I don't want what you can buy me.

(MARTHA *is shaken, in distraction, finishes packing her gifts in the stroller.*)

MARTHA: (*Weakened by* CLAIRE*'s strength.*) I guess I should go.

(MARTHA *works blindly in the confusion of her emotion. She is literally losing it: Her purse drops, spilling keys, money. She is on the brink of breaking down.*)

MARTHA: What do you want me to do? I'll do it.

(*Desperate, looking up from the floor.*)

Do you want me to have a brunch? My treat. At a nice restaurant . . .

(*The* OTHERS *look at her stonily.*)

MARTHA: (*Continued.*) I was having a good time.

NINA: You were having a ball.

MARTHA: I thought it was a wonderful party . . . considering the location.

JESSIE: Thank you. So glad you could come.

MARTHA: I haven't had so much fun in years. Since we all lived in the same building.

SUE CAROL: Oh, go home to Donald, that pussy-whipped wimp . . .

MARTHA: I wish he was pussy-whipped . . .

(*She decides to offer her real gift: an honest admission.*)

I didn't want to go out with him tonight . . . I wanted to stay here . . .

LISBETH: You missed a great dinner.

MARTHA: And who do you think would have had to pick up the check?

SUE CAROL: (*Elated.*) You have to pay with him too!

JESSIE: (*Hushing* SUE CAROL.) *Sssssh.*

(*The* OTHERS *lean in, needing to hear* MARTHA*'s ultimate truth.*)

MARTHA: You'll be happy to hear I pay all the bills, make all the reservations . . . He doesn't even speak to me at meals. He just lowers his head into a bowl and makes sounds . . .

JESSIE: You support Donald!

SUE CAROL: I suspected it, I suspected it . . .

CLAIRE: (*Restraining* SUE CAROL*'s glee.*) Hold on . . .

MARTHA: Ask him to "contribute" and he says his money is all tied up . . . huh . . . in his sock! He won't even open *a joint account.*

SUE CAROL: And how's his joint?

NINA: Yeah, how is it?

MARTHA: (*Laughing on the verge of tears.*) Ha Ha . . . you don't know the half of it. He only makes love to me on my birthday. August 7th. I have to get on top and do all the work. Things are slipping fast . . . His doo-hickey isn't as strong as it used to be. It has a pleat. It folds . . . like an accordion. I don't know that I can fix it in time for the wedding . . .

(*She makes a helpless gesture, as if repairing an accordion.*)

MARTHA: (*Continued.*) Oh, God, I'm getting tired of trying . . .

LISBETH: Do you love him?

MARTHA: Sweetie, his pupils don't even focus. There's no one home.

SUE CAROL: So why all the bullshit with the QE II, and the earrings?

MARTHA: I decided to marry him, anyway.

OTHERS: Why?

MARTHA: (*Defeated.*) It's easier. I can still go to a good restaurant.

JESSIE: That may not be the pinnacle of human experience . . .

NINA: It can be pretty close . . .

MARTHA: Well, I love lobster places. Can you imagine me, alone in a bib? I'd feel absurd. Where am I supposed to go? To the coffee shops, where the plates are chipped, and the glasses are all spotty? So some waitress can plunk down my dinner, and say, "There you go"?

SUE CAROL: Hey, I'm on the other end of that. There *I* go!

MARTHA: You all hate me . . . and you're my best friends!

(MARTHA *is crying, has scooped up most of her belongings, and is wheeling next to the door. She presses the elevator.* CLAIRE *takes pity on her, takes her hand from the elevator button, holds it.*)

CLAIRE: Oh look . . . All friends have arguments, little ripples . . . undercurrents . . . It doesn't mean we don't *care* . . . Listen, some of what you said made sense . . . I've grown old, but I haven't grown up . . .

MARTHA: (*Weeping.*) I didn't mean that personally. We belong to the first generation that refused to give up sneakers. We're still young but we've been young for so long . . .

CLAIRE: God, you just put things the wrong way . . . But in a way, I ought to thank you . . .

(MARTHA *perks up.*)

CLAIRE: You made me so mad . . . it cleared my head . . .

MARTHA: (*Apologizing.*) Maybe I was a little outspoken.

CLAIRE: Well, you lit a fire under me. Running out and running back up here is the most action I've seen since the fruit store . . . God, there may not be a right way, or a wrong way to do this . . .

(*She touches her belly.*)

We each have to find our own way. Our children are our choices, and this is mine. I'd rather have the child of that night than the offspring of some lifelong "accommodation". . . I don't want my life to be some long shlep to the finish . . .

MARTHA: (*Sarcastic but resigned.*) Thanks.

CLAIRE: I think it's just as scary to play it safe. If I lose out, at least I lose *big!*

MARTHA: I envy you . . . and believe me, I wish you well . . .

CLAIRE: I know you do . . . We don't hate you.

MARTHA: I'm sorry, I'm sorry! I'd never hurt you!

(*They collapse into a weeping, group huddle.*)

NINA: Don't cry . . .

LISBETH: I can't stand to see *you* cry . . .

MARTHA: I should never have opened my mouth!

SUE CAROL: I'm sorry I said you had a mean streak . . .

MARTHA: That hurt.

JESSIE: I'm glad I had this here . . . This is what I wanted.

CLAIRE: Oh, God, I love you all.

OTHERS: We love you.

(*They are crying, laughing, clinging.*)

CLAIRE: You've all given me so much. Let's face it. This may be as good as it gets . . .

LISBETH: You mean we won't get to meet new people?

(*They close in, laughing at themselves, as dawn seeps into the loft, bleaching away the cityscape, and leaving the women, exposed to one another.*)

BEDTIME

Mary Gallagher

BEDTIME premiered at the Ark Theatre Company in New York City in June 1984. It was directed by Liz Diamond; the set design was by Michael Pillinger; the lighting design was by Rick Pettit; and the production stage manager was Sydney Lloyd-Smith. The cast was as follows:

KITTY	Heather Nicole Rose
TINA	Laurie Robyn

TIME

The fifties. A few minutes after KITTY and TINA turned out the light to go to sleep.

PLACE: Their bedroom. They are lying in separate twin beds.

CHARACTERS

KITTY, 12
TINA, 10

These characters can be played by children *or* by actresses, who must play them simply and naturally.

TINA: Kitty?

KITTY: What?

TINA: Do you ever think about God?

KITTY: Ohhh . . . come on, will ya? I'm trying to sleep.

TINA: Sorry.

(*Pause.*)

KITTY: I wish you hadn't said that.

(*They giggle.*)

TINA: Yeah, I know. It's sort of . . .

KITTY: *Sort* of?

(*They giggle.*)

TINA: Yeah, but . . . sometimes I do think about it, you know.

KITTY: Well, think about it in the daytime.

(*Pause.*)

KITTY: And anyway, you're a funny one to be talking about God, after you went in my drawer and took my brand new sweater. (*Beat.*) And then leaving it under your *bed*. You got dust all over it.

TINA: I said I was sorry.

KITTY: Well, it's *my* sweater!

TINA: I know it.

KITTY: I hadn't even ever worn it, hardly!

TINA: Okay.

KITTY: At least you could have put it back—

TINA: Okay!

KITTY: So don't do it again.

TINA: I won't!

(*Pause.*)

KITTY: Well, what about God?

TINA: Never mind.

KITTY: Come on, hurry up. *I'm* thinking about it now . . . you noodnik!

(*They giggle.*)

TINA: Yew nooood-nik!

(*Variations on this with giggles.*)

KITTY: (*Giggling.*) No but really.

TINA: No but *really.*

KITTY: (*Trying to stop giggling.*) No, come on, be serious. Come on, quit it . . .

TINA: (*Giggling.*) Be *serious* . . .

KITTY: (*Sharply.*) Quit it! You started this. You woke me up—

TINA: (*Overlapping.*) You were not asleep—

KITTY: (*Overlapping.*) —and made me think about it, and you know I hate to think about a lot of stuff at night. So come on, get it over with.

TINA: Well . . . I was just thinking about . . . forever. You know.

KITTY: Forever?

TINA: Yeah.

(*Pause.*)

KITTY: What about it?

TINA: Well, do you ever think about that?

KITTY: What do you mean?

TINA: Forever. I mean, *really* forever.

KITTY: Well . . . yeah, I guess . . . I don't know . . .

TINA: Because if we live *forever* . . . in heaven or hell or anywhere . . . don't you think that's scary?

KITTY: No. I'd rather be around forever than be dead.

TINA: Not me.

KITTY: Of course you would. You don't want to be dead, do you?

TINA: No. But . . .

KITTY: Well, what's scary about forever?

TINA: I don't know. But when I think about it . . . that there wouldn't be any days or nights, or any clocks, or any holidays or any school . . . just everything all the same, all the time . . . and it would never end, never ever ever ever—

KITTY: Quit it, would ya?

(*Pause.*)

TINA: When I really let myself think about it . . . I get sick to my stomach . . . like when you play the bottom part of "Heart and Soul" on the piano, you know, over and over and over?

KITTY: What are you talking about? First you're talking about God, now you're talking about playing "Heart and Soul" on the piano—

TINA: I'm talking about forever!

KITTY: You said you wanted to talk about God!

TINA: Forever *is* God—

KITTY: Will you shut up about forever! (*Pause.*) Sometimes you're really creepy, you know it?

TINA: (*Tearful.*) I can't help it.

KITTY: Oh, geez . . . are you *crying*?

TINA: Well, I'm scared.

KITTY: You don't have to be scared *now.* It isn't going to happen *yet.*

TINA: How do you know?

KITTY: What do you mean? How could it happen now? . . . You mean what if you get hit by a car or something? You're not gonna get hit by a car.

TINA: You don't know.

KITTY: You're *not*. Just look where you're *going* for a change.

TINA: But it isn't just a car, or something you can *see.* A lot of things can kill you. And some of them, you don't even know what's happening to you. You just go to sleep . . . and you don't wake up . . . and you don't even know it. And forever starts.

KITTY: Why wouldn't you wake up?

TINA: It could be gas, you know.

KITTY: Gas? What kind of gas?

(*Beat; outburst of mutual giggles. They pretend to fart and die from the gas.*)

TINA: (*Giggling.*) Quit it! This is serious . . . The kind of gas that's in your house. For the stove and stuff. It's invisible. You can't smell it even. And it's poison. And my teacher told us about this one family, they had a gas leak in their house, but they didn't know it, and it was winter so they didn't have their windows open, so no good air could get in, and they were breathing poison gas but they didn't even know it.

KITTY: So what happened?

TINA: Well, they were all unconscious, and, but, finally someone called them on the phone, and the ringing woke the mother up, and she sort of staggered to the phone, but still she didn't know that there was anything wrong, and so . . . so she answered the phone, and the person who called her thought she sounded real strange and slow, and so he sent the police to their house. But the police couldn't get in because they were all asleep and couldn't answer the door. And so finally the police broke the windows. But it was too late. And they all died.

(*Pause.*)

KITTY: Who told you that?

TINA: My teacher. And she said it was true, too.

KITTY: Huh.

TINA: And she told us about this family that used to go mushroom-picking in the woods and then they'd eat them, and everybody warned them that you shouldn't go picking mushrooms all on your own like that, because you could get a poisoned toadstool by mistake, because they look just the same, and only a trained expert should do that. But they wouldn't listen and they went out and picked mushrooms anyway, and they took them home and cooked them up and ate them, and they all died. Except the baby, because the baby didn't eat any mushrooms.

(*Pause.*)

KITTY: We should play that.

TINA: Yeah . . . but *still.*

KITTY: Is that why you told Mom you don't like mushrooms all of the sudden?

TINA: They could be poison. You can't tell—

KITTY: Oh, so we all die and you get off scot free!

TINA: You shouldn't eat them either, then!

KITTY: Your teacher's cracked, if you ask me.

TINA: It's not just her. It's true. The bad mushrooms look just like the good ones. And one bad one can kill a whole family. They could get just one bad one mixed up with—

KITTY: But you can't go around worrying how everything you eat or everything you breathe might kill you all the time.

(*Pause.*)

TINA: There's something else to.

KITTY: Now what? (*Long beat.*) *What*?

TINA: . . . Well . . . what if the world ends tonight?

KITTY: *What*? Did your teacher tell you that?

TINA: No. But it *could* end tonight.

KITTY: Oh, that is just . . . so . . . sometimes I think you are really batso. You're actually lying here thinking that the world might end tonight?

TINA: I don't try to think about it. But sometimes when I'm falling asleep, all of the sudden it pokes up in my mind. That the world might end, any minute . . . and forever will start . . . and there's nothing anyone can do about it. I start getting really scared . . . and sick to my stomach . . . just like when I play the bottom part of—

KITTY: "Heart and Soul," I know. (*Beat.*) Look. Why don't you try . . . you know . . . thinking about really *nice* things instead?

TINA: (*Gloomily.*) Like what?

KITTY: Like what you'd do if yo had a million dollars. Or your dream house, what it would be like. Or having a horse . . . you know.

TINA: (*More gloomily.*) Yeah . . .

KITTY: Probably you shouldn't even think about God and stuff like that at all, if you wind up getting all—

TINA: But you think about God.

KITTY: Yeah, but not like that.

TINA: Well . . . how?

KITTY: Well . . . I don't know. Just . . . you know, trying to be a good person, and . . . wondering if there's really a heaven and hell and all that . . . because nobody knows, really. Nobody knows if there's even a God, really, so there's no point in—

TINA: Mom knows.

KITTY: Mom doesn't know.

TINA: She told me.

KITTY: She told you what?

TINA: There's really a God. Mom said.

KITTY: Well, geez! Why don't you tell *her* all this creepy stuff about forever and the end of the world—

TINA: I wanted to ask you.

(*Pause.*)

KITTY: Okay. I'm sorry I got mad.

TINA: That's okay. I don't care.

KITTY: But sometimes you can be really weird, the things you think of.

TINA: I know.

KITTY: But listen, okay? Mom told you there's a God and you believe her, right?

TINA: Yeah.

KITTY: Well, now I'm telling you, the same as Mom would. Okay. There might be a forever. Okay? Yes, we might all live forever. But we don't know for sure, just like with heaven and hell. But, maybe. *But.* If there *is* a forever, then it's God who thought of it, and who, you know, who's in charge of it . . . and if God loves everybody so much, like they always say, then forever isn't creepy and boring. Forever's really nice.

TINA: . . . Nice, how?

KITTY: I don't know. But really nice. A hundred times nicer than now.

(*Pause.*)

TINA: . . . Well . . . maybe . . .

KITTY: And anyway, forever doesn't start till the end of the world. And I am telling you right now that the world is not going to end tonight, or any other night, just because you're lying here and worrying about it.

TINA: But it *could*, it *could* end tonight—

KITTY: It won't! You know how I know? Because in the first place, we would've been warned. The scientists would've seen signs . . . or there would've been prophecies, or *something.*

TINA: Yeah?

KITTY: Of course! I mean, what's it gonna be? A big explosion, right?

TINA: I don't know, but it says in the Bible that the world is gonna end, and the whole world and the universe and everything will be destroyed, right?

KITTY: (*Warily.*) . . . Right . . .

TINA: And all the planets will fall out of the sky, and everything will be burning and exploding . . . and there'll be tidal waves and hurricanes and earthquakes, all happening at the same time—

KITTY: Oh, great . . .

TINA: And then Jesus and Mary and all the apostles and angels and everyone who ever lived . . . they'll appear.

KITTY: Appear where?

TINA: In the sky?

KITTY: Everyone who ever lived? Like outside our window?

TINA: Yeah. Everybody's window. They'll be in the sky. Like the moon. So everyone can see them and know that it's the end of the world.

KITTY: Right. So here we are, you in that stupid nightgown with the rip down the back, and me in my old ratty pjs with the tulips on them . . . and suddenly they all come surfing in, on the planets, I guess, Jesus and Mary and everybody who has ever lived, surfing right toward our window . . . Come on, can you *see* that? For the end of the whole *world*? That's ridiculous!

TINA: (*Giggling.*) I guess.

KITTY: Come on! Our car's in the driveway. Mom and Dad are downstairs watching TV. And the world ends in our bedroom? Get serious!

TINA: Yeah . . .

KITTY: You noodnik!

TINA: Yew nooooodnik!

(*Noises and giggles. Finally they subside. Brief silence. Then:*)

KITTY: Go to sleep now, okay?

TINA: Okay. Can we sing a song?

KITTY: (*Beat.*) . . . Yeah . . . okay. Don't sing too loud or Mom and Dad'll hear us. What do you want to sing? Like a hymn or something?

TINA: No. "What Coral Bells."

KITTY: Okay.

(*Beat. Then they sing in unison, softly:*)

BOTH: *"White coral bells, upon a slender stalk.*
Lilies of the valley deck my garden walk.
Oh, don't you wish that you could hear them ring.
That will happen only when the angels sing."

(*Still very softly, they sing it again as a round, as lights slowly fade. Then:*)

KITTY: Good night.

TINA: Good night.

KITTY: Sweet dreams.

TINA: Okay . . .

(BLACKOUT)

THE MOST MASSIVE WOMAN WINS

Madeleine George

THE MOST MASSIVE WOMAN WINS premiered at the Public Theater in New York City as part of the Young Playwrights Festival in October 1994. It was directed by Phyllis S. K. Look; the set design was by Allen Moyer; the costume design was by Karen Perry; the lighting design was by Pat Dignan; the production stage manager was Elise-Ann Konstantin; and the dramaturg was Sarah Higgins. The cast was as follows:

SABINE	Candace Taylor
CARLY	Amy Ryder
RENNIE	Elaina Davis
CEL	Suzanne Costallos

CAST OF CHARACTERS

CARLY: Thirty-one years old. In acid-washed jeans, a rhinestone-studded denim jacket, and a sweatshirt with high-top Reebok sneakers.

CEL: Twenty-six years old. In a long dress. Her name is pronounced "Seel;" it's short for Celia.

SABINE: Twenty-five years old. In à la mode nineties office wear.

RENNIE: Seventeen years old. In overalls and flannel. She is a high school senior.

SCENE: The play takes place in a liposuction clinic waiting room.

TIME: 1990s.

MUSIC

Preshow music: "Dr. Feelgood," "The Weight." Playout: "Satisfaction," all by Aretha Franklin. Preshow music should be completely out by the time the house goes to half.

GENERAL NOTES

—All four women do not have to be overweight.
—Rennie is the only bulimic.
—It is important that the play be established as humorous from the outset.
—A great deal of the "dialogue" is directed out to the audience; the characters are often able to pick up on each others' thoughts without speaking straight at one another.
—The chants are genuine hopscotch, jumprope, and hand-clap rhymes from our own childhood and other children in Amherst, Massachusetts.
—We used blocking inspired by children's games: London Bridge and Mulberry Bush for the scoliosis check, Red Rover for the thesis defense, Musical Chairs for Carly's job interviews.

MONOLOGUE NOTES

—Each monologue is delivered out to the audience.
—The three women not speaking at any one time should not look at the speaker, but some way should be found to indicate that they are listening—stomps, thigh slaps, or claps that punctuate moments of tension or anger, for example. In the "dance, run, jump, fly" sequence at the end of Cel's monologue, the other three women do a slow flap of their arms, reprising the bird movement from earlier in the play. At that point they also turn to look at Cel.
—Carly talks hard and fast and never gets sentimental, but she loves her kid.
—Sabine is extremely hard on herself and never gives herself a break; instead of getting sad she always gets angry, right through to the very last line.
—Rennie is perpetually panicked and jumpy; it's as if there's nothing holding her down to the floor. She laughs a lot to disguise her fear.
—Cel is not crazy. Her monologue is driven by her own need to tell her story. She does not relive the moment of her self-immolation, she tells us about it (this is important). Realization and catharsis come at the very end of the monologue, not before.

SETTING: *Waiting room of a liposuction clinic, furnished with four chairs.*

AT RISE: *The light is bright and sterile.* SABINE, CEL, CARLY, *and* RENNIE *are seated on the chairs. For several minutes they stare at their magazines, fidget, cough, cross and recross their legs, and flip magazine pages, in an otherworldly, choreographed little dance.*

RENNIE: I'm about to have my body surgically removed.

CEL: (CEL*'s chant runs underneath the others' comments.*) Cinderella dressed in yella . . .

RENNIE: They're taking stuff out—big chunks, sloppy hunks.

CEL: Went to the ball to meet her fella . . .

SABINE: I'm here for the ass and inner thigh combo.

CEL: On the way her girdle busted . . .

CARLY: He said my butt and my gut is the parts he would pay for.

CEL: How many people were disgusted?

CARLY: Aw, shit, I hate waiting. If I'm gonna do this I just wanna do it, you know?

RENNIE: Scared?

CARLY: It's not that . . .

RENNIE: If you're here you're here because you want to be here.

ALL: On the way her girdle busted
How many people were disgusted?

RENNIE: One—

SABINE: Two—

CEL: Three—

CARLY: Four—

ALL: (*Addressing the audience.*) Five—

CARLY: The other night my boyfriend goes to me, he's spread-eagle on the couch giving his gut some air watching Monday Night Football and during the commercial he goes, "We don't have steak anymore. How come is it we never have steak?" I'm about to say, "You want steak, buy steak. Take it out a your paycheck, if you want steak so bad," but then he says to me, like, right in the same breath he goes, "What am I saying? You're too fat for steak. Last thing you need is fatty red meat." Just like that, then he tips back his beer and the conversation's over.

SABINE: What did you say to him?

CARLY: I don't know, nothing. It's like I can't tell him off. Then later he leaves me this liposuction ad he clipped from the classifieds on my bedside table with a signed blank check. Is the guy subtle or what?

SABINE: Shit . . .

CARLY: You think it doesn't make me sick? What's the matter with me that I can't tell Frank Nowak where to stick it? I'm a weenie, that's what. A big fat wimp. How am I supposed to look my own kid in the face?

ALL: *My boyfriend gave me peaches*
My boyfriend gave me pears
My boyfriend gave me fifty cents
and kicked me down the stairs!

CARLY: C'ai play too?

RENNIE: She's too fat for jumprope.

CARLY: That feeling, you know it, it's the one you've been getting since you were six years old.

ALL: *Miss Suzy had a baby*
She named her Mary Lynn
She put her in the bathtub
Just to see if she could swim
She drank up all the water
She ate up all the soap
She tried to eat the bathtub but it wouldn't go down her throat!

CARLY: It starts like a tidal wave under your feet and grows and grows until you forget your name and the people you love and all you know is you have to eat.

CEL: You think if you dared to open your mouth all of creation would get sucked right in.

SABINE: You think about eating alone in your bed, making love to a Twinkie, devouring it desperately, HUNGry for it.

CARLY: You sneak out of bed, you don't think he hears you, you run down the stairs to where you hid the Sugar Smacks behind the TV, you're alone at last and you're eating great fistfuls, hand over hand. It tastes like everything you never had.

SABINE: It rises from a moan to a wail in your ears, it's pulsing through your body, it's chocolate you're hearing. It's the middle of the night and there's a winter storm warning you're about to drive across town for a 52-ounce bar of Toblerone love.

RENNIE: Now you're gorging, cramming it thick down your throat, all Chewy Chips Ahoy and no room to breathe, you have to you have to you have to have it, then you're doubling over, spitting and shaking, face in the toilet, so sorry, so ashamed.

CARLY: You eat and you eat until you can't fit another bite into your body, you're bloated, drowned from the inside out.

SABINE: A beached whale, you can't move an inch.

CEL: You're done.

SABINE: You're done for.

RENNIE: So you throw out the evidence. Flush down the rest.

SABINE: Regain control.

CARLY: And you go back to doing what you were doing before.

(*They reprise the waiting dance.*)

SABINE: But you know you did it.

RENNIE: You may be making like everything is fine fine fine but you know what you've done, you bit it, you blew it.

CARLY: It's your fuckin fault—you lost control.

CEL: You know better than that.

SABINE: So it's time to make an adult decision.

CARLY: (*Smacks her own butt.*) Throw out the evidence.

RENNIE: You think of every sin in your past—

CEL: Every slice of pie—

CARLY: Every french fry—

SABINE: Every chocolate croissant—

RENNIE: You know it's all in there, simmering under your skin, and this nice man is gonna get rid of it all. Purify you.

ALL: Clean slate.

RENNIE: The ultimate purge.

SABINE: You are responsible for your own behavior.

ALL: You are responsible.

RENNIE: You are guilty.

(*Lights shift, a whistle is blown.*)

CEL: (*Bellowing.*) Scoliosis check!

(CARLY, RENNIE, *and* SABINE *scramble into position down center.*)

CEL: Shirts off!

CARLY: (*To* RENNIE.) She's such a fatso.

RENNIE: (*To* CARLY.) She weighs a hundred and four, I peeked at the scale.

CARLY: (*To* RENNIE.) Oh gross, look, she's getting boobs.

CEL: Bend at the waist!

CARLY: If you get them early it means you're a slut.

CEL: Rotate to face me!

RENNIE: I hope I don't get them.

CEL: Touch your hands to the floor!

CARLY: It's her fault cause she always eats two desserts at lunch.

CEL: Rotate again!

CARLY: We'll never get them like she's got them.

CEL: Stand up!

RENNIE: We'll never be so disgusting as her.

(*Lights shift, a whistle is blown.*)

SABINE: Look who's not playing.

CEL: (*Sassy.*) She's excused.

CARLY: She's always excused. Bitch.

CEL: She can't play dodgeball, she's ginormous!

SABINE: Gigundo!

CARLY: Gigantoid!

CEL: (*Yelling to* RENNIE.) Hey fatso, what position are YOU playing, huh?

RENNIE: (*Quietly.*) Offense.

(*Lights shift, a whistle is blown, they scramble into a new formation.*)

SABINE: (*Announcing.*) In defense of my thesis: "Images of Women in Cold War and Post-Cold-War-Era Media Colon Self-Denial and Self-Esteem." (*Confidently.*) I refer you once again to both Kruger and Wolf as well as to Baudrillard's discussion of the hypnotizing image. (*She takes a deep breath, then speaks quickly.*) In conclusion I would like to emphasize my belief that this and related subject matters are pertinent, if not crucial, to our postmodern society. Although inquiry into such subjects is somewhat scarce in journals today, I predict that as the information age hits its stride, and as feminist thought becomes more seamlessly integrated into mainstream American consciousness, we will see a proliferation of influential and powerful work concerning the subjugation of women's bodies through media images. Thank you.

RENNIE: Ms. . . . Rowe . . . Can you explain again ex-act-ly how this subject is relevant? I can't see how this topic merits scholarly investigation when it has such a minute effect on the population as a whole.

SABINE: If eating disorders are as prevalent among women as recent studies show, and if women comprise as they do 52 percent of the population, I think you'll find this is quite a relevant subject for investigation—

CEL: (*Cutting in.*) I fail to understand why these women can't simply "get over" disorders that you claim are caused by looking at two-dimensional images.

SABINE: Obviously it's a bit more complicated than that—

CARLY: (*Cutting in.*) As every person is responsible for his own attitudes about himself, it should be a simple matter for a person to alter his image of self, should it not?

SABINE: (*Stumbling over words.*) Once again I'd like to remind you that studies show physical appearance, that is, conformity to societally established standards of beauty, has a much greater impact on women's lives than on men's; this includes social status, marital status, income, and work-related achievements—

RENNIE: (*Cutting in.*) It seems to me you're getting a little emotional about this. I can understand why—this hits a little close to home for you. For that reason I would have advised you to choose a topic you could remain somewhat objective about.

(*Lights shift, whistle.*)

CARLY: What about benefits?

RENNIE: (*Strongly emphasizing the "Mizz."*) We haven't yet decided if this is an appropriate job for you, Ms.—

CARLY: Kinski.

RENNIE: Let's hold off our discussion of fine points and sundries until we are able to come to a full understanding.

CARLY: Sure thing, sir.

(*Whistle.*)

SABINE: Let me be frank, Ms.—

CARLY: Kinski.

SABINE: I don't think you have fully considered the physical taxation that is put on a person in this line of work.

CARLY: Sir I been in food service all my life.

SABINE: The waitstaff here are part of our family. And because of the extreme demands placed on their persons I demand that every member of the family be in peak physical condition.

CARLY: Alls I'm saying sir is I can do this job and I just wanna know about the benefits you—

(*Whistle.*)

CEL: (*Overlapping.*) I'm afraid I'm not fully getting through to you, Ms.—

CARLY: Kinski, Kinski.

CEL: Allow me to speak as plainly as possible. I really don't think the restaurant can use a woman of your—stature at this time. Please don't take this personally, but with the aesthetic atmosphere I am trying to cultivate there are certain, hmmm, discrepancies that cannot be tolerated.

CARLY: I been trying to tell you—

(*Whistle.*)

RENNIE: (*Cutting in.*) Most of the girls I hire are eighteen, nineteen years old.

(*Whistle.*)

SABINE: They haven't been through what you've been through I'm sure.

(*Whistle.*)

CEL: I hope you won't be unduly upset by this.

(*Whistle.*)

RENNIE: Not everything can be fair in this world, I'm afraid.

(*Lights shift, whistle is blown. During* CEL*'s trial* SABINE *paces the perimeter of the stage calling off,* RENNIE *and* CARLY *become* CEL*'s reflected image in the mirror.*)

CEL: My husband has a theory. He's figured it out.

SABINE: Cel!

CEL: My husband says to me Cel, can't you see yourself in the mirror? I say Yeah.

SABINE: Cel!

CEL: He says so why don't you do something about it, it's for your own good he says. You know about the heart failure and the brain tumors and amputations, but how many times I have to tell you what really happens to girls who get too big—

SABINE: Celia!

CEL: (*Bitter, completing the quote.*)—honey.

SABINE: (*Calling for her.*) Honey?

CEL: He says fat girls go crazy more than thin girls do.

SABINE: Goddamn it girl, where did you get to now?

CEL: It has to do with metabolism, he says, he read it in the encyclopedia, because fat girls let their cells get unbalanced.

SABINE: Ce-lie, it's freezing in here!

CEL: See, your body has to send more blood down to the fat so it can't spend the time it should in your brain. It's like there's this system inside you and everything in it has to balance, if you add a little too much of one thing you throw off the rest.

(The mirror reflections begin to flap their arms like birds, then turn away from CEL, *released.)*

SABINE: For Christ's sake, Cel, what is going on here in the middle of November? Every window and door is swung out on its hinges, the place is a mess, there are birds flying by me in the goddamn kitchen, what's the matter with you, girl? What is wrong with you, woman?

CEL: *(Still to the audience.)* That's why he said maybe a surgical cure, so I can get rid of that parasite fat. I can maybe start acting more normal he says.

(Lights shift, final whistle is blown.)

ALL: *Little Baby Sally was sick in bed*
Sally called for mama and her mama said
Little Baby Sally you're not sick
All you need is a peppermint stick.

(Lights shift, hospital gowns fly in, the women stand behind them and undress during the next exchange, then put the gowns on.)

CARLY: My mama was—she used to say "plump and juicy."

RENNIE: My mother said for big girls like me it was ugly to let people see the stuff you were made of. Especially legs and shoulders and the inside of your mouth.

SABINE: Our mothers all taught us the same thing.

CARLY: Hush up, Carly girl.

SABINE: Sit still till we get to grandma's and mama'll give you a cookie.

CEL: If you're good you can lick the bowl.

CARLY: Do you kiss your mother with that mouth?

RENNIE: Sit up straight and eat only what you're offered.

SABINE: Children are starving in Denmark.

CEL: Eat your peas.

SABINE: Or was it Detroit?

CARLY: Open wide!

RENNIE: What's the matter, don't you feel well?

CARLY: What's wrong, don't you want dessert?

SABINE: Here, darling, have some of mama's homebaked cherry pie.

CEL: Chicken-fried steak.

RENNIE: Chocolate mousse.

(*They all laugh and "mmm" in agreement.*)

CARLY: Baby, you are so be-yoo-tiful, just like a calendar girl with those big brown eyes and that beautiful skin!

RENNIE: Why did everyone always tell me I had beautiful skin?

CARLY: And babes, some day you'll thank me for letting you put on that extra padding. When your airplane crashes on the highest peak of the Himalayas all those skinny passengers are gonna starve to death seven ways till Sunday and you will survive for months and months, living only off what you have stored in your tush.

SABINE: Mama's always right. You just wait.

(RENNIE, CEL, *and* SABINE *return to their corners to sit, lights up on* CARLY *in the center.*)

CARLY: No my mama was not always right. No, you shoulda seen her when he'd come home nights, the whole place'd get quiet like the grave, I swear, she'd be pussyfootin around him jumping like a sick kitten every time he made a move . . . all you could hear was him chewing with his mouth open and his silverware hitting the plastic plate.

It's too late for my mama, it's too late for me now. But the day my kid was born I made it a promise that she was gonna know who she was. No one was gonna walk all over my kid. No one was gonna give her a goddamned blank check.

Then the other day I come home from work and there she is, my stupid kid, sitting on the bathroom floor, leaning against the tub, and her long blonde hair is dyed pitch black, I swear, black as tar, and it's dripping black rivers all down her face and her neck . . . I could have killed her right then and there, I wanted to knock her head off of her skinny little neck.

Instead of killing her I say, Jesus, Christ, what the hell did you do to your hair, and she's crying and choking and she goes, Ma! and points at the counter. I looked and I swear I thought I was going to toss my cookies. She has got one of these EPT plus pregnancy tests laid out there, you know, the little stick kind? Pink, pregnant, white, not pregnant . . . there's that little stick leaning up against the box it came in and the end is as bright pink as an Easter egg, pink as all fuck, pardon my French, pink like a baby's butt is pink. Talk about history repeating itself. Suddenly I'm sixteen again with that sinking feeling in my stomach looking at the little test tube, holding it up against the light bulb in the upstairs closet . . .

So I'm trying to figure out what exactly the black hair has got to do with the pink stick. I say, Is that or is that not an EPT plus pregnancy test? and she nods, so I say, Is that or is that not a pink stick you got there? and she says, It's pink. I say, So you're pregnant, so you dyed your hair black? She starts sobbing and wailing and she goes, I knew you wouldn't understand, you never understand anything about me! She bangs past me and stomps down the hall and slams the bedroom door behind her. I'm thinking, what's to understand? You're totally nuts!

I'm standing there alone in the bathroom. The place looks like a tornado hit, there's little bottles and vials and tubes all over, with that little pink baby-positive stick lying right in the middle like the eye of the hurricane, the evil eye, more like, still and pink and sticking its tongue out at me. Ha. You lost. You fucked up. I'm thinking, what happened? I thought only fat girls didn't know what they were doing. My kid's a beauty, gorgeous, skinny, tall, why the hell didn't she stand up for herself? How could she let this happen? She's got no goddam spine!

Then I'm back to the time when she was just two years old, the first time I saw her throw a tantrum. It was in the kitchen, over a purple popsicle. I was so surprised at the force inside her little body. She stamped her bare feet on the kitchen floor and balled up her fists and bared her tiny white teeth at me, and when I said, No, and shut the refrigerator door with the toe of my shoe she looked up into my face and squinted, she wasn't three feet tall, and her mouth got tiny like the . . . head of a nail, and I knew I had someone to contend with then.

So I go into the bedroom, sit down on the edge of the bed and pat her on the back. Stacey, sweets, hey, hey, it's alright. You got to be strong and make your own choice but whatever decision you want to make, I'm behind you, okay? We'll do whatever you choose. She stops sniffing. She breathes in and out. I say, So, listen, uh . . . have you talked to the guy about this yet? And she says, nasty, No, Ma, God. Boys don't like girls who boss them around.

(Lights down on CARLY, *up on* SABINE *in her corner, during the course of the monologue she moves center.)*

SABINE: Like my friend Michael. Michael and I, we are best friends. We go for sushi and foxtrot once a month at the full moon. The thing is, all our conversations go like this: Michael tells me about his love life, I support him. Michael whines about his girlfriend, I console him. Michael moans about the horrors of latex, I sympathize, I hug him, I make him tea, and recently I have found myself possessed with rage absolutely every time I lay eyes on him. Because I am so very tired of being everyone's warm and fuzzy sounding board. I want to be a full-blown sexual threat right now. I want to get down on my hands and knees and do it, sweaty, hot, savage, wrong, morally rep-re-hensible . . . If my mother could hear me now . . . she wasn't out of her foundation garments long enough to have sex. I was an immaculate conception. My father stuck his tongue in her ear and bang, there I was, I appeared just like that on the kitchen counter in an attractive presentation basket. That's how we fat women do it, you know. We just close our eyes and think beautiful thoughts and our offspring arrive with the afternoon mail.

In undergrad psychology we learned about these people, they were called split-brain patients, and each hemisphere of their brain could work on a task without the other half knowing. In the films they showed us they taught this one guy to build blocks into towers with his left hand only. Then separately they taught his right hand to tear block towers down. On the last day of the experiment they let both hands work together—the guy actually fought with himself in this film—his left hand tried to build a tower while his right hand constantly wrecked whatever he made. The hands started slapping each other and wrestling with the same block . . .

The one half of me, see, won't take no for an answer. This me's gonna go out there and take the corporate world by storm, if that's what I decide I want to do, or climb mountains, or pump gas, or write for TV, or . . . become a stock broker if I happen to feel like it. I do not need male approval to achieve my life goals. Like a fish needs a bicycle, and so on and so on.

But I just can't ignore my pathetic other side—it's so whiny and "needy" inside of me. I yearn for . . . human touch, God, it's embarrassing, sometimes all I want is to be looked at, admired, soothed and caressed. I still want the power, I still want to make money and go mountaineering. But the thing I want most right now, God, Santa, Gloria Steinem, is some person to love me and sleep in my bed.

First I hate myself for it, then I forgive myself lovingly, then I yell at myself for going soft on myself. Then I cry, usually, and then I get sullen and scowl. Stomp around the place dropping dishes and breaking bric-a-brac. Backlash! I scream, backlash, Sabine! You're contributing to the undeclared war against women! How could you! How dare you! You ought to be shot! Then I usually have a marshmallow sundae to calm myself down.

The saddest thing is, I've got no one to blame. God damn, I wrote my dissertation on this, I know the eight key symptoms and the ten warning signs and the twelve-step recovery program like the back of my hand. How can I be so smart and so stupid?

So I've made a very adult decision. If I can't change the world, I have to change myself. I'm gonna lay on my back and suck up the gas and fall into a deep sleep, and when the prince kisses me I'm gonna wake up and be beautiful. And then I'm gonna flush all my feminist morals down the can and I'm gonna sashay my butt out into the glittering suburban night and I'm gonna get laid, goddamnit. Like my mom used to say—you've made your cake, now you have to eat it. I hear you, Ma. Ain't it the truth.

ALL: (*Quietly.*) *This is the way we bake our cake*
bake our cake
bake our cake
This is the way we bake our cake
So early Friday morning.

(*A flashbulb pops and* RENNIE *is propelled into center.*)

RENNIE: The first picture of me is at my first birthday party. In this one I am screaming with laughter and holding my hands up to show the camera that I am covered with chocolate cake. My face is smeared with it, it is all over the front of my pretty pink dress. Apparently I was quite verbally advanced, and my parents were showing me off when my uncle Jake said, Oh yeah? How smart is she? She's a genius, says my mother, she understands everything. Try it. She'll do anything you say.

So . . . Rennie, says my uncle Jake, smush that chocolate cake all over your face, sweetheart. Will do you that for me?

And I did it of course because I was just that smart and I ruined my dress and they took a picture of me humiliating myself when I was twelve months old.

(*Flashbulb pops.*)

This one is my mother's favorite. It's of her and me on one of our mother-daughter days, we're on the steps of the Met looking very close and what you don't see is Mother boring her knuckles into the small of my back saying straighten up, sweetheart, it lengthens your neck. Now glow, come on, glow. We want this one to glow.

For awhile there is an absence of photos—when tummies are no longer little-girl cute. Mother hides me at family gatherings and I seem always to end up behind pieces of furniture. So we have no extant record of the long years of wanting, of wanting and wanting and being denied. Reaching for bread and peanut butter and having Slimfast thrust into my twelve-year-old fist. Mother says No, I am putting my foot down. She is putting her foot down, I see, and I see that to want and demand things is bad.

And when I finally want nothing, nothing at all, when I finally want so little I can barely get up in the morning, my head feels like a ten ton brick on my shoulders, my knees buckle walking from class to class, when I want so little the gentlest sounds scrape my ears and my skin is sore and my hair falls out, finally my mother pulls me out from behind the chaise longue and says This is my daughter Rennie! This is my wonderful, beautiful daughter. Out comes the camera!

(*Flashbulb pops.*)

The pictures reappear. All the while Mother says Sweetheart, you're beautiful. You really do glow.

(*Flashbulb pops.*)

In this one I am standing outside my own house, in a hideous dress I do not recall choosing, it is blue and it feels like a garbage bag next to my skin. I am wearing a floppy white orchid on my wrist and man, am I glowing. I am really fucking glowing. My smile is about this wide on my face though I don't know what I am smiling about because Andrew Marino has his hand on my back. We haven't even left the house yet, my mother is still snapping pictures and there he is, slinking his hand up my dress. Later we are in the dark and he is breathing so hard he is fogging the windshield and I say to him Andrew. No. No. And he says to me Rennie, you're beautiful. Please Rennie please, will you do it for me? I am saying, No, I am saying, Stop, but he does not hear me, I am not loud enough. I am so—weak. I am just . . . too . . . weak.

(*Flashbulb pops.*)

In this one my mother is getting remarried. She is a vision in indigo organdy, she looks half her age, her husband's in real estate. But heavens, where's Rennie? Rennie's not in this one. Rennie is wearing an attractive off-white linen pants suit, but she is not in her place at her mother's side because she is in the parish hall kitchen, devouring the three-foot-tall wedding cake meant to serve one hundred and eighty guests. It was just so pristine, floating there, with no one to guard it, no one to witness . . . I ate and I ate and I ate it all up until there wasn't one crumb left, not a single frosted rosette, and I held that whole cake inside my body, I had it all to myself. And then I threw it all up on the kitchen floor and I walked out the back door into the night.

(RENNIE *runs back to her chair, lights shift.*)

CARLY: I wonder what it'll actually be like.

SABINE: I've researched the procedure, I'll describe it if you want.

CARLY: Thanks but no thanks.

SABINE: You'll be knocked out, you won't feel a thing.

RENNIE: What are you afraid of? It's what we've been waiting for.

(*Lights shift, up on* CEL *in her corner. During the course of the monologue she moves up center and then progressively further downstage.*)

CEL: It starts with a girl maybe six maybe seven, looking down at herself seeing how—horrible she was! How gross like a monster. She didn't look anything like the other kids from 4-H, they were all skinny as rats from dragging goats through the mud and bending over fields in the blazing hot sun. In summer all kids' legs were scabby—but nobody had marks on them like I did, like Cel, Cel had some scars.

The first one came when I was six. I had split open my knee climbing through barbed wire and mama drove me to the hospital to get the thing stitched up with ugly dark thread, that's how deep it was. But I took those stitches out with scissors when I got home. I told my mama they came out in the bath but I could tell by the way she looked at me sidewise frying the eggs that she didn't believe it. All that summer I worked on my knee and by the time Labor Day rolled around my leg looked like it had been caught in a thresher, maybe.

After that she just seemed to find them, Cel, these cuts in her skin, these holes. They seemed to pop up without her even noticing. Some she put in there herself with the kitchen knives for killing the chickens or shears for the garden or the awl daddy used for punching holes in saddles. Mama didn't know what to do with her girl. At first she didn't say anything, just folded her arms like so across her chest. What's happened to the backs of your feet she asked. You're picking those cuts of yours apart aren't you? What are you doing to yourself Celie? Why do you want to do such a thing to yourself? So she started buying extra boxes of bandaids and leaving them about the house in places she thought I might be likely to come across them. But I wanted to—take myself completely apart. I had dreams of my body parts spread out in the yard for everyone even the neighbors to see.

All the way through high school I did it at night when no one was looking. After my shower, when the skin was still soft. It was my thing to know. Then one day my husband found me on the floor of the bathroom, busted in without knocking . . . After that he kept watching me, keeping track where I went. I tried to lay still. I forgot things . . . left them to burn on the stove. My husband paced around and slammed the door on his way out. He accused me of letting the heat out in winter, letting animals in, stray cats and birds.

So I needed a final solution. Get rid of all the flesh at once. I was poking a roaster chicken full of cloves getting ready for Sunday dinner and I went to light the broiler with a hard wooden match. Then it came to me. My body—I wanted to light it on fire. Hear the fat sizzle into smoke. With all the fat gone I could dance—more than that, I could run and jump and fly maybe even, just me and my bones running naked through the meadows feeling the breeze. It seemed so obvious—why hadn't I thought of this before? I struck one of the matches, stroked it smooth cross the rough edge of the box and I could feel the flame sparking and growing and swallowing the match head. I held it in front of my face. It flickered in my own breath. My thighs would go up first I thought then the rest of me would catch on quick. I lifted my leg and dropped the match onto my pants. For a moment—nothing, then—warm hot my leg started to jump—my skin was on fire! I screamed without meaning to Oh my God! I reeled around to face the counter my hands out in front of me reaching desperate—something, anything! Towel potholder glass of water . . . In my mind I heard Miss Moser from in front of the black board—stop, drop, and roll, she said, if you ever catch fire just stop, drop and . . .

Later I went to the phone to call 911, shivering, numb. I caught fire, I said calmly into the phone. I was cooking a chicken. It escaped.

(RENNIE, SABINE, *and* CARLY *come over to* CEL *and touch her one by one. They all look at each other, then, embarrassed, start to return to their chairs.* CARLY *stops them by beginning the candy store chant.* SABINE *joins in, then* RENNIE, *so it sounds like a round. When they hit the "Doctor doctor will I die" line they each continue to chant that until they all say it together, including* CEL.)

ALL: *I met my boyfriend at the candy store*
He bought me ice cream
He bought me cake
He brought me home with a belly ache
Mama mama I feel sick
Call the doctor quick quick quick
Doctor doctor will I die?

CARLY: Count to five and you'll survive.

RENNIE: One.

SABINE: Two.

CEL: Three.

CARLY: Four.

ALL: Five.

(*They look at each other, then simultaneously take off their gowns and drop them on the floor. In their underwear, they walk together downstage and stand facing the audience. The last few lines are light and full of relief.*)

CARLY: Once upon a time there was a very beautiful woman who hardly ever wanted or asked for anything until one day when she suddenly got—very extremely hungry.

CEL: So she said to her husband, honey, climb over that wall and get me some of them radishes I see growing down there in that garden.

SABINE: But this was no ordinary garden.

CARLY: This was no ordinary woman.

RENNIE: This was no ordinary hunger.

(*Two beats, lights bump out. End of play.*)

TEA

Velina Hasu Houston

This play is dedicated to the Japanese women of Kansas; especially my mother, Setsuko, and Kazue Logan. With thanks to Patti Yasutake and Julianne Boyd.

TEA received its professional premiere at the Manhattan Theatre Club, New York, in October 1987. Lynne Meadow, Artistic Director; Barry Grove, Managing Director; Jonathan Alper, Producer; Tom Szentgyorgyi, Literary Associate. It was directed by Julianne Boyd. The cast was as follows:

SETSUKO BANKS	Takayo Fischer
HIMIKO HAMILTON	Patti Yasutake
CHIZ JUAREZ	Jeanne Mori
TERUKO MACKENZIE	Lily Mariye
ATSUKO YAMAMOTO	Natsuko Ohama

ORDER OF SCENES

Prelude	Invitation to Tea
Scene One	The Art of Tea
Scene Two	Selecting Tea
Scene Three	Serving Tea
Scene Four	Cold Tea
Scene Five	Perfect Drinking Temperature

The play is to be performed without an intermission.

TIME AND PLACE

1968. The home of Himiko Hamilton in Junction City, Kansas, and an obscure netherworld where time moves at will.

SETTING

The stark set includes both a presentation of the netherworld (in which time is elastic and the spirit can journey) and a representation of the home of Himiko. The home is a combination of 1960s Americana and things Japanese, including a raised area that abstractly comprises a Japanese tatami room bordered by linoleum. In the room are a pile of zabuton (flat Japanese sitting cushions), an antique, round-hooded trunk overflowing with Japanese cloth materials, kimono, etc.; and an oval, red lacquer tea table. The reality is distressed.

DRAMATIST'S NOTES

This play is based on virtually undocumented historical fact of communities of Japanese "war brides" who have lived in Kansas over the last 20 to 40 years. Over 100,000 native Japanese women married American servicemen during the American occupation of Japan. These families returned to the U.S. between the years 1946 and 1960. Depending on the time of their return, any American servicemen married to "Oriental" women were required under the Army's resettlement policies to be stationed at remote forts, such as Fort Riley, Kansas. Hence, in an area of Kansas known mostly for German and Irish American Protestants and agriculture, there came to exist dispersed communities of Japanese women and their multiracial, multicultural children. This background and my family history were the catalysts for this play, in addition to extensive interviews with fifty Japanese women residing in Kansas who were international brides.

PRELUDE

Invitation to Tea

(In the darkness, an unaccented, female American voice belts out "The Star Spangled Banner." A traditional Japanese melody—perhaps "Sakura"—cuts into the song's end as lights FADE IN *slowly to half to suggest a netherworld.* HIMIKO *kneels* DSC. *She is a pale, delicately-boned woman wearing a feminine but mysterious dress, over which is a kimono of distorted colors. The dress is long and muted in tone; its skirt, short in front, trails the floor in back and the outer hems are ragged. In its little-girlishness and antiquity, the dress suggests a different era. A white petticoat hangs underneath it, its shredded edges peeking out. Quiet, traditional Japanese* MUSIC *haunts the background. Crumpled like paper,* HIMIKO *rises gradually, relating to a presence that we cannot see. She is beautiful, but beaten, and exudes an aura of sultry mystery. There is no lunacy in this woman, rather the sense of one who has been pushed to the edge, tried desperately to hold on, and failed. She is, indeed, resolute.* HIMIKO *reaches out to the presence and speaks in a voice that carries the weight of the world, moving from a hoarse whisper to a more audible tone.)*

HIMIKO: Billy. Can't you see it's me? Himiko Hamilton. You gave me your name and, this day, I give it back. You have forsaken my spirit and it is left shaking in the cold mist left behind by your restless breath. As you walk. Fast. And always away. Leaving me to wander between two worlds forever. (*A quiet smile appears.*) But listen, Billy, listen. I have learned your Christian prayer: "Now I lay me down to sleep. I pray your Lord my soul to keep. And if I die before I wake. I pray your Lord my soul to take."

(*Himiko's attention is suddenly drawn to another presence which absolutely delights her; she moves toward it slightly.*)

HIMIKO: Mieko-chan? This is your mother. Come close. Let me smell the confusion of your Amerasian skin. For you are the only gift I ever had. Beautiful half-Japanese girl, fill the holes in my kimono sleeves with your soft laughter. Lead me to peace.

(*Himiko removes a pistol from her kimono sleeve, bows as she offers it to time and space, and places it before her. She kneels and looks again toward her vision of Mieko.*)

HIMIKO: Mieko, my child.

(*She looks in the opposite direction.*)

HIMIKO: Billy, my beloved husband.

(*She looks* DSC.)

HIMIKO: (*Her voice louder, but not too loud.*) Mother? Can you hear me? Wait for me, Mother. I am coming to have tea with thee.

(*Himiko lifts the pistol and aims it toward her throat.* BLACKOUT *as a* GUNSHOT *followed by a deafening atomic-like* EXPLOSION *fills the theater, leaving behind trails of smoke.* HALF LIGHT UP *as, from various dark corners,* TERUKO, ATSUKO, CHIZ, *and* SETSUKO *enter one by one and take staggered positions.* SPOTLIGHTS *simultaneously* FADE IN *on the women, who bow as they speak their first lines. The style of the bows reflect their personalities.*)

SETSUKO: Shall we have tea at three?

TERUKO: Please come over for tea.

ATSUKO: Join me for tea, just the two of us.

CHIZ: Tea. O-cha. That's our word for it.

SETSUKO: I drink it hot in a pretty Japanese cup.

TERUKO: I like it cool. Any cup will do.

ATSUKO: Lukewarm in a fancy Japanese cup.

CHIZ: Very hot. In a simple cup.

TERUKO: Tea is not quiet.

ATSUKO: But turbulent.

SETSUKO: Tremblings.

CHIZ: So fine you can't see them.

SETSUKO: So dense it seems to be standing still.

TERUKO: We Japanese women drink a lot of it.

ATSUKO: Become it.

SETSUKO: Swallow the tempest.

CHIZ: And nobody knows.

ATSUKO: The storm inside.

TERUKO: Ever.

SETSUKO: We remain . . .

TERUKO: Peaceful.

CHIZ: Contained.

ATSUKO: The eye of the hurricane.

SETSUKO: But if you can taste the tea.

TERUKO: If it can roll over your tongue in one swallow.

ATSUKO: Then the rest will come to you.

CHIZ: When the tea leaves are left behind in the bottom of a cup.

(*Himiko reenters carrying Ray-Ban sunglasses and a long, blonde wig; she comes* USC.)

HIMIKO: When we are long gone and forgotten.

(*Himiko puts on the sunglasses and holds out her arms in welcome to the audience as the other women exit.*)

HIMIKO: Come . . . it is time for tea.

(Himiko pulls on the wig, CROSSFADE to the tatami room.)

SCENE ONE

The Art of Tea

(ATSUKO *and* TERUKO *drift to the tatami room, where piles of books and a wild-looking wig are on the floor. They take off their shoes outside of the room and enter.* ATSUKO *has brought her own booties and puts them on. She removes her sweater, and studies the room with mixed feelings of revulsion and attraction, as if she has vicariously imagined this room's experiences. She sniffs the air with displeasure, and covers her nose and mouth with a handkerchief. They set up the Japanese-style table and place four zabuton [Japanese sitting cushions] as* HIMIKO *observes from the darkness. Whenever* HIMIKO *speaks to the audience, it is as if she is on trial and offering a matter-of-face defense.*)

ATSUKO: Ugh. How were you able to have tea here with this stench! (*Studies the floor.*) Maybe we should keep our shoes on.

TERUKO: It didn't smell here before, Atsuko-san!

ATSUKO: Yes, it did. You said it did.

TERUKO: I said it smelled like liquor and burnt candles.

ATSUKO: Well, you know that's from bringing home men and making sex.

TERUKO: (*Insistently protective.*) Before her husband died, Himiko lived a quiet life.

(ATSUKO *picks up the wild wig as if to negate* TERUKO*'s statement.* TERUKO *starts to exit to the kitchen.*)

TERUKO: I'm going to find the teapot and cups.

(ATSUKO *hurriedly drops the wig and looks around the room as if she has seen or suspects ghosts.*)

ATSUKO: Don't leave me alone!

TERUKO: We must begin.

(TERUKO *exits to kitchen.*)

HIMIKO: (*To audience.*) Yes, we must begin . . . Tea for the soul; tea to cleanse the spirit.

(ATSUKO *examines the room carefully as if afraid of getting dirty and begins to put things away. She puts on her glasses.*)

ATSUKO: Himiko was so wild after her husband died. Maybe she was like that in Japan, too. I don't know how she passed the screening tests for Army brides. They took so long and the Yankee officers asked so many stupid questions.

HIMIKO: (*Addresses* ATSUKO *as if echoing a reminder, encircling her as she speaks.*) "Are you a Communist? Why do you want to marry this man instead of one of your own native Japanese? Do you think moving to America will afford you personal financial gain? Are you suffering from insanity? Are you an imbecile or idiot?" (*A beat.*) "Are you now—or have you ever been—a prostitute?"

ATSUKO: The nerve of that Amerikan Army! Did the Army ask you if you were a prostitute?

(TERUKO *returns with a teapot, cups, lacquer coasters, and two clothes—one wet and one dry—all on a lacquer tray. She handles them delicately.*)

TERUKO: Yes. I told them we weren't all bad girls just because we fell in love with Amerikans. (*Looks around the room as if drinking in* HIMIKO*'s life.*) Poor Himiko.

ATSUKO: Where is Setsuko Banks? I thought she was the one most friendly with Himiko. (*looks around the room eerily*) I heard the tatami was covered with blood. It's funny, isn't it, how one moment someone is full of life and the next, they are ashes.

TERUKO: Atsuko-san, ne, if you're that uncomfortable, go home. Setsuko and Chiz (*Pronounced like "cheese."*) and I can take care of this.

ATSUKO: As head of our Buddhist chapter, how would it look to headquarters if I didn't do everything I could to help a member? (*A vicarious smile as she peers over her glasses.*) Besides, I wanted to see the inside of this house.

TERUKO: Well, Setsuko-san went home to pick up o-sushi.

ATSUKO: And "Chiz" is always late. Her nickname sounds so stupid. Like food. She even wears pants now and grows her hair long like a hippie. (*Removes a crocheted green-and-purple poodle toilet paper cover from the trunk and shakes her head at its oddity.*) She's just as silly as Himiko was.

(ATSUKO *takes out her own tea cup, admires it, and places it on the table.* TERUKO *wipes* HIMIKO*'s tea cups, first with a wet cloth, and then a dry one. She carefully arranges the cups with coasters and teapot on the table.* ATSUKO *moves* HIMIKO*'s tea cups away from her own.*)

TERUKO: (*Removes a folded newspaper article from her wallet; reads from it with officiousness.*) Listen. I cut this out. "Death Notices. September 9, 1968. Himiko Hamilton, 39, widow of Chief Warrant Officer William Hamilton, passed away in her home from a self-inflicted gunshot wound. She was preceded in death by her husband and, recently, her daughter, Mieko, 18. A Japanese war bride, Mrs. Hamilton was a resident of Junction City for twenty years. She leaves no survivors."

HIMIKO: (*To audience with quiet dignity.*) But, still, I ask you to listen. Please. (*A beat.*) I am suspended between two worlds. There is no harmony here (*Indicates the women in tatami room.*) nor here (*Indicates her soul.*).

TERUKO: Well, she *did* leave survivors.

ATSUKO: Who?

TERUKO: Us.

ATSUKO: Not me! Just because I'm Japanese doesn't mean I have anything to do with her life. Dead is dead, Teruko-san, so what difference does it make? Who knows, ne. Maybe next it will be me. Do you think the Japanese women in this town are going to pray for my soul just because I happen to come from Japan?

TERUKO: (*Shocked at* ATSUKO*'s callousness.*) Atsuko-san. We must respect the dead.

ATSUKO: Only because they no longer have to fear the darkness. The rest of us must wait, without any idea of when our time will come to an end.

TERUKO: (*As if she feels* HIMIKO*'s presence.*) No, sometimes even the dead must wait. In limbo.

ATSUKO: (*A smile.*) Well, Himiko should wait forever after what she did to her husband.

TERUKO: But you know what he was doing to her.

ATSUKO: Nobody really knows.

HIMIKO: Nobody would listen.

ATSUKO: Maybe she wasn't a good wife.

HIMIKO: I was the *best* wife.

TERUKO: He never let her out of the house and hardly let her have guests. Remember during the big snow storm? The phone lines were down and—

HIMIKO: —I didn't have any tea or rice left. Billy had gone to Oklahoma to visit his family. He said, "Don't leave the house" and took my daughter, Mieko, with him. So there I was, starving to death, standing behind—

TERUKO: (*Overlapping with* HIMIKO*'s last two words.*)—Standing behind the frosty glass. She looked like she was made of wax.

HIMIKO: (*Smiles at herself.*) I asked him once. I said, "Why did you marry me?" And he said he wanted a good maid, for free.

ATSUKO: Maybe she wanted too much.

HIMIKO: I never asked for anything. Except soy sauce and good rice. And dreams . . . for Mieko.

(HIMIKO *glows with love for her child, turns around and seems to see her as a tot, and beckons to her.*)

HIMIKO: Mieko-chan! My little girl!

(HIMIKO *exits as if chasing "Mieko."*)

ATSUKO: Teruko, I saw your daughter last week. (*A compliment.*) She looks Japanese. That's nice. Too bad she isn't friends with my girl. My girl's always with Setsuko-san's daughter. Have you seen her? Looks Indonesian, not Japanese at all. Shame, ne.

TERUKO: But Setsuko's daughter is the only one who cooks Japanese food. My daughter likes hamburger sandwich and yellow-haired boys.

ATSUKO: My daughter always goes to Setsuko-san's house. I've never been invited.

TERUKO: Setsuko likes her privacy.

ATSUKO: She invited you to tea.

TERUKO: Well, if you're not willing to be genuine with her, how can you share the honor of tea together?

ATSUKO: She invited Himiko, too!

TERUKO: Yes, even after the incident. Even though everyone was afraid.

(*A siren wails as a deafening* GUNSHOT *echoes in the air and all lights* BLACKOUT. ATSUKO *and* TERUKO *exit to the kitchen in the darkness.* HIMIKO, *without sunglasses, drifts from the darkness and stops* CS. *The siren* FADES OUT *and a spotlight* FADES UP *immediately on* HIMIKO, *who crouches as if shooting a pistol. She smiles and rises gracefully. She speaks matter-of-factly to the audience.*)

HIMIKO: (*Imitates the sound of* SHOTS, *pronounced "bahn" like in bonfire.*) Ban! Ban! Ban! Yes. I am Himiko Hamilton. The murderess. I married and murdered a gentleman from Oklahoma. And they let me go on self-defense. It took one shot—right through the heart I never knew he had. Now that he's gone, I can speak freely. Please listen. I wasted my life in Kansas. The state—of mind. Not Kansas City, but *Junction City,* a stupid hick town that rests like a pimple on an army base called Fort Riley. Where the Army's resettlement policy exiled our husbands because they were married to "Japs."

(HIMIKO *indicates her own face as* CHIZ *and* SETSUKO *enter from opposite corners carrying food in a basket and furoshiki, respectively.*)

HIMIKO: They won't tell you that because they're real *Japaneezy* Japanese.

(CHIZ *and* SETSUKO *smile and bow formally to each other in greeting;* SETSUKO *bows a second time.*)

HIMIKO: See what I mean? Well . . . I'm about as Japanese as corn flakes, or so they say, and I killed my husband because he laughed at my soy sauce just one time too many. (HIMIKO *smiles whimsically and turns away from the audience.* CHIZ *and* SETSUKO *drift* DS. *They are unaware of* HIMIKO*'s presence.* SETSUKO *and* CHIZ *stand outside of the house.*)

SETSUKO: Oh, Chizuye-san, I wish Himiko-san could have seen all the Japanese women at her funeral.

HIMIKO: (*To the audience.*) All the Japanese women who were too ashamed to say hello to me in public because I was "no good."

CHIZ: (*Adamant with characteristic exuberance.*) Ever since she shot her husband two years ago, she's kind of haunted me. It made me remember that underneath my comfortable American clothes, I am, after all, Japanese. (*A quick smile.*) But don't tell anybody.

SETSUKO: Well, after all, you were the one who went looking for her.

CHIZ: Someone had to. The rest of you were too afraid of what you would find. (*Looks into space as she recalls.*) I forced her door open and, there she was, paler and bluer than the sky over Hiroshima that strange August. She had pulled her kimono over her American dress, as if it might make her journey into the next life a little easier. But I took one look at her and I knew nothing was ever going to be easy for her, not in life or in death.

HIMIKO: I would have given anything to have tea with Japanese girls. I drank alone.

(SETSUKO *and* CHIZ *approach the house and remove their shoes.* SETSUKO *straightens hers and* CHIZ*'s.*)

CHIZ: What'd you bring?

SETSUKO: Maki-zushi.

CHIZ: (*Smiles to poke fun at her friend.*) Figures. I brought spinach quiche, Sue.

SETSUKO: My name is not Sue. My name is Setsuko. Chizuye-san, I tell you many times not to call me by this nickname you made up.

CHIZ: But it's easier.

SETSUKO: Like "Chiz." (*Pronounces it "cheese."*)

CHIZ: (*Laughs; pronounces it with a short "i."*) No, Setsuko, like "Chiz." That's what my customers at my restaurant call me, but you can call me anything you like.

(*The enter the house and* CHIZ *looks toward the kitchen.*)

CHIZ: Hello? Hello? Ah, Teruko! Hello.

(TERUKO *appears from the kitchen with food, including fruit.* SETSUKO *scurries to help her.*)

TERUKO: Hello! Hello! Look, Atsuko-san is here, too.

CHIZ: (*Much surprise and a touch of contempt.*) Atsuko?!

SETSUKO: Well, what an unexpected pleasure.

ATSUKO: Setsuko-san! I rarely see you, but you look younger every time I do. I was sorry to hear about your husband.

SETSUKO: Yes, well, it was his time to . . . to move on.

ATSUKO: Negroes don't live very long. The food they eat, you know.

SETSUKO: My husband ate almost entirely Japanese food.

TERUKO: Atsuko-san's husband hates Japanese food. (*Giggles.*) And he's Japanese Amerikan!

ATSUKO: He does *not* hate Japanese food! (*To* SETSUKO *and* CHIZ.) Why are you both so late? We cleaned the kitchen already. And, of course, we must have tea.

SETSUKO: Oh, yes, tea sounds very good to me now.

TERUKO: Why, yes. Everything must start with tea.

CHIZ: (*Laughs.*) Tea is *just* a drink.

SETSUKO: Oh, it's much more than that.

ATSUKO: I couldn't live without tea.

HIMIKO: Yes . . . it brings everything into balance.

ATSUKO: I think it improves my eyesight.

SETSUKO: (*Laughing.*) And my insight.

(TERUKO, SETSUKO, *and* ATSUKO *have a good laugh over this as* CHIZ *looks on deadpan. Finally she smiles and lights up a cigarette.*)

CHIZ: Hey, enough about tea. Who else is coming?

TERUKO: More than four would be too many. I stopped asking for volunteers after Atsuko-san spoke up.

CHIZ: How many were there?

TERUKO: At least fifty Japanese women!

CHIZ: Fifty? Jesus. You'd think it was a blue-light special.

SETSUKO: Chizuye-san! Shame, ne! After all, this is a difficult occasion for us: the first time a member of our Japanese community has passed on.

CHIZ: What "community"?

HIMIKO: (*Again, to audience.*) Yes, what community? We knew each other, but not really . . . We didn't care enough to know.

CHIZ: Who's got time to chit-chat, right, "Ats"? (*Pronounced with a short "a," like "ahts."*) Now that I'm finally having tea with the great Atsuko Yamamoto, you get a nickname.

ATSUKO: Thank you, but you can keep your . . . gift. (*A beat.*) It's obvious we're all from different neighborhoods.

SETSUKO: But we are all Army wives—and we are all Japanese.

CHIZ: So what? That won't buy us a ticket to Nirvana. Let's face it, girls, after we get through dealing with our jobs and our families, we're ready to go to sleep. And, if any of us are willing to drive across town and have tea, we don't even talk about what's really on our minds—whether coming to Amerika was such a good idea. (*She smiles.*) Countries last; love is mortal.

SETSUKO: But we're here today because we're Japanese.

CHIZ: We're here today because we're scared.

HIMIKO: Scared they will be next to die or their souls will be left in limbo like mine.

(ATSUKO *can hardly contain her excitement at finally being able to ask a question she's pondered for years:*)

ATSUKO: Tell us, Setsuko-san. Is it true about Himiko being a dance hall girl in Japan?

SETSUKO: If that's what she said. I never really knew her until after her husband died. I would see her walking in the middle of a humid summer day in a heavy coat and the yellow-haired wig.

HIMIKO: (*Reliving that day.*) "Hello. I am Mrs. William Hamilton. May I have a glass of water? Oh, thank you, thank you. You are so kind."

ATSUKO: (*Gesticulating that* HIMIKO *was crazy.*) Kichigai, ne . . .

CHIZ: She was *not* crazy.

TERUKO: It is the Japanese way to carry everything inside.

HIMIKO: Yes. And that is where I hid myself.

ATSUKO: She came from Japan, but the way she dressed, the way she walked. Mah, I remember the district church meeting. She came in a low-cut dress and that yellow-haired wig (*Mocks how she thinks a Korean walks.*), walking like a Korean.

SETSUKO: Atsuko-san, ne, we have something in common with all the Oriental women here, even the Vietnamese. We all left behind our countries to come and live here with the men we loved.

ATSUKO: Okay, okay. It's not that I didn't like Himiko-san. So many things she did were not acceptable. If she acted like that in Japan, people would think she was . . . well, a prostitute. Something was not right inside her head. I mean, whoever heard of a Japanese shooting her husband with a rifle? I told you that day at the cemetery.

(HIMIKO, *having had enough, rushes forward and the women* FREEZE.)

HIMIKO: (*Defiantly calls them back into the past with a roll call, stamping her foot as she calls out each name.*) Teruko. Setsuko. Atsuko. Chizuye.

(HIMIKO *exists through the kitchen as the music for "Taps" sets the mood. The women drift from the house as if answering the roll call. The lights* FADE OUT *on house and* FADE UP DS. *They stand as if around a headstone at a cemetery as* HIMIKO *enters. A black-veiled hat, black coat and black pumps complete her widow ensemble. She carries a black bag out of which she pulls a can of beer. The women watch in shock as* HIMIKO *opens the beer and pours it over the "grave" by which they stand.* SETSUKO *runs to her and takes the beer.*)

HIMIKO: Mah, there must be a thousand graves here!

SETSUKO: Shame on you, Himiko-san! Pouring beer on your husband's grave!

HIMIKO: I am celebrating. First Memorial Day since he "left me." He liked beer when he was alive. Why shouldn't he like it when he's dead?

CHIZ: Sounds pretty fair to me.

ATSUKO: Teruko-san, come. We've seen enough.

(ATSUKO *pulls away a reluctant* TERUKO, *who beckons to* CHIZ. *All three exit.* SETSUKO, *concerned, lingers as* HIMIKO *suddenly looks up at an invisible object in great shock.*)

HIMIKO: I'm sorry, Billy. That's right. I forgot. You like Budweiser beer. This is cheap kind, brand X. See? (*Points at the can.*) Just B-E-E-R. Billy, what are you doing here? I believe in reincarnation, but this is a little soon. I planned on being gone before you came back. I'm sorry I didn't bury you in your favorite shirt. I couldn't fix the hole in it from when I shot you. No, no. I don't want to go with you. (*Fighting.*) No, I want to stay here with our daughter. She's not mad at me for what I did. She says you deserved it. No, I don't want to be alone with you anymore. I don't want to kiss and make up. (*Pushes away at unseen presence.*) Setchan! Help me! Billy's going to take me away. (*The presence knocks her off her feet.*)

SETSUKO: (*An antithetical picture of solitude, she draws near.*) Himiko-san. Let's go home now. We'll make tea and talk.

HIMIKO: Help me, Setchan. He's going to beat me up again.

SETSUKO: Come, Himi-chan. You must go home and rest.

HIMIKO: There is only unrest. It is like the war never ended.

SETSUKO: (*Sympathetically.*) Oh, Himi-san. (*Not knowing what else to do, she releases* HIMIKO *and bows her head sorrowfully.*)

HIMIKO: (*Enervated, to herself.*) I wish I would have died in World War II. It was an easier war than this one.

(HIMIKO *exists offstage as* SETSUKO *removes her shoes and returns to the tatami room and lights* CROSSFADE *into Scene Two . . .*)

SCENE TWO

Selecting Tea

(*Lights* UP *on the house where* ATSUKO *stands wearing an apron over her clothing.* TERUKO *sits at the table arranging three tins of tea, a porcelain tea pot, and the tea cups.* SETSUKO *sorts through the trunk, removing such things as a photo album, materials, and green and purple crocheted poodle toilet paper covers. A tea kettle* WHISTLES *loudly from the offstage kitchen. The noise jars everyone.*)

ATSUKO: (*To the offstage Chiz.*) Chizuye-san. What kind of tea would you like?

CHIZ: I'm looking for coffee. Isn't there any coffee around here?

TERUKO: (*Gets up, prepared to go.*) I'll go to the store and buy some for her.

ATSUKO: Why do we need to waste time with that? There's tea.

SETSUKO: She just wants coffee. She's tired.

ATSUKO: She just wants to have coffee because we're having tea. She even brought egg pie. Ugh.

TERUKO: I like egg pie. (*On a look from* ATSUKO.) Sometimes.

CHIZ: (*Enters holding up a jar triumphantly.*) Instant coffee! What will we Americans think of next?

ATSUKO: Did you learn that at English class?

CHIZ: Why? You want to go to class with me, Ats?

TERUKO: (*Interested.*) What do you learn there?

CHIZ: English. (*A beat; smiling.*) *You* should learn English.

ATSUKO: She knows English!

CHIZ: I mean real English. (*To* TERUKO.) Ever seen "My Fair Lady"? (TERUKO*'s face is blank.*) You know Audrey Hepburn?

TERUKO: Yes! Yes! *Breakfast at Tiffany!* (*A beat; excitedly but with surprise.*) She goes to English class, too?

CHIZ: No, no, no. But in *My Fair Lady,* she starts out like you and ends up like me.

(CHIZ *laughs, something* ATSUKO *doesn't appreciate.* ATSUKO *gets back to the matter at hand by tapping a spoon on the side of a tea cup.*)

ATSUKO: We have plain green tea, roasted rice tea, and just a little premium green tea.

TERUKO: Plain tea, please.

ATSUKO: Plain tea?

CHIZ: It's peasant tea, Teruko.

TERUKO: I like it.

ATSUKO: You have such simple tastes.

TERUKO: Makes life easier, *yo.*

SETSUKO: Well, roasted rice tea is fine.

ATSUKO: I like premium.

CHIZ: Of course.

SETSUKO: We'll let Atsuko choose.

(TERUKO *starts to open the premium tin, but* ATSUKO *pulls out a pretty tea tin from her bag and smiles like a reigning queen.*)

ATSUKO: I brought my own! Shall I treat you?

(*Everyone but* CHIZ *nods.*)

CHIZ: Once in a while, I still drink green tea, but I choose my drink like I chose my husband: strong, dark, and with a lot of sugar.

ATSUKO: (*Extremely offended.*) Really, Chizuye-san!

CHIZ: Aw, loosen up, Ats!

ATSUKO: (*Repulsed.*) Did you husband teach you to talk like that?

CHIZ: (*Ready to take her to the mat.*) You don't know anything about my husband.

TERUKO: (*Leaps into the conflict to avoid confrontation, hands each woman a plate of food.*) Well . . . what do you think our husbands thought about us when they met us?

(*The other women look at* TERUKO *with accustomed strangeness.* CHIZ *isn't quite ready to relinquish her fight, but does so out of respect for* TERUKO *and* SETSUKO.)

TERUKO: I mean, there they were, in a strange land full of people they had never seen before. We were 18 or 19, didn't speak too much English. Why do you really think they wanted to marry us?

SETSUKO: For the same reason we wanted to marry them. We were young and we fell in love. So many of us.

CHIZ: I don't think there were that many.

SETSUKO: Oh yes. My daughter read that over 100,000 of us married Amerikans after World War II.

CHIZ: That many?

TERUKO: (*With her customary amusing innocence.*) That's a lot of love!

(*As the lights* FADE OUT *on the house,* HIMIKO, *without sunglasses, enters and comes* DCS. *She wears a pretty, youthful kimono. A light* FADES UP *on her and the* SONG, *"Don't Sit Under the Apple Tree with Anyone Else But Me"* FADES IN *to mark the post-war era in Japan. The other women drift* DS *and occupy various background positions of the stage as they don pretty kimonos as well. Note: special kimono can be built with obi already attached.*)

HIMIKO: War's over. Strange-looking tall men with big noses and loud mouths are running our country. Our new supreme commander is called MacArthur, the great military savior who will preserve our ravaged nation . . . but who cannot preserve the common soul. (*A beat.*) Last night, coming home from a wedding, I see my mother in her best kimono walking by the river. She takes off her geta and puts her feet in the water. Her face is peaceful. So lovely, like the moon in the shadows of the clouds. She slips her small hand into the river and picks up a large stone. Looking at it for only a moment, she drops it in her kimono sleeve. Suddenly, she begins filling both sleeves with stones. I try to stop her, but she fights. The same stones I played with as a child sagging in her kimono sleeves, she jumps into the currents. I watch her sink, her long black hair swirling around her neck like a silk noose. Her white face, a fragile lily; the river, a *taifun*. I wondered what it felt like to be a flower in a storm.

(*"The Wedding March"* STRIKES UP *and the women move as if in an American ceremony toward* CS, *all formally except for* HIMIKO. *All come* DSC *looking outward, their expressions a varied repertoire.* SETSUKO *smiles confidently.* TERUKO *is meek, but decided.* HIMIKO *is arrogant.* ATSUKO *smiles uncertainly.* CHIZ *stands and joins them. The music* RISES *to an uncomfortable pitch and* CEASES. *Though facing the audience, the women share experiences happily as if stripped of inhibitions. Their demeanor and carriage reflect their youth.*)

TERUKO: (*A pert, cute bow.*) I come from Fukuoka.

SETSUKO: (*An elegant, formal bow.*) Me, from the great port city of Kobe.

CHIZ: (*A quick, crisp bow.*) Yokohama.

ATSUKO: (*An official bow.*) Nagoya.

HIMIKO: And me from the capital of the magnificent Empire of Japan: Tokyo. (*She bows, flipping her hair back.*)

(*Lights* WIDEN. *The women relax and take staggered positions. The lights* FOCUS *from one to one.*)

TERUKO: We live in a small house next to my father's lumber business. I'm hanging clothes to dry as the white Yankee walks by. He says, "Why, hello, sugar pie! (*Pronounced "shuga pie."*) Ain't you the purtiest thing!" I say no. He says yes. I say okay.

SETSUKO: And Father says, "Don't look at them! They'll rape you." He even confided to me they had tails. But on the way home from dressmaking school, the Yankee soldier's helmet falls off at my feet. What can I do? I give it back to him. For the first time, I look into the gentle eyes of a man the color of—soy sauce!

ATSUKO: (*Removes a fan from her kimono sleeve and uses it girlishly.*) Coming home from countryside to visit my aunt, I stop at market. Suddenly . . . there he is! A Japanese man in Amerikan uniform from California. He speaks bad Japanese. Sounds cute! He wants to give me a ride. (*Sharply slaps the fan closed against her leg.*) But I can hear my mother: (*Speaks as if she's become her mother, an adamant and proud Japanese.*) "Japanese Amerikans not Japanese anymore! They speak loud and marry foreigners. They don't even take a bath every night." (*Again, the fan opens and moves girlishly.*) He looked clean! But I say to soldier, "Sorry. No thank you, sir." (*Bragging with joy.*) He followed me all the way to the train station!

HIMIKO: It's tough in Tokyo after the Yankees take our country. I have six sisters. My father screams about all the daughters my mother left him with. "Too crowded, no money." If I want a new dress, I have to work for it. There is this cabaret. My girlfriend says let's go be dancers. I think she means on-stage. Like movies, dancing in pretty dresses while people watch and clap. I find out too late it means dancing with Amerikans. Fifty yen-a-dance.

CHIZ: My mother died when I was born so it's always just Father and me. His best friend runs a restaurant that's pretty popular after the war with all the Amerikan boys. The first time I see Gustavo is there. Father and his friend—and his friend's marriage-hungry son—have me surrounded on all sides. But what they don't have covered is my heart.

(*All exit except for* TERUKO *and* CHIZ. MUSIC—*"Tokyo Boogie Woogie"—sets the post-war mood in Japan again.* CHIZ *immediately assumes the persona of an older, intrusive matchmaker. She stands behind the effervescent* TERUKO *as if sneaking up on her.*)

TERUKO: 1947. The business is picking up. We hold the yearly national barber competition and I win! First woman to win! Since the day he walked by my house, Master Sergeant Curtis Mackenzie comes to our barber shop again and again. He comes too much! Soon he will have no hair left!

CHIZ: Excuse me.

TERUKO: Yes.

CHIZ: That Amerikan. That nice-looking Texas man over there? He wants to take you to a movie. He's very nice. I cut his hair every week.

TERUKO: Explain to him.

CHIZ: Come on, Teru-chan, give him a chance. One little date. I won't tell anybody.

TERUKO: Tell him I can't be seen with a Yankee.

CHIZ: He said he will take you and a girlfriend to a movie. In fact, he said he will take everyone at the barber shop to a movie.

TERUKO: What? The four of us plus the three girls in back?

CHIZ: Yes. If that's what it takes to get a date with you.

(CHIZ *disappears in the darkness.*)

Teruko: We walk on opposite sides of the street. Seven women on one side; you on the other. At the movie house, as if by chance, we sit next to each other. For a year, we go just like that, every week. Maybe fifty movies. Seven women. You spend a lot of yen, ne, just to get to know this silly country girl.

(BLACKOUT *on* TERUKO; *simultaneous spotlight* GOES UP *on* HIMIKO, *who dances romantically to a slow American 1940s rhythm and blues* SONG.)

HIMIKO: It was simple; it was a job. "Good evening. Welcome, welcome. Fifty yen. Do you want a dance, soldier?" (*Mimics taking money and stands in surprise.*) Five hundred yen! No, no. Too much. Take it back, please. (*Offers it back.*)

CHIZ: (*Immediately appears and stands close to* HIMIKO; *the persona of the matchmaker continues, but in the style of a dykish, dance hall madam.*) Girl-san. That Yankee soldier over there. He wants to take you to dinner.

HIMIKO: I don't leave with customers.

CHIZ: Ah, but one date won't hurt, will it, Himiko-san? No one has to know. (*Touches* HIMIKO *sexually, who is taken aback by this.*) After all, like he says, this is a dance hall.

HIMIKO: Yes. That is exactly what we do and all that we do—dance.

CHIZ: You'll never get anywhere thinking like that.

(CHIZ *disappears in the darkness.*)

HIMIKO: His name was Billy, a cute white boy from Oklahoma. He came back every week and danced only with me. Never said too much, but he brought me flowers every time. He taught me how to do the "lindy hop," (*She begins dancing and twirls around, finally stopping full of laughter; it settles into a smile.*) . . . among other things. (*A beat.*) It was my first time.

(*A beat.*) There was a teacher. Japanese. He taught at a university at Aoyama. He liked me. Truly. I was going to marry him. Good family. But I can't tell him I wasn't working at the trading company as an operator anymore. I can't tell him I am no longer respectable. So I just say I am sorry. I say my family won't accept the marriage. And I go back to the cabaret and wait for Billy.

(BLACKOUT *on Himiko; spotlight on* ATSUKO *and* SETSUKO, *unaware of each other's presence. They come forward.*)

ATSUKO: We are shopping at the market.

SETSUKO: We are waiting for a train.

ATSUKO: Mr. Kazuhiro Yamamoto, the Californian, is buying fish. So cute his face. He says, "Buy. Fish. This one. (*Indicates fish.*) Kore," and looks at me for help with his Japanese—as the shopkeeper laughs and overcharges him! I say it's wrong to cheat him and protect my *Japanese* Amerikan fiance.

SETSUKO: It begins to rain. Will the color of his skin wash off? I watch his wrist and wait, but (*To her pleasure.*) it stays brown. He is a "military policeman" with great power. But he has gentle eyes; I don't know how he could have killed in the war. (*A beat.*) Most of my girlfriends who married Amerikans are long gone. Creed goes, too, but we write—my bad English and his bad Japanese. He gets stationed in Tokyo after Korean war and, for five years, we date while I care for my Mother. One August, I hold her and she dies in my arms. My bond with Japan gone, I can now leave. (*A beat as she smiles.*) Creed and I marry. He says it's not like Dick and Jane getting hitched in Peoria.

(*The women address the unseen presences of their husbands.*)

TERUKO: You are so white, like a ghost, ne. How can I be sure you will never look at another woman? I hear you have many yellow-haired girls in Amerika. How can I be sure my black hair and different eyes will still be what you want?

SETSUKO: You say we may live the Japanese way wherever we go. I can't give up being Japanese even in your Amerika. This war drove my father to take his life. I gave up enough. I want peace.

ATSUKO: Well, you look Japanese. It isn't like marrying a real Yankee. Well, it isn't!

CHIZ: You keep telling me you're Mexican and that life isn't always easy in America. I'm not sure what that means, but you have taught me this word "love" and I think that's what I feel for you. Life is short, Gustavo, and I have never felt like such a woman before. Take me with you. Hurry, before I see the tears in my father's eyes.

HIMIKO: My father doesn't want me to show my face at home again. "Look at your big belly," he shouts, carrying Yankee-gai-jin baby. Shame. Shame." Billy, you have to take me to Amerika now. There's no life left for me in Japan. People whisper "whore" in the streets and spit at my feet. You brought the war into my heart. (*A beat, as if getting married.*) Yes. I do. Until death do us part.

TERUKO: They are taller.

SETSUKO: And kinder.

ATSUKO: And cleaner.

HIMIKO: And richer.

CHIZ: Our men have lost their spirit.

TERUKO: It is hard after the war.

SETSUKO: We will soon be twenty.

ATSUKO: Soon too old for marriage.

HIMIKO: I am tired of living in the Tokyo the Yankees left us with.

(They look outward and begin removing their kimonos to reveal their original outfits underneath. They put the kimono away.)

CHIZ: Father, forgive me. I should be here to take care of you when you're old.

TERUKO: Mother, please, stop crying. I'm not crazy. I love him.

SETSUKO: Dear mother, thank you for your blessing of Creed and me.

ATSUKO: My parents stop talking to me. I can't help it. He's the one I want to spend my life with. Forgive me. *(Bows low.)*

HIMIKO: Goodbye Father . . . *(Regret and sadness.)* . . . sisters. You shall never see me again.

CHIZ: Father weeps like a grandmother. "Write me, Chizu-chan!" he cries. "If you don't like it there, let me know and I'll come and get you myself." "Sayonara," he says, addressing me like a son. And I depart, my heart divided between two men like a dark, shameful canyon.

SETSUKO: We are a casualty the Japanese do not care to count.

CHIZ: Excess baggage Amerika does not want to carry.

TERUKO: And so the country watches as thousands of us leave Japan behind.

ATSUKO: And it aches.

HIMIKO: And it cries.

CHIZ: And it hopes we will not be lucky.

SETSUKO: Or brave.

TERUKO: Or accepted.

ATSUKO: Or rich.

HIMIKO: But between the hate they have for us.

CHIZ: The disdain.

SETSUKO: The contempt.

TERUKO: There is a private envy.

ATSUKO: Silent jealousy.

HIMIKO: Longing.

CHIZ: Yes.

SETSUKO: They want to wear our shoes.

TERUKO: Leave Japan and their war-ragged lives behind.

ATSUKO: Because the mess finally seems too much to clean.

HIMIKO: And Japan finally looks as small as it really is.

CHIZ: The war makes them see Japan is not the strongest or best.

SETSUKO: It makes us see—just once—beyond our tiny country and our tiny minds.

TERUKO: (*Salutes, mocking an American Army officer in a booming voice.*) "Attention!"

ATSUKO: "All wives of American military personnel must wear pants on board ship during the entire fifteen-day journey."

HIMIKO: "Attention, all wives of American military personnel, socks and shoes must be worn at all times."

CHIZ: "I repeat socks *and* shoes."

SETSUKO: "Husbands and wives will be confined to separate sleeping quarters."

TERUKO: "That's all."

HIMIKO: (*As herself, quietly.*) For now.

(*A single spotlight of interrogation grows* TIGHT, CS, *as the women are drawn to it as if by mandate. All crowd together and stand at attention.* HIMIKO *is less serious than the others.* TERUKO, *unsure, follows* ATSUKO*'s movement and attitude. The women clear their throats. As they speak, they exchange looks which indicate unsure commitment to or a lack of understanding for the words.* SETSUKO *and* ATSUKO *raise their right hands.* TERUKO *raises her left and then changes to her right, following* ATSUKO*'s example.* ATSUKO *glances at* HIMIKO *who, with great boredom, raises her right hand. Only* CHIZ *is confident, and she says the words well and with command.)*

WOMEN: (*In unison; with difficulty, stumbling over various words as this is the first time they have seen or read these words; some can say almost none of the words.*) "I hereby declare, on oath, that I absolutely renounce all allegiance to any foreign state or sovereignty of which I have heretofore been a citizen; that I will defend laws of United States of Amerika against all enemies; that I will bear arms on behalf of United States; and that I take this obligation freely without any mental reservation: So help me God."

CHIZ: (*With pride and a sense of great accomplishment.*) That's it.

ATSUKO: What? Did anybody understand any of that?

SETSUKO: Defend against all enemies? Aren't we enemy?

HIMIKO: Yes. Bear arms?

TERUKO: (*Nodding at* ATSUKO *for confirmation.*) Freely?

CHIZ: Without *any* mental reservation!

SETSUKO: So help me . . .

ATSUKO: God?

(CHIZ *sings "My Country Tis of Thee" and enjoins the others to sing along.* TERUKO *is willing and joins in. They hold hands and smile and sing with joy.* SETSUKO *softly sings the Japanese national anthem, "Kimi Ga Yo."* ATSUKO, *after studying* CHIZ*'s choice for a brief moment, ioins* SETSUKO *and sings. But, as* HIMIKO *begins singing "My*

Country Tis of Thee" in a jarring, life-or-death manner, the women all grow quiet and sing the final lyrics with her, but with altered words. They sing with a sense of fear.)

WOMEN: "Land where our souls will die. Land of our children's pride. From every mountainside, let freedom ring."

(CROSSFADE *to Scene Three as* CHIZ, TERUKO, ATSUKO, *and* SETSUKO *return to the tatami and lights* FADE UP. HIMIKO *moves to side stage and observes:)*

SCENE THREE

Serving Tea

(*Atsuko pours tea as the others begin to examine the trunk's contents.*)

CHIZ: (*Holds up her coffee cup.*) Here's to fairy tales—and the dust they become.

HIMIKO: (*To audience, insistently.*) No, no, they must drink for hope.

(SETSUKO, TERUKO, *and* ATSUKO *lift their tea cups and sip.* TERUKO *reacts as if she burned her tongue.*)

TERUKO: A-cha-cha-cha-cha!

ATSUKO: Don't drink so fast, ne. Burn your mouth. (*Tastes it.*) It's not hot at all.

HIMIKO: It's hard to find the perfect temperature.

SETSUKO: It's fine. I like it this way, too.

CHIZ: Funny. You two like your tea the same way, your daughters are best friends, your husbands used to go hunting together—and you two probably haven't said a dozen words to each other over the last fifteen years. Is this the first time you've ever had tea together?

HIMIKO: It is, isn't it, Setsuko-san?

SETSUKO: I'm busy with my family. And I have so much sewing to do.

HIMIKO: What is your excuse, Atsuko-san?

ATSUKO: I keep busy with the church.

HIMIKO: And Teruko?

TERUKO: I try to visit everyone, but I like to play Bingo with my sugar pie. And, you know, three times a year we go to Las Vegas.

CHIZ: I don't have time either. After Gustavo left the Army, we spent all our time together. Then . . . he was gone and, well, I started classes.

HIMIKO: Everyone has an alibi for silence.

CHIZ: (*Smiles at the women to tease them.*) Besides, no one ever invited me to take tea but Setsuko.

ATSUKO: I thought you didn't like tea.

CHIZ: Don't hand me that bull, Ats. You know damn well you didn't want me in your house because my husband was Mexican. (*Slowly, without hostility as she moves from woman to woman.*) Atsuko believes she's the only pure soul left. But, Ats, I have to tell you . . . you have no soul.

(ATSUKO, *taken aback, gets up and moves away.* CHIZ *stands and walks toward her.*)

CHIZ: Don't worry—I don't either.

TERUKO: Chizuye-san!

CHIZ: And, Teruko, you think your white husband buys you a

position in town society, but, deep down at heart, you're still a "Jap" to them and you always will be. (SETSUKO *looks away.*) Setsuko, you live like a social worker. You've had to deal with so much prejudice you don't want *any*body else to feel pain.

SETSUKO: I enjoy taking tea. With any of you.

TERUKO: My husband doesn't like when we speak Japanese. He says it sounds like silverware dropping. So it's better if I take tea at someone else's home.

ATSUKO: Well, I'm not ashamed to say it: I only take tea with my very best friends.

CHIZ: Which is to say you don't take it very often.

(ATSUKO *boldly faces* CHIZ, *who does not back off.*)

ATSUKO: Chizuye, there's no reason to spite me because my husband is Japanese Amerikan.

CHIZ: (*Laughs.*) Do you think I have any respect for Japanese Americans?

ATSUKO: (*Quickly, adamant.*) They're our people. My husband's parents died in a concentration camp in the California desert, just because they were Japanese.

CHIZ: They're not "our" people. They hate us more than Americans because we remind them of what they don't want to be anymore. They made a choice; most of us haven't. They don't like you either, Ats, because you're a "war bride."

ATSUKO: (*Indignant.*) I'm not a war bride. I didn't marry the war.

SETSUKO: Maybe we did.

CHIZ: And then we came here—to Kansas. Not quite the fairy tale ending you ordered, eh, Ats?

(*As* CHIZ *laughs gruffly and darkly, the truth of this statement jars them. Clouded with discomfort, they lift their tea cups and drink, except for* CHIZ, *who stares off into the distance. Lights* FADE OUT *on the tatami area.* DSC, *a spotlight* FADES UP *on* HIMIKO. *She wears her black sunglasses. A typically 1950s Kansas song—"How Much Is That Doggie in the Window"—*FADES IN *as* HIMIKO *pirouettes and then speaks in the manner of a carnival barker. In the background in dim* LIGHT, *the others kneel as if just having arrived in Kansas. When* HIMIKO *addresses them, they smile, unaware that they are the joke.)*

HIMIKO: "Welcome, welcome, to the Land of Milk and Honey, the Bible Belt; the land of great, wide plains and (*With pride.*) narrow minds. On behalf of the tourism bureau, we'd like to welcome you to Kansas, the Sunflower State. We know all about you people. We read the magazines. We saw the cartoons. We saw 'Sayonara.'"

(HIMIKO *bows ridiculously and the women respond sincerely with bows;* HIMIKO *returns to her own persona.)*

HIMIKO: It was more than racism. It was the gloating of victor over enemy. It was curiosity about our yellow skin, about why in the hell their red-blooded Amerikan boys would want to bring home an "Oriental." (*She indicates the other women.*) Some of them liked us; most of them didn't. (*Exits; the music* FADES OUT, *and the others move* DS.)

ATSUKO: Tell me, miss, do you have a Japanese restaurant here? I want to surprise my husband. No Japanese restaurant? *Ara!* What kind of restaurant do you have? Steak? Barbecue? (*Pronounced bah-bee-q.*) What is barbecue?

SETSUKO: Excuse me. We are looking for a hotel. What? Interracial couple? What does that mean? You reserve the right to refuse service? But what did we do wrong? My husband works for your government. We just need a place to stay for the night. I *am* speaking English!

TERUKO: (*Fearfully.*) Please stop staring at me like I am an animal. I just want to buy groceries. (*Less fearfully.*) What? You want to be my friend? Oh, how . . . how nice! (*She mimics shaking the person's hand, something she finds strange. She bows at the same time and then, uncomfortable, draws her hand back without malice.*) You have such beautiful yellow hair. Like the color of Japanese pickles!

CHIZ: (*Determinedly and to the point.*) Listen, lady, you give me a hard time about opening a checking account just because I'm Japanese, and I'll give you more hell than you bargained for. *I'm an American citizen now.* (*But she slightly mispronounces the word "citizen."*)

TERUKO: I miss sashimi!

CHIZ: It would be nice to bite into o-manju.

SETSUKO: I can taste the crisp nashi.

ATSUKO: Sasa-dango.

TERUKO: Kushi-dango.

CHIZ: Hot oden.

SETSUKO: Kaki. There's nothing like Japanese persimmons.

ATSUKO: He never told me there would be no Japanese food.

SETSUKO: He never told me about "we reserve the right."

CHIZ: I never thought he would die and leave me here to be an American without him.

TERUKO: I never thought they would be scared of us, too.

(*The shrill* WHISTLE *of a tea kettle blasts through the air, bringing the women back to the tatami room.* HIMIKO *enters and drifts. Periodically, she rests and rubs her feet as if they are sore.*)

TERUKO: More tea.

HIMIKO: (*To audience.*) Yes. Please. They *must* keep drinking.

ATSUKO: You didn't mix up the tea cups, did you?

(*The women react to* ATSUKO*'s idiosyncrasy.*)

TERUKO: I think this one is mine.

SETSUKO: This one is mine.

(TERUKO *serves fresh tea to everyone and* TERUKO *freshens* CHIZ*'s coffee.*)

CHIZ: Now, Ats, take it easy.

ATSUKO: She talks just like the women at the grocery store.

TERUKO: Yes, but she gets through the checkout line faster than any of us, too.

SETSUKO: She's always adapted faster than us.

ATSUKO: So, ne, I could never even get used to Amerikan bed. In Japan, I always sleep right on the edge of the blankets so my nose could smell the sweet straw of the matting. I come to Amerika and every night for months I fall out of bed!

SETSUKO: One day—I am so embarrassed—Creed sees me in the bathroom. He says, "Setsuko! You're standing on the toilet! Sit down." So I sit—facing the wall. Next time, he laughs and says, "Honey, you're sitting on it backwards. Turn around."

TERUKO: You know this car wash on Sixth Street? I want to surprise my sugar pie by washing the car for him. So I drive through about 25 miles an hour! The machines scrape the car. When I come out of there, there are bumps all over and I tell that manager he better pay me for the damage. He just laughs and calls my husband.

SETSUKO: (*Looks at the placid* CHIZ.) Was it always so easy for you?

CHIZ: Well, I live *here*. I make the best of it.

SETSUKO: Japan. Amerika. Maybe it doesn't matter where we go. Back home, country papa-san says to me when my first is born, "Bring *it* here for me to see." He wants to see how ugly she is. But she is pretty, and the Japanese crowd and stare. She doesn't look Japanese, they say, and she doesn't look Negro. And I am glad because I have created something new, something that will look new and think new."

CHIZ: (*A chuckle which she knows will irritate* ATSUKO.) Hybrid Japanese.

TERUKO: Mixed Japanese kids at school are very smart. Teachers say they've never seen anything like it.

ATSUKO: That's only because they're half Japanese.

CHIZ: Ats, may your daughter marry a Mexican.

(ATSUKO *almost chokes on her tea at this remark.*)

TERUKO: Japanese-Mexican girls are pretty.

ATSUKO: I don't expect Chizuye to understand the importance of being Japanese.

CHIZ: Oh, Teri's (*Notes Teruko.*) all right because her daughter came out looking Japanese. Buddha was good to her for chanting all these years. (*Rubs her hands together to make fun of chanting.*)

ATSUKO: At least none of our girls turned out like Mieko Hamilton.

HIMIKO: But they are like Mieko. They're between two worlds. We put them there.

ATSUKO: Mieko was just like her mother.

HIMIKO: Yes. And like her father.

ATSUKO: Himiko was crazy and she drove her husband crazy.

CHIZ: And I think you're crazy, so it's all relative, Ats.

TERUKO: It's nice to be together again, *ne.*

(CROSSFADE *lights from tatami to* DSC *as women march quietly in military formation to a period military* SONG *and* DRUMBEAT. HIMIKO *comes centerstage.*)

HIMIKO: Our husbands didn't know what they were getting into. They brought us to Kansas: their Japanese wives dressed up in Amerikan clothes. We were little, breakable dolls to them. I don't think they ever really understood us, but they loved us. Even when the memories of the war crashed through their heads like an endless nightmare, they tried hard to keep on living like normal people and to be the husbands they had dreamed about being when they laid their lives on the line for their country.

(*As the women file into place and stand at attention,* HIMIKO *joins them. They appear rigid, stoic with the carriage of men.* SETSUKO *breaks line and takes on the persona of a gentle, urban Negro.*)

SETSUKO: Uh, Baby-san, why are you staring at the washing machine? The clothes should have been done an hour ago. Yes, I said you don't have to do a thing. Yes, I promised it's all automatic. But, honey, even when it's automatic, you have to push the button to turn it on.

(SETSUKO *falls back into formation.* ATSUKO *takes on the persona of a mellow, California nisei and steps forward.*)

ATSUKO: Hey, Atsuko, where'd you put my hammer? I gotta finish these shelves and I know you never put it back when you use it. Now don't get upset. I'm not trying to say you don't ever do anything right. I just want my hammer. Are you on the rag or what? (*The imaginary hammer comes flying through the air and he barely catches it.*) Okay, okay. Sorry. I didn't mean it. Aw, honey, please don't make me sleep on the couch. (*Apparently,* ATSUKO *has hit him on the head.*)

(ATSUKO *falls back into line.* CHIZ *falls out.*)

CHIZ: Hey, Chizuye. I'm happy you've learned to cook Mexican food, but can you cook some Japanese food for me? The paella is fine, but I love Japanese food. What do you say you teach me how to make yaki-soba?

(CHIZ *falls back into line.* TERUKO *breaks line and takes on the persona of a robust, swaggering Texan.*)

TERUKO: You did *what* to the car at the car wash? Shit, Teri, ain't you got any sense in that little Japanese head of yours? You don't drive *through* the car wash. You just sit in the damn car and let the machines roll the car. I'll be damned, my new car lit'rally gone down the drain. (*Reacts to a crying* TERUKO, *softens.*) Now, honey, don't cry. We'll just have to get the car fixed. (*Falls back into formation.*) Again.

HIMIKO: (*Falls out of formation with the persona of a scrappy Oklahoman with an edgy, rural voice.*) Himi, I didn't stay out late. I told you. I was fishing with Kaz Yamamoto. Okay, okay, so I fished all night and only brought home two fish. What can I say? I'm a bad fisherman. You want to go out for ice cream? There's a Peter Pan store right up the street. I'll get you some Oregon blackberry. I'll bet you never had that flavor before. What? Wait a minute, these ain't frozen fillets from the grocery store. Shut up before I knock your fuckin' teeth in, you hear me, Himi?

(HIMIKO *falls back into formation. The "men" break line and ad lib hearty greetings. Two go through the motions of cleaning and loading rifles; two open the beers and mimic drinking. Campsite activity ensues.*)

TERUKO: Yo, beer.

ATSUKO: Yeah.

HIMIKO: Ain't nothing' like a huntin' trip to clear out the lungs, ain't it, boys?

TERUKO: Kinda like shooting at Japs again. (*Men look at him.*) Ooooooops. I didn't mean it that way. Y'all know how it was during the war, "do this to the Japs," "do that to the

Japs." Sorry. Slip of the tongue. 'Course mine always has been kinda swinging' on a loose hinge. (*As he pats* ATSUKO *on the shoulder.*) I mean, you know I got a good heart. (*He turns and mimicks shooting a basket.*) Two points.

ATSUKO: (*He takes his turn at shooting, makes the basket and ad libs victory.*) My friends said I married one of my own kind. Uh-uh. I spent my life trying to be American, not Japanese American. Being American was better.

(ATSUKO *and* SETSUKO *exchange a handshake of fraternity.*)

SETSUKO: I grew up hard in New York. I had chicks throwing a lot of fast words and a lot of fast ass in my face for years. When I met Setsuko, I knew I could live the quiet life I love, and she'd be right there with me. Forever.

TERUKO: Before World War II, I never dated anything but white tomatoes. When I laid my eyes on Teri, I said to myself, "Fella, you are just about to cross the big boundary line." And I crossed it and there ain't a yellow rose in all of Texas who'll ever turn my heart like her.

CHIZ: (*He shoots a basket and misses; the other "men" kid him.*) I never even saw a Japanese until the war. I just fell in love with this strange girl. She happened to be Japanese, and she happened to be pretty ballsy and bright. She may be less Japanese now, but I think that's her way of survival. I hate to think what a loner I'd become without her, and vice versa.

ATSUKO: (*Mimics urinating with back turned to audience.*) Ats and I are a good example of opposites attracting, but she's the only person who calls me Kazuhiro . . . just like my mom used to.

TERUKO: Aw, well ain't that cute.

(TERUKO *and* ATSUKO *mimic tagging each other, shooting two baskets competitively.*)

TERUKO: Two points. Whoosh.

ATSUKO: (*Joking.*) Wimp. (*Shoots and revels in victory.*)

(TERUKO *and* ATSUKO *do a quick "Three Stooges" exchange.*)

ATSUKO: Women. You can't live with 'em and—

HIMIKO: And you can't shoot 'em. Not anymore. Even though they're Japs. (*Dark, reverberating laughter that disturbs the other "men."*)

ATSUKO: (*Approaches* HIMIKO.) Hamilton, I'm tired of hearing that word. What should I call you? White trash?

HIMIKO: I'm the only real American here. (*With pride.*) All-American mutt. (*More somberly, threateningly to* ATSUKO.) Fightin' Japs . . . marryin' Japs. Yellow skin and slit eyes. Just like the man in the jungle. Wanting me to die so he could live.

TERUKO: I remember the time your wife ran out of your house wearing a slip. She said you'd had a fight and you told her you wanted to kiss and make up. (*A beat as the others relive this, too.*) And you kissed her, all right—and bit off part of her lip. They had to sew it back on.

HIMIKO: What can I say. There's nobody like her. Never has been. (*A beat.*) Never will be. She's the only fuckin' prize I ever won.

(*The others eye him like a hurry and* HIMIKO *laughs.*)

SETSUKO: What did you expect, Hamilton? You'd bring her home and she'd sprout blue eyes and whistle "Dixie"?

HIMIKO: (*Anger simmering just under the surface and finally busting loose.*) Hey, what do you want me to do? Huh? She crawls under my fist like an orphan beggin' for love and my knuckles come down like a magnet. Like a fucking magnet, man. I got eight younger brothers and sisters and I lived in a trailer the size of a pencil box, working three jobs while you guys was jabbin' broads in the alley. Fuckin'-ay man, give me some room to breathe in.

(HIMIKO *spins away as lights* BLACKOUT *on the "men." Spotlight simultaneously* FADES UP *on* CHIZ, DSL.)

CHIZ: Gustavo always said, "Chiz, you're gonna love Kansas. It's real slow, I know, but we'll have a house and a business, and Mama's going to spoil you rotten." He was going to teach me how to build a snowman, our project for that first winter in Kansas. So the snow came and we waited. He said it had to be just the right wetness so we could pack it tightly, so we could make a snowman who would outlive all other snowmen. A *perfect* snowman. That afternoon, Mama Juarez and I were making cinnamon-hot chocolate for when Gustavo came home. Snow was falling around the steaming window. The icy streets looked like a distorted mirror. And, somewhere where I couldn't hear him call, where he couldn't grab my hand for help, Gustavo was sliding into another world, thinking only of me as the ice cut into his beautiful face. The next day, the snow was perfect for building our snowman. But I didn't know how to build anything without Gustavo. And I told myself I would never not know how again. (*A beat, a vow to herself.*) Perfect.

(SETSUKO *enters the light and hovers over her.*)

SETSUKO: My youngest takes home economics. She taught me how to make cooky and milk. I'm almost done. The phone rings. "Mrs. Banks?" the army doctor says, "We regret to inform you Sgt. Banks passed away at fourteen hundred thirty-two hours." The nightmares of war had chased his heart away. (*A pause.*) The girls come home, their sloe-shaped eyes full of the sun. I ask them if they want to go "home"—to Japan. Or to California, where there are more (*Smiles.*) "hybrid Japanese." They say they want to go with me. That I am home. And so, I have a family to raise and my house. I'm staying right here and I dare anyone to move me.

CHIZ: Setsuko.

(CHIZ *holds onto her, a move that makes* SETSUKO *uncomfortable at first but then becomes necessary for both of them.*)

SETSUKO: Yes.

CHIZ: (*With unbitter puzzlement.*) It wasn't perfect.

SETSUKO: But at least it was. At least we had it. Once.

(*Lights* DIM *on them with an immediate spotlight* UP *on* HIMIKO.)

HIMIKO: (*With quiet, determined dignity without a shred of anger or self-pity.*) No, we didn't. We never had it. All we had filtering through our fists was the powder left when a dream explodes in your face and your soul is left charred with the memory of what could have been if there was no war, if there was never a drink to help him forget, never a place like this where our dignity was tied to a tree and left hanging for strangers to spit on.

(HIMIKO *exists as* CHIZ *and* SETSUKO *return to the tatami room and lights* CROSSFADE *into Scene Four:*)

SCENE FOUR

Cold Tea

(*The women reflect exhaustion and contemplation. They appear to be sitting closer, except for* ATSUKO, *who is distant both physically and psychologically.*)

SETSUKO: The tea is cold.

ATSUKO: Well, we must make a fresh pot. (*Exits to kitchen to do so.*)

TERUKO: We've been talking so much.

SETSUKO: Yes, things get cold when neglected.

TERUKO: (*Checks* ATSUKO*'s tea tin and calls out to* ATSUKO.) We're out of your tea, Atsuko-san. May we drink "peasant" tea?

ATSUKO: (*From the kitchen.*) Have what you want.

(ATSUKO *returns with fresh hot water for tea.*)

TERUKO: I've been in Kansas so long, I don't know good tea from bad.

CHIZ: Oh, Teruko, come on. You've adjusted the best; you're an entrepreneur. You and Curt started from scratch: Japanese barber comes to Kansas.

TERUKO: Curtis wants to stay here. Maybe buy a farm. I think that's okay. Setchan, what about you? Do you think you'll marry again and stay here?

SETSUKO: If a nice man comes along . . . maybe. I will be fine.

CHIZ: How many Kansas rednecks are there who can think of a Japanese as anything but a geisha or Tokyo Rose? Even the most beautiful Japanese in the world couldn't find a redneck for miles who'd see her as a real person. (*A beat.*) I don't want to love again. It hurts too much when they go away.

ATSUKO: Well, I suppose you all envy me, thinking I'm the lucky one. (*The women react to her again.*) But my husband promised he'd leave the army and we'd move to California. He's still in the army and we're still here. (*A beat.*) It's so unfair that I have to die in Kansas.

TERUKO: (*Tired of* ATSUKO*'s ridiculous fears.*) Atsuko-san, you're going to live a long time.

ATSUKO: So? What difference does it make? When we're dead, no one will remember there were Japanese in Kansas.

TERUKO: What will happen to the last one? Who will bury her?

ATSUKO: When it comes down to it, we're alone. Just like Himiko. She died alone.

SETSUKO: But she's not alone now. I am with her.

ATSUKO: Oh, spare me. She'd dead. Who cares about death unless it's happening to you?

HIMIKO: They must care. If my journey leaves me stranded here, they, too, will have no passage.

TERUKO: I am with Himiko-san, too.

ATSUKO: Well, I'm not and I never was. (*Starts gathering her cup and goodies.*) In fact, I'm ready to go home. I've wasted my day and, let's face it, all the cleaning in the world isn't going to change Himiko's life or help her find a new life that's any better.

SETSUKO: Maybe it's really not Himiko's life you're worried about. Maybe it's yours, Atsuko-san.

(ATSUKO *looks outward. Her eyes lock with* HIMIKO*'s for a moment.* HIMIKO *bows her head toward her invitingly.* ATSUKO *shakes her head as if she has seen something and then turns to the women again. She is uneasy and caustic.*)

ATSUKO: Come on. Let's be honest. Since when has anyone really cared about Himiko Hamilton? We've always known she was crazy. Poor Teruko, you had to live in the same neighborhood as her. You couldn't even go into your front yard without her bothering you. Of course, Himiko was scared of Chizuye so she didn't bother her too much. She admired you, Chizuye. Yes. You had become a model Amerikan. She used to talk about your "perfect Amerikan" accent. Said you sounded just like a television star.

CHIZ: Atsuko, shut up before I lose my temper. I've been saving it up for you all these years, so if it gets loose . . .

TERUKO: (*Gently, again trying to deter confrontation.*) It *was* Chizuye who finally came to check on Himiko when she disappeared. She found her here. Sleeping.

CHIZ: Dead. For at least three days. To think of it.

SETSUKO: No. She died many years ago. Of a broken heart.

ATSUKO: Oh, you all make me laugh. Such tragedy in your eyes. I can just hear the shakuhachi playing in the background as you weep for her spirit.

SETSUKO: That's enough, Atsuko-san.

ATSUKO: Enough what? Enough laughter for the joke the war played on my life? Enough tears for having no allegiance except what I practice in the silence of my soul? Excuse me for not being strong like you, Setsuko. We all have our own problems to worry about. Maybe you think you can bear the weight of the world, but I can't.

CHIZ: What you can do for me is shut up. You've always been a mean, selfish bitch, Atsuko.

ATSUKO: (*Quite taken aback, she tries to collect herself.*) Teruko, let's go! (TERUKO *shakes her head firmly.*) Teruko!

TERUKO: (*Highly upset, the words spill out uncontrollably.*) Atsuko, I know you're afraid because the first of us is dead. Maybe you think soon we'll be having tea like this after you die. And maybe that is what will be. You can't control that. But you *can* control how you treat people.

SETSUKO: And the respect you owe the dead.

ATSUKO: Oh, just leave me alone. I wish I'd never come here today.

CHIZ: But we did, didn't we? Like the good Japanese ladies we are. (*A beat.*) We're not here because we have to be. Japanese manners don't require us to pay homage to some loon of a woman, even if she *was* Japanese. No, we're here today because we hurt inside like we never have before. Because when the first of us goes so violently and it's all over the papers, it wakes us up. For the first time in our lives, we gather

together all the pieces of our used-up hearts and come running here hoping we'll find some kind of miracle that will glue it all back together and send us into our old age with something to hold onto.

TERUKO: But today we *have* all gone a little farther with each other than we ever have before.

CHIZ: Tomorrow it'll be status quo again.

SETSUKO: No, it won't ever be like it used to be again.

ATSUKO: Speak for yourself. (*A challenge, desperately trying to maintain the control she has always enjoyed over* TERUKO.) *Are you coming, Teruko?* (*She begins to move toward an exit; she is full of anger and suppressing tears. She turns once again to look at* TERUKO. SETSUKO *stands supportively behind* TERUKO. *The words bite out of* ATSUKO*'s mouth.*) Teruko . . . this is your last chance.

(*To her shock,* TERUKO *even more firmly turns away. Devastated,* ATSUKO *moves toward the door and then, defeated, falls to her knees;* HIMIKO *immediately comes to her side.*)

HIMIKO: Atsuko-san, stay. If you leave now, no one will rest.

(HIMIKO *stands in front of* ATSUKO *and, without touching her, helps her to stand and maintain, using her hands as delicate guides.* ATSUKO *fights with herself and then turns back to the women. She bows in apology to* TERUKO, *who bows back. She turns toward the door again, but* SETSUKO *bows to her. Feeling better,* ATSUKO *returns the bow. Still uncomfortable,* ATSUKO *glances at* CHIZ, *who motions kindly for her to sit down. She does and the other women follow suit, except for* TERUKO.)

TERUKO: The only time we have taken tea together is whenever something bad happened to a Japanese "war bride." We have the best tea and realize how little we understand about each other's choices: in husbands, in raising our children, in whether or not we choose to embrace Amerika. Amerikans don't want us. Japanese Amerikans too busy feeling bad themselves. We can't go back to Japan. That's why I say family is the most important thing. What makes us the most happiest? Our children. Our children.

(CHIZ *exits as lights* CROSSFADE *to the tatami area and music—"Runaway"—*FADES UP *rapidly. The women dance onto the tatami area as young girls. The "girls" assume positions as if enjoying themselves at a slumber party: manicuring,* TERUKO *rolling someone's hair, putting on cosmetics, etc.* ATSUKO *mimics smoking. The women are playing their daughters. They sing the "wa-wa-wa" lyrics of the song and burst into laughter.*)

ATSUKO: Can you believe it? My mom won't let me go out for cheerleading. She said it's too "sexual." (*Imitates mother's accent.*) "Don't do skiing. Japanese don't ski. Don't do motorcycle. Don't do skydive." She even thinks life insurance guarantees you don't die. When I was born, she bought me a hundred-thousand dollar policy.

SETSUKO: My mother worries about life, not death. (*Imitates mother's accent.*) "Did you eat your raw egg and fermented soy beans today? Did you have bowel movement?" (*She laughs.*) Mom's so funny. We were separated in a store and, over the intercom, I heard: "Japanese mother lost in dry goods. Will her daughter please claim her?"

TERUKO: My mother doesn't worry about anything except my dad. When she starts licking the bottom of his shoes and gets that look in her eye, (*Mimics her mother doing this.*) I can say, "Mom, hi, I'm going to join the Marines, become a lesbian, screw the football team." She'd just say, (*Imitates mother's accent.*) "Okay, Linda. That's good. Have to fix dinner for sugar pie now."

ATSUKO: (*Does breast exercises.*) Man, the only thing that really bugs me after all these years is having to take my shoes off in the house.

SETSUKO: I thought I was going to die when my date picked me up for the homecoming dance. While he waited for me, my mother put shower caps over his shoes!

(*Except for* HIMIKO, *the "girls" laughed and ad lib sounds of embarrassment.* HIMIKO *is eerily silent.*)

TERUKO: Mieko, what about *your* mother?

(TERUKO *can't help giggling, although she tries hard to suppress it. It is contagious.*)

TERUKO: She came to our house wearing that blonde wig. She slurped her tea and crocheted those green and purple poodle toilet paper covers. Ugh.

(*All but* HIMIKO *laugh nervously, unable to restrain themselves, despite* HIMIKO*'s cold stare.*)

HIMIKO: (*Without feeling, no sense of bitterness, with an eerie smile.*) I hate the world. (*Fresh laughter from the other "girls."*)

ATSUKO: So take a number, Mieko.

HIMIKO: You guys don't know anything about what life really is. Life is about relationships. Relationships with guys.

TERUKO: Oh, Mieko. We all date guys.

HIMIKO: It isn't about dating guys. It's about being *fucked* by guys.

(*Their laughter is cut short by* HIMIKO*'s remark. Whatever they are doing, their motions grind to a halt:* TERUKO *in the middle of putting on lipstick,* ATSUKO *in the middle of a laugh, and so on. They are shocked at this language and eye one another uncomfortably.* MIEKO *seems to enjoy this power.*)

HIMIKO: In fact, it's about being fucked by everyone: your mother, your father—and even yourself. (*A beat as she looks away from the girls and then she hits the table with the palm of her hand, frightening the other girls.*) Don't ask me about my mother. Because then you're asking me about myself . . . and I don't know who the hell I am.

(*She spins away from the other girls, moving to one side of the stage and folding herself into a ball, and the other "girls" exit quickly. A light* FADES UP *on* HIMIKO, *now having reassumed the persona of* HIMIKO, *the spirit.*)

HIMIKO: I was born in a storm and it's never stopped raining. My only blessing is Mieko, my half-Japanese girl. I love her so much, but she was born in my storm, too. For years, I tried to talk to her, but she wasn't ready. (*A sad laugh.*) Mieko is so fast, I only know what she looks like from behind. Because she's always leaving, her big Japanese o-shiri swaying like a flower, out looking for dreams she thinks men are going to give her. So it was a Saturday in May. Mieko wants to make me worry, so she *hitchhikes.* She's gone three days. Then the big policeman comes. "Do you have a daughter named Mieko? When's the last time you saw her, Mrs. Hamilton?" (*Breathes hard and fast; forces composure.*) The last time I saw Mieko is in the dusk. She looks so Japanese, her shoulders curving like gentle hills. "Perfect kimono shoulders," her grandmother would say. (*A beat.*) Mieko came home today. Someone made her dirty, stabbed her in the chest many times and then raped her as she died. Left a broom inside my little girl's body. Her brassiere was shredded by the knife. (*A beat.*) There is no one for me; there never was. Even my sisters of Japan cannot bless me with sandals to cover my blistered feet as I prepare for the longest journey. (*Looks around.*) Billy, is that you? Before it's too late, tell me the truth. You loved me, didn't you? Once. Once there was nobody like me. Now that I know, I can go on without you, Billy. I see you there, waiting in the mist, your strong arms ready to hold me for one last dance. But I'm going another way. Like bamboo, I sway back and forth in the wind, bending but never breaking. Never again. The war is over. Mother? Is that you? Are you waiting for me, too?

(*Brief, absolute delight, addressing Mieko when she was five.*) Mieko-chan, I see you dancing in my best kimono: all light and laughter and . . . clean! (*The delight fades.*) No, you all have to let me go now. I have a long walk ahead of me. All ties are unbound, as completely as if they never existed.

(*She exists as lights* DIM *and we bridge into the next scene. Wind chimes* TINKLE *in the darkness:*)

SCENE FIVE

Perfect Drinking Temperature

SETSUKO, ATSUKO, CHIZ, TERUKO: (*From various corners of the stage, they chant in the style of Buddhist chanting; in English the ancient poem means: "I don't care / What anybody says. / I will never stop / Loving you."*) *Hito wa dono yo ni, i oo to mamayo.*

SETSUKO: Tsunor'ya.

ATSUKO: . . . suru to mo . . .

TERUKO: . . . yami . . .

CHIZ: . . . wa senu.

SETSUKO: Hito wa dono yo ni . . .

ATSUKO: . . . i oo to mamayo . . .

TERUKO: Tsunor'ya suru to mo . . .

CHIZ: Yami wa senu.

SETSUKO: Himi-chan.

ATSUKO: Himiko.

TERUKO: Himiko-san.

CHIZ: Searching.

SETSUKO: For peace

TERUKO: Finally free.

CHIZ: Himiko-san.

(*As if drawn to the power of their harmony,* HIMIKO *enters dressed in resplendent kimono. She moves gracefully, winsomely, and comes* CS *as the chanting continues.*)

SETSUKO: Your sisters call.

TERUKO: Come.

ATSUKO: Come unto us.

ALL: Come to tea with us.

(*They study each other thoughtfully, and then surround* HIMIKO *with warmth.* HIMIKO *kneels before them, facing the audience and bows her head low.*)

ALL: (*A whisper.*) Gan'batte.

SETSUKO: (*A whisper in the shadow of "gan'batte."*) Persevere.

(*The women return to the tatami room,* WIND CHIMES *marking the transition.* HIMIKO *follows and watches them.*)

CHIZ: I am glad I came here today. Somehow, I feel at home with you women, you Japanese women. (*Smiles.*) Today.

SETSUKO: We should have let anyone who wanted to help come over. Today, even taking tea is different.

ATSUKO: Yes, even tea tastes different.

CHIZ: Maybe we will have tea again. All of us?

SETSUKO: Yes, Chizuye-san. Soon.

TERUKO: As you wish it.

SETSUKO: Atsuko-san?

ATSUKO: (*Looks around the room as if she senses a ghost; answers slowly.*) Yes? (*A frightened beat.*) Himiko is here, isn't she?

TERUKO: Oh, please, you're scaring me. Let's not talk about ghosts.

ATSUKO: But maybe that's the fate that awaits us all. A black space where the war dead and us, the war wounded, must sit out eternity.

SETSUKO: If it is our destiny, then—

CHIZ: Then it is our destiny.

TERUKO: *So, ne.*

SETSUKO: (*The women look solemnly at one another as Setsuko bows in honor of* HIMIKO.) *Okagesama de.*

CHIZ: (*Takes a cup for* HIMIKO *and acknowledges her.*) In your honorable shadow. (CHIZ *puts a fifth cup on the table.*) Please join us for tea.

(*The women sit for a last drink of tea.* HIMIKO *joins them. They lift their cups simultaneously and slightly bow their heads to one another.* HIMIKO *forms a cup with her hands and drinks from it in unison with the others. She looks happier.*)

HIMIKO: Perfect.

(*The minute that word is uttered, the women pack up their things, ad lib farewells in Japanese—"sa," "ikimasho, ne," "mata, ne," "ato de denwa shimasu," etc.—except for* CHIZ. *She is the last to speak and says "bye-bye," and* TERUKO *responds with "bye-bye." They exit in different directions.* SETSUKO *lingers as if trying to absorb* HIMIKO*'s energy from the air. She bows deeply. Then she, too, exits as traditional Japanese* MUSIC *fades up. Taking each cup of tea and bowing to the woman who left the tea before,* HIMIKO *pours the remnants into her cup. She gathers strength from this and moves* DSC, *where she kneels. Holding the cup outward, she bows gracefully to the audience, and then* *drinks the tea with extreme thirst that appears to be satisfied from the drink. She sets the cup down in front of her and smiles a half-smile, perhaps like that of Mona Lisa, to the audience. She bows low, all the way to the floor.* BLACKOUT. CURTAIN.)

THE END

APPEARANCES

Tina Howe

CHARACTERS

IVY WALL: an inexperienced shopper; in her thirties.

GRACE MATTHEWS: the woman who guards the fitting room; in her fifties.

SCENE

A ladies' fitting room in a department store. Rows of dressing rooms are visible off to one side. A desk guards the area. Standing nearby is a rack of discarded clothes.

TIME: Late in the afternoon of a winter day.

The Curtain Rises.

GRACE *is sitting at her desk reading a paperback. The joyous soprano-alto duet "Jesu Der Meine Seele" from Bach's Cantata 78 plays.*

IVY: (*Dressed in a bulky winter coat, comes staggering up to* GRACE *with twenty-four dresses falling out of her arms.*)

GRACE: Just one minute! You can't bring all of those in here!

IVY: (*Dropping them right and left.*) Oooooooopppppppppps . . .

GRACE: You're only allowed to try on six items at a time!

IVY: (*More and more distraught.*) I'm sorry . . . uh-oohhh . . .

GRACE: Miss! Did you hear me . . . ?

IVY: (*Scooping them up off the floor.*) They keep falling off the hangers.

GRACE: You'll have to put some of those back!

IVY: (*Has finally gathered everything up in a huge ball, but loses her balance and flings everything on* GRACE*'s desk, herself included.*) WOOOOOPS!

GRACE: HEY . . . WHAT'S GOING ON HERE?!

IVY: (*Laughing with embarrassment.*) I lost my balance . . . I was just trying to . . . oh God, I'm sorry . . . they keep falling off the hangers . . .

GRACE: How many items do you have there anyway?

IVY: (*Picking them up.*) Here we go: one, two, three, four, five . . .

GRACE: Who was helping you out front?

IVY: six, seven, eight, nine, ten, eleven . . . (*Starts to teeter under her load.*)

GRACE: (*Rises to protect her desk.*) OH NO YOU DON'T.

IVY: (*In an effort not to drop it all again, lurches into the first dressing room and hurls everything onto the little stool, which immediately tips over.*)

GRACE: (*Running after her.*) HEY . . . COME BACK HERE! I DIDN'T ASSIGN YOU THAT ROOM!

IVY: (*On the floor picking everything up.*) I'm sorry, I was just trying to . . . Oh God . . .

GRACE: The customers don't select their dressing rooms, *I* do!

(*She unwittingly stands on the dress* IVY *is trying to pick up.*)

How do you expect me to keep track of the merchandise unless I know how many items pass through here?

IVY: (*On her hands and knees trying to move* GRACE*'s foot off the dress.*) Excuse me, I'm afraid you're . . . uh . . . I'm sorry, could you just . . .

GRACE: (*Doesn't budge, oblivious.*) There are certain rules which customers have to follow, I don't care *who* you are . . .

IVY: . . . lift your foot half an inch to one side . . . just move a tiny bit . . .

GRACE: . . . Miss America or the Queen of England.

IVY: . . . thaaaaat's the way . . . just ease over this direction . . . thaaaat's it . . .

GRACE: First they have to let me count the number of items

they're going to try on, and second, they have to wait for me to assign them a dressing room.

(*Moves her foot to one side.*)

IVY: (*Trying to move it further.*) Yes, yes . . . keep going, that's it . . .

GRACE: Running a fitting room is not as easy as it looks!

(*She stands on another part of the dress.*)

Thousands of dollars worth of merchandise passes through here every day.

IVY: . . . just one inch more, you're doing fine.

GRACE: The customers would steal you blind if given half a chance!

(*She steps off the dress.*)

IVY: (*Snatches it up.*) Thank you very much!

GRACE: (*Helps her gather up the rest of the pile.*) I once caught a woman trying to sneak the entire length of carpeting off the floor. That's right, over seventy-five yards of wall-to-wall carpeting . . . Here, give me those . . . Let's go back to my desk so I can count all of this.

IVY: (*Scoops up the rest of the dresses and follows* GRACE *to her desk.*)

GRACE: (*Starts making order of it all, hanging the dresses on one side of the reject rack.*)

God's truth! She brought this huge canvas bag with her. I told her she'd have to check it with me at the desk. "Oh no," she says, "I've got all my try-on blouses in here plus a few extra pair of shoes. I always bring this bag in with me!" . . . Like an idiot I tell her it's all right, just this once . . . and the next thing I know, my desk and chair start sliding down the hall . . . so I go charging into her dressing room and there she is, down on her hands and knees prying up the edges of the carpet with a crowbar and stuffing it into that bag of hers. I couldn't believe my eyes! How she thought she could possibly *fit* seventy-five yards of wall-to-wall carpeting into that bag and then just tiptoe out of here without anyone noticing it trailing behind her . . . I mean, what did she take me for . . . a total idiot? . . . OK, now, let's see how many items you've got here . . .

IVY: I need something for a party.

GRACE: Who was helping you out front?

IVY: We're having a party at our office tonight. I want to look wonderful.

GRACE: Do you remember her name? It was probably Irene.

IVY: (*Showing* GRACE *her dress under her coat.*) I thought this dress would be perfect, but when I looked at myself in the mirror during lunch hour I realized it was all wrong. It's too mousy.

GRACE: A big woman with short orange hair . . . I think she's wearing a green blouse today.

IVY: I want to stand out.

GRACE: (*Finally has all the dresses hung up.*) OK, let's see what you've got here . . . (*Going through them.*) two, three, four, six, eight, ten, twelve, fourteen, sixteen, eighteen, twenty, twenty-two, twenty-four . . .

IVY: (*Breathless.*) Alex London will be there.

GRACE: (*Pulls out a nightgown.*) What's *this?!*

IVY: He's our new managing editor.

GRACE: It looks like a nightgown. How on earth did you get a nightgown in here?

IVY: You know how some people send off a kind of . . . animal thing?

GRACE: Lingerie is on the third floor!

IVY: They make you feel like they don't have any clothes on and you're afraid to look at them because well, you know . . . you might see something you're not supposed to.

GRACE: Do you have other things from different floors in here? (*She pulls out a feathered bed jacket.*) *What* is this?!

IVY: Of course they *do* have clothes on, they just have this way of suggesting that maybe . . . well, they're showing you something . . .

GRACE: (*Reading from the tag.*) Department 215B?! Department 215B is all the way down in the basement!

IVY: (*More and more embarrassed.*) . . . and then you start imagining *you're* showing something, that it's peeking out and you're afraid to breathe because then everything will fall off and you'll both be stark naked! And you think you're losing your mind because everyone else is fully dressed walking around answering telephones and writing memos!

GRACE: OK. Which things do you want to try on first? You can pick out four.

IVY: (*Looking at her watch.*) Oh dear, I don't have much time. I've got to be back at six to help set up. You see, I never planned to go shopping in the first place. I snuck out.

GRACE: After you finish trying on the first four, just come back and I'll give you the next batch and so on until you find the one you want.

IVY: Which should I try on first? (*Looking through them all.*)

GRACE: It doesn't matter, just pick four that you like . . . but no more than four.

IVY: It's so hard to choose.

GRACE: Normally, I could never hold all these back here for you, but since it's slow I don't mind. It's nice to have some company.

IVY: (*Still going through them.*) Oh God . . .

GRACE: Here, would you like me to choose for you?

IVY: *Would you??!*

GRACE: No problem! (GRACE *matter-of-factly counts off the first four and hands them to* IVY.)

One, two, three, four. There you go!

IVY: (*Heads for the first dressing room.*) Gee, thanks a lot.

GRACE: HEY, WAIT A MINUTE! I HAVEN'T ASSIGNED YOU A ROOM YET . . .

IVY: (*Returns.*) Oh yes.

GRACE: (*Writes on a slip of paper, which she puts into a time-punch machine and then hands to Ivy.*)

Here, take them into Room 22.

IVY: (*Takes the slip and heads into Room 23.*) Thank you.

GRACE: Honey, I said Room 22! It's across the hall!

IVY: Oh, sorry! (*Lurches into Room 25, which isn't across the hall, but down the aisle.*)

GRACE: The *other* side, dear! The even-numbered rooms are on the other side!

IVY: (*Creeps out, hiding her head within the dresses.*) Sorry . . . sorry . . . (*And stands in the middle of the corridor, lost.*)

GRACE: (*Rises from her desk and leads* IVY *into Room 22.*) Room . . . 22! Here we go! (*She returns to her desk.*)

IVY: (*Enters the room, which is completely visible to the audience. It's small, windowless, and painted yellow, with a ratty beige carpet. It's seen real battle. The floor is littered with broken hangers, torn off labels, and a showering of straight pins. A free-standing three-way mirror is pushed into one corner. The room is entered through a neck-high, cantilevered swinging door, which is hung on a perilously tight spring.*)

HEY, THERE'S NO STOOL IN HERE! WHERE WILL I PUT EVERYTHING?

GRACE: Use the hook on the wall.

IVY: What hook?

GRACE: It must have been stolen. Listen, you're lucky you've still got a mirror in there. (*Pause.*) You *do* have a mirror, don't you?

IVY: Ahh, here's a piece of hook left . . .

(*She gingerly hangs up her selection and takes off her coat.*)

COULD I BRING IN THAT LITTLE STOOL FROM THE OTHER DRESSING ROOM? I HAVE NO PLACE TO PUT MY COAT.

GRACE: I'm sorry, but you're not allowed to move stools from one room to another.

IVY: (*Slings her coat over the mirror, completely covering it, and then looks through her selection of dresses. She chooses a long-sleeved grey wool number, looks for a place to put it, and places it over her coat. She then takes off her dress, which she puts on top of the grey one. She returns to the other three dresses to make sure she chose the right one. After looking through them, she returns to the grey one, but can't find it since it's hidden under her dress. Panic-stricken, she retraces her moves until she finally spies it. She pulls it off the mirror, dragging down her own dress with it. She neatly folds the latter and places it in a corner. Then she tries on the grey one but can't see anything since her coat is covering the mirror, so she whips off her coat and slings it over the cantilevered door. She returns to the mirror. The dress is* not *a success. She strikes deliberately ugly poses and adds a belt, which makes it look even worse. Finally, she takes it off and leaves it on the floor. She selects the next one, a bright red whorish number, which she quickly slides over her head, keeping her eyes shut. She spreads out her arms like a diva and opens her eyes. She strikes several outlandish poses and then quickly whips it off, rolling it up into a ball and kicking it behind the mirror. Two more dresses are left. She chooses a long-sleeved grey wool that's identical to the first one she tried on . . . only much bigger.)*

What's this? I thought I already tried it on! (*She looks at the ticket.*) Ohhh, it's a different size . . .

IVY: (*She puts it on. It's so big it makes her laugh. She starts playing in it, pulling her arms and head down into the bulk of it so that nothing shows except her legs. She flails around inside it, laughing, and finally takes it off, putting it over her coat on the door. She tries on the last dress, a blue print that's not bad except she can't reach the zipper in the back. She flings her arms this way and that trying to get hold of it.*)

I can't reach the . . . DAMN . . . I ALMOST HAD IT! . . . There we go . . . that's it . . . steady . . . steady . . . almost . . . If I can just sneak up on it . . . yes . . . almost . . . almost . . .

GRACE: What's going on in there?

IVY: (*More and more frantic.*) I CAN'T REACH THE ZIPPER . . . Help . . . That's it . . . just . . . *fling* the arm back and reach . . .

GRACE: Well, come on out, I'll help you.

IVY: (*Makes one last desperate attempt, grunting and flailing.*)

GRACE: COME ON . . . !

IVY: (*Her arms wrapped around her body, she tries to push out through the door, but it won't move since her coat and dresses clog the two halves. Finally she lowers her head like a bull and comes charging out, her clothes flying every which way.)*

AAAAAAHHHHHHH!

GRACE: (*Catches* IVY *in her arms.*) ATTA GIRL!

IVY: I CAN'T REACH IT . . . I JUST CAN'T . . .

GRACE: Come here, turn around.

IVY: I'm afraid it's too small, that's why I . . .

GRACE: Well, no wonder! The zipper pull's broken off! The dress is defective! You'll have to go back out front and look for another one.

IVY: Defective . . . ?

GRACE: That is, if there *is* another one out there. I don't recall ever seeing this dress before. Did you get it on this floor?

IVY: Just my luck! A broken zipper! And this was my favorite.

GRACE: Honey, I'm not selling you damaged merchandise, you'll have to go back out there and see if you can find another one.

IVY: I don't mind, I'll use a safety pin for the time being.

GRACE: (*Taking the dress off her.*) I'm sorry, but you cannot buy a defective dress! (*She hangs it at a far end of the reject rack.*) How were the others you tried on?

IVY: Terrible!

GRACE: Well, if you like this one so much, see if you can find another one!

IVY: (*Walks out of the fitting room into the store. Several moments pass.*)

GRACE: (*Starting to run after her.*) HEY, WAIT A MINUTE! YOU CAN'T GO OUT THERE IN YOUR SLIP . . . !

(*More moments pass.*)

GRACE: (*Calling to her.*) Psst . . . honey . . . you're just in your slip . . . yoo hoo . . .

(*More moments pass.*)

IVY: (*Heaving with laughter, comes careening back in, her hands covering her crotch and bosom.*)

I was only in my slip . . . What if somebody from the office had seen me . . . (*Roaring with laughter.*) What if Alex London . . . had seen me . . . ?!

(*She tears into her dressing room.*)

GRACE: Boy, I'll be glad when this week is over! My daughter is getting married on Saturday and it's not going to be your average intimate gathering of family and friends . . . Guess how many people are coming . . . Two hundred? . . . Three hundred? . . . Five hundred? Try 850! That's right, 850 strong . . .

IVY: (*Returns to* GRACE*'s desk with her overcoat on over her slip.*)

Hi . . . I'm back. I can't believe what I just did . . .

(*She starts looking through the dresses on the reject rack.*)

GRACE: My future son-in-law works for the Mayor. He's one of his chief speech writers and a very bright boy. Everyone's crazy about him. All of City Hall is coming and half of the Albany legislature . . . No, no, honey, I put your things on the *other* end! Those are items other customers have rejected.

IVY: (*Pulling out a dress.*) Gee, this one's nice.

GRACE: But it's not yours.

IVY: (*Holding it up to herself.*) It's a great color.

GRACE: But it's not your size. It's much too small. Look, would you let me give you some advice?

IVY: (*Pulling out another one.*) OH . . . THIS IS THE BEST!

GRACE: (*Shaking her by the shoulders.*) HELLO?

IVY: THIS IS REALLY BEAUTIFUL.

GRACE: Forget the blue dress with the broken zipper . . . stop looking through things you didn't even pick out . . . and try on the rest of your selection!

(*Silence.*)

IVY: Really?

GRACE: Really! You'll save yourself a lot of time! (*She counts out the next four dresses and hands them to* IVY.)

One, two, three, four. There you go!

IVY: (*Heads back to her dressing room.*) Thanks a lot.

GRACE: WAIT A MINUTE, I DIDN'T GIVE YOU YOUR SLIP YET! . . . Oh, to hell with it, I know where you are.

IVY: (*Back in her dressing room, looks for a place to put her latest batch. She tries the remnant of the hook, but everything falls to the floor. She scoops it up and slings it all over the door and then takes off her dress, which she lays in a corner, as . . .*)

GRACE: (*Fusses with some inaccurately printed price tags.*) I'm telling you, I'm dropping with fatigue! I've never made out so many lists in my life: invitations, seating plans, thank-you notes . . . I'm taking off the rest of the week to recover. I should have taken off the entire month, but frankly we need the money. I don't want to tell you how much this wedding is costing, though the Mayor, bless his heart, insists on taking care of the reception afterward. He's holding it in the ballroom of Gracie Mansion, all expenses paid! It's a great honor for Kenny and Donna and a Godsend for me! I'm a widow, you see, and have been going it alone for eleven years . . .

(*As* . . .)

IVY: (*Selects her first dress, a white polyester number with wide sleeves and a full skirt. She holds it up to herself and smiles, playing with the skirt. Before she puts it on she combs her hair and adds a fresh touch of lipstick. Then she slides it over her head. It looks nice. She eyes herself from several angles and does a few little dance steps. She looks remarkably like a bride.*)

GRACE: You ought to see the dress Donna picked out! It's straight out of a fairy tale! Miles of taffeta, ruffles everywhere, seed pearls sewn onto the bodice and sleeves. When I saw her at that first dress fitting, I thought my heart would stop. She's a very pretty girl to start with but in that dress . . .

IVY: (*Takes the dress off, lays it on the floor, and selects the next one, which is identical in fabric and style except it's maroon. She holds it up and sashays around. She slips it on and stands way back to get a better look.*)

GRACE: Of course Kenny's no slouch in the looks department either, he's as handsome as the day is long. He's been after Donna for years. He comes from a nice family, simple people, hard working. He's one of eleven. Can you imagine having eleven kids?! Boy, I could no more deal with eleven kids than fly to the moon! It was all I could do to raise Donna, but to have ten more as well . . . all those lives to worry about . . . I'd be a total nervous wreck! I don't know how Kenny's mother does it. That woman is a saint, an utter saint! You see there are some problems in their blood . . . well, I guess you'd call them more than "problems" . . . they're more like disabilities, severe disabilities . . .

(*As* . . .)

IVY: (*Lurches very close to the mirror and then backs off like a yo-yo gone haywire.*)

GRACE: It's so tragic. They're such a darling family, and then to have all that . . . that . . .

IVY: (*Reaches for the white dress again and holds it up over the maroon one, trying to decide which one looks better. She does a few turns, then takes off the maroon dress and puts the white one back on.*)

GRACE: One of Kenny's sisters was born without legs and another one has extra fingers. I could never handle that. Having handicapped children who break my heart every time I look at them. No thank you! But Kenny's family is wonderful with them, treats them as natural as you please. You can guess who the star attractions of that wedding are going to be in their matching flower girl dresses and little white gloves . . . Kenny adores those girls, takes them everywhere with him. Even brings them down to the Mayor's office sometimes. The Mayor is crazy about them, has their picture right up on his desk alongside the photos of his own kids. He says they're an inspiration to the entire human race.

(*As . . .*)

IVY: (*In a burst of brilliance, puts the maroon dress on* over *the white one. It takes some doing, but she manages it so you can't tell she has on two dresses at once. She poses first in the maroon and then flips it over her head and poses in the white . . . back and forth.*)

GRACE: The one without the legs has these custom-made artificial legs that she hooks onto herself. They're amazing, they're so lifelike, the exact same color and texture as her own skin. The thing that really gets me about her, though, and I'm probably a little strange to notice it . . . is every day she's got on a fresh pair of socks. That's right, each night she discards the pair she'd been wearing and selects a clean pair for the next day. If you stop and think about it, you realize there's no way those socks ever get dirty since she doesn't have feet that get them all sweated up. She's just a stickler for appearances and insists on fresh socks every day because fresh socks look better than wilted ones! Well, when I look down and see those spanking white socks hugging those little plastic ankles of hers, the cuffs folded just so . . . it brings tears to my eyes! That little girl really takes pride in how she looks! She knows she's been born with a handicap, but she doesn't let it get to her. And active . . . ? She does everything any normal ten-year-old would do: run, jump, play sports. She's amazing the way she tears around. And sense of humor? She's a real mimic, that one . . . you ought to hear her imitate the pop singers . . .

(GRACE *imitates the child imitating a pop singer.*)

(*As* . . .)

IVY: (*Goes crazier with indecision, flipping the dresses back and forth.*) I CAN'T DECIDE!

GRACE: . . . though to be perfectly honest, she *does* give me the creeps a bit; I don't like being around her. There *is* trouble in Kenny's genes and I'm nervous as a witch about him and Donna having normal kids. Two of his sisters born with missing or extra extremities. One of his brothers has something queer growing out of his ear, and there's another child no one has ever seen! You can't turn your back on those things! Kenny and Donna are a very high-risk couple. I know Donna's anxious about it too. She doesn't look well, she's lost a lot of weight, but she refuses to talk about it. "It's between Kenny and me," she says. "I love him and I want to give him children. They'll be all right, I *know* they'll be all right!" . . . Well, it's in God's hands, there's nothing any of us can do about it . . . though I'll tell you, I haven't slept through the night since the invitations were sent out . . . It's too late to call it off now, 850 friends are rooting for them and the decorators have already turned Gracie Mansion into a pink and white valentine. What will happen, will happen . . . but if Donna has a legless baby, I don't know what I'll do . . . I mean, can you imagine watching a toddler trying to get around without any legs . . . ? I'd kill myself, just put a gun to my head, I couldn't take it . . . but then I'd have to take it, wouldn't I? . . . Put on a brave face like Kenny's little sister changing her socks every day. People adjust . . . I just don't know if I have it in me. I'm very weak on courage and always have been! I can't even help a blind person cross the street! As soon as I see one coming with their tapping stick, I try to disappear, hoping to God they can't really see me after all . . . It's a terrible failing. I wish I could change. It's my most fervent prayer, "Please God, make me more accepting!"

IVY: (*Bursts out of her dressing room.*) I CAN'T DECIDE!

GRACE: Oh, I like that on you! That's very nice.

IVY: But what about *this* . . . ?! (*She lifts up the maroon dress to reveal the white one.*)

GRACE: You're wearing two dresses at once?

IVY: I can't make up my mind. (*Starts sashaying around in the white one.*) What do you think . . . ?

GRACE: (*Starts laughing.*) You're too much!

IVY: This one . . . or this?

GRACE: I hope you're not planning to sneak out of here in one of those . . .

IVY: The wine brings out my color, but there's something romantic about the white one.

GRACE: (*Flipping the dresses up and down.*) It's really amazing, no one would ever know you've got two dresses on!

IVY: (*Whirling around in the maroon dress.*) What do you think . . . ? You've got to help me decide. You see it's my one chance to catch his eye . . . If he could just notice me for ten seconds.

GRACE: That *is* nice! It gives you a flush!

IVY: (*Flips it over her head and whirls in the white one.*) But then there's something ethereal about this one . . .

GRACE: Well, it's a question of which he'd respond to more . . . a hectic flush . . .

IVY: (*Whirls in the maroon.*)

GRACE: . . . *or* romantic pallor!

IVY: (*Whirls in the white.*)

GRACE: You can't have both at the same time!

IVY: (*Launches into an extraordinary flamenco-type dance in which she's fire and passion in the maroon, and then demure innocence in the white. She whips her skirts faster and faster, stomping her feet and tossing her head.*)

GRACE: (*Watches, dumbfounded. She gradually gets into the spirit and starts singing an accompaniment and clapping.*)

IVY: (*Finishes in a burst of brilliant alternating dips.*)

GRACE: (*Applauding wildly.*) BRAVO! . . . BRAVO! . . . I HAD NO IDEA YOU COULD DANCE LIKE THAT! YOU WERE REALLY TERRIFIC!

IVY: (*Out of breath.*) Thank you.

GRACE: SENSATIONAL!

IVY: Thank you. Thank you very much.

GRACE: You didn't tell me you were a dancer.

IVY: Thank you.

GRACE: You're incredible, absolutely . . . incredible!

IVY: It was nothing . . . really.

GRACE: I never would have guessed you could dance like that . . . never!

IVY: So, which one do you think I should get? (*She starts taking off the maroon dress.*)

I was supposed to be back at the office ten minutes ago. I promised Panda Schultz I'd help set up the appetizers.

GRACE: Here, let me help you.

IVY: The editorial department is doing the food and the art department is doing the drinks. The party starts at 6:30 sharp. Panda and I have got to have the appetizers ready and out by 6:30! The whole place is in an uproar because this is our first office party since Alex London joined the company and everyone is crazy about him . . . men as well as women! When he walks into a room secretaries collapse and senior editors walk into glass partitions. It's ridiculous! We're like a bunch of hysterical teenagers swooning in a locker room . . . (*Lowering her voice.*) You see, aside from his "animal thing," Alex London has the most beautiful mouth you've ever seen! It's the sort of mouth people jump off bridges for . . . you know, the kind with a very plump lower lip that's divided into two little mounds that are shaped sort of like rose petals . . . He isn't really all that good looking . . . medium height with greying hair, nondescript eyes, and a rather sallow complexion . . . he just has this phenomenal lower lip that drives everyone into a frenzy.

GRACE: (*Putting* IVY*'s dress over her arm.*) You don't have to tell *me* about lower lips! Kenny has a dimpled one and it's all Donna can do not to bite it off every time she sees him. It's half the reason she's marrying him, if you ask me.

IVY: It's going to be impossible to be noticed, everyone's dressing to kill!

GRACE: (*Holds the dress up to her.*) The trouble is, you can't really get the full effect when they're on at the same time.

IVY: All I'm hoping for is just three or four seconds of being *seen!* He doesn't have to speak to me. All I want is to be held in his eyes for a moment, actually *see* my reflection caught in his pupils . . . He's my boss, for God's sake! We speak to each other every day, but I can't seem to materialize when he looks at me! It's very scary because I feel as if I'm on fire with my whole body in flames . . .

GRACE: (*Holding the maroon dress up to herself.*) If only there were somehow *two* of you . . .

IVY: (*Starts taking off the white dress.*) Sometimes when I think about him, I feel myself starting to glow. It's true! Once when I was on the crosstown bus, I thought I saw him out the window and my face began to burn. I shut my eyes, afraid I was starting to radiate, my arms and face glowing like some huge iridescent firefly. Ever since the party was announced, I've been having this dream . . . well, it's more like a nightmare actually . . .

GRACE: (*To herself.*) I've got it, I've got it.

IVY: The big day has come, Panda and I have set up all the appetizers, and I'm standing over a plate of stuffed vine leaves and cherry tomatoes, marveling over the way she's arranged them in alternating rows of red and green . . . when far away, I see Alex London walking toward me . . . Well, the flush begins and I start popping vine leaves into my mouth. (*She reaches for the maroon dress.*) Maybe I should try on *this* one first . . .

GRACE: No, no, I have a hunch about the white one. Try it on.

IVY: But what about . . . ?

GRACE: Come on, just do what I say. I've got an idea.

IVY: The white one?

GRACE: (*Helping her into it.*) Honey, we don't have all day!

IVY: So, there I am . . . glistening with rice and olive oil all over my face as Alex London inches closer, and I mean . . . *inches!* It takes him forever to reach my table, but finally his face is right over me: the sallow complexion, the dull eyes, and of course that incredible mouth . . .

GRACE: Ah yes, don't forget the incredible mouth!

(*And she starts taking off her own dress . . .*)

IVY: I begin thinking of all the clever things I'll say to him. I try them out softly and my voice sounds marvelous, all deep and sexy like a movie star's . . . "Yoo hoo, Alex! I'm over here by the antipasto! My, but don't you look dashing tonight!"

GRACE: (. . . *and inconspicuously eases into the maroon dress.*)

IVY: But as usual, he doesn't see me. So I start jumping up and down, waving my arms . . . "HERE I AM . . . OVER BY THE VINE LEAVES AND CHERRY TOMATOES . . . YOO HOOO . . . !" Nothing . . . He looms closer and closer until his face is the size of a mountain range . . . "OVER HERE, ALEX, LOOK DOWN!" . . . I jab my elbows into his arms and stomach and then suddenly he's gone and Panda is standing next to me, wild-eyed and sobbing . . . "Have you heard?" she asks . . . "Alex London left the company. He cleared out his office this morning and no one has seen him since!" . . . For some reason, I'm not surprised or upset, but the rest of the office is in an uproar! Secretaries throwing themselves into punch bowls, research assistants slashing their wrists with hors d'oeuvres forks; broken glass everywhere. . . . It's now around two in the morning, everyone's gone home, and I'm at my desk typing: tappity tap tap tap tap tap! . . . When I notice something strange about the keys . . . they feel oddly soft and moist. I look down . . . Instead of keys, there are these tiny mouths . . . They're all Alex London's mouth! . . .

I'm so surprised, I try and pull my hands away, but they won't let go. They clamp their little lips around my fingers and hold on for dear life! It feels so strange because there are so many of them and they're so small . . . like exquisite tropical fish . . . "Alex, is that you?" I ask . . . "Are you hiding in my typewriter?" . . . but of course he doesn't answer. There's just this light smacking sound . . . My surprise gives way to delight as they swarm around my fingers, nibbling and sucking. Their lips are so soft . . . It's hard to describe because it sounds rather disgusting, when it was really quite . . . uh . . . *nice!*

GRACE: I thought *I* had strange dreams . . .

IVY: Eventually all the mouths become this one . . . huge . . . mouth, glistening and pulsing . . . reaching for my arms and shoulders, my neck and face . . .

GRACE: Please! No more!

IVY: Everything started to flood and dissolve . . .

GRACE: (*Linking arms, pulls* IVY *toward the mirror.*) Come on, that's enough of that! We've got to make our decision before the damned store closes on us.

IVY: Moonlight gushed through the window . . .

GRACE: (*Arms still linked, does a little pirouette.*)

IVY: (*Finally sees her.*) OH . . . MY . . . GOD!

GRACE: (*Enjoying the attention, does a deeper pirouette.*)

IVY: LOOK AT YOU! You put on the maroon dress . . .

GRACE: (*Twirling to show off all sides.*) Well . . . ?

IVY: (*Awestruck.*) You look . . . fabulous!

GRACE: (*Bursting with false modesty.*) Oh, it's nothing . . . really . . . I just . . .

IVY: WOW!

GRACE: Come on dear, I'm trying it on for *you!* So we can see them side by side . . .

IVY: I just never pictured you in a dress like this.

GRACE: Which do you like better?

IVY: (*More and more excited.*) WE LOOK LIKE TWINS!

(*They do a few chorus line kicks together.*)

GRACE: Come on, concentrate!

(*They eye themselves and then each other. A long pause.*)

IVY:	GRACE:
The white!	The white!

IVY: The white!

GRACE: The white!

IVY: NO CONTEST!

GRACE: The white.

IVY: (*Hugging her and spinning around.*) We did it, we did it!

GRACE: We did it, all right!

IVY: You were great, really great!

GRACE: Well, that's the first time I ever took my clothes off for a customer!

IVY: I couldn't have done it without you! (*She kisses* GRACE.) Thank you so much.

GRACE: Don't mention it.

IVY: You saved me. You really saved me!

GRACE: Well, I enjoyed it, though to be honest, I don't know what came over me. I mean, trying on the merchandise during store hours.

IVY: If Alex London doesn't notice me tonight. . .

GRACE: Oh, he'll notice you all right, don't worry about that! All you need is the right attitude!

IVY: (*Spinning and laughing.*) LOOK AT ME!

GRACE: It's like with Kenny's sister . . . she isn't born with legs, so she goes out and finds herself a pair!

IVY: LOOK . . . just . . . look!

GRACE: She doesn't lie around in some wagon or grocery cart waiting for someone to push her. She hauls herself over to the medical supply store and *gets* those legs with a nice little pair of feet to match!

IVY: (*Starts pulling the two sides of the mirror in on herself, sending out showers of light.*)

I'M BEAUTIFUL . . . I'M REALLY . . . BEAUTIFUL!

GRACE: When you stop to think about it, we're all hanging on for dear life! . . . This one has no legs, that one has a bunch of extra fingers, I'm deaf in one ear, you have trouble materializing . . . The whole thing is to keep going . . .

IVY: (*Giddy, pulls the mirror faster and faster.*)

LOOK . . . LIGHT IS POURING OUT OF ME . . . I'M LIKE A TROPICAL SUNSET . . . SOMETHING YOU SEE AT THE END OF A MOVIE . . . OH GOD . . . LOOK AT ME . . . JUST . . . LOOK!

(*Bach's soprano-alto duet returns as* IVY *shimmers and dazzles and . . .*)

THE CURTAIN FALLS

DAVID'S REDHAIRED DEATH

Sherry Kramer

DAVID'S REDHAIRED DEATH premiered at the Woolly Mammoth Theatre in Washington, D.C., in July 1991. It was directed by Tom Prewitt; the set design was by Keith Belli; the costume design was by Constance Campbell; and the lighting design was by Christopher Townsend. The cast was as follows:

JEAN	Kate Malin, Jennifer Mendenhall
MARILYN	Jennifer Mendenhall, Kate Malin

In the premiere production, the actors alternated the roles nightly.

CAST

JEAN: Her hair is deep, rich, dark auburn red. She is thirty.
MARILYN: Her hair is bright red, true, light red. She is thirty.

SETTING

The redhaired world is created, and then lost during the play—a transforming, non-static setting, constantly evolving or de-evolving.

The Redhead's bed is perched on what might be a ledge of a tall skyscraper—but there are elements of the natural world that have encroached on the man-made aspects of the structure. The 1970 royal blue Pontiac Tempest should be suggested in some way, and all set pieces should have active interaction with the characters and the two stage technicians.

All sound effects are created by the technicians, including music—a redhaired world melody, on vibes or some other bell-toned instrument is recommended, as is scoring throughout the play.

Costumers note: Redheads tend to wear deep forest green, not shades of red.

ACT ONE

JEAN: (*To the* AUDIENCE.) There was a time a person had only a hundred deaths, at best. In remote, isolated places forty or fifty had to do. When a man died, the only people who had his death were the members of his family, and those close enough to know him, day by day. And so consequently, no one ever went through life carrying the weight of more than several dozen deaths on top of them.

We have death differently now. The sheer volume of death in the global village demands it. Think how many people had Judy Garland's death, for instance. Hundreds of thousands. If not millions. In fact, she's still having them, in bars where female impersonators reign; in homes where late night movies are watched, alone; in poster shops; in the costumes of Halloween; in little girls' dreams down the yellow brick road.

I had a handful of those Judy Garland Deaths. I didn't know it at the time.

Since then I've had about a couple hundred thousand deaths, I guess. These are my deaths, in part:

My grandfather. Chips, our boxer. Ophelia. JFK. Christine Polchef, hit by a train on her way to church. Little Jim Carmichael, thrown from a car. Faust. Carmen. Everybody in *On the Beach,* the movie, and then much later, the book. Oscar Werner as a young German soldier turned traitor in a movie I can't remember, near the Berlin Wall. My mother's best friend. Tony Curtis in *Tarus Bulba*—Yul Brynner shoots him for betraying the Cossacks to the Poles. A bullet, through the shining Polish armor, straight into Tony's wavy black-haired heart—and mine. My father's mother. One fresh-faced crew member per week on *Star Trek*. During syndication, one a day. Villains in Westerns, spies during the '60s, boys in Vietnam—deaths I did not really have, but borrowed, the way I tried on a bracelet for a nineteen-year-old missing in action, whose name I forget, who never came home. Sydney What's-His-Name in *A Tale of Two Cities*. Eight nurses in Chicago. The six million who died. And David.

There are so, so many people in the world. All having deaths, over and over. We are not far away, I'm afraid, from a moment of critical mass, of geometric progression, when we are all carrying so many deaths that the system must collapse, like a black hole, must just consume itself in its own weight.

I feel the irreversible heaviness, the unnatural slowness already. Our deaths pile up on top of us. And one day their weight makes taking a step toward a person you love like carrying a brontosaurus on your back while dodging across eight lanes of L.A. traffic, with your teeth sunk into the dinosaur's tail to keep it from slipping. Once it falls you will never, ever be able to lift it up again. You will never be able to shoulder the weight of your deaths. And move toward someone you love.

When my brother David died he had—oh, at least a couple thousand deaths. And he's still having them, in all the people that loved him, and that he loved. A remembered joke he told—a pair of shoulders shaped like his, seen for an instant in a crowd—the most ordinary detail of the most ordinary day—reminds us of him . . . and David dies again. In those he loved.

This is the story of one of David's deaths. This is the death of David's that was had by two redheads. This is David's Redhaired Death.

(*Running her hand through her hair.*)

There have been times I've let it slip back into brownette, it's true, and in certain light, only my hairdresser can tell for sure. But I will always think of it as red, even after it is gray. Of course, even after it is gray, it will still be red—at least for awhile. Now the Redhead—

(*Lights up on* MARILYN. *She lies on a bed, on white sheets, asleep. The bed is perched on a ledge that suggests that of a tall skyscraper.*) (*Jean moves toward the bed.*)

—the other redhead—is a more honest redhead. Her hair is naturally the color mine is on purpose. She takes it several steps redder—brighter, but notice—

(*She lightly touches the* REDHEAD*'s hair.*)

—no brassy highlights—no give-away tones—she takes it to a shade found only on young Irish girls who live in the green hills where the deaths are still numbered in hundreds. Not hundreds of thousands.

This is the redhaired death of David's, one of many, not complete, not ever finished. Someday it will fade, like my hair, to a shade, a shadow, one lost in a crowd of shadows, like a mousy blond lost in the streets below. This is the redhaired death. The death of David's that was had by the two redheads, Marilyn and Jean—in this room, on this bed, in these arms.

David's Redhaired Death.

(*Two stage technicians appear as the light changes to a kind of moonlight. The technicians are tall, dark-haired men.*

JEAN *leaves the bed area.*

One technician begins the transformation of the bed area into the magical redhaired world—perhaps he hangs shell- and shrimp-colored mythic lingerie from a flying buttress, perhaps he spreads a luscious magenta-colored duvet over the sleeping REDHEAD*'s body—or perhaps the colors are green, deep forest green—and red arrives later in the transformation.*

The other technician blows a bit of dust into JEAN*'s hair, takes a large McDonald's Coke, and holds it up so* JEAN *can take a sip from it—the lid is loose, some spills down her blouse. He hands her a road map, a pair of sunglasses, a Shell credit card.*

She gets into her car.)

The road came up to meet me in Pennsylvania, then Ohio. I was on my way to the Redhead's in a royal blue 1970 Pontiac Tempest—a high seas cruiser of the highway, a six-cylinder, pre-auto emission standards Tempest—a boat of a car. But—as the sailors say—the water is your friend. It's the land you have to watch out for.

(*The Tempest makes hideous engine trouble sounds.*)

I ran aground outside Chicago.

(*The Tempest makes "grinding to a halt" noises.* JEAN *gets out, goes around to inspect the engine.*)

I pulled into a Texaco station, and trusted my car to the man who wears the star.

(*One of the technicians pops the hood, and looks inside. He shakes his head, sadly.*)

It was the transmission. Now the transmission turns out to be a closed black box, not unlike Pandora's. Once you open it up, you're stuck—there's no shutting the lid and going on. The sensible traveler, faced with transmission trouble, takes the roadside mechanic's advice and turns around and heads for home.

(JEAN *slaps the hood of the car shut, and climbs back in.*)

I ignored the mechanic's warning. What did a roadside mechanic know? I was on my way to the Redhead's. The mythical, magical redheads. And no power on earth could have gotten me to turn around and head for home.

(*One of the technicians holds a phone, some distance away from the stage. It rings, with a far-off sound.*)

MARILYN: At a midtown Holiday Inn hotel, a desk clerk is calling the fire department. This is the first of the calls that will trap us with David's death. There is a fire on the fourteenth floor.

JEAN: (*She puts the car in gear, continues driving. The Tempest makes unobtrusive, but odd engine noises.*) The Tempest raced strangely through the fading hills. I bought a few moments of daylight, chasing the sun west. Astronauts in space see the sun rise and set seven times a day. This is my version of *Fiddler on the Roof,* in space:

(*She starts off slow, then sings* VERY FAST.)

Sunrise, sunset. Sunrise, sunset. Sunrise sunset. SunriseSunset. Sunrisesunset Sunrisesunsetsunrisesunset.

(*Pause.*)

Anyway, the best the Tempest could do, from a dead stop, was sunrise, sunset . . . period. I knew that. It didn't stop me, though. I was on my way to the redhead's, the mythical, magical redhead's—and when I got there, it would be wonderful.

I remembered the first time.

(JEAN *takes a step in* MARILYN*'s direction.* MARILYN *gets out of bed and walks toward her. They stop several feet from each other.*)

MARILYN: Hi. You must be Jean.

JEAN: You're Marilyn.

MARILYN: Hello.

JEAN: I've heard a lot about you.

MARILYN: From Bob?

JEAN: From Bob.

MARILYN: Me too.

JEAN: Funny, you look different from the way I imagined you.

MARILYN: You too. You're a redhead.

JEAN: So are you.

MARILYN: You don't meet that many redheads.

JEAN: No, you don't.

MARILYN: Real redheads, I mean. Most redheads you meet come out of a bottle. Lady Clairol.

JEAN: L'Oréal.

(*Pause.*)

MARILYN: (*Lying.*) I'm a real redhead.

JEAN: (*Lying.*) So am I.

MARILYN/JEAN: You can always tell.

MARILYN: One redhead to another can always tell.

JEAN: (*To* AUDIENCE.) It was love at first sight. It was lots of giggling, lots of phone calls, lots of hidden picture looks across crowded rooms. We looked so special to each other. We looked so right. We each had a redhaired heart to look inside of, and see it as if it were our own hearts beating. No one could look at us the way we looked at each other.

People used to fear the redheaded woman—she had, they claimed, the power to witch a man, enchant him. As it turned out, the Redhead and I had tested out our powers on men for years. For all our lives. Now it was time to try it on an equal.

(*To* MARILYN.)

Nice to finally meet you.

MARILYN: Nice to meet you.

(*They cross the few feet between them, extend their hands and shake.* JEAN *realizes she has a French fry in her hand.*)

JEAN: Oh . . . I'll bet you're wondering what I'm doing with this French fry . . .

MARILYN: It is late when you arrive.

JEAN: No—

MARILYN: You are tired—

JEAN: Not yet—

MARILYN: You come to bed—

JEAN: (*To the* AUDIENCE.) A fall from a great height changes everything.

JEAN: Take a penny, for instance. If you drop one on the floor you probably don't—

MARILYN: Jean—(*She sighs.*) Bob warned me about you. (*Louder, insistent.*) BOB WARNED ME ABOUT YOU.

(*Jean stuffs the French fry back in her pocket, returns to Marilyn.*)

JEAN: Bob warned me about *you*.

MARILYN: He did?

JEAN: Bob's a slime.

MARILYN: Yes, he told me all about you.

JEAN: He told me about you.

MARILYN: Bob's a slime. I'll bet none of the things he told either of us about the other are true.

JEAN: He said be careful of Marilyn. She's a redhead.

MARILYN: He said be careful of Jean. The first time I met her, she wore a see-through blouse.

JEAN: It wasn't *really* see through.

MARILYN: *Mine was.*

(*Pause.*)

JEAN: Look—it's none of my business, but Bob told me that you and he were—

MARILYN: I'm not surprised. He says that about everyone.

JEAN: Everyone?

MARILYN: Yes. The story he told about you and him and a baby grand was sublime.

JEAN: The slime. Even if he were the last man on earth, I wouldn't touch him.

MARILYN: Yes. I'd let the human race die out before I'd touch that slime.

JEAN: You know, Bob has no shame.

MARILYN: None at all. One time I had to sit there and listen to him tell the story of my conquest of a Nobel Prize winner. He had this whole story, this fantasy, and he had the nerve to tell it to someone while I was sitting right there in front of him.

JEAN: So—what happened when you denied it?

MARILYN: The more you deny it, the more the other person thinks it's true.

JEAN: Was it?

MARILYN: Yes. A completely different Nobel Prize winner, but Bob is occasionally a lucky son of a bitch.

JEAN: So—what was it like?

MARILYN: Well, if you've heard Bob's version—

JEAN: No, tell me the real one. I've always wondered what it would be like with a Nobel Prize winner.

MARILYN: So did I. In many ways, Bob's version was far superior to mine. In Bob's version, the old man performs like a boy of seventeen, has a heart attack, and dies.

JEAN: And in yours?

MARILYN: The old man remains an old man. It takes a hell of a long time to win the Nobel Prize. I put on my clothes, he calls me a cab, I go home.

JEAN: And the heart attack—

MARILYN: Three days later.

JEAN: Had nothing to do with you.

MARILYN: Well . . . three days is a long time, but a girl can dream, can't she? I mean, he was a very old man. I mean, come on, haven't you ever . . . you know, wanted to believe you could kill a man by the way you looked? Construction workers, come on, you know. You're trying to get across the street, they're throwing their lunch buckets down in front of you, their tongues are hanging out, and they all claim to know exactly what you like to do at night. You can't tell me you don't want to turn toward the one who's yelling "Hey there, Red, I could die for you, baby"—open your coat wide, and give him the good long look that buries him?

(MARILYN *opens her robe, seductively, toward* JEAN. JEAN *takes a step in her direction, then hurries back to the Tempest.*)

JEAN: (*To* AUDIENCE.)It is almost dark. I am beginning to wish

I'd taken the mechanic's advice. But no one ever takes sound advice. In the story of Rapunzel, we focus on the Prince who makes it, on the one in a hundred who carries Rapunzel down her golden rope of hair. We forget all about the other ninety-nine guys who didn't make it. All the poor slobs who should have heeded the witch's warning, but didn't, who saw no reason why they shouldn't be the one to wrap their legs around Rapunzel's heavy plait of shining hair. And so I had faith that I would make it to the Redhead's. And that when I got there it would be wonderful.

This was our second meeting. On the way over to see her, I'd stopped at the 7-Eleven, to get some smokes. There are no accidents, and the Redhead and I smoked the same brand.

(*A technician gives her two packs of Camel filters.*)

Ever notice there's a naked man in the camel on the front of the pack?

(*She tosses one of the packs to* MARILYN. *Along with it at least one French fry goes sailing through the air.* JEAN *realizes she is still holding a French fry as well.*)

Oh—I'll bet you're wondering what I'm doing with this French fry.

MARILYN: It is late when you arrive.

JEAN: No, please, not yet—

MARILYN: You are tired.

JEAN: (*To the* AUDIENCE.) A fall from a great height changes everything.

MARILYN: What do you think you're doing, Jean!

JEAN: Take a penny, for instance. If you drop one on the floor, you probably don't even bother picking it up anymore.
If you drop a penny from the top of the Empire State Building, however, that penny transforms itself into the weight of—

MARILYN: This is not the way it happens, Jean.
It is late when you arrive.
You are tired,
you come to bed.
The phone rings.

(THE PHONE RINGS)

(*A technician carries the phone closer to the stage as it rings, still rings, still with a far-away sound.* JEAN *continues, falteringly.*)

—transforms itself into
the weight
of a thousand
or more pounds
on its way to the . . .

(JEAN *can't continue.*)

At the fire department, the central dispatcher is calling for backup, for extension ladders, for special upper-story crews. And in the Holiday Inn the alarms are ringing on every floor, in the hallways, in the bar, the coffee shop, the lobby. Guests are scurrying from their rooms, half-packed suitcases under their arms.

MARILYN: They are flooding into the elevators. They are rushing headlong down the stairs. They are pouring onto the street and staring up at the flames.

(*The technician moves the phone closer, it rings insistently.*)

An ambulance is called. The door to the burning room is jammed, or barricaded, and inside someone has started to scream.

JEAN: Ever notice there's a naked man in the camel on the front of the pack?

MARILYN: Jean, let's get it over with.

JEAN: Here's his leg, right where the camel's leg is—I can't believe Bob didn't show you too.

MARILYN: This just makes it harder. Let's get it behind us, move on—

JEAN: Here's his arm—he's holding it like this—

(*She demonstrates, using her arm.*)

MARILYN: Come to bed, Jean, let's get it over with—

JEAN: And here is his—

(*She indicates a large penis.*)

MARILYN: Jean I can't—

JEAN: You can't say you don't see it, Marilyn. It's the size of a small nuclear submarine.

MARILYN: I can't. Do this. I—

JEAN: Oh. I didn't realize it was so late—you must have other plans for dinner, I'll leave.

(*She turns, and starts to go.*)

MARILYN: NO!

JEAN: (*Pause.*) No, what?

MARILYN: Jean. Please. Don't do this.

JEAN: (*Prompting* MARILYN.) No, I don't have other plans . . .

MARILYN: (*Resigned.*) No, I don't have other plans.

JEAN: (*Still prompting.*) Do you want to go out . . .

MARILYN: Do you want to go out?

JEAN: And get . . .

MARILYN: And get . . .

(JEAN *waits.* MARILYN *gives in.*)

. . . something to eat?

JEAN: (*Thinks about it for an instant. Lightly.*) No.

MARILYN: (*Monotone, still an unwilling participant.*) You're sure? Because if you're on a diet or something, I know this great salad place, all kinds of—

JEAN: (*Seductively.*) Oh, I never bother with diets, not really. If I gain a pound or two, I just instinctively stop eating for a couple days. Don't you?

MARILYN: (*Can't help laughing. She is drawn in again.*) No. What planet are you from?

JEAN: (*They are both laughing now.*) It's just I ate already. At McDonald's. It's silly. Crazy. I have this thing about McDonald's.

(*To* AUDIENCE.)

The Redhead never even saw it coming. A McDonald's story was not exactly the usual redhead attack. Here we were, both orchestrating the subtle ways we would prove who was the stronger redhead, the better redhead, the deadlier redhead.

But I could tell that I didn't stand a chance against the Redhead with the usual redhead array, sultry looks, unspoken promises, that sort of thing. I had seen that right away.

So I circled around back and got the drop on her. With the McDonald's story.

(*To* MARILYN.)

I have this—thing—about McDonald's.

MARILYN: Tell me.

JEAN: (*As if embarrassed.*) Oh, no, you don't want to know.

MARILYN: But I do.

JEAN: Not really.

MARILYN: Cross my redhaired heart and hope to—

JEAN: Redhaired heart?

MARILYN: Yes. Don't you think of it like that?

JEAN: (*To* AUDIENCE.) This is the moment in the chronology of the redheads when the redhaired heart is officially carried out into the open like a 4-H club's nativity scene in a Christmas parade.

(*To* MARILYN.)

Yes.

MARILYN: I really want to hear about this thing you have about McDonald's. Cross my redhaired heart and hope to die.

JEAN: (*As if reluctant.*) Okay. If that's what you want.

(*She sits down next to* MARILYN *on the bed.*)

I was at McDonald's, ordering a Quarter Pounder with cheese—

(MARILYN *kisses her wrist.*)

—a large Coke—

(MARILYN *kisses the inside of her elbow.*)

—and a large fry—

(MARILYN *kisses her neck.*)

And in a midtown Holiday Inn hotel, my brother David . . .

(*She stops, lost, confused. She pulls away from* MARILYN, *leaps off the bed.*)

NO! . . . I was at McDonald's, ordering a Quarter Pounder with cheese, a large Coke, and a large fry, because ever since I was thirteen years old, and my parents told me I had to have a goal in life, I've had this plan. I wanted to order the exact same thing—a Quarter Pounder with cheese, a large Coke, a large fry—in Louisiana, in Mississippi, in Hawaii. In every state, in the map I got from McDonald's marking every Golden Arch-marked town. I wanted to say the same eleven words, pay with a five-dollar bill, receive the exact same change. Eat identical food, identically, ritualistically—three French fries, one bite of burger, one sip of Coke. I knew in advance that the decor would inevitably vary—Townhouse McDonald's, with their fake exposed brick. Country Cottage McDonald's, with rough-hewn plastic stones littering the floor. And in Missouri, they say, there is the Taj Mahal of McDonald's—costing over a million dollars to build, with three different theme eating areas featuring one hundred thousand dollars worth of rare antiques, all bolted down. And in the Dutch decorated room is a portrait of Ronald McDonald after the school of Van Eyk. And in another, the French room, he's painted in a Renior-like shimmer of light. And in the third, he's the all-male Western Ronald, sitting high in the saddle on a brave, earth-tone range. His ten-gallon hat pushed jauntily back, on his mop of bright red hair.

(*To* AUDIENCE.)

Of course, things rarely work out the way they're planned. Here I was expecting a nice, easy fight—while I was charming the Redhead with the story of my life plan for McDonald's—which is a true story, but an insane one, its insanity being the secret of its charm—I'd be bringing up my heavy artillery on the side. Bring the Redhead under my spell, and waste her.

Instead, the Redhead decided to get the drop on me.

If there was any hope of our avoiding a very intense, very

messy, very up and down, up and down kind of unnatural redhair affair, after what was only the tip of the iceberg of the McDonald's story, it was gone as soon as the Redhead made the first move. To her cigarettes.

(*Marilyn opens her pack of Camel filters.*)

It was a standard in the redhaired arsenal. I reached for mine.

(*She does.*)

The lighting up, while gazing into the eyes.

(*They light up, gaze into each other's eyes, etc. They are like gunslingers, facing each other down.*)

The long inhale . . . the longer exhale. The gauzy smoke caressing the face. The cigarette that makes the victim think she's looking across at the mysteries of Greta Garbo—who wasn't a redhead, but should have been.

(*They continue to smoke and seduce.*)

I matched the Redhead's movements. She matched mine. She was good. She was complete. She thought she had the drop on me.

And then it happened.

MARILYN/JEAN: (*Starts seductively, on the exhale.*) A LITTLE CLOSER TO HEAVEN . . . WITH A CIGARETTE IN MY HAND . .

(*They look at each other, incredulously.*)

A little closer to heaven with a cigarette in my hand?

Oh—

(*They begin laughing.*)

I don't believe it—

MARILYN: The exact same line—

MARILYN: (*Very slow.*)	JEAN: (*Very fast.*)
I don't	I don't believe it! (*Normal speed.*)
believe it!	It's one of my favorite
(*Normal speed.*) Yes, I guess Bob told you it was *my* favorite line.	lines!
Oh, God.	But I don't remember using it on Bob—he must have seen me use it on someone else.
What?	The slime.

JEAN: Well who else could have told you?

MARILYN: Told me what?

JEAN: That line, told you to use my favorite line.

MARILYN: That's my favorite line.

JEAN: I don't believe it—

MARILYN: I don't believe it!

JEAN: (*To* AUDIENCE.) We couldn't fucking believe it. We quickly checked to see if we were the same person.

(*To* MARILYN, *as the technicians make the final changes that transform the bed area into the mythical, magical redhaired world.*)

I've got a younger brother, an older brother.

MARILYN: I've got a younger brother, an older brother.

JEAN: I've got a grandmother I call Nano.

MARILYN: I've got a grandmother I call Nana.

JEAN: Nana?

MARILYN: Nano . . .

JEAN: Well, adjusting for regional dialect differences—

MARILYN: Yes, it's exactly the same.

JEAN: I love my family.

MARILYN: I love mine too.

JEAN: I loved my family, very much, but growing up I knew I was different.

MARILYN: I loved my family, very much, but I didn't fit in.

JEAN/MARILYN: Every day of my life I had to wear this scarlet letter that said: DO NOT PASS GO.

MARILYN: DO NOT FIT IN.

JEAN: It started fading—but it was—

JEAN/MARILYN: —too late by then.

MARILYN: It started fading too late to fit in.

JEAN: (*Pause. They both pull back, overwhelmed.*) Spooky, huh?

MARILYN: Coincidence. Coincidence, that's all it is, it's just—

JEAN: I have been waiting all my life to recognize someone the way I recognize myself.

MARILYN: The way I recognize you.

JEAN: The way I recognize you.

MARILYN: Here's what I've done while I've been waiting. Here's what I've been doing while I've been hunting you: I love Sam Shepard's plays. I wear Ralph Lauren perfume. I eat Chinese food. I prefer blue ink over black, black clothing over blue There are the facts of how I've hunted you.

JEAN: Me too. And we both smoke Camel filters.

MARILYN: Which will be very convenient, when one or the other of us runs out.

JEAN: I'm really trying to quit.

MARILYN: Who isn't? I'll bet every pack of Camel filters that's sold is bought by a Camel filter smoker who wants to quit.

(*They smoke.*)

JEAN: Once I fell in love with a man I thought I recognized.

JEAN: I must have met that man a hundred times.

JEAN: But the more familiar he looks over dinner, the better the chances are he'll be almost unrecognizable by midnight.

MARILYN: A total stranger by three A.M.

JEAN: A bad memory by morning.

MARILYN: You think you recognize him every time, but it turns out he doesn't want anything interesting—

MARILYN: Or remarkable—

JEAN: —or enduring from you.

MARILYN: It turns out, that if most men were women, you'd call them—

JEAN/MARILYN: Whores.

JEAN: You'd think a redhead would be immune.

MARILYN: But even a redhead can't help going back for more.

JEAN: (*A sigh of longing.*) Men.

MARILYN: All those men.

JEAN: So what if they're whores—the things you can find out from them!

MARILYN: Amazing, isn't it?

JEAN: And for a redhead, so goddamn easy.

MARILYN: Like taking candy from a baby.

JEAN: All those men.

MARILYN: You know, it's funny, but I don't think any of them were ever redheads.

JEAN: I wonder why.

MARILYN: I never consciously ruled out redheads.

JEAN: Just aren't that many of them around.

MARILYN: Maybe only redhaired girls grow up to be redheads. I remember my father telling my brothers, when we were little: You can take out all the flashy blondes you want, do what you want with them in the back seat of the car. But when you marry—marry mousy brown.

JEAN: Your father really said that?

MARILYN: But what do you do with the redheads, I wanted to ask him. He never said, he knew. Redhaired girls are supposed to fade into brown! That's where all the little redhaired boys are, Jean. Everyone of them's faded into marrying brown.

JEAN: But not us.

MARILYN: Not us.

JEAN: Not yet.

MARILYN: If I have one life to live—

JEAN: Let me live it as a redhead.

MARILYN: Let me make it to the drugstore before the roots start to show.

JEAN: Let me choose a soft, natural, but vibrant color.

MARILYN: With no brassy highlights, no give-away tones.

JEAN: Lead me not into temptation by colors called—(*Painful to say.*) Racy Spiced Wine.

MARILYN: Red Hot Rose.

JEAN: Fuchsia Plum.

MARILYN: I almost bought some Fuchsia Plum the other day.

JEAN: Me too!

MARILYN: I took it from the shelf. I had it in my hand!

JEAN: I couldn't do it. I chickened out.

MARILYN: So much for your brave, true redhaired heart, I said.

JEAN: But if we went in together—

MARILYN: The two of us together—

JEAN: The redhaired badge of courage—

MARILYN: We'd be strong enough together.

JEAN: We'd buy all the Fuchsia Plum they had. To hell with "only your hairdresser knows for sure."

MARILYN: To hell with 'em all! Let 'em know, the minute we walk into a room. Our hair dyed the exact same shade.

JEAN: Double your redhead pleasure.

MARILYN: Double your redhaired fun.

JEAN: And be twins.

MARILYN/JEAN: (*They lock arms.*) PRESENTING—FOR ONE LIFE ONLY—THE SWEET AND FUNNY REDHAIRED TWINS!!!!!

(*They do a little vaudeville bit, kicking and swaying to the theme song from the Patty Duke show.*)

They dye their hair alike
They smoke alike
They love alike
They joke alike
You could lose your miiiiiiiind—

(*The phone rings.* MARILYN *pulls away from* JEAN, *leaving her in the middle of the big kick.*)

JEAN: When redheads—are—two—

MARILYN: That was just a game.

JEAN: It was a real game.

(*The phone continues to ring.*)

MARILYN: Maybe to you.

JEAN: It was real.

MARILYN: Not any more.

JEAN: It was a real game and we loved to play it. No matter how many times the phone rings, we loved to play that game.

MARILYN: (*The phone continues to ring, as the technician brings it almost to the edge of the stage.*) The calls are getting closer, tracking Jean down. They are getting a bead on her from the imprint on the Master Card David used when he checked in to the hotel. A computer somewhere in Atlanta is printing out a phone number and an address.

(*Marilyn moves toward the bed area.*)

It is late when you arrive.

JEAN: It wasn't a game—

MARILYN: You are tired—

JEAN: You wanted this. You wanted a sister to stand up for you when your brothers teased you.

MARILYN: You come to bed—

JEAN: (JEAN *grabs* MARILYN, *whispers in her ear.*) You loved your family, your family loved you, but right there at the beginning, it was always there—the raven black-haired family wheeling along the baby carriage filled with red hair.

MARILYN: (*Insistently.*) It is late when you arrive.

JEAN: "You can't be our little sister, our little sister has black hair."

MARILYN: (*Still trying.*) You are tired, you come to bed.

JEAN: "Somebody stole our real little sister and gave us a flame head. A carrot top."

MARILYN: (*Can't help joining in.*) "A marmalade brain."

JEAN: "Scarlet O'Heada—"

MARILYN: "We're gonna trade you in an' get our real sister back."

JEAN: My brother Jim said there was just one chance.

MARILYN: To be like them.

JEAN: To finally fit in.

MARILYN: If I cut it all off, all the way down, when it grew back in, it'd grow in black.

JEAN: I asked my brother David, but he just laughed. Even if I pulled it out by the roots, he said, it still wouldn't grow in black.

MARILYN: I had all this lovely, long golden red hair. Everybody was always telling my mother it would be a tragedy to cut it. It would be a crime to wear it short.

JEAN: I wasn't strong enough, but my brother Jim said he would help me do it. We went into my bedroom, and Jim locked the door. He had me hold onto the doorknob, and then he took a big handful of my hair.

He started pulling. It hurt. It burned. I screamed but he wouldn't stop. David pounded on the door, he yelled for Jim to stop. Jim had me by the hair, he was dragging me across the room. I grabbed a hanger from the closet and swung it at Jim as hard as I could. It was an accident, really.

(*They are giggling together.*)

It caught him through the lip. I had him on the hook of the hanger like a big black-haired fish.

(JEAN *stops laughing.*)

And then the door gave way. David rushed in, my father right behind him, he took one look at Jim's lip, and came at me with his belt. But David wouldn't let him touch me.

I cried all night and David held me. He said "I'm going to hold you until it's all right." And in the morning, when he let go of me, it was.

It took a year for the hair that Jim had pulled out to grow back in. A whole year I waited for it to grow in black.

MARILYN: But it didn't grow in black.

JEAN: No. It grew in mousy brown. It didn't grow in black. And I never looked the same.

(*They are touching each other's hair, stroking it softly.*)

But if I'd had a redhaired sister—

MARILYN: (*Whispering.*) A redhaired sister . . . I always wanted a redhaired sister . . .

JEAN: (*Whispering.*) All my own.

(*They continue to touch and caress, but they don't kiss. They continue until the phone rings.*)

MARILYN: (*Dreamy.*) Do you believe in miracles, Jean?

JEAN: I believe in McDonald's.

MARILYN: You've got a point. McDonald's is not exactly likely. Given all the possibilities for life on earth, McDonald's is not what you'd expect.

Do you think, on the scale of things, that what is happening to us is more probable than McDonald's, or less?

JEAN: (*To* AUDIENCE, *as they embrace, over the* REDHEAD*'s shoulder.*) The Redhead couldn't believe what was happening to her. Neither could I. We were hypnotized, but wide awake at the same time. No matter what I said, it was right. No matter what the Redhead did, it was perfect. This was love—infinite, redhead, and pure. There were no odd angles, no extra digits, this was it. This was the enchanted redhead world where no matter what story I told, it was always the McDonald's story, and the McDonald's story was anything I goddamn wanted it to be.

I held the Redhead close. It was . . . confusing . . . I wanted to hold her, to do nothing but hold her, to not stop holding her, but when we touched, her skin was dry, and rough, like sandpaper, she scraped against my skin. It was confusing . . . but it was also wonderful. It was part of the redhead world, wasn't it?

(*To* MARILYN.)

Marilyn, I—

MARILYN: Yes?

JEAN: Marilyn, I want to—

MARILYN: Yes?

JEAN: Marilyn, I—

MARILYN: Say it, Jean.

JEAN: (*About to kiss* MARILYN.) Marilyn, I—

(*The phone rings, as the technician brings it to the edge of the stage.* JEAN *breaks away from* MARILYN, *returns to the Tempest.*)

(*To* AUDIENCE.)

I am a hundred miles away from the Redhead's, on the outskirts of Madison when it happens.

MARILYN: The fire has grown, engulfing the hotel room, billowing out from it like a giant red flare. The ladder has been extended, a fireman smashes the flames back with a stream of water and leans in through the shattered window. He extends his hand. The man in the room looks at him, confused, pushes him aside, and goes out the window. He reaches the ground in less time than it takes to say, less time than it takes to tell.

(*The phone rings again as the technician moves it onto the stage.*)

JEAN: A call makes its way to my mother and father within an hour. They are listed as credit references on my brother's Master Card.

(*A technician hands* JEAN *a gift-wrapped package as she steps out of the Tempest.*)

MARILYN: You know what I want?

(MARILYN *lights up a cigarette, offers one to* JEAN.)

JEAN: This was our third time together. Things were happening fast, even for redheads. And redheads like things fast. It's not how long you make it—it's how you make it long.

(*She takes the cigarette.*)

MARILYN: I want a cigarette that shuts off at exactly the right instant. I want a Camel filter that knows.

(JEAN *surprises* MARILYN *with the gift—it contains a sexy negligee.* MARILYN *puts it on.*)

JEAN: I do too. All the things you're thinking, I'm thinking too. I am thinking how you smell, I am thinking that I also wear Ralph Lauren's perfume. I am thinking I like Sam Shepard, Chinese food, prefer blue ink to black, black clothing over blue. I am thinking about what touching you will do. I am thinking we are in trouble, or in Paradise.

(*To* AUDIENCE.)

Who had time to choose?

(*To* MARILYN, *as she comes out to model the negligee.*)

I love you.

MARILYN: I love you.

(*They touch each other's hair, then stop.*)

Well. What do you think we should do about this?

JEAN: We could call up Bob. He's spreading some very interesting rumors about us.

MARILYN: We could call up Bob, ask him what he's been saying about us, and then do it.

MARILYN/JEAN: He's such a slime.

JEAN: It'd almost be worth it just to do it, just so we could call him up and thank him for introducing us. Rub it in that we're doing it with each other and not with him.

MARILYN: Yes. It's the kind of thing that could kill a slime like Bob.

JEAN: This is getting confusing, Marilyn.

MARILYN: I know.

JEAN: Really, really confusing.

MARILYN: I know.

JEAN: I'm not used to things like this being confusing.

MARILYN: No, not for a redhead.

JEAN: Never for a redhead.

MARILYN: It wasn't even all that confusing when I was with that woman before.

JEAN: It didn't sound confusing.

MARILYN: It wasn't. It was really fun. Good, clean schoolgirl fun.

JEAN: I remember when everything was good clean schoolgirl fun.

MARILYN: Yes.

JEAN: Where I went to school, it was just thought of as part of the liberal arts degree. Since then, I really haven't thought about it at all.

MARILYN: I thought it would be sweet, and funny. And easy. It's always been easy before, right?

JEAN: Always. Even when it looked like love.

MARILYN/JEAN: It always looked like love.

JEAN: But this is hard.

MARILYN: And it is love.

JEAN: And it's confusing.

MARILYN: (*She sighs.*) Maybe we should have done it before . . . before we got to be twins.

JEAN: I wonder why we didn't think of it then.

MARILYN: Just think, it'd be out of the way, we could get on with being the redheads.

JEAN: But we'll still be the redheads after, won't we?

MARILYN: Of course.

JEAN: I mean, even after it's—over?

MARILYN: Jean—who says it's ever going to be over?

JEAN: Oh.

(*Beat. They pull away from each other by a fraction of an inch. To* AUDIENCE.)

We had reached a critical impasse in the redhaired affair.

MARILYN: (*Sighing.*) Do you know what life is like, Jean?

JEAN: I know what McDonald's is like.

MARILYN: This can't go on, Jean.

JEAN: I know.

MARILYN: We have to move on—

JEAN: I know.

MARILYN: Next time.

JEAN: All right.

MARILYN: Cross your redhaired heart?

JEAN: Cross my redhaired heart. I promise. Next time.

(JEAN *returns to the Tempest, as* MARILYN *lies down in bed, and sleeps. To* AUDIENCE.)

I was almost at the Redhead's. Just another thirty or forty miles. I had not taken the mechanic's advice and I had made it. Not only that, but I was making it in record redhead to redhead time.

(*The technician moves the phone to the* REDHEAD*'s bedside table. The phone rings, at the* REDHEAD*'s.*)

The Redhead is a heavy sleeper, the Redhead is a deep, unreachable dream. My mother lets it ring and ring and ring.

(*The ringing stops.*)

An hour later, she'll have to make the call again. But for the moment, for an hour, David's death has been delayed.

And I am racing toward it. Eighty-five, ninety miles an hour. How did the crippled Tempest manage such speeds? Like a horse in the Black Stallion series, whose leg has been shattered in the crush of flying hooves at the starting gate, and runs to the finish line on heart alone.

(*The Tempest makes valiant transmission dying noises.*)

I had worn the transmission down to the bone, the way the princess in the fairy tale wore out three pairs of stone shoes and broke three stone walking sticks on her way to her true love. She also sucked three stone loaves down to pebbles. I went to . . . McDonald's.

(*As if McDonald's employees at a drive-through, the two technicians prepare and load a McDonald's bag for* JEAN, *and hand it to her.*)

I ordered a Quarter Pounder with cheese, a large Coke, and a large fry. I was ten miles from the Redhead's, but I needed that last sacred pit stop. The drive-through is a blessing for the traveler who cannot turn back.

(*The Tempest races on for an instant, then sputters to a halt, and dies* JEAN *leaves the Tempest. She opens the bag, takes out a French fry, and places it on the ground behind her. She leaves a trail of French fries, as she arrives at the* REDHEAD*'s.*)

I arrived at the Redhead's.

This was it. We had it all mapped out. We had a double redhead plan. Cross our redhaired hearts. We had agreed.

(*She bends down and kisses* MARILYN *lightly on the forehead.* MARILYN *wakes, reaches out to* JEAN, JEAN *reaches to embrace her. They both realize* JEAN *has a French fry in her hand.*)

Oh—I'll bet you're wondering what I'm doing with this French fry.

MARILYN: As a matter of fact, I am.

JEAN: (*To the* AUDIENCE.) A fall from a great height changes everything.

MARILYN: Stop it Jean—there's no where else to go, Jean—JEAN!

JEAN: Take a penny for instance. If you drop one on the floor, you probably don't even bother picking it up anymore.

MARILYN: You are tired, you come to bed.

JEAN: If you drop a penny from the top of the Empire State Building, however—

MARILYN: You do not tell this story. It is too late. You come to bed. The phone rings.

JEAN: (*To* MARILYN, *triumphant.*) But the phone rings *after* I come to bed. It is late when I arrive, I come to bed, and the phone rings *after* I come to bed, right?

MARILYN: Right, but—

JEAN: No buts. Here we go.

A fall from a great height changes everything. If you drop a penny from the top of the Empire State building, that penny transforms itself into the weight of a thousand or more pounds on its way to the ground. On a good day, not too much wind, the penny will be embedded a good foot into the concrete, straight down. If you drop a woman from the top of the Empire State Building, however—

MARILYN: No.

JEAN: No what?

MARILYN: It's not your story.

JEAN: Maybe I didn't start it well enough. All right. I'll start it again. A FALL FROM A GREAT HEIGHT CHANGES—

MARILYN: It's not your story! So it doesn't matter how you start it or if you finish it. The phone rings. Come to bed.

JEAN: I was at McDonald's—

MARILYN: You do not tell a McDonald's story! It is late, you are tired, you come to bed. The phone rings.

JEAN: If the phone hadn't rung, I might have told it.

MARILYN: You didn't.

JEAN: I meant to. I meant to tell you the most magnificent McDonald's story of them all. And maybe it would have taken forever to tell. Maybe, with the laughing, and the holding, and the smoking, I could have made the McDonald's story last until the end of time. Told it until there was only you and me and the McDonald's story. The story of each of the billions sold. You and me in each other's arms.

I ask you—one redhead to another—can it be done?

MARILYN: No.

JEAN: I think you're lying. I think that in a world, a parallel redhead world where the McDonald's story is always being told, the phone doesn't ring. Maybe there are no phones. Maybe Alexander Graham Bell was dropped on his head as an infant or something, I don't know. But in that world, as long as the McDonald's story is being told, David is still alive.

MARILYN: It is late when you arrive.

JEAN: No.

MARILYN: You come to bed.

JEAN: (*To the* AUDIENCE, *desperately, she returns to the Tempest area.*) I was at McDonald's, you see, and I'd had all this car trouble. Radiator, water pump, thermostat, it was coming every fifty miles or so—

MARILYN: (*She's had enough.*) Jesus Fucking Christ—who the hell do you think you are, Jean!

JEAN: —but nothing my Shell credit card and I couldn't handle. Then the transmission started acting up outside Chicago.

MARILYN: You've got French fries all over my room—

JEAN: I should have turned around and headed home—

MARILYN: —you change the subject every thirty seconds or so—

JEAN: —any sane person would have. I have, but nooooooo-ooo—

MARILYN: And this fucking negligee—

JEAN: I was on my way to the Redhead's. The mythical, magical Redhead's. I'll be safe if I can just make it to the Redhead's.

MARILYN: —don't let me get started on this fucking negligee, I'm warning you—

JEAN: You never loved me.

MARILYN: OH FUCK OFF.

(*Pause.*)

I did love you.

(*Pause. Gently.*)

Once I fell in love with a redhead.

(*She reaches out her hand to* JEAN.)

Once I looked at her. And when she looked at me, we were both the double redheads, the most powerful woman in the world. The redhead seen by the redhead seeing the redhead. If we had wanted, we could have been the redhaired death of the world.

JEAN: (*Crying.*) Then why didn't it work, why?

MARILYN: It is late when you arrive. You are laying a trail of French fries up to my bed.

(*She can't help a little smile.*)

I did love you. You know I loved you.

(MARILYN *gets back into bed, as* JEAN *takes another French fry out of the bag, slowly puts it down. She arrives at the* REDHEAD*'s, as before, and wakes her, as before.*)

JEAN: Oh. I bet you're wondering what I'm doing with this French fry?

MARILYN: Well, as a matter of fact—yes. I am.

JEAN: Isn't it obvious?

MARILYN: No.

JEAN: I'm leaving a trail so I can find my way back to the Tempest.

MARILYN: Something's happened to the Tempest—

JEAN: Yes.

(*She is laying down more French fries, she is almost to the bed.*)

It's tragic.

(*She plops down on the bed.*)

It's the transmission.

MARILYN: I'm sorry. What is the transmission, really?

JEAN: I have no idea. Except it's gone.

MARILYN: Where did you have to leave the car?

JEAN: Two blocks. Two blocks, and I would have made it. It could be worse. If it had happened out on the highway, I would never have had enough French fries.

MARILYN: Oh, Jean, I'm sorry.

JEAN: Well, anyway, I'm here.

MARILYN: Jean—you've been crying.

JEAN: It was a very difficult parting.

(*Pause.*)

I'll tell you all about it in the morning.

(*Pause.*)

So.

(*Pause.*)

Anyway, I got here.

MARILYN: Yes.

JEAN: I've missed you.

MARILYN: I've missed you.

(*They start to really kiss, but quickly shift to fast pecks on the cheek. Nervously, stalling:*)

So. You made good time, though?

JEAN: Yes. All things considered.

(*They attempt to kiss and embrace again, but back off shyly again.*)

MARILYN: You . . . hungry?

JEAN: Well, I stopped at—

MARILYN: Oh, right—

JEAN/MARILYN: McDonald's.

(*Pause. They try to kiss again.*)

JEAN: But if *you're* hungry—

MARILYN: No, not really, I—

(*She leaps out of bed.*)

THIS IS MAKING ME CRAZY!

JEAN: The sweet and funny twins lose their minds. Over nothing, really.

MARILYN: We agreed—

JEAN: I know. No more dancing around it.

MARILYN: No more talking it to death.

JEAN: No more talk. Action!

MARILYN: We agreed. I am not seducing you. You are not seducing me. We are both in this together.

MARILYN/JEAN: We both get to be the redhead.

MARILYN: I am not going to wait for you to kiss me. You are not going to wait for me to kiss you.

JEAN: All right.

MARILYN: Okay.

(*They both wait. They cannot keep a straight face after a moment or two.*)

JEAN: What are you waiting for Marilyn?????

MARILYN: What are you waiting for, Jean????????

JEAN: Marilyn?

MARILYN: Jean?

JEAN: I'm not the one waiting.

MARILYN: Well it's certainly not me.

JEAN: I think you're waiting . . .

MARILYN: Not me . . .

(*They are playing cat and mouse on the bed.*)

JEAN: You were too—

MARILYN: No, you were the one waiting—

JEAN: I saw you waiting . . . I definitely saw you waiting . . .

(*To* AUDIENCE.)

We didn't know it, of course, but we were waiting. For the phone to ring.

MARILYN: You are really asking for it.

(*She starts tickling* JEAN. JEAN *tickles back.*)

JEAN: Who me?

MARILYN: Yes, you!

(*She tickles* JEAN *more aggressively.*)

Come here—

(*She grabs* JEAN, *they kiss for an instant on the lips,* JEAN *pulls back.*)

JEAN: You promise we'll still be the redheads?

MARILYN: I promise.

JEAN: No matter what?

MARILYN: We'll be the redheads forever. No matter what.

(*They come together, a long true kiss. The phone rings, they explode into laughter.*)

Oh, no.

(*They are laughing too hard to continue the kiss. They flop on their backs, giggling.*)

Should I answer it, or let it ring? Maybe it'll stop.

JEAN: Maybe, if we just ignore it—

MARILYN: Go back to where we were—

JEAN: Now, where were we—

(*They try to embrace and kiss again, but the phone keeps ringing, and they're laughing too hard.*)

You might as well get it. Maybe it's Bob, with sex tips for girls.

MARILYN: (*Marilyn crawls toward the phone.*) How CAN you bring up Bob at a time like this!

(*Answering the phone.*)

Hello?

JEAN: (*Sudden light change—spotlight on* JEAN.) And so David's Redhaired Death begins like this.

(*blackout*)

ACT TWO

MARILYN: (JEAN *lies on the bed, as at the end of* ACT ONE. MARILYN *moves downstage, addressing the* AUDIENCE.) A fall from a great height changes everything.

If you drop a penny from the top of the Empire State building, that penny transforms itself into the weight of a thousand or more pounds on its way to the ground. On a good day, not too much wind, the penny will be embedded a good foot into the concrete, straight down. If you drop a woman from the top of the Empire State Building, however, she is transformed into that famous picture that appeared in LOOK. She is lovely, and young, and perfectly dressed in a trim suit. Her blonde hair flows gently in waves that frame an angelic face. She is wearing gloves, but her shoes are gone, as if she has only just kicked them off before falling into what looks to be a deep, soft, rich feather bed. She lies there, an innocent, peaceful smile on her face, like an exhausted child who has succumbed to sleep the instant she hit the bed, too tired to pull the covers over her, too weary to squirm and disturb the perfect impression she has made on the satin coverlet—each line leading into the valley that cradles her body is clean, sharp, distinct. The photographer must have caught her in the instant after she lay down to sleep—in a moment, of course, the feather bed will flatten out, the satin—a dark, silky satin that shines where it catches the light—the satin will smooth out again, all the lines will be erased. But the caption under the picture reads: A TRAGIC SUICIDE. The soft, bright feather bed beneath the beautiful girl is in fact the crumpled roof of a Dodge. And they can carry the broken girl's body away, the photographer can take his prize and go on home. But the imprint of the body on the roof of the Dodge will remain.

I saw that picture for the first time in my pediatrician's waiting room, I was in for a polio booster, or a tetanus shot. I was eight or nine years old.

Later the photograph turned up in a collection of THE BEST FROM LOOK that we kept on our coffee table. I could look at that picture for hours. She was so beautiful. She was as lovely as Snow White, as Sleeping Beauty—lovelier than both of them rolled together. But there was a catch. She would sleep, and there would be no prince. She was sleeping for no one. It would be forever wasted sleep.

I knew that she must have done it for love, but I was too young to really care. No, what bothered me was the Dodge. What I thought about while I looked at that picture was the moment after the picture was taken. When the owner of the Dodge returned.

I imagine the man, with his family—a family like our family, his nicely dressed wife, his three spoiled children, just down from a trip up the Empire State Building. The children are fighting about who will sit in the middle this time, I sat in the middle last time. Their father herds them along, he is in a hurry, worried about the meter. They have wasted too much time at the souvenir stand, parking tickets are expensive, do his children think money grows on trees? They round the corner, and come upon the place where they have parked their car. It takes several seconds for them to realize that they are looking at their Dodge.

And I wondered, too, just how romantic the photograph would have been if the family had not been at the souvenir stand so long. If they had been all loaded up and ready to go, the children squirming and elbowing each other in the back seat, their father checking a road map in the front. If they had come between a falling body and the ground.

The world is full of things that are falling.

(*She returns to the bed, touches the phone.*)

It was Jean's mother on the line.

(MARILYN *moves away from the bed.* MARILYN *uses a controlled, blank tone for* JEAN*'s mother and father, no color, only calm, relentless pain.* JEAN *builds in terror and loss.*)

JEAN: (*Sitting up.*) Mom? What's wrong—

MARILYN: Is Marilyn with you?

JEAN: Yes, why? What's—

MARILYN: Jean, it's David.

JEAN: What's wrong.

MARILYN: There's been a . . . accident.

JEAN: No.

MARILYN: Honey, he's . . . Jean, he's dead.

JEAN: Mom—

MARILYN: We don't know really how it happened, we're all in . . . shock, they say.

JEAN: No.

MARILYN: (*Pause.*) Marilyn is with you?

JEAN: Yes.

MARILYN: Good. That's good.

JEAN: Where's Dad?

MARILYN: Right here.

JEAN: Can I talk to him?

MARILYN: Yes.

JEAN: (*Pause.*) I love you mom—

MARILYN: (*Cutting her off.*) I love you too so very, very much—

(*As* MARILYN, *to* AUDIENCE.)

Jean's mother cannot go on. She has no right, she knows, to have gotten this far.

JEAN: Daddy?

MARILYN: "We want you to know how much we love you" Jean's father says, in half a voice.

JEAN: I know, I know. Daddy I wish I was with you, I—

MARILYN: I know. We've already made the reservation—there's a flight that will get you here a little after noon. Leaves at six-thirty your time. Can your friend Marilyn drive you?

JEAN: Yes.

MARILYN: Good. That's good.

JEAN: (*She begins to get hysterical.*) But the Tempest—I can't leave the Tempest, the transmission—

MARILYN: What?

JEAN: I had to leave the Tempest on the road, it—it—

MARILYN: Don't worry about the car right now, honey.

JEAN: Okay, Daddy, okay.

MARILYN: Sweetheart?

JEAN: Yes?

MARILYN: I love you.

JEAN: I love you Daddy. Daddy—

(*She begins to break.*)

MARILYN: I have to see about your mother, she—

JEAN: (*Keeping it in.*) Okay.

MARILYN: You'll be all right?

JEAN: Yes.

MARILYN: I hate you being up there all alone, honey.

JEAN: I'll be home tomorrow, I'll be home.

MARILYN: Tomorrow. Yes. If we can just make it through—

JEAN: Daddy—Daddy—

(*It comes rushing at her again.*)

—how can this be happening to us—

MARILYN: You try and get some sleep.

JEAN: This can't be happening—

MARILYN: Sweetheart I love you.

JEAN: Daddy it can't be happening—

MARILYN: We've got to call Jim still, sweetheart.

JEAN: (*Pause. She holds it in again.*) Okay.

MARILYN: You try and get some sleep.

JEAN: I will.

MARILYN: You call us tonight if you need to, no matter how late—

JEAN: Okay.

MARILYN: All right?

JEAN: I will.

MARILYN: Tomorrow when we're all together we can—

JEAN: Yes, you're right. You're right.

MARILYN: Your friend Marilyn, she'll take care of you.

JEAN: Yes.

MARILYN: Good.

JEAN: Daddy?

(*Wrenched out of her.*)

Do you want me to call Jim?

MARILYN: (*Pause.*) No, sweetheart.

JEAN: Because I will if—

MARILYN: "No" says Jean's father, and the weight of his son's death, the weight of the death multiplying itself like a tidal wave, sweeping up the force of David's death as it hits his daughter Jean, the death it will be in five minutes when it strikes his son Jim—"No," her father says, and the weight pushes his head down under the waves, and holds it there.

(JEAN *begins to cry—she leaps off the bed, bolting for escape,* MARILYN *grabs her and holds her while she sobs.*)

Jean—what's wrong—Jean—

JEAN: I can't—I can't—

MARILYN: Tell me what's wrong—

JEAN: No, I just can't. It's so sad.

MARILYN: I'm here, Jean. Tell me what's happened—

JEAN: So terribly sad.

MARILYN: You have to tell me, Jean.

JEAN: It's not fair, it's not fair, he can't be dead, he can't be dead—

MARILYN: Oh, Jean—

JEAN: Make it all right. Make it go away.

MARILYN: I'll take care of you.

JEAN: Hold me.

MARILYN: I'm holding you.

JEAN: Tighter.

MARILYN: I'll take care of you.

JEAN: Make it all right.

MARILYN: I promise. I'll make it go away.

(*She is rocking* JEAN *in her arms, stroking her hair and comforting her.* JEAN *is quiet for only a few moments.*)

JEAN: You shouldn't have promised me that, Marilyn.

MARILYN: I meant it.

JEAN: All the same. You shouldn't promise something if you don't really know what it means.

MARILYN: I tried to take care of you. I meant it.

JEAN: You meant it, but—(*She shrugs.*) You couldn't even get me to the airport the next morning on time.

MARILYN: That's not true.

JEAN: I wanted to go to the airport right away, but you said there was plenty of time—

MARILYN: That's not how it happened!

JEAN: Didn't you say the plane wasn't for hours? Didn't you say that?

MARILYN: Yes, but—

JEAN: I wanted to go, but you wouldn't take me.

MARILYN: That's not how it happened! You wanted me to hold you, so I held you. You fell asleep, in my arms. I woke you up in plenty of time. YOU TOLD ME TO HOLD YOU!

JEAN: No. I told you *not* to hold me.

I told you you could take me to the airport right away, or you could hold me. But if you held me, I wouldn't stop crying until you made it all right.

You were warned.

MARILYN: I held you anyway.

I held you, and you cried all night, even after you fell asleep. I didn't think a person could cry in their sleep like that. (*Al-*

most yelling.) I didn't hold you so you could keep on crying, Jean. I held you because I wanted you to stop.

JEAN: I can't get free, Marilyn. I can't get out from under this one. I can't—

MARILYN: (*Under* JEAN.) It is late when you arrive, you are tired—

JEAN: I know you want me to be the person who gets out from under it—

MARILYN: (*Under* JEAN.)—you come to bed, the phone rings, and I hold you. I hold you all night, and in the morning—in the morning—

JEAN: —you want me to be the person who can carry it on top of me. But I can't.

MARILYN: I woke you up in plenty of time.

(JEAN *lies down, or is lying down with her head on a pillow, in* MARILYN*'s lap.* MARILYN *hands* JEAN *a Kleenex.*)

Here—

JEAN: (*Taking it,* JEAN *dries her face, blows her nose, and puts her hand on the pillow.*) Your pillow—I've gotten it all wet—

MARILYN: Don't worry about it.

JEAN: What time is it?

MARILYN: A little before five.

JEAN: Good.

MARILYN: You feel okay?

JEAN: I don't know. Sort of like I'm in a dream. You know what I want?

MARILYN: Here—

JEAN: You can't say no to me—my brother's dead, I get anything I want. MY BROTHER'S DEAD AND I GET ANYTHING I WANT.

MARILYN: Okay, Jean, okay. I'm sorry.

JEAN: I'm sorry.

MARILYN: It's okay.

JEAN: I'm sorry.

MARILYN: It's okay, Jean. It's okay. (*Pause.*) Jean, you can stay right here another few minutes, it's okay, but I have to go warm up the car. Okay?

JEAN: No.

MARILYN: All right, then we'll get your things and go out together, we'll sit in the car together, okay?

JEAN: No.

MARILYN: Your father's going to be there waiting, if we don't leave soon—Jean, he thinks you're coming home today, he—

JEAN: Then call him! Call him and tell him I can't come! Call him and tell him I'll be there tomorrow, tell him . . . tell him I just can't come.

MARILYN: I can't do that.

JEAN: Of course you can. I can't leave until I've gotten the Tempest off the road, now can I? He'll understand.

MARILYN: Jean, I'll take care of that for you—

JEAN: You don't know where it is—

MARILYN: You'll show me on the way to the airport—

JEAN: You don't know what's wrong with it—

MARILYN: So I'll take it to someone who does—

JEAN: You don't know how to drive it right—

MARILYN: (*Desperate whisper.*) It's just a car, Jean. It's just . . . a . . . car. Come on—

JEAN: (*Exploding.*) DON'T YOU KNOW WHAT IT'S GOING TO BE LIKE THERE? Oh, sure, it's bad here, but there—David's death is going to be everywhere. Everywhere I look, everything I touch . . . I'll sit there with my parents, with my brother Jim, we'll sit at the kitchen table and say things to each other but all we'll really be doing is screaming WHERE'S DAVID. WHY ISN'T HE HERE! Why doesn't he drive up in his car, why doesn't the door open, why doesn't David come walking in. We don't get together much, the way we're all spread out, but at least at a time like this you'd think your brother David would be here. We're a family and we don't get together much, but when it matters, we are all here. Why is David so late?

I'm not going, Marilyn. If you love me, you won't make me go home.

MARILYN: But you went anyway, not that day but the day after. You went and waited with your family at the kitchen table. David did not come home. I had the Tempest towed into the shop. David did not come home. I stood and stared at the empty box that had held the transmission. Jean sat in the funeral home and waited with her family. I authorized the purchase of a rebuilt transmission. Jean waited for David to sit up in his coffin and yell "Surprise!" He didn't. I drove the Tempest home, parked it in the drive. They lowered the coffin into the ground, and the earth began to pile up on top of it and it was David's last chance to pull the joke off, his last chance to leap out of the coffin and laugh his loud laugh at his very good joke, his best joke ever, he had taken them all in, it was a very good joke but it was time for the joke to end. It was time for David to pop up the lid like a Jack in the Box and . . . but the weight of the earth would be too much for him. All right—then he would dart from behind a tombstone. Any minute now. He would flag down the funeral procession on its way out of the cemetery. He would beat them home and be waiting at the kitchen table—having a late breakfast or lurking in the hallway to chase Jean up the stairs—or lying on his bed in his room reading science fiction—or barricaded in the bathroom reading something else. He was in the living room scuffing up the furniture with his big, boat-sized boots, and he was in the basement sneaking a smoke, and he was out in the carport riding his first bicycle and he was in the back yard mowing the lawn, and he was everywhere in the house, in the yard, he was a little boy and a grown, magnificent dark-haired man.

So the day ended, and Jean and her family sat at the kitchen table and they didn't wait any longer. David was not coming home and they had to go on and they would go on.

And as they sat there together the next morning at breakfast, Jean's father believed for the first time that they actually would. He was still drowning, he knew they were all still drowning, but now and then as they struggled up toward the surface, a luminous gray patch of light appeared.

And then the letters David mailed on the day of his death arrived like a giant meteor shower crashing into earth, exploding entire continents, ripping the atmosphere away.

So Jean returned to me, and the Tempest. She came up for air, or tried to—in bed beside me. That was the way I wanted it. We were young, and I loved her, and I wanted to hold her and make it all right. I thought that would be enough for her. I thought you could love another person enough to be the thing that lets them enter the world, and stand in it.

But the world is full of things that are falling.

And two years later, here we stand.

JEAN: (*Turning back to* MARILYN.) I did love you. I do love you.

MARILYN: If you love me, come to bed—

JEAN: No.

MARILYN: Let's get it over with, get it behind us, move on.

JEAN: As long as I stay here I'm safe.

MARILYN: From what?

JEAN: David's death.

MARILYN: That's not fair.

JEAN: Of course it's not fair. I love you.

MARILYN: If you love me—

JEAN: NO! As long as I stay here, the story about David is not about you.

MARILYN: That's your choice.

JEAN: It happened the way it happened. It tracked me down and it found me here. How can you say it was my choice? How can you say I had any choice in what happened here?

MARILYN: All right. But we can change it back.

JEAN: I can't, I'm sorry, I can't.

MARILYN: Don't be sorry, be the redhead.

JEAN: I can't, Marilyn, I'm afraid—

MARILYN: Your choice.

JEAN: No.

MARILYN: It is.

JEAN: He did not choose to fall.

MARILYN: I don't care anymore, Jean—if he did, if he didn't. It's too long ago. We didn't know then, did we? We don't know now. We will never know. Are you telling me that knowing will change things for us?

JEAN: I can't change it back—I can't.

MARILYN: And I can't tell you why. That's what you really want from me, isn't it? You want me to make it all right. But I don't know why, and I can't make it all right. There are three things you can get if you come to bed with me. But one of them is never knowing why. You can't get that from me no matter how hard you try. And you have tried.

I don't care anymore, Jean, I don't care. It's too long ago. We will never know.

Come to bed.

JEAN: Come to bed, come to bed, what did we do when I did come to bed? One kiss, two? We hated kissing each other.

MARILYN: We didn't.

JEAN: Liar.

MARILYN: Is that really the way you want the story to end, Jean? It is late when you arrive, you are tired, you come to bed, the phone rings, and we hated kissing each other?

(*No response from* JEAN.)

All right, then. We hated kissing each other.

JEAN: We were going to be the aunts of each other's children. We were going to walk down the street together, pushing our baby carriages filled with redhair.

MARILYN: Wheel them down the street in matching prams.

JEAN: We could get by with words like pram when we were the redheads.

MARILYN: Oh. So you're saying we're not the redheads, is that what you came all this way to say?

JEAN: No—no—you know that's not—you know that's not what I want.

Shit.

I was really looking forward to coming here, to seeing you again. I'm sorry about all this other crap I can't help laying on you. I'm sorry.

(*She starts picking up all the French fries.*)

I thought—I thought it would be different. I thought we'd—go back to where we were and start again, and it would have a different ending. I thought—I'm sorry, Marilyn. About everything. About that awful negligee. And these French fries.

(*She takes one off the bed, starts to eat it. Can't. She throws the rest of the French fries out.*)

I shouldn't have gotten these. I haven't been able to eat a McDonald's French fry in . . . in a long time.

MARILYN: I thought you loved McDonald's.

JEAN: Yes. I loved McDonald's. And for a long, long time, I thought McDonald's loved me. But that's crazy. McDonald's is a multimillion-dollar operation.

MARILYN: Want a cigarette?

JEAN: Yeah.

(*They smoke.*)

I'm sorry.

MARILYN: That's not what I want from you.

JEAN: What do you want?

MARILYN: Come to bed.

JEAN: (JEAN *perches on the edge of the bed, awkwardly.*) Now what?

MARILYN: Comfortable?

JEAN: (JEAN *moves so she is beside* MARILYN.) Yes.

MARILYN: Now you finish the McDonald's story. You finish the story that includes each of the billions sold. And then we go on. Wherever it is we're going. No matter what is left for us, together, after the story is finished. We go.

JEAN: I was at McDonald's, ordering a Quarter Pounder with cheese—

(*They kiss.*)

—a large Coke—

(*They kiss.*)

—and a large fry.

(*They kiss. From far away, the phone rings.*)

And in a midtown Holiday Inn hotel, my brother David wedged a chair against the door and lay down on a bed with a cigarette that did not know when to stop in one hand, and in the other the largest quantity of cocaine that the credit limit on his Master Charge could stand. He planned to slip away quietly away from this world, on a bright, chemical dream. And instead, he woke up and found he had ridden into a trap. Oh, he had left this world, all right. No mistaking that. This world is easy to leave. Not the world he found himself in now. He found himself in a world that did not offer easy escape.

David woke up in hell, in a Holiday Inn hotel room filled with flames. From the hallway, from the world he had left and to which he could not return, he heard the frenzied pounding on the door. He stood up, unsteady, confused.

The things that were lacing up his life in the still, small places in his blood gave him no shade, no cool sweet resting place to hide from the crushing flames.

And the sounds of the sirens came to him. Called him to the window, where a fireman reached out his hand. But it was too late. The letters had been written, and sent and he was gone already, and so he went. The fire reached out to touch him as he started on his way down. He was my redhaired brother for the fourteen stories it took him to reach the ground.

My brother David was falling, a red halo around his head, and I was at McDonald's, and I was in your arms, and my brother David is falling, and I was ordering a Quarter Pounder with cheese, and I am in your arms, where my brother David is always falling.

He will always be here falling, Marilyn. He will always be here. In this bed.

(MARILYN *gets out of bed, moves away from* JEAN.)

I'm sorry, Marilyn. I'm—

MARILYN: (*Bitterly.*) Yes. It is late when you arrive, and you are sorry.

(*She lights a cigarette, does not offer one to* JEAN. *Smokes alone.*)

I wanted to be your redhaired twin, Jean. I really did.

JEAN: I know.

MARILYN: I tried.

JEAN: Sometimes I wish you hadn't tried so hard.

MARILYN: I'm still trying.

JEAN: But you'd like to stop.

MARILYN: I have to stop, Jean.

JEAN: Then stop, once and for all. Just stop and let this thing pass on by.

MARILYN: We'll have to start over, from scratch, we'll have to start over and we can't ever be the redheads again.

(*One of the stage technicians enters, removes or changes one aspect of the redhead world.*)

JEAN: Not even at Christmas?

MARILYN: Not even at Christmas.

(*Another stage technician enters, and the redhead world is swiftly dismantled.*)

JEAN: And at our weddings, we can't be bridesmaids?

MARILYN: No, we'll send each other invitations, along with a hundred others. We'll send a gift but we won't come.

JEAN: I read this story, a long time ago, about two girls playing on a school playground, each wearing the exact same plaid dress. One was on the teeter-totter. A hideous freak wind came along and swept her away, they never saw her again. Well, the other girl wearing the same dress saw it all and went insane.

MARILYN: I was watching an old episode of Ben Casey the other day. "Man, woman, birth, death, infinity"—that's the way they all start out—and I only caught the tail end of it, but it was about a man who had a twin brother who was in for emergency surgery. Well, the brother insisted that everything his brother felt, he felt too. So they wheel the sick one into the operating room, and start to cut, and the other brother drops writhing to the floor. He describes the incision, he feels the knife probing inside him. "Get this man into surgery" Ben Casey commands. "But Doctor, you're not going to operate" the nurse demurs. "No," he replies, "But we're going to get him under anesthesia, do everything we can. I told him earlier we've never lost the brother of a patient yet." Poignant pause. "Now I'm not so sure."

I have to stop.

(*The redhaired world has been dismantled, transformed back to the ordinary.*)

JEAN: (*Watching the technicians carry off the last of the redhead world.*) We're not the redheads any longer?

MARILYN: No. Not ever again.

JEAN: It shouldn't have happened like this.

MARILYN: But it did.

JEAN: Maybe if we—

MARILYN: What?

JEAN: Maybe if we went to every McDonald's in America, a sort of pilgrimage—

MARILYN: We could go to every McDonald's in the world, and it wouldn't change what happens when we do this.

(*She kisses* JEAN, JEAN *pulls away.*)

Wake up, Jean, we're not the redheads any longer. The McDonald's story don't cut no shit with me.

JEAN: Then what does?

MARILYN: Good question.

JEAN: Marilyn—

MARILYN: Yes?

JEAN: Do you think that in a parallel redhaired world where the McDonald's story still cuts through—

MARILYN: Jean, don't—

JEAN: Last time, I promise.

MARILYN: Cross your redhaired heart?

JEAN: You're as bad as me.

MARILYN: You promise this is the last time?

JEAN: Yes.

MARILYN: Okay.

JEAN: Do you think that in the parallel redhaired world, where the McDonald's story still cuts through all the shit there is, that even though David is not alive, even though the phone call came, and all the things that came with it came on and on—do you think that the redheads are still the redheads? Do you think they still love each other?

MARILYN: Yes.

JEAN: Good.

MARILYN: Is that enough?

JEAN: (JEAN *returns to the Tempest area. To the* AUDIENCE.) I will never know if the deaths that were David's to carry grew too heavy, and had to be set aside. It is also possible that he tried to move too quickly toward someone he loved—the monster that he carried on his back shifted unexpectedly, catching David off balance, he struggled for a moment, but then—then the weight was gone. It must have seemed to him that angels felt no lighter than he did, for that one, long instant before he hit the ground.

And his fall, that was a leap, from a high place, landed right on top of me. David's death piled up on top of me. And kept me from taking a single step toward a person I loved.

(*She gets into the Tempest.*)

I was driving along, and I saw this woman, crossing the

street to the side of me. And I smiled, because it was you, Marilyn. You the way you would look when you were sixty-five. There—that's Marilyn at sixty-five, I said to myself. And I smiled. You were someone's mother, someone's grandmother, someone's aunt. You were carrying a red bag, and your hair was gray, and you were very nice and neat, you looked good. You looked very good. I could see that you had lived through the redhaired death nicely—I could see it from the way you moved across the street. And I wanted to call out to you and tell you that I had too. I wanted to tell you that I had learned how to shoulder the weight—that I had learned how to carry it.

And I wanted to tell you that I had learned that it is not the weight of our deaths, in the end, that is the hardest thing to carry. It is our regret. For all the steps we wanted to take, and didn't, toward someone we love.

I wanted so badly to call out to you, to say "Marilyn, I'm all right."

(*Lights fade on* MARILYN.)

And that was the last time I saw you.

(*Blackout.*)

END OF PLAY

CATHOLIC SCHOOL GIRLS

Casey Kurtti

***

Dedicated to Walter Hadler

The Off Broadway Production of CATHOLIC SCHOOL GIRLS opened at the Douglas Fairbanks Theatre on April 1st, 1982. Directed by Burry Fredrik; setting by Paul Leonard; lighting by Paul Everett; costumes by Sigrid Insull. Presented by Lucille Lortel and Mortimer Levitt in association with Burry Fredrik and Haila Stoddard. Ben Sprecher, Associate Producer. The cast was as follows:

ELIZABETH MCHUGH/SR. MARY THOMASINA	Lynne Born
WANDA SLUSKA/SR. MARY AGNES	Maggie Low
MARIA THERESA RUSSO/SR. MARY GERMAINE	Shelley Rogers
COLLEEN DOCKERY/SR. MARY LUCILLE	Christine Von Dohln

TIME: 1962–1970

PLACE: St George's School, suburb in New York State.

AUTHOR'S NOTES

CATHOLIC SCHOOL GIRLS is obviously a memory play. It is my intention that the audience drift in and out of that reality. That is why there are no costume changes when the students "become" their teachers. When casting, the director should not be concerned with the youth of the actors, the concern should be with a strong ensemble. (Technically the Catholic school girls would be in their early thirties.) In addition, I would like to point out that the text is very well suited to non-traditional casting, and I vigorously encourage you to do so. In the Off-Broadway production we used very realistic props, costumes, sets, etc.; however, in Australia everything was left to the imagination. Either way, the play works.

ACT I

SCENE: *Music begins playing as lights gradually come up on a Catholic school first grade classroom in 1962. There are six student desks in a row, an oak teacher's desk and chair, a wastebasket, and an American flag by its side. A blackboard, two bulletin boards, a crucifix, and a big clock decorate the backstage wall.*

AT RISE: *After a few moments,* ELIZABETH, COLLEEN, WANDA, *and* MARIA THERESA *enter. They are dressed in white uniform blouses, blue ties, white cotton slips, knee socks, and brown oxford shoes. They are carrying their uniform jumpers. They each stand by a student desk and begin to dress as the music continues. They look around the classroom and at each other as they dress. Then* ELIZABETH *raises her skirt to pull her blouse down neatly. All follow suit, straightening their blouses. When they are finished,* ELIZABETH *shouts.*

ELIZABETH: I'm ready!

(*The lights come up quickly. The music stops. It is the first day of first grade, 1962.*)

COLLEEN: (*Polishing apple, while watching* MARIA THERESA *crawl under a desk.*) Where's the teacher? I wanna get started.

WANDA: I saw the teacher in the bathroom. She said to pick a seat.

MARIA THERESA: The teacher's in the bathroom?

(COLLEEN *begins to eat the apple.*)

WANDA: She's throwing up.

COLLEEN: Boys are supposed to sit over there. You retarded or something? What's that?

ELIZABETH: My mother pinned it on me. It's a Holy Medal for the first day. I live on Remsen Road in an apartment—

COLLEEN: (*To* MARIA THERESA:) I live near you.

COLLEEN: You got that white car with the back door off. It's a circus car right? Right?	ELIZABETH: I have four brothers and two sisters. We ARE going to get a house—someday.

MARIA THERESA: No!

COLLEEN: You live down by Carvel's. I seen your family there, your father's fat.

WANDA: I know where Carvel's is . . .

ELIZABETH: (*Crosses to statue.*) Hi, Jesus. Come here, Mr. Gunderson, say hi.

WANDA: Who's Gunderson?

ELIZABETH: My friend, she stays with me. Mr. Gunderson is a girl. She's got a red dress on, with lots of bows. She doesn't like this uniform.

COLLEEN: I don't see her.

ELIZABETH: She's invisible to people.

MARIA THERESA: (*Waves furiously in wrong direction and crawls under desk again.*) My name is Maria Theresa Russo.

ELIZABETH: She has long hair.

MARIA THERESA: I see it.

WANDA: Is she your sister?

ELIZABETH: No she's my friend. I don't talk to my family.

COLLEEN: (*Crosses to front.*) I have my own room. My brothers are slobs. They jump on the couch when my mother is not home. We are the only Catholics on the block, the rest of the families are Jews.

WANDA: I know some Jews.

COLLEEN: Shut up. My second best friend, Kitty, is a Jew. She has a little doll house with lights that turn on and off and—

WANDA: There were lots of Jews where we used to live.

COLLEEN: (*Getting furious.*) They go to church on Saturday and they all go to public school.

MARIA THERESA: When is the teacher going to stop throwing up? I don't like it here.

COLLEEN: That's a sin, you have to go on Sunday, right? Right?

ELIZABETH: I don't know.

COLLEEN: Well I do, because I'm going to be a nun. Got a little doll that's a nun. Sister is going to let me try on her bride's veil . . .

MARIA THERESA: Do they have any hair underneath that bride's veil?

WANDA: Oh yes.

COLLEEN: Who says?

WANDA: Mamow—My Mother. She taught me a special hymn for the first day to sing to sister, wanna hear?

COLLEEN: No.

ELIZABETH: Yes.

WANDA: The Ave Maria by Wanda Sluska . . . Zdrowa's Maryo, Laskis Pelna, Panz Toba . . . (*Air raid siren sounds.*)

COLLEEN: Yuch, stupid name.

MARIA THERESA: Lunch time, already?

ELIZABETH: That sound means the communists are sending a bomb over here. We all have to go home.

WANDA: But we just came here.

COLLEEN: This is Cheez Whiz. What you got? I'll trade you.

MARIA THERESA: I have a meatball hero. I think this is my sister's lunch.

ELIZABETH: There is a bomb shelter in my apartment building. I got to call my grandmother so she can get on the bus and come over to my house before it goes off. She lives in the Bronx. My grandfather isn't coming, he's already dead. You guys can come over and hide, but no boys allowed.

WANDA: We are supposed to hide here.

COLLEEN: Who says?

MARIA THERESA: We have bunk beds. Maria Diana sleeps on top of me. Maria Rose sleeps on top of Maria Ann. Anthony sleeps on top of Salvador Jr. Cosmo sleeps on top of Joseph.

ELIZABETH: Red fiery stuff comes out of that bomb and if it falls on you it could burn your skin right off. (MARIA THERESA *pulls out sweater.*) That won't save you. You need a raincoat.

WANDA: I'm getting the teacher. (*Exits.*)

ELIZABETH: This Chinese guy got hit by the bomb the last time while he was riding his bicycle. He got squished right into the ground. You can go over there and see him right now. He is still lying there all flattened out with his bicycle.

COLLEEN: (*Stops eating.*) Is the guy dead?

ELIZABETH: Yes.

COLLEEN: Hey, wait for me.

ELIZABETH: One second. (*She grabs Jesus.*)

MARIA THERESA: I'll get the mother.

COLLEEN: Don't touch the snakes, they could come alive. (SISTER MARY AGNES *enters.*)

SISTER MARY AGNES: Boys and girls. My name is Sister Mary Agnes. (*Writes it with the holy water.*)

MARIA THERESA: Sister, are you finished throwing up?

SISTER MARY AGNES: What was that, dear?

COLLEEN: I gotta ask you something about that bride's veil.

SISTER MARY AGNES: Take your seats, first graders, and good morning. My name is Sister Mary Agnes.

MARIA THERESA: Sister, there is a bomb coming over here. We're going to this girl's house. You wanna come?

SISTER MARY AGNES: This is just a test. We hide here at school, in the basement. Now, even though this is a test and for some reason Sister Rose Gertrude, your principal, decided to pull the alarm on the first day of school, in the very first hour of the new year, we must pretend it is real, so we will know what to do in case we are attacked. I have been assigned to take you down to the basement.

COLLEEN: You want me to get that sick, Sister?

SISTER MARY AGNES: No, Sister Mary Claire has a big heart, but a very weak stomach. She'll join us downstairs just as soon as she can. Put Jesus back in his spot, dear. Now, pick partners . . .

COLLEEN: Sister, how old are you?

SISTER MARY AGNES: Sixty-six.

COLLEEN: Wow.

ELIZABETH: Sister, that's how old my grandmother is. Do you know her?

SISTER MARY AGNES: Follow me.

ELIZABETH: Lorretta Stokes.

SISTER MARY AGNES: Pleased to meet you.

(*All exit, turn right, pass behind blackboard. Lights cross fade as they reenter classroom through far* S.R. *door, into* SISTER MARY LUCILLE*'s second grade classroom, 1963.*)

ELIZABETH: (*Going over her lesson.*) Honor thy mother and father. Honor thy mother and father. Honor thy mother and father.

SISTER MARY LUCILLE: (*Entering classroom.*) Good morning, boys and girls.

ALL: (*Not at all together.*) Good morning, Sister Mary Lucille. Good morning, Sister Mary Lucille. Good morning, Sister Mary Lucille.

SISTER MARY LUCILLE: Saints preserve us. Second graders, if you find an air raid drill so exhausting, God help you when the real thing comes along. You've been running up and down from the basement for a year and a half. It's about time you developed some stamina. Second graders, take a crack at that word.

WANDA: (*Raising her hand.*) S-T-A-M-I-N-A. Stamina.

SISTER MARY LUCILLE: That's it. (*To all:*) . . . Boys and girls, it will take hard work to maintain the reputation that Catholic schools all over the country have earned. Please try to rise to the occasion or get out. (*Pause.*) Take your seats.

MARIA THERESA: (*To* WANDA:) Ask me. (*Passes candy.*) Here.

WANDA: (*Taking candy.*) What are the three kinds of sin?

MARIA THERESA: Number one, Original Sin: that is what you are born into. Number two, venial sin: that is when you tell a lie or do something that is not very nice to a stranger or your family. Number three, mortal sin: that is when you kill someone or knife them.

SISTER MARY LUCILLE: Second graders, please stop cramming and put those Baltimore Catechisms away. Donna Maria Gianetta, if you don't know it now, you never will. McHugh, stand up. Who made you?

ELIZABETH: (*Standing.*) God made me. (SISTER MARY LUCILLE *gestures and* ELIZABETH *stands.*)

SISTER MARY LUCILLE: Why did God make you?

ELIZABETH: God made me to feel this heart and when I'm all done with that to go back to his house in Heaven.

SISTER MARY AGNES: Where did you get that answer?

ELIZABETH: I asked God and He told me.

SISTER MARY AGNES: Don't you dare lie to me.

ELIZABETH: I'm not lying, Sister.

SISTER MARY LUCILLE: Saints in heaven preserve us. Don't you dare stand in front of me and tell me that our Lord gave you that answer.

ELIZABETH: Sister that's what he said

SISTER MARY LUCILLE: Well that's the wrong answer. Are you trying to tell me that God gave you the wrong answer? Because God is never wrong. Miss McHugh I don't know who you are talking to but it is not God. You will go home tonight and you will memorize the Baltimore Catechism or you will never receive the Body and Blood of Jesus Christ. Do you understand me? Sit down.

ELIZABETH: Yes, Sister. But I . . .

SISTER MARY LUCILLE: There will be no "buts" about it. Miss Sluska the seven sacraments in order.

WANDA: (*Sing-song.*) Baptism, penance, First Holy Communion—

SISTER MARY LUCILLE: Louder. The boys in the back can't hear you.

WANDA: (*Shouting.*) Confirmation, Matrimony, Holy Orders, Extreme Unction.

SISTER MARY LUCILLE: Miss Sluska, very good. Miss Sluska, please thank your father for me and all the other sisters in the convent for his generous donation of roast beef for our Sunday dinner. There was not a line of gristle in that roast. He is fondly remembered in our morning prayers.

WANDA: Yes, Sister.

SISTER MARY LUCILLE: Miss Sluska is well on her way to making her first Holy Communion, which is more than I can say for a few select individuals in this classroom. Miss McHugh. Your parents are going to be in for the shock of their lives when all the other boys and girls are marching down the aisle to receive their first Holy Communion and you are not in line with them. Don't laugh, Mr. Crawford, a few of you are headed in the same direction. Now, let us stand and review what we will say when we go into the confessional for our first confession.

SISTER MARY LUCILLE: (*Blesses herself.*) Bless me, Father, for I have sinned. This is my first confession.

GIRLS: (*Bless themselves.*) Bless me, Father, for I have sinned. This is my first confession.

(*All except* ELIZABETH *kneel and stay frozen during the monologue.*)

ELIZABETH: Okay, everybody. This is church. This is God's house. If you ever have to talk to him just come right in and kneel down in one of these long chairs and start talking. But not too loud. In here you have to be real quiet. You might wake up the statues and they are praying to Jesus. (*Bows her head.*) Oh, I forgot to tell you something. Whenever you hear the name "Jesus" you have to bow your head or else you have a sin on your soul. Now, over there is the statue of Jesus' mother. Her name is The Blessed Virgin Mary. She is not as important as Jesus, so you don't have to bow your head when you hear her name. All the girls sit on her side when they go to mass. One time I heard that Margaret Mary O'Donahugue, a sixth grader, was in church saying the rosary, that's the necklace with beads on it for praying, she said that the Blessed Virgin Mary statue started crying right in the middle of Mass. I believe it, too. Sister says that there are miracles, magic things that happen to people that are real good. Margaret Mary never gets in trouble. In class she always gives the right answers, so I guess she deserves to see a miracle. Well, I'm going to get a miracle someday, too. Anyway, the boys sit on the other side of the church, the one with the statue of Saint Joseph. He is Jesus' father. (*Bows head.*) Hey, you forgot to bow your head. Don't do that cause you'll have a black spot on your soul and you'll go straight to hell. Now in hell it is real hot and you sweat a lot and little devils come and bite you all over. If you are real good you get to go to Heaven. In Heaven they have a big refrigerator full of stuff to eat. M&M's, ice cream, little chocolate covered doughnuts, anything you want to eat and it never runs out. But the best thing about Heaven is that you get to meet anyone you want. Let's say I wanted to meet Joan of Arc . . . no . . . no . . . Cleopatra. I would go to one of the saints and he would give me a permission slip and I would fill it out and give it to Jesus. (*Bows head.*) Hey, you didn't bow your head. Okay, I warned you. Then I would fly across Heaven, cause when you get in they give you wings, and I would have a chat with Cleopatra. The only thing is that I hope everyone I like gets accepted into Heaven or else I would never see them again. Jewish people can't even go to Heaven. So if any of you are Jewish I would change into a Catholic or else you have to go straight to Hell. Jewish people can't even go to church. If I saw a Jewish person in church I would stand up and tell the priest that there was a Jewish person in church, and he would stop the Mass until they left. One time I heard this story and I know it is true, that a Jewish person went to church for two weeks disguised as a Catholic. He got communion every day except he took them out of his mouth so that they wouldn't melt and he put them in his kitchen cupboard so they would be safe. Then when he had gotten enough, thirteen or so, he put them in a frying pan and he cooked them and blood started dripping from the ceiling and it was Jesus' blood. (*Bows head.*) You see that crucifix up there. That's how Jesus died. The Jewish people put him up there and they killed him. If a Jewish person walked in here, that statue would turn bloody. Jesus would start hurting from the nails. That's all I wanted to say. I just wanted to tell you a few important things. I hope I haven't hurt anyone's feelings but that's just the way it is. Oh, one more thing, if you ask Jesus a question, make sure you write the answer down real fast, so you don't mess it up. 'Cause if you mess up an answer from him it could get you in real bad trouble.

(*Lights come back. Girls rise and assemble* U.S., *each pantomiming putting on communion veil. They talk until ready to form a line and enter the "church" area.*)

COLLEEN: I'm starving. I can't wait to get hold of that host.

WANDA: That's disgusting, Colleen, and now you have a black spot on your soul and you can't receive.

COLLEEN: You believe anything.

WANDA: You thought about it. So that's a sin, too. You better get off this line or you'll have a mortal sin. (*They start walking into church.*)

COLLEEN: I don't care. I decided not to be a nun.

WANDA: You could change your mind again when you get into high school, and then what would happen? (*Raising hand.*) Besides, I'm telling.

COLLEEN: (*Pushing her arm down.*) No, you're not. Hey, look, your father. He's standing up to take your picture. You better smile.

ELIZABETH: Maria, look at Wanda's dress. It has these little sparkles all over it, it's pretty.

MARIA THERESA: I had to wear my sister's old dress. Look, it's ripped right here. My mother didn't even have time to sew it.

ELIZABETH: I have on my sister's, too. My grandmother couldn't come today but she gave me a little white rosary.

COLLEEN: My Aunt got me these new shoes. Hi, Aunt Dorothy. I have a white pocketbook with a silver dollar from my uncle in it.

MARIA THERESA: My father gave me this new watch. He almost had to go to work this morning but he's here. He's right there. (*She waves to him.*) Hi Daddy. He sees me. (*All have knelt except* MARIA THERESA. ELIZABETH *pulls her down.* MARIA THERESA *notices the priest approaching them.*) Hey, Father Moyhnihan is four away.

ELIZABETH: (*To* COLLEEN:) Four away. I can't wait.

COLLEEN: (*To* WANDA:) Four away.

WANDA: (*To imaginary person next to her.*) Four away.

(*They repeat in the same progression "three away," "two away," "one away." When the priest gets to* MARIA THERESA, *she sticks her tongue out to receive the host. She nudges* COLLEEN *and this pattern is repeated until completed. They end by crossing themselves.*)

ELIZABETH: You guys, I bit the host.

MARIA THERESA: Which part? Maybe you bit off the arm of the baby Jesus.

ELIZABETH: You mean I have the arm of baby Jesus in my stomach. Oh, no.

MARIA THERESA: Uuch. It could be a leg.

WANDA: Elizabeth, you make me sick.

ELIZABETH: Jesus is dying inside of me. I feel it.

COLLEEN: Wanda your father is getting to me with that camera. Go stand somewhere else.

WANDA: Come on, Sister is calling our row.

ELIZABETH: Don't tell Wanda please.

(*They rise and sing as they circle back into the classroom.*)

ALL: *OH, HOW I LOVE JESUS.*
OH, HOW I LOVE JESUS
OH, HOW I LOVE JESUS
BECAUSE HE FIRST LOVED ME.

SISTER MARY LUCILLE: All right, class. You all looked beautiful on Saturday. That was one of God's small miracles, and I am glad to see you have the spirit of the Holy Ghost inside of you. I hope to see a marked improvement in your conduct from this day forward. Don't disappoint me or the Sacred Heart of Jesus or you will pay the consequences. (*Passing out construction paper.*) Now I would like you all to draw something to decorate the classroom for Thanksgiving. I will take ten minutes from my valuable class time. (*Removing old decorations.*) These Halloween decorations are a little passé. (*Takes Mission Box from shelf.*) Miss Russo, go around with the Mission Box. It's obvious you don't suffer for lack of food. I will be watching to see who puts how much in. Mr. Vaccaro, squeeze that pocket. I have eyes in the back of my head, or didn't you know that? They were put there by Jesus Christ himself. Now, perhaps some of my students have reflected over the weekend and have come up with some things that they are thankful for this year and I am sure they would like to share those thoughts with Sister Mary Lucille and the rest of the class. (WANDA *raises her hand.*) Yes, Miss Sluska, why don't you start? (MARIA THERESA *returns box to* SISTER MARY LUCILLE.) One minute. (MARIA THERESA *puts coin in box.*) This is a disgrace. (*Turns to crucifix and shakes box to show how little is in it, before replacing it.*) This is what the second grade in Yonkers, New York, has collected for you today. Sluska, go on.

WANDA: I am thankful that we have made our First Holy Communion this year and that we have a Catholic president.

SISTER MARY LUCILLE: An Irish Catholic president.

WANDA: Yes, Sister.

SISTER MARY LUCILLE: Very nice, Miss Sluska. Please remind your father that cameras and flashers do not belong in church. I do not like distractions during the consecration and thank him for that lovely leg of lamb.

WANDA: Yes, Sister.

SISTER MARY LUCILLE: Saints preserve us, Maria Theresa Russo. Don't suck your thumb in Sister Mary Lucille's classroom. When your parents have a thousand dollars worth of orthodontist's bills to pay, I will be happy to tell them that you sat in my classroom, like a bump on a log, sucking your thumb. Your parents can't afford to take care of the nine children they have now, what kind of selfish daughter would expect them to pay for her bad habits in their later years? And tell your mother to scrub you down, you look like a stray cat. McHugh next. Keep that thumb out of your mouth. If you cannot control yourself, sit on your hands.

ELIZABETH: Was Jesus a Jewish person? Some kids I know said that our God, Jesus is Jewish.

SISTER MARY LUCILLE: In the two years you have been attending St. George's School, has there been any mention of Jesus, other than as a Catholic?

ELIZABETH: No, Sister, but I thought. . .

SISTER MARY LUCILLE: You are not paid to think. Boys and girls, there is one thing, and only one thing to be aware about the Jews. They killed Jesus and that is the beginning and the end of it.

ELIZABETH: I am thankful for . . .

SISTER MARY LUCILLE: Hold on there, Miss Tish. Is that Cray-Pas on your desk? We use Crayola Crayons in this classroom. Don't we class?

ALL: Yes, Sister.

ELIZABETH: These are my grandmother's. She used to be an artist. She said if I was real careful, I could bring them to school and I could . . .

SISTER MARY LUCILLE: Class, Miss McHugh's grandmother is an artist.

ELIZABETH: No. She used to be.

MARIA THERESA: I know, Sister.

SISTER MARY LUCILLE: The class is not impressed. Your grandmother is/was an artist, who cares? (SISTER MARY LUCILLE *takes Cray-Pas and throws it into the wastebasket.* ELIZABETH *sits at desk and begins to cry.*) No one told you to take that seat, young lady. I would like to know, as I am sure the whole class would, what you are thankful for this year?

ELIZABETH: (*Trying to avoid looking at her.*) I am thankful for . . .

SISTER MARY LUCILLE: Miss McHugh, you do not face the wall when Sister asks you a question. You face Sister.

ELIZABETH: I can't really be thankful for anything because the good things always turn bad.

SISTER MARY LUCILLE: Why do they turn bad?

ELIZABETH: Well, Sister, a lot of the time you make them turn bad.

SISTER MARY LUCILLE: Come here, Miss McHugh. (ELIZABETH *reluctantly crosses to teacher's desk.*) I joined the convent at thirteen years of age in the tradition of my country and my family and I began teaching when I was sixteen. I am now forty-seven years old. How many years have I been teaching, class?

WANDA: Thirty-one?

SISTER MARY LUCILLE: Right on the button. God willing I will be here for another thirty-one years, teaching long after you have gone. One day you will return and thank Sister for all she has done. Boys and girls, the sisters are not here to be popular. We are here to teach you and to discipline (*Pulls out ruler.*) you, in spite of your bold and brazen ways. Miss McHugh, I have a personal message from me to you. In all my years of teaching, I have never met a spirit I couldn't break. Sometimes it takes one lesson and sometimes it takes one hundred. (*Slaps* ELIZABETH *with ruler. Tapping is heard on the public address system.*) God, give me strength. Am I going to get any teaching done today?

VOICE ON THE P.A. SYSTEM: Boys and girls, this is your principal, Sister Rose Gertrude. I have a serious announcement to make and I hope you will cooperate by putting away what you are doing and listen carefully.

SISTER MARY LUCILLE: Fold your hands on top of your desks.

(Lights dim slightly as news of President Kennedy's assassination is announced, though not verbally. SISTER MARY LUCILLE *rises, takes picture of Kennedy from bulletin board, and places it under crucifix. This pantomime begins transition into fourth grade, 1965.* ELIZABETH *exits to return as* SISTER MARY THOMASINA. *As lights come back up* COLLEEN *and* MARIA THERESA *are "twisting"* D.S.R. *in front of the teacher's desk.)*

MARIA THERESA: Show me again, how do they do it, Colleen?

COLLEEN: You're so dumb. Just copy me. Just like this.

MARIA THERESA: I'm not dumb, Colleen. Am I doing it right now?

COLLEEN: Hold out your hands and shake.

WANDA: Maria, it's like drying yourself with a towel.

COLLEEN: Who invited you, Miss Know-It-All? You stay out of here, Wanda.

MARIA THERESA: You could show me. Just a little, come on, Wanda.

COLLEEN: Maria, you're a little turncoat. Don't you dare listen to her, or I am not your friend.

WANDA: Colleen, I take dance classes.

COLLEEN: So what? Get out the book and show Maria the pictures.

WANDA: I didn't get the twist out of any book, Colleen.

COLLEEN: Yeah. Hey, if you think you're so great, why don't you just get up on that desk and show the whole class.

MARIA THERESA: Yeah, get up on the desk.

MARIA/COLLEEN: On the desk. On the desk. . . .

WANDA: Okay, okay, you guys. Watch Maria Theresa.

COLLEEN: If you look at her, I'll never talk to you again Maria. (COLLEEN *covers her eyes.* MARIA *watches.)*

MARIA THERESA: I'm sorry, Colleen, but I've got to. Hey, you're good. Am I doing it right? It feels like it.

(COLLEEN *notices* SISTER MARY THOMASINA *by the doorway and sneaks back to her desk.* MARIA THERESA *notices too late, so does* WANDA.)

SISTER MARY THOMASINA: What are you doing by my desk?

MARIA THERESA: I left my book up here, Sister Mary Thomasina.

SISTER MARY THOMASINA: Are you in the habit of dropping things on my desk? Sit down. (MARIA THERESA *sits.* WANDA has been trying to lower herself into her chair. SISTER MARY THOMASINA *catches her midway down.*) No. Wanda. Don't you sit down, just yet. I would like you to go on with what you were doing. Go on, go ahead.

WANDA: It's just the twist, Sister.

SISTER MARY THOMASINA: Well, let's see it. (WANDA *twists again.*)

MARIA THERESA: She does it good, Sister.

SISTER MARY THOMASINA: So I see. (COLLEEN *laughs.*)

MARIA THERESA: She's better than you.

SISTER MARY THOMASINA: Colleen, if you think this is so funny, you may join her. No? I didn't think so. Now, girls, I don't think it is necessary to make a spectacle of yourselves, especially in front of the boys, do you, Wanda?

WANDA: No, Sister.

SISTER MARY THOMASINA: Wanda, get down.

(WANDA *stands beside her desk.* SISTER MARY THOMASINA *writes SIN OF PRIDE on the blackboard.*)

SISTER MARY THOMASINA: There is a sin called the "sin of pride." It is when we call attention to ourselves or when we boast about our talents, that we are guilty of this sin. Now Wanda it is obvious that you are guilty of this vice, and that you need to develop a little humility. Until I see examples of humility accumulating in your character, I am going to have to strip you of your responsibility as fourth grade classroom monitor. Hand over your little book, please. (WANDA *takes off book, from around her neck,* SISTER MARY THOMASINA *hands it to* COLLEEN.) Colleen, you need help to develop a little responsibility. Let's see how you do.

WANDA: Are you going to tell my parents, Sister?

SISTER MARY THOMASINA: I see no reason to report to your parents . . . at least not at this point. You may be seated.

COLLEEN: Maria, aren't you going to congratulate me?

MARIA THERESA: I'm sorry, Wanda.

COLLEEN: Oh, you're just a sore loser.

SISTER MARY THOMASINA: All right. We have something to discuss. (*Draws thermometer on blackboard.*) Now as you all know, The Catholic Church is going through a fiscal crisis. If we cannot raise enough money this year to meet the cost of running the school, the government will come in here and we will be ordered to take down our statues and crosses and we will not be able to have any more religion classes. We could never mention God. We would be just like public school . . . For the past five years, my classroom has led in all areas of financial collection. Now Mr. McCarthy, Kevin's father, who is in the Knights of Columbus, has come up with an idea to raise money. The Knights of Columbus is going to sponsor a Talent Show. First prize will be twenty-five dollars. The boys have already come up with an idea and I think the girls could contribute some of their talents instead of wasting them during Sister's valuable class time.

WANDA: What are the boys doing, Sister?

SISTER MARY THOMASINA: The boys are going to do the Beatles. With the wigs and everything. Greg, stop tapping on that desk . . . I don't think we need a Ringo just yet.

COLLEEN: I've come up with an idea, Sister. Do you think we can have a few minutes to discuss it? Just a couple of us girls, in private?

SISTER MARY THOMASINA: That's the spirit, Colleen, but just a few minutes. The boys and the rest of you girls can use this time to clean out your desks. Frank, go around with the wastepaper pail.

(*The girls gather around* COLLEEN*'s desk. Including* ELIZABETH *who "breaks" from* SISTER MARY THOMASINA *character.*)

COLLEEN: Listen, I got a great idea. Why don't we do Diana Ross and The Supremes?

MARIA THERESA: Great idea. I can borrow my mother's high heels.

WANDA: Wait a second. I have a better idea. Why don't we all do Nancy Sinatra? Then we can wear white go-go boots. Besides, there are only three Supremes and there are four of us.

COLLEEN: You just go ahead and do Nancy Sinatra all by yourself. I don't want you in my act, got it? You're always trying to be different. Why don't you give it up, Polack?

ELIZABETH: It's not really a bad idea. If we do the Supremes we'd have to paint our faces black.

MARIA THERESA: No we wouldn't. Besides, the boys wouldn't recognize us.

COLLEEN: Look, who has the go-go boots, huh?

WANDA: I do.

COLLEEN: No kidding. Only child Polack gets everything she wants. Well, my mother won't get them for me.

MARIA THERESA: Mine either. And we would need them. I'm sorry, Wanda. Colleen, who is going to play Diana? I volunteer.

COLLEEN: I get to play Diana, it was my idea. I get to decide.

ELIZABETH: Colleen, you can't play Diana.

WANDA: I agree.

COLLEEN: Why?

WANDA: You are Irish and most of them have red hair and they look like "I Love Lucy." Everyone knows, Lucy can't sing and you can't either.

COLLEEN: What?

ELIZABETH: Maria does sing best.

COLLEEN: She can't dance.

WANDA: I'll help her. I know tap . . . almost. Maria, we'll make you into Diana. Let me see your skin.

MARIA THERESA: Wanda, I'll get Maria Rose to do the wash for me, she owes me. I'll be able to practice every day. I can't wait till my father sees me on that stage.

ELIZABETH: Let's take a vote. All for Maria as Diana, raise your hand. (*All raise hands except* COLLEEN.) Majority rules. Maria plays Diana.

COLLEEN: No. We will have a tryout and if I lose, which I won't, I still get to stand in front, got it!

ELIZABETH: Yeah, yeah.

WANDA: Let's go over to my house and rehearse after school.

COLLEEN: We'll go up to my room after school.

WANDA: I have a TV in my room and we can all watch "Dark Shadows."

COLLEEN: You better knock it off. You are showing off again. I'll tell Sister and she'll make you stop. I have her wrapped around my little finger and don't you forget it. She'll kick you right out of that talent show.

WANDA: Tell, I dare you.

COLLEEN: (*Raises her hand. All exit as* COLLEEN *says following, except* WANDA *who stands in center.*) Sister, I think we have something to discuss. (*After all exit* WANDA *begins.*)

WANDA: My father comes home from work every night and before he even takes off his gray hat with the skinny feather, he drops a bag of leaky, smelly meat on the table for my mother. She waits to see if she should kiss him or not. If it is just hamburger, she grunts. If it is liver, she practically goes to Mars. I hate liver. I hate all things sometimes. Even things I like. My ballet lessons, my pedal pushers, my dolls on the shelf, and I hate my smartness. You know why, because they were given to me. I am working on something that's mine. I have been for a long time. After school I go home and do my homework right away so I can go down to my father's store. He's not really a bad man, I just don't like him or something. While he is in the back room, sawing those bones out of the big legs of meat, I take soda cans and crush them onto my shoes. I move some sawdust into a little pile on the floor and I begin to dance. Not like Nancy Sinatra or Diana—oh, I am so much better. As I'm dancing, my mind just lets go and all these little movies come into my head. My favorite—I'm on the Ed Sullivan Show. (*Mocks being handed a microphone.*) Thank you, Eddie. I'm singing a song. Fake snow is falling all around me. I have on a sexy dress. It's sort of a sad song and I look so incredibly beautiful, that some people in the audience are starting to cry. Well, I break into a tap dance just to cheer them up. Later on Ed Sullivan brings me backstage to the Beatle's dressing room and Paul asks me to marry him. I say, maybe in a couple of months, because I have my career to think about. I become an international superstar and I go live in a penthouse apartment right on top of Radio City Music Hall. (*Starts to put on go-go boots.*) So for now I don't mind rehearsing in my father's store. He stays out of my way. I don't care if my hands and feet stick out a little too much, that can be fixed. I don't mind being Nancy Sinatra, I like these go-go boots a lot anyway. I made my mother buy them for me at S. Klien's. So here is DAWN GABOR, who used to be Wanda Sluska, coming to you live, right after eighth grade, to sing and dance, just because she feels like it. So you just get those TV sets warmed up, because even if it is a sin, I don't care, I'm going to be famous. Wait. Watch for me. Okay? (WANDA *does a baton twirling introduction to Diana Ross and the Supremes.*) I am happy to present, Sister Mary Thomasina's fourth grade class doing their rendition of "Stop In The Name of Love."

(*Scratchy version of song begins to play.** ELIZABETH *and* COLLEEN *enter followed by* MARIA THERESA *as Diana Ross. All wear feather boas.* MARIA THERESA *flirts with audience.* COLLEEN *tries to upstage her.* WANDA *tries to get into the act via her baton, streamers, and bubbles.*)

(*After finishing the number, straggle offstage,* MARIA THERESA *yanking* COLLEEN *off.*)

COLLEEN: Wait a minute, this was all my idea.

(*They circle back into the classroom, still wearing feather boas,* WANDA *twirling her baton. They enter singing the theme song from a popular 1960's television show.*)

COLLEEN: Maria, what happened to your father? He never showed up, did he?

WANDA: Shut up, Colleen.

COLLEEN: I'm talking to my ex-friend Maria, so butt out.

*Cautionary Note: Rights to produce the play do *not* include permission to use this song in production. For permission, producers must procure rights from *Stone Agate Music;* 6255 Sunset Blvd.; Los Angeles, CA 90028.

MARIA THERESA: My mother was there, he had to babysit.

COLLEEN: Your mother had the baby with her, Maria.

MARIA THERESA: So what, Colleen, we have more than one baby, you know. I don't care about him anyway. Eddie saw me . . . He said I was great.

COLLEEN: Sure. Sure. (SISTER MARY THOMASINA *enters.*)

SISTER MARY THOMASINA: Good morning, boys and girls.

ALL: Good morning, Sister Mary Thomasina.

SISTER MARY THOMASINA: I have a short announcement to make. Miss Carlson, the lay teacher in the eighth grade will be leaving us. She is getting married at the end of June.

COLLEEN: It's about time.

SISTER MARY THOMASINA: . . . and therefore a new teacher has been assigned . . .

MARIA THERESA: I hope it is a guy.

SISTER MARY THOMASINA: Maria Theresa, it is certainly not a guy. Sister Mary Lucille will be moving up from the second grade. So there is a possibility that she will be seeing some old familiar faces in her class.

MARIA THERESA: Oh, God, yuuch.

SISTER MARY THOMASINA: Also, class, the talent show was an enormous success and we have the first prize winners, right here in class.

(*She looks from the boys to the girls while holding trophy and money. She moves toward girls. They cheer.*)

COLLEEN: I don't believe it.

MARIA THERESA: It was my Diana.

SISTER MARY THOMASINA: Let's hear a round of applause. Wanda, I liked your introduction.

WANDA: Thank you, Sister.

COLLEEN: Oh that was my idea, Sister.

SISTER MARY THOMASINA: Really, Colleen, I'm not surprised. Boys, it's too bad your wigs weren't on a little more securely. I'm sure you would have won second prize. Girls, I'm sure you want to be very generous and donate your prize earnings to the. . . .

COLLEEN: I have plans for this money.

SISTER MARY THOMASINA: . . . to the missions.

MARIA THERESA: I'll get the box.

(MARIA THERESA *gets the box and collects the money from* COLLEEN. *Then* MARIA *starts back to her seat.*)

SISTER MARY THOMASINA: The Knights of Columbus raised $256.75 on the little beer garden after the talent show. We are now in the 60th percentile. (SISTER *grabs* MARIA THERESA*'s boa as she passes.*) And girls, please put those boas away. I think that there is a good chance, with our continued effort, that the school will be saved.

ALL: St. George's. St. George's. St. George's. (WANDA *twirls her baton.*)

SISTER MARY THOMASINA: Wanda. (WANDA *puts her baton in desk.*) Now, will you take out your math text books, please. Wanda, would you please pass these papers out so we may get started? (WANDA *passes paper to* MARIA THERESA. MARIA *hands* WANDA *a candy.*)

MARIA THERESA. Wanda, pssst, what's the answer to seven times seven?

SISTER MARY THOMASINA: No talking, boys and girls. Maria Theresa, are you having some sort of problem?

MARIA THERESA: Sister, I was just wondering, are we having a test?

SISTER MARY THOMASINA: This is not a test. This is your math homework for tonight. I would like it done neatly and signed by both your parents. And I would appreciate it, Maria Theresa, if you did not speak out in class. I would like to see your homework. Get it out. Quietly. (WANDA *returns from boys' side, clomping.*) Wanda, please stop clomping around the classroom like an elephant. And remove those go-boots. (WANDA *does so as* SISTER MARY THOMASINA *crosses to* COLLEEN*'s desk.*) Colleen, your homework please. I don't believe I see a signature here. This homework is not signed.

COLLEEN: I told my parents to sign, Sister. The problem was that my dog had a heart attack and we had to take him to the hospital. So I guess my parents, just sort of forgot . . .

SISTER MARY THOMASINA: I want you to do this over, twenty-five times. I want you to have each copy signed by your parents. And Colleen, I don't want to see such negligence again. I do, however admire your imagination. Wanda your homework, please. Nice and neat and tidy. I wish all my students were as conscientious as you. 100 percent, Wanda. What's this ball point pen? We use Scheaffer fountain pens in the fourth grade. I don't like sneaks, Wanda. That will cost you, let's see . . . 85% that's fair.

WANDA: Sister, what about the Honor Roll?

SISTER MARY THOMASINA: Maria Theresa, your homework, please.

MARIA THERESA: (*Hands* SISTER *a torn and holey paper.*) I had to erase a little, Sister.

SISTER MARY THOMASINA: This is very messy. I told you if you could not erase completely to please make a new copy of your work. I know I did say this to the entire class. From now on I will no longer accept papers in this condition. This is not public school. Boys and girls, you will not get away with this here. If you want to go to public school, please take your books (*She piles everything in desk, on top of it.*) and messy papers and go down the street and go to public school. (MARIA THERESA *doesn't move.*) Fine. I didn't think so. Then do the work the way I want it done. I don't want to see dog-eared pages, no erasures, and if you must rip pages out of your notebook, please trim the edges before you come to class. (*A model airplane flies onto the floor.*) Bernard, does this belong to you? Oh, it does. Well, join it in the wastebasket. Now I would like to have a math quiz. Two volunteers come to the front of the classroom. I will ask the times tables. The winner will be allowed to skip the math homework and choose a holy card from Sister's own collection. Who would like to start? (WANDA *raises her hand.*) Let's have some new hands, for a change. (COLLEEN *raises her hand.*) What a pleasant surprise. Colleen come up front. Maria Theresa, how about you? I'm sure since you have such a difficult time with math you may want to have some fun with it. Come on, spit spot.

MARIA THERESA: Yes, Sister.

(MARIA THERESA *and* COLLEEN *stand by teacher's desk.*)

SISTER MARY THOMASINA: We will start with the easy ones. Maria Theresa, five times five?

MARIA THERESA: Twenty-five.

SISTER MARY THOMASINA: Six times five?

COLLEEN: Thirty.

SISTER MARY THOMASINA: Four times four . . . Four times four?

MARIA THERESA: I thought you would call on us, four times four equals sixteen.

SISTER MARY THOMASINA: Maria Theresa, please do not repeat the question.

MARIA THERESA: It helps me to repeat the question.

SISTER MARY THOMASINA: Maria Theresa, we have been doing these times tables since the beginning of this year. I think you have had sufficient time to get them into your head, don't you agree?

MARIA THERESA: Yes, Sister.

SISTER MARY THOMASINA: Nine times six?

COLLEEN: Fifty-four.

SISTER MARY THOMASINA: Eight times eight? (*Pause.* COLLEEN *whispers answer to* MARIA THERESA.)

MARIA THERESA: Sixty-four.

SISTER MARY THOMASINA: Maria Theresa, did Colleen whisper that answer to you? Did I hear an answer whispered? I do not like that one bit. If you do not know an answer perhaps you should go stand in front of the blackboard and review your eight times tables. (MARIA THERESA *crosses* D.S.R.) Turn around and put your nose against that blackboard. (MARIA THERESA *places her nose against the blackboard so that she is facing front.*) The rest of the class is dismissed for lunch. Timothy, did you blow a bubble? Take that gum out of your mouth and place it on your nose and leave it there for the entire day. Colleen, I'd like a word with you privately. (*All exit except* MARIA THERESA *who starts her monologue.*)

MARIA THERESA: Late at night when I'm lying in my bed, I ask myself some math questions and I get all the answers right. Then when I wake up and go to school and all the way there and all the way through religion class and on the line to go to the lavatory, the answers are still in my head. But just right before math class, they have fallen out of my brain when I wasn't thinking to hold them in. I am not stupid, even though my parents and Sister think so. If we had math first thing, maybe they wouldn't go away. Sometimes, if my father comes home from work early, he helps me with my math homework. I don't want him to because if I give the wrong answer he gets mad and hits me. Usually my mother makes him stop but sometimes she is giving one of the babies a bath and she doesn't hear me. I think about math almost every single night. I can't help it. It makes me feel weird so I usually make a plan for a good happy dream so that when I do fall asleep I won't have a scary one. My favorite dream right now is that I live with someone else's family. Like I live with Donna Reed and I am the only child except that I have an older brother and sister. Donna Reed sends me to a school where there is no math or spelling. When I come home from school, my older brother takes me for a ride to the candy store in his yellow convertible. I make him put the top down and I sit in the back and my older sister combs my hair gently for a whole hour and lets me play with her make-up. Then we all get dressed up for dinner and we go downstairs. Donna Reed always cooks something real good for dinner. Stuff like steak or turkey with mashed potatoes and gravy. She never makes eggplant parmesan and tuna casserole. Dessert is always on the table so right after you finish your dinner you can just grab your dessert and eat it. Usually it is My-T-Fine chocolate pudding because Donna Reed knows that is my favorite. After the family is finished we are excused from the table and we go into the living room and everyone gathers around while I play the piano. Then my father, Mr. Reed, picks me up and carries me up the stairs to my room and tucks me into my very own canopy bed. He puts my stuffed animals around the bed so I will be safe and he leaves my Raggedy Ann and Andy night-light on so I won't be scared. Donna Reed kisses me on the forehead and tells me what a wonderful and beautiful daughter I am and how glad she is that she adopted me and I fall asleep. Sometimes I pray to Jesus about something. Jesus tells me not to think that my parents don't love me. He says that they will probably not get mad at me if I bring home another bad mark in math and spelling. So I believe him, but something always happens when I get home anyway.

(ELIZABETH *enters.*)

ELIZABETH: Maria, she's gone. (MARIA THERESA *doesn't respond.*) Maria, she went to the convent to have lunch, come on.

MARIA THERESA: Elizabeth, do you think it is a sin to pray to Jesus and ask Him to kill certain people in a car crash?

ELIZABETH: Yes, I think so. But I think you can pray and ask Him to send them to a hospital for a little while. I don't think that counts as a sin.

MARIA THERESA: Okay, repeat after me . . . "Dear Jesus . . ."

ELIZABETH: Maria Theresa, this is your prayer, I don't have to say it.

MARIA THERESA: But if two people say it, He is going to listen harder, maybe. Please.

ELIZABETH: . . . "Dear Jesus . . ."

MARIA THERESA: Please send Sister Mary Thomasina . . .

ELIZABETH: (*Crossing her fingers.*) Please send Sister Mary Thomasina . . .

MARIA THERESA: and my whole family . . . especially my father . . .

ELIZABETH: (*Crossing her feet.*) and my whole family . . . especially my father . . ."

MARIA THERESA: To Saint Bernadette's Hospital . . .

ELIZABETH: To Saint Bernadette's Hospital . . . Amen."

MARIA THERESA: I didn't say Amen yet. " . . . at least until I graduate from eighth grade. Thank you very much, signed Maria Theresa Russo, fourth grade, Saint George's School, Yonkers, New York. Amen."

ELIZABETH: ". . . at least until I graduate from eighth grade. Thank you very much. Maria Ther . . . (MARIA THERESA *nudges her.*) Elizabeth, fourth grade, Saint George's School. Amen."

MARIA THERESA: You have to say your last name.

ELIZABETH: McHugh. Elizabeth McHugh.

MARIA THERESA: Okay, great. Elizabeth, you are my very best friend. Let's go eat. (*Starts out of room.*)

ELIZABETH: (*Calling after her.*) Wait for me outside, I forgot my Chinese jumprope.

MARIA THERESA: (*Exiting.*) Okay, hurry.

ELIZABETH: (*Races back to where she stood for prayer.*) Jesus, this is Elizabeth, Elizabeth McHugh, fourth grade, Saint George's School. Please forget everything I just said about the hospital and everything. I was only kidding and besides I had my fingers crossed just in case you didn't notice. Please don't forget to take my name off the list. Thank you very much. I'm sorry we haven't been talking that much lately. Listen, can I ask you something? A couple of us girls were wondering, are you Jewish? Let me know as soon as you can, okay? I love you, Elizabeth.

(*Starts to exit, then runs back, genuflects, and exits as the lights dim.*)

END OF ACT I

ACT II

Patti Smith's "Gloria" is playing as the curtain rises.* GIRLS *enter as if returning from lunch. They enter the lavatory and* ELIZABETH, COLLEEN, *and* MARIA THERESA *begin to groom themselves.* WANDA *pre-*

*Cautionary Note: Permission to produce this play does not include permission to use this music in productions. Producers must procure rights from the copyright owner.

pares her "experiment "and when she is ready she signals the girls to watch. She has a tampon, which she unwraps, dunks in a glass of water, and as it expands, all squeal and giggle with delight. COLLEEN *grabs it away from* WANDA *and, threatening* MARIA THERESA, *chases her out of the lavatory, down the hall, and into the classroom.* WANDA *is in hot pursuit. Sixth grade, 1967.*

WANDA: (*At classroom doorway, grabs tampon.*) Colleen, you make me sick. Put that thing away. Someone will see it, the boys or something.

COLLEEN: Wanda, my brothers see these all the time. No big deal about it.

WANDA: Really. I don't think my father knows about it.

COLLEEN: God, he's got to know about it.

WANDA: Hey, Colleen how come Maria's not in school today?

COLLEEN: Mr. Russo is in jail.

WANDA: What?

COLLEEN: It's true. I swear. My mother told me. Somebody pushed him out of line in the A&P. And he hit the guy on the head with a can of grapefruit juice.

WANDA: Really?

COLLEEN: Yeah, the cops came and everything. The whole family went to pick him up this morning. My mother told me I can't go over to Maria's house anymore, but I think I can still talk to her in school.

ELIZABETH: (*Entering.*) Hey, you guys, guess what?

COLLEEN: Thanks for calling me back last night, Elizabeth.

ELIZABETH: I'm sorry. My house was nuts last night. But I've got great news, my grandmother is moving in next week.

COLLEEN: Great.

WANDA: Is everyone excited?

ELIZABETH: No. No one wants her but me. She's going in my room. Mary Pat is moving into the living room. I can't wait.

COLLEEN: Good luck.

ELIZABETH: Why?

WANDA: Watch out, Colleen's turning green.

ELIZABETH: Why, what's the matter?

COLLEEN: Just that when my grandmother moved in with us everything got creepy. She was always complaining. And she even had her own room. I wouldn't sleep with her.

ELIZABETH: Why not?

COLLEEN: 'Cause she could just die right there while I was sleeping.

ELIZABETH: My grandmother wouldn't die on me, Colleen.

COLLEEN: (*Reading from* True Confessions.) "It was just a little game but we didn't know all the rules. He only did it half way, yet I got pregnant. God help me if Momma finds out who I played with."

WANDA: Let me see that. "Nightmare in the Classroom." "They stripped me naked just for kicks while so many hands and lips did dirty things to me." Wooooh, Colleen, where did you get this?

COLLEEN: From my baby-sitting house. They have *Playboy* too. And she, the lady, has those little birth control pills.

WANDA: She's not a Catholic.

COLLEEN: No kidding.

ELIZABETH: Could I see that?

COLLEEN: No, get your grandmother to show you. Wanda, look at this.

WANDA: How do they fit together like that?

ELIZABETH: Wait a minute. My grandmother may be coming to live with us but we're still best friends, I swear. She's sick and she can't move around too much for awhile. So after school I may go home to see her, but that's it.

COLLEEN: What about basketball?

ELIZABETH: I can still go. Come on. I'm not a flat leaver. (*Grabs magazine.*) Page 45, a sexy word quiz. "A fun fill-in puzzle for women who know the language of loving." Fourteen down. Sixty-nine. Wanda, what does sixty-nine mean? I heard you knew.

WANDA: Get lost.

COLLEEN: I happen to know what it means. It means the guy's thing is six inches long and in nine months you have a baby.

ELIZABETH: That's not it.

COLLEEN: Or that he sticks it in you and in nine months you have a six-inch baby.

ELIZABETH: That answer has too many letters.

COLLEEN: You're right.

ELIZABETH: After school we'll go to the library and look it up.

COLLEEN: Wanda, you're not invited.

SISTER MARY GERMAINE: (*Entering.*) Good afternoon, boys and girls.

ALL: Good afternoon, Sister Mary Germaine.

SISTER MARY GERMAINE: You may all be seated. Now Colleen has a little announcement to make. (WANDA *raises hand.*) Yes, Wanda.

WANDA: Sister, I have an announcement about cheerleading.

COLLEEN: Copy cat.

SISTER MARY GERMAINE: We'll hear about that tomorrow, thank you, Wanda.

COLLEEN: Ha.

SISTER MARY GERMAINE: Boys, file quietly to the back one by one and remove your sneakers and things from the cloakroom for physical fitness. Row one, Francis, you may start. Go on, Colleen.

COLLEEN: Saturday afternoon at 1:30 Father Moynihan is going to unlock St. Steven's auditorium and all the girls are going to meet for the first round of basketball tryouts. Sister Mary Redemptor will show us what we need to know. But I happen to know a few "secret" plays. Pick and roll, and split the post, which I can show to a couple of the girls. My brothers taught them to me. Boys' basketball is different from girls' basketball but we can still use these plays because they don't look too rough even though they really are. My brother T.J. (*A look from* SISTER MARY GERMAINE.) Thomas James, says "it's not the strength, it's the skill," and he should know because he plays for Iona College. (WANDA *is making faces to distract* COLLEEN.) Now don't forget sneakers so that you won't scratch the gym floor. Oh, and bring some shorts so that you can jump real high and still be modest. And no chewing gum . . .

SISTER MARY GERMAINE: Colleen is there something the matter?

COLLEEN: Yes, Sister, Wanda is trying to make me laugh.

WANDA: I was not.

COLLEEN: Was too.

WANDA: Was not.

SISTER MARY GERMAINE: Wanda, cut it out. Please. Try to practice some self control. Russell, check that fly!

WANDA: Did you see it?

ELIZABETH: I think I saw a little pink.

COLLEEN: . . . gum chewing because it could go right down your throat and strangle you. Oh, and this year we are going to get new uniforms, better than the cheerleaders.

WANDA: I doubt it.

COLLEEN: Fact of life.

SISTER MARY GERMAINE: Colleen, wrap it up, please.

COLLEEN: Yes, Sister. And it is good for school spirit and the church gets to make a lot of money because it costs fifty cents a head to get in.

WANDA: Who's going to pay to see a bunch of girls, huh?

ELIZABETH: When we start winning, they'll be busting down the doors.

COLLEEN: That's right. That's all for today, Sister.

SISTER MARY GERMAINE: That was very nice public speaking, Colleen, you may be seated. Now, boys, are you all packed up? Good. File down to the gym. I don't want to hear a single sound on that line. Terrence, take names. Now, who are the two girls who will report to us today? (WANDA *and* COLLEEN *raise their hands.*) Now last week we were discussing puberty during health class . . . acne, fried foods, regular bathing.

WANDA: Yeah, until Richard Krause busted right in the classroom, without knocking.

COLLEEN: Dick Krause.

SISTER MARY GERMAINE: . . . deodorants, etc. Now, today, girls, the assignment was to consult the "Little Pictorial Lives of the Saints" and report back to the class on what you found particularly relevant under the title Saint So-and-So, Virgin, comma, martyr. Then, right after these two reports, we will have another brief discussion on personal hygiene. Which one of you would like to start? (WANDA *raises her hand.*)

WANDA: (*Crossing to in front of teacher's desk.*) January 21st, Saint Agnes, Virgin, Martyr.

SISTER MARY GERMAINE: Sister Agnes' patron saint, yes, Wanda, go on.

COLLEEN: Brown nose.

WANDA: St. Agnes, virgin, martyr, was twelve years old when she was led to the altar and was commanded to offer incense which was part of the rules in Rome at the time. She didn't want to offer incense because it was against her religion, so instead, she raised her hand to Jesus, and made the sign of the cross. The King got really mad when he saw . . .

SISTER MARY GERMAINE: People get mad, dogs get angry.

WANDA: Yes, Sister. The King got really angry when he saw this and he had her tied up but the bandages would not stay on and so he made her take off all her clothes and stand in front of the pagan crowd. But nobody could see her because Jesus performed a miracle and made a blinding light appear so everyone had to look away. One person, a guy, did not turn away because he wanted to see St. Agnes naked. But the light made him blind and he had to be carried away. The King was really mad—angry now and he had a death sentence passed and he had St. Agnes' head chopped off in one blow. Just before she died she managed to say, "Christ is my spouse. He chose me first and His will be done." After she died the angels came to get her body and took it straight to Heaven.

SISTER MARY GERMAINE: Now, Wanda, in your own words, can you tell the class what that story means to you?

WANDA: Well, that saint made up her mind that she wanted to follow Jesus and nothing was going to tempt her.

SISTER MARY GERMAINE: The Saint also represents youth. After all she was only twelve years old. It illustrates how hard you must try to keep your innocence, doesn't it, class?

ALL: Yes, Sister.

SISTER MARY GERMAINE: Also the part of the story we haven't discussed, was when the young man was blinded as be tried to gaze at the body of the young Saint. Now, girls, God protected St. Agnes from this man and even though God is all-knowing, He can't be in all places at all times. You must take some responsibility yourselves. Now I have something for you girls. Wanda please come up to my desk and pass these out. Girls these are some sanitary napkin kits for you to take home. They were donated by Mr. Lorenzo. He has asked me to remind you to tell your parents that all members of our parish are eligible for a 10 percent discount. So please patronize his store. Take these home and show them to your mothers. They will explain.

COLLEEN. My mother explained it already. (WANDA *looks in bag.*)

SISTER MARY GERMAINE: Please do not be gazing at those things here in my classroom. There is a proper place and time for everything. Girls, all eyes up here. You are at the age where you are beginning to provoke the boys. I don't want to see legs crossed in my classroom and I don't want to see uniform skirts that are shorter than regulation length. As a matter of fact let me check them now. (*Girls kneel .*) Elizabeth, when was the last time you took an iron to that skirt? That skirt is too short, Colleen. Take it down two inches by tomorrow. Wanda, perfect.

WANDA: I iron my own uniform blouses.

SISTER MARY GERMAINE: All right back to your seats. (WANDA *raises hand.*) Yes, Wanda.

WANDA: (*About something in bag.*) Sister, I was just wondering what's this for?

COLLEEN: Oh, brother.

SISTER MARY GERMAINE: Wanda, ask your mother. Colleen, let's hear from you. Nice and loud and clear.

COLLEEN: (*Crossing to teacher's desk.*) I have Saint Agatha, virgin, martyr, February 5th. She was from Sicily.

SISTER MARY GERMAINE: Which is in Italy.

COLLEEN: And she was going to be Jesus' spouse, too. A judge sent for her when he heard how pretty and how rich she was. So she went because he made it into a law but she asked Jesus to help her not be harmed by him. When she got there she was thrown in jail because she refused to fall into sin with him. She was locked into a cell until she could change her mind. She didn't change her mind so the judge got real angry and started to torture her. The next thing he did was to strip her of her clothes and send her to a place where the sheep were. Then he took one of her breasts and cut it off. (*Starts to laugh.*) And then Jesus heard her scream and sent one of the apostles to put it back on. (*Laughs some more.*) And then Jesus accepted her prayer of wanting to join him in Heaven so he ended her life and took her to Heaven. (*Composing herself.*) I'm sorry.

SISTER MARY GERMAINE: Sorry or not, Colleen, I have a few important things to say to you. The life of a saint is a very important and holy thing and I will not have that life mocked at in my classroom. It is sacrilegious and perhaps even a sin, I will check into that. Second, Colleen, and I want all the girls to listen closely to this because it concerns some of you. I have been keeping an eye on you and I am sorry to say that you are going right down the drain.

COLLEEN: Sister, I am not.

SISTER MARY GERMAINE: You might be dragging some of your friends down with you. There is a type of girl that gets into trouble, that gets a bad reputation. Colleen, stand over by that blackboard. Face us. Now, girls, looking at Colleen you may not be able to tell from her outward appearance that her soul has turned black and shriveled up smaller and smaller, so that it has almost entirely disappeared . . .

ELIZABETH: I disagree.

SISTER MARY GERMAINE: And who are you to disagree, Elizabeth? What kind of girl might choose Colleen for a friend or even an acquaintance? I would venture to guess and say someone who has a soul in the same sad condition.

ELIZABETH: You can't see Colleen's soul.

SISTER MARY GERMAINE: Elizabeth, take yourself for a little walk down to the principal's office.

ELIZABETH: What should I say to her?

SISTER MARY GERMAINE: Tell her you are doubting the word of Sister Mary Germaine and the Catholic church.

ELIZABETH: Yes, Sister.

COLLEEN: Score one for their side.

(ELIZABETH *exits.*)

SISTER MARY GERMAINE: Enough said. You can use the rest of the time to clean your desks and get your own gear ready for physical fitness. Monica, go around with the waste basket.

(*Lights down except for* COLLEEN *monologue spot.*)

COLLEEN: I used to go out with this guy, Ricky. I liked him a lot for awhile. We hung around Cross County Shopping Center on Saturdays. We used to get red pistachio nuts and then we'd wait till our hands got all red and sweaty. Then we'd go upstairs on the escalator to the Wedding Shop and smear all the white dresses with our hands. It looked like The Bride of Frankenstein, I swear. One time we went to the movies on a Friday night. Me and Ricky saw "Born Free." It was okay for awhile but then toward the end it got bad. The girl lion gets killed and it's really sad. I started to cry even, but I didn't let that Ricky see. I hate to let a boy see me cry. The day we broke up, Ricky and me were sitting in the back of his father's car in the garage. He gave me his ID bracelet and then he tried to put his hand somewhere. I ran right out of that car but I kept the bracelet just for spite. I told my mother about it. Me and my mother are just like this. (*Holds two fingers together.*) She told me I did the right thing. Then she started giving me a speech about sex stuff. She told me about the change and how it was part of becoming a woman. She told me when I got it, it would be such a happy day that we would go out to lunch and have a party all day long. Just me and her. Ha. I don't want to be a woman. I like myself the way I am. My chest is growing, and I think there is hair coming out of, you know, down there. Well anyway, Sister told everyone to finish up with their desks and to pack up. I felt something. I tried to close my legs so it would stop. I held my stomach in, real hard, but it kept leaking. I didn't know the whole thing was so messy. I didn't want to move. I took my sweater off and I wrapped it around me. I knew what it was. After Monica put the wastebasket back, Sister Mary Germaine told me to take my seat. But even before I started to move, she asked me about my sweater. She thought I was trying to show off with sex or something, I guess. She said, "Take that sweater off, it's seventy degrees in this classroom." "My stomach hurts, it makes me feel better." "I'll ask you one more time, take it off." The boys began to come into the classroom, she didn't care, she let them. I couldn't look at her. She hit me. I put my hands to my face and she ripped the sweater off, digging her nails into my side. I just stood there against the blackboard. Everyone was looking at me. Then she made an announcement to the class, that in all her years of teaching, she had never come across someone with such a lack of concern for their personal hygiene. She said these things right in front of the boys. I thought I was going to die. A couple of drops of blood got on the floor. She made one of the boys go down to the janitor's closet and get a mop. The nurse came in and took me out of class. I never want to go back there again. She is trying to make me feel guilty. I do feel guilty. I am a jerk. I wish I was dead, and never had to see you or anybody else again. I wish I had never become a woman. I'm no good at it. Is that what you wanted to hear, Sister? All right, I'm no good at it.

(COLLEEN *exits. Lights return. Eighth grade, 1969.* MARIA THERESA *has a transistor radio plugged into her ear. We hear a 1960s type ballad playing.* ELIZABETH *has been rummaging through her purse, as they enter.*)

MARIA THERESA. Elizabeth, hi. I missed you soooo much. How was your summer?

ELIZABETH: It was great . . . except my grandmother had another heart attack.

MARIA THERESA: Oh, no.

ELIZABETH: She's better now. Hey did you see those guys walk on the moon?

MARIA THERESA: Nah, I fell asleep.

ELIZABETH: It was neat. I was scared, for a minute. You know, Maria, they made up that, "one giant step . . ." slogan, months before. Rip off. (COLLEEN *enters wearing sunglasses.*)

COLLEEN: Hey you guys.

MARIA THERESA: I got your postcard. "Wish you were here." Ha ha.

COLLEEN: I wanted to bring back an alligator pocketbook, but my mother said it was too ugly. We don't get along like we used to. She's getting crazy. My brothers and I palled around mostly. All the guys down there thought I was in high school, I swear.

MARIA THERESA: Big deal.

COLLEEN: Let me see that. (*Puts radio plug in her ear.*)

MARIA THERESA: My father got it for me.

COLLEEN: It isn't your birthday till December.

MARIA THERESA: He bought us all presents because he threw the dining room table against the wall, one Sunday during breakfast. Everyone got real upset. Eggs were hanging off the wall.

COLLEEN: He's nuts.

MARIA THERESA: No, he's not.

ELIZABETH: Hey, did you see Wanda? She's got these cool aviator glasses. She wears them just like Gloria Steinem.

COLLEEN: Who?

MARIA THERESA: The women's libber.

COLLEEN: They're crazy. My father says, watch out if a girl becomes president.

ELIZABETH: How come?

COLLEEN: They could get the curse in the middle of something and cause World War Three.

ELIZABETH: I'm glad we didn't get Lucy for homeroom. Do you think she'll recognize us?

MARIA THERESA: How could she forget? Maria Theresa says, Agie is great, though. She says Agie's got one foot in the grave.

(SISTER MARY AGNES *enters. She is carrying a shopping bag and sprinkles holy water on the class and room as she enters.*)

SISTER MARY AGNES: Good morning, boys and girls.

ELIZABETH: Steady girl.

MARIA THERESA: Sister, watch my hair please.

SISTER MARY AGNES: Good morning, boys and girls.

ALL: Good morning, Sister Mary Agnes.

COLLEEN: Didn't we do this already?

MARIA THERESA: She forgets things, and I think she's gotten worse. (SISTER MARY AGNES *writes her name on the blackboard.*)

SISTER MARY AGNES: Sister—Mary—Agnes.

COLLEEN: We heard, Agie.

SISTER MARY AGNES: Would two of you children come up here and pass these out? This will be a very big year for you eighth graders. We have a great deal to discuss. Now this year you will be graduating . . .

MARIA THERESA: Are we going to have a boy/girl dance?

MARIA THERESA: I have a dress, all picked out. It's lay-away. Wait till you see it.	SISTER MARY AGNES: In spite of that punch being spiked last year . . .

SISTER MARY AGNES: . . . there will be an eighth grade dance. Sister Mary Lucille will be handling the details. Oh, and we have to discuss the co-ops.

SISTER MARY AGNES: Now at my first dance, I had the prettiest dress. White, of course, with small pearls around my neck. My mother was a seamstress. She made all my things. My brother, Jed, played the piano. I loved that dress. I had a lovely time, too. Rufus Quinn brought me a small bouquet of lilies of the valley, with a lilac ribbon around them. Rufus had some scent on too. He smelled so nice: like wood. After the dance, we had a snack. Shortenin' bread and milk with a little taste of honey in it . . . Oh, and then we sang a hymn. (*Begins to hum song.*) "Ah humm . . . I need thee, precious Jesus, for I am filled with . . . filled with?

COLLEEN: It was so long ago, she probably danced with a brontosaurus rex.

ELIZABETH: When are the co-ops, Sister? That's our ticket out of here?

COLLEEN: So what did your mother do?

MARIA THERESA: When? Do you like my hair like this?

COLLEEN: Put it over more. Hold it. When your father went nuts.

MARIA THERESA: She just went into the kitchen and did the dishes.

COLLEEN: I wouldn't take that.

ELIZABETH: Me neither. I'm never getting married.

MARIA THERESA: They might get a divorce.

ELIZABETH: What?

COLLEEN: Maria's parents are getting a divorce.

MARIA THERESA: God, don't announce it. I swear, I hope they do. Mind your own business, Anselm.

COLLEEN: Who would you go live with?

ELIZABETH: Maria, you'll still be in high school with us, right? Oh, it would be the worst if we couldn't all stay together. What about open house about St. Mary's? What about the co-ops?

MARIA THERESA: Hey, Sister, I'm not singing any hymns at that dance.

COLLEEN: She can't hear you, watch this. (COLLEEN *drops books on the floor with a loud bang.*)

ELIZABETH: Is she ever going to get to the co-ops?

SISTER MARY AGNES: Oh, look, you dropped your books, dear. Now what was that song? Rufus had a good strong voice, didn't you, dear? Oh, yes . . . "I need thee precious Jesus, for I am filled with . . ."

COLLEEN: Filled with what, spit it out?

SISTER MARY AGNES: "Filled with . . . sin," thanks Rufus. (*Girls applaud.*) Oh and after we sang that hymn, I bent back my head and Rufus kissed me, right like that.

MARIA THERESA: She actually made out with a guy?

ELIZABETH: What do you think she used to look like?

MARIA THERESA: A dog.

COLLEEN: Sister have any of the other nuns made out with guys? What about Sister Mary Germaine?

MARIA THERESA: Another Bow Wow Club member,

SISTER MARY AGNES: Oh, yes, dear, Sister Mary Germaine was quite a looker in her day. I have seen pictures.

COLLEEN: I'd love to get my hands on those negatives.

MARIA THERESA: Sister, what happened to Rufus, is he a priest or something?

COLLEEN: He ditched her.

SISTER MARY AGNES: After high school, he enlisted in the Army. He was blown up.

MARIA THERESA: Yuuch.

ELIZABETH: So you had to join the convent?

SISTER MARY AGNES: I didn't have to join the convent. I wanted to. I had another beau after Rufus. We used to take long walks, arm in arm, around the trails of West Point.

ELIZABETH: Sometimes, I don't think God knows what He is doing.

SISTER MARY AGNES: God always knows what He is doing, Loretta.

ELIZABETH: Sister, my name is Elizabeth.

COLLEEN: She called you by your grandmother's name. She's spooky.

SISTER MARY AGNES: Did someone have a question?

MARIA THERESA: She's a witch. A nun-witch. Look at that nose real close . . .

SISTER MARY AGNES: No questions, good let's move on.

ELIZABETH: Sister, I have a question, the co-ops?

SISTER MARY AGNES: The results come in the mail. The children just line up by that phone in the hallway and the noise is . . . well, I tell them that patience is a virtue, but you can't tell children anything these days. The co-ops are the entrance exams you must take if you want to get into Catholic high school. Did we do this already? When you are as old as I am, one year just blends into the next.

COLLEEN: No, Sister.

SISTER MARY AGNES: Thank you, dear. Now I will be teaching math and current events and . . . something else . . . well, don't worry it will come back to me, it always does. Lucille will be teaching English and science in the class across the hall.

COLLEEN: I love Lucy.

MARIA THERESA: (*Trying to read handwriting in* SISTER MARY AGNES' *book, which was left on her desk.*) Look at the way she spells co-ops. March 5th. I can't read her writing.

SISTER MARY AGNES: Dear, is there something the matter with your eyes? That says Blessed Sacrament High School. You should get those bangs cut. What was your name, Mary Alice?

MARIA THERESA: Maria Theresa.

SISTER MARY AGNES: Well, Mary Thomas, don't you think you should get those bangs cut? I remember a story about a young lady who had a hairdo she liked so much . . . I believe you would call it a beehive. How can you see from behind all that hair? Well, she never washed her hair because she didn't want to ruin it. About two months later, she went to the doctor's . . . Eugene, could you please stop shaking him? Thank you . . .

MARIA THERESA: What happened to the girl with the beehive?

SISTER MARY AGNES: Who? . . . oh . . . yes. Well, when she went to the doctor's he found bugs all in her hair and they were eating her brains out. Now we all want to see your pretty face, don't we, dear?

COLLEEN: Yeah, we all want to see her pretty face, don't we, Eddie?

MARIA THERESA: Drop dead. I think it's time to change classes, Sister.

SISTER MARY AGNES: Thank you dear. Let me check.

ELIZABETH: Sister, are you looking for something? Are you looking for your glasses?

SISTER MARY AGNES: I know I put them some where . . . now, just one second . . .

ELIZABETH: Sister, they are around your neck.

SISTER MARY AGNES: So they are. I put them there so I wouldn't forget them. Isn't that funny?

MARIA THERESA: Hysterical, we're all dying. Let me out of here.

SISTER MARY AGNES: It *is* time to change classes. Would you like me to walk you?

COLLEEN: No. It's right across the hall. Hey, Sister, thanks again. (COLLEEN *and* MARIA THERESA *exit.*)

SISTER MARY AGNES: Have a nice afternoon. Good bye, Loretta.

ELIZABETH: I said my name is Elizabeth.

SISTER MARY AGNES: (*Ignoring her and singing.*) I need, precious Jesus . . . (ELIZABETH *looks at her and exits.*) Rufus, there is one thing I have been meaning to . . .

(SISTER MARY AGNES *exits. The girls circle around and change to* SISTER MARY LUCILLE*'s classroom.*)

MARIA THERESA. Wanda, did you ever show up at Saint Mary's open house yesterday?

WANDA: Yeah. I was in the science lab for most of it. Maria, we get to dissect frogs in sophomore year.

MARIA THERESA: Oh.

WANDA: The science teacher showed me these little dead mice in jars. It was really neat.

MARIA THERESA: Well, I didn't brownnose with any teachers. I was in the cafeteria. You got to check out that food. Every Wednesday, they have little fried chicken wings with gravy and lasagna.

ELIZABETH: Did you see the principal? She's real young. She doesn't wear a habit. That place is perfect.

MARIA THERESA: What if I don't get in?

WANDA: You'll get on the waiting list, at least. Don't worry. (SISTER MARY LUCILLE *enters.*)

SISTER MARY LUCILLE: Sit down. How many times do I have to tell you I don't want to hear any stressing or laughing in that hallway? I will just sit back and see who gets into Catholic high school and who doesn't. I have left students back in the eighth grade and I will do it again. Watch your P's and Q's. Now, business at hand. In three short weeks the archdiocese of New York will hold the Seventh Annual Forensic Tournament. Six students have submitted speeches on the theme for this year, "Outstanding Current World Leaders." Mr. Farrell and Miss Howes, your marks are not satisfactory. I want my class to capture that First Prize trophy—fourth year in a row. Mr. Mackenzie, your lisp, while I admire your determination, disqualifies you. Mr. Egan, "Selected Works of Archbishop Fulton Sheen," approved and good luck. And finally, Wanda Sluska—"The Inaugural Address of our Late Great John Fitzgerald Kennedy," wise choice, Miss Sluska. (ELIZABETH *raises hand.*) Between your elocution and style, Jack Kennedy's words, and my careful coaching, God will surely be on our side. First prize is . . . Yes, Miss McHugh, what is it?

ELIZABETH: Sister, I submitted a speech. I was wondering . . .

SISTER MARY LUCILLE: I was coming to that, Miss McHugh. Patience is a virtue. Miss Sluska, good luck. Miss McHugh I have rejected your speech.

ELIZABETH: Sister, it's under eight minutes. I timed it twice.

SISTER MARY LUCILLE: I have no quarrel with the length, Miss McHugh, it is the subject matter. In all good conscience, I cannot allow a student in my classroom to enter the Seventh Annual Forensic Tournament with the words of a non-Catholic.

ELIZABETH: But he *was* a Christian.

SISTER MARY LUCILLE: "I Have a Dream" by Martin Luther King Jr., leave it to the public schools. Who exactly did Martin Luther King lead anyway? Miss McHugh pick another speech. From a Roman Catholic author, this time. Perhaps you should look at the words of Pope John the XXIII, his work in the ecumenical council. No more Latin Mass. Guitars. Dialogue with other faiths. Right up your alley.

ELIZABETH: But I prepared—there isn't enough time to choose a new . . .

SISTER MARY LUCILLE: End of discussion. We have three and a half minutes to spend on the dance, no more, no less. (ELIZABETH *throws a note to* WANDA.) You are very bold and brazen, who do you think you are?

WANDA: Nobody, Sister.

SISTER MARY LUCILLE: Well, Miss Nobody, hand Sister that note. (*She reads the note and crumples it.*) Miss McHugh, if you expect me to be shocked and annoyed at your behavior, you are going to have to do a lot better than this. Grow up, Miss

McHugh, and find stronger ammunition if you want to tangle with me. Take the seat furthest away from me and sit there for the remainder of the year. Do you understand me?

ELIZABETH: Yes, Sister.

SISTER MARY LUCILLE: Don't use that tone with me, young lady. Sluska, read that note.

WANDA: Do I have to, Sister?

SISTER MARY LUCILLE: Don't defy Sister, read that note.

WANDA: "Sister Lucy plays bongo drums with Monsignor Ricardo in the closet."

SISTER MARY LUCILLE: Now, I would like you two to diagram this sentence for homework, one hundred times. As a matter of fact, the whole class can do it so nobody gets itchy fingers. Write that note on the blackboard, Miss Sluska.

MARIA THERESA: Thanks a lot, you guys.

SISTER MARY LUCILLE: P.S., girls, not funny. (ELIZABETH *sneezes. This is the signal to start humming the theme song from a popular '50's TV sitcom.*) The theme for the dance will be . . . stop that this instant or there won't be a dance. (*Humming stops.*) The theme for the dance will be "Spring Flowers." Now, as for the chaperones, we will need four to handle this crowd, plus the faculty. Maria Theresa, how about your father? He is a nice, big, beefy man and your sisters always brought him.

MARIA THERESA: I think he will be working nights then, Sister.

SISTER MARY LUCILLE: I think he can get off for just one night, right, Miss Russo?

MARIA THERESA: Yes, Sister.

SISTER MARY LUCILLE: Miss Sluska, we expect a cold cut donation from your father. A few rules for the dance. No Beatles music. You will not bring any of the filth that is running around, outside the school, via the dance. None of the long hair, the cigarettes, or those Brits from Liverpool who run around saying that they are better than Jesus Christ. Also it is semi-formal. That means, girls, no mini skirts, no long gowns . . .

MARIA THERESA: But I just finished my last payment.

SISTER MARY LUCILLE: Please, girls, no fishnet stockings, no make-up, no jewelry, and perhaps some wristlength white gloves. Boys, jackets, white shirts, and navy blue ties.

ELIZABETH: I don't believe it. (*She sneezes, class hums.*)

SISTER MARY LUCILLE: Well you better believe it or there won't be a dance. Now, boys and girls, you have heard a rumor about an incident that occurred in my classroom last year. That I took James Fowley's head and smashed it against the blackboard. This is not a rumor, this is a fact. (*Humming stops.*) That boy provoked me. That boy's parents marched right up to this school and walked through that very classroom door . . . and they thanked me. The same thing will happen to you if there is any sort of misconduct at that dance. No smoking, no drinking, and if there is any slow dancing, I want the couples to dance an arm's length apart. That is enough room for you and the Holy Ghost. Have I made myself clear? HAVE I MADE MYSELF CLEAR?

ALL: Yes, Sister Mary Lucille.

(*All move* D.S.R. *and bunch together at the dance. 1960s dance music is playing.*)

COLLEEN: Look at the boys, they're all squished up there by the band. Nobody is going to dance with us. What a bomb.

WANDA: Well, if nobody asks us to dance, we can dance with each other.

COLLEEN: Like a bunch of lesbos, forget it. If it wasn't for you, Elizabeth, we wouldn't have to wear these stupid uniforms.

ELIZABETH: Hey, Colleen, you were the one who carried it too far. I was just going to put the bongo drums on her desk. You didn't have to play them like an "ass" in the bathroom.

MARIA THERESA: Hey, look, here comes Eddie.

WANDA: First comes love, second comes marriage, then comes Maria and a baby carriage.

ALL: Hi, Eddie. (*They push* MARIA THERESA *forward but the imaginary* EDDIE *asks* COLLEEN *to dance.*)

COLLEEN: Yeah, sure, Eddie, I'd love to. Toodles, faggots. (COLLEEN *dances offstage.*)

WANDA: What a traitor.

MARIA THERESA: I called dibs on Eddie. He was supposed to be mine. I just want to do something to her.

ELIZABETH: Sic your father on her.

MARIA THERESA: Don't mention him.

COLLEEN: (*Dancing over to the girls.*) Hey, Wanda, I have a message for you. Five o'clock shadow wants to know if you want to dance?

WANDA: Francis?

COLLEEN: That's what I said

WANDA: Okay, but I'm not dancing anything slow with him, he sweats a lot. (WANDA exits.)

ELIZABETH: Look, Maria . . .

MARIA THERESA: I'm changing my name. Call me Terry.

ELIZABETH: Hey look, Terry, your father is dancing with Lucy.

MARIA THERESA: Arm's length apart, Sister. Perfect couple.

ELIZABETH: Hey, look, they're doing the bunny hop, Maria.

MARIA THERESA: Terry.

ELIZABETH: Hi, Eugene. Let's go do it. He's calling us.

MARIA THERESA: He's calling you.

ELIZABETH: You don't need a partner.

MARIA THERESA: Just go, huh. (ELIZABETH *exits.*)

COLLEEN: (*From* O.S.) Put your arms around me, Eddie, and you better hop.

MARIA THERESA: (*Stands alone listening to music.*) Oh hi, Daddy. Get lost, huh? I'm not dancing cause, I don't feel like dancing. I'm in a watching mood. I am not B.S.ing. Don't curse around me, please. I'm having a great time. I just don't want to dance, because my legs are a little tired. I don't want to dance with you. No it's not because you dance weird, no it's not because you're fat. It's because of a guy I know. Which one? That one. Daddy, lower your voice! No, I don't want you to break his legs. Daddy, I got to tell you something. I've always been afraid of you and you've always been afraid of me. How come, huh? All right, I'll dance with you. And Daddy let's bash into Eddie every once in awhile, okay?

(MARIA THERESA *dances awkwardly with her imaginary father,* S.R. *as* COLLEEN, WANDA, *and* ELIZABETH *do the bunny hop, entering from the left. Finally* MARIA THERESA *joins them and they "hop" into the classroom scene.* WANDA *is at the blackboard, erasing. Spring 1970.*)

ELIZABETH: Wanda, Wanda, are you deaf?

MARIA THERESA: Leave her, she's in love.

ELIZABETH: I guess so. Mrs. Francis Crawford, yuch.

MARIA THERESA: My parents went out on a date the other night. To Carlo's.

WANDA: You're kidding.

MARIA THERESA: Nope. And they haven't fought for three days straight. They decided to call the divorce off.

ELIZABETH: (*Reading the Encyclopaedia Britannica.*) That's great, Maria.

MARIA THERESA: I think she might be having another baby.

WANDA: Your family multiplies like rabbits.

MARIA THERESA: How crude. At least we multiply, only-child-Polack. What's the matter with your mother, huh?

ELIZABETH: Hey, you guys, shut up. After a week of scientific research in Yonkers Public Library, I have found this little tidbit. Ready? (*Reads from encyclopedia.*) "The earnest *Jewish* piety of Jesus' home, the character of his parents and especially his mother . . . blah, blah, blah . . . all this helps us to understand the profound religious development of the *man* Christ Jesus. The MAN Christ Jesus.

WANDA: Let me see that. They don't even think Jesus was God.

ELIZABETH: Yeah, I know. And some people don't think there is a God.

MARIA THERESA: They're wrong, right?

WANDA: Are you going to show this to your parents?

ELIZABETH: Nope. I'm copying this and three other things and I'm going to send them to Sister Mary Lucille.

MARIA THERESA: Are you crazy?

ELIZABETH: I may deliver them personally, depending on her behavior.

WANDA: When?

ELIZABETH: I'll know when the time is right.

WANDA: Yeah, well don't send it till after graduation.

MARIA THERESA: You're taking your life in your hands.

ELIZABETH: I am not.

WANDA: Don't be too sure. (SISTER MARY LUCILLE *enters.*)

SISTER MARY LUCILLE: Quiet down. I can hear that ruckus all the way across the hall. Sister Mary Agnes won't be in today . . .

ELIZABETH: Is she all right?

MARIA THERESA: Did she die?

SISTER MARY LUCILLE: She fell on her way from the convent. I will be taking both classes for the day. Oh, does someone want to register a complaint? Just stand right up and say so. Fine, I didn't think so. Elizabeth McHugh pack up your books and get your things together. (ELIZABETH *does so.*) Now I will pass out these book reports. Mr. Joseph Ross, "Johnny Tremain" an F. Mr. Ross, it is not sufficient to report on only one page of a book. The page where Johnny Tremain gets his hand encased in silver may hold a fascination with you, but I fail to see this as the outstanding literary event of the twentieth century. No, this won't do. Read the entire book, please. Wanda Sluska, "Atlas Shrugged" by Ian Rand.

WANDA: It's Ayn Rand, Sister.

SISTER LUCILLE: IAN-ayn, Miss Sluska, see me after class. And tell your father, I don't like kidneys.

ELIZABETH: I'm ready.

SISTER MARY LUCILLE: Class, if a girl refuses to learn her lessons, time and time again, God has a way of making his displeasure known. Elizabeth you continue to disobey my will, which is God's will, and therefore he has sent you a personal message of disapproval that I have been entrusted to deliver. Your mother called in to Sister Rose Gertrude and I am sorry to tell you this; but your grandmother passed away this morning.

MARIA THERESA: Elizabeth, I'm sorry.

SISTER MARY LUCILLE: Down in your seat.

ELIZABETH: What time this morning?

SISTER MARY LUCILLE:: Keep your mouth quiet.

ELIZABETH: (*softly*) Jesus was a Jew.

SISTER MARY LUCILLE: Excuse me?

ELIZABETH: Jesus was a Jew.

SISTER MARY LUCILLE: Shut it, young lady.

(SISTER MARY LUCILLE *slaps* ELIZABETH *across her face.* ELIZABETH *exits.* WANDA *stands with the encyclopedia.*)

WANDA: Jesus was a Jew and I have the facts to back it up.

MARIA THERESA: (*Bars the door to the classroom with a pointer.*) Jesus really was a Jew, read it, Wanda.

WANDA: "Jesus was the promised Messiah of Jewish expectation, that is, the exalted, semi-divine King of Israel, in the glorious age to come . . ."

SISTER MARY LUCILLE: Who gave you that information?

MARIA THERESA. . . . And Jesus may just be an ordinary, old human. Just a regular guy, sort of smart.

SISTER MARY LUCILLE: Mr. Reynolds, sit down, or I will cut the legs from underneath you. Hand me that book, Sluska.

WANDA: (*Tosses the book to* MARIA.) Maria. "In the end it was the Jerusalem hierarchy and the officers of the Roman army of occupation who put Jesus to death." Catch, Maria. (MARIA THERESA *catches book.*)

MARIA THERESA: Jesus probably wasn't any good at math, either.

(MARIA THERESA *exits with the book,* SISTER MARY LUCILLE *follows her and then* WANDA *exits.*)

WANDA: Wait 'till the Pope hears about this.

(*Lights fade as* ELIZABETH *reenters. Spot light comes up on her.*)

ELIZABETH: (*To God, as if she is in church.*) Hey, come on out, I want to talk to you. It's me, Elizabeth. You can hide behind any statue in this place, but you better listen to me. I don't know if you know this but after my grandmother moved in with us, everything was different. We used to sit in my room, after school. She'd ask me questions about all sorts of things. Then she'd listen to my answers real close because she said I was an important person. Some nights, after we went to bed, I would hear her talking to my grandfather in the dark. If I made any noise she'd stop. Because it was private. One night I saw that she was crying. I made some noise and she stopped. Then she asked me if I remembered my grandfather. I did, she liked that. We fell asleep on her bed like sisters. Sunday mornings were kind of strange. Nobody would give up eating bacon and some smells made her sick. My father would tell her if the grease bothered her so much, to take her eggs and go into the bedroom and wait until breakfast was over. I helped her stuff towels into the cracks under the door; but the smell got in anyway. Then my father would make me come back to the table and eat with the rest of the family. I'd go, but I wouldn't eat that bacon. Sometimes, if she was feeling a little better we'd take short walks. After we had rested, she'd tell me stories about my mother and bring along pictures that I had never seen. I didn't know why my mother was so sad and neither did my grandmother. One day, my father came home from work and told me that my grandmother would have to move back to the Bronx. He said it was just not working out. She needed more care and besides she was making the family crazy. I told him that she wasn't making me crazy. I told him she let me be near her. He didn't understand that. And now I see that you didn't either. You took her and I don't think that's fair. You're supposed to do the right thing, all the time.

I don't believe that anymore. You just like to punish people, you like to interrupt their lives. You didn't let me finish. She doesn't know what I think, and I was almost ready to tell her. Why don't you take my mother next time? Oh, you like to take little kids, don't you? Grab one of my brothers next, they're all baptized. Why don't you take my whole stinking family, in one shot, then you won't waste any time. That would be some joke. But I want to tell you something. It's a personal message, I'm delivering it, myself. Don't you ever lay your hands on me, cause if I ever see you, you can strike me dead . . . try . . . I will spit all over your face, whatever it looks like. Because you and everyone else in this world are one big pack of liars. And I really think I hate you. Something else: You don't exist.

(ELIZABETH *turns from audience. Spot out and* ELIZABETH *exits. Classroom lights up on* SISTER MARY AGNES*'s class.* COLLEEN *and* MARIA THERESA *enter dragging field hockey sticks, followed by* ELIZABETH.)

COLLEEN: We got burnt.

MARIA THERESA: How embarrassing. We'll never beat Lucille's homeroom like this. Elizabeth, you let everything fly right by.

COLLEEN: Maria, you didn't do much better. Elizabeth, don't worry.

MARIA THERESA: I'm nervous about the co-ops results. You don't care about them, so what's your excuse, huh?

ELIZABETH: Maria, don't bug me.

COLLEEN: Elizabeth, I beg you, don't give up, don't go to public school. Don't let Lucy ruin your life.

ELIZABETH: It's not her, it's him. You know if you are a Catholic and you have something you like, he . . .

MARIA THERESA: He who?

ELIZABETH: God.

MARIA THERESA: Oh.

ELIZABETH: He finds out about it and then he takes it away. Just to punish you. So I don't care about anything, anymore.

COLLEEN: Oh, that's not true. God is going to let you into Saint Mary's.

ELIZABETH: No, he's not.

MARIA THERESA: I agree with Elizabeth.

ELIZABETH: You do?

MARIA THERESA: Yup. How come I'm always failing math, huh? Punishment.

COLLEEN: Punishment for what?

MARIA THERESA: I don't know. (SISTER MARY AGNES *enters.*)

SISTER MARY AGNES: Girls, your minds were not on the game. Eight to . . . humm . . . to what?

MARIA THERESA: Eight to one. Ask her.

COLLEEN: Sister, the reason we couldn't concentrate is because, well, the co-op admission slips are in the mail today. And we were wondering if we could get out a little early to call our mothers.

SISTER MARY AGNES: (*Looks around in her shopping bag.*) Well, I don't know, you girls are so noisy by that phone.

COLLEEN: Sister, you have to. I'm going to kill myself if I have to wait till three o'clock.

MARIA THERESA: I'll take names.

COLLEEN: Have a heart.

SISTER MARY AGNES: What was I looking for?

MARIA THERESA: A phone.

SISTER MARY AGNES: A bone. Oh no, a foot, yes. Here is a rabbit's foot for each of you to hold on to, while you are on the phone. Mary Steven, (*to* MARIA THERESA) you get two, you're going to need them.

MARIA THERESA: Thanks, Sister. That's sweet.

COLLEEN: You're a sly devil, Sister.

SISTER MARY AGNES: Don't thank me, thank Rufus. It was all his idea.

MARIA THERESA: Thanks, Rufus.

COLLEEN: Thanks, Rufus, can we go, Sister?

SISTER MARY AGNES: Yes, but be quiet by that phone.

(MARIA THERESA, COLLEEN *exit,* ELIZABETH *hesitates.*)

COLLEEN: Elizabeth, come on.

SISTER MARY AGNES: Get going, dear, don't forget your rabbit's foot, Loretta.

ELIZABETH: I don't care about dumb old Saint Mary's. And I don't believe in magic.

SISTER MARY AGNES: What do you believe in, dear?

ELIZABETH: Facts. I think it's only fair to tell you that I am not a Catholic anymore, Sister. God hates me and I hate God. Sister Agnes, you're really nice for a nun and all, but you're all wrong about God.

SISTER MARY AGNES: What do you mean?

ELIZABETH: God is just a killer. He killed my grandmother and he killed Rufus. You probably forgave him, but I never will. Never.

SISTER MARY AGNES: That's up to you. Stay angry, as long as you like. But I've got some bad news: God will never give up on you. And I don't think you'll be able to keep that heart of yours closed forever.

ELIZABETH: Don't bet on it, Sister. (ELIZABETH *begins to exit.*)

SISTER MARY AGNES: Elizabeth, you forgot something.

ELIZABETH: What?

SISTER MARY AGNES: Your rabbit's foot, dear. (ELIZABETH *takes it and exits.*)

COLLEEN: (*Lights up on phone area.*) Stop pushing, will you? Don't you have any class?

MARIA THERESA: Good luck, Eddie. (WANDA *enters area.*)

WANDA: Who's got change of a quarter?

COLLEEN: Oh, God. Glad you could make it, Elizabeth.

ELIZABETH: I didn't have a choice. I didn't feel like listening to her singing and talking to Rufus.

COLLEEN: Who's first? Not me, that's for sure. Maria, you go ahead, you first. Come on dial, I'm dying.

MARIA THERESA: Hello, Mom, Dad? Daddy, how come you're home from work? Nothing's wrong? I just wanted to call and see if the mail was there yet, Daddy. Daddy, let Mom get it please. They're fighting to see who gets to open it. Ma, hi, yeah, what does it say? I got in. I'm real glad. No, tell him I'll talk to him later . . . Ma, there are other people waiting. Hi, Dad, yeah, I got in. Gotta go. I did it. I made it. Go ahead, Wanda.

WANDA: Tak man. Jestem bardzo podniecona. Czy otrzymalam stypendium? Skad?

ELIZABETH: She doesn't show any expression.

WANDA: Ze Swietej marit Swieteco Ignaca. Wspaniale. Do Zubaczenia.

COLLEEN: She probably got a scholarship.

WANDA: Kocham cie . . . Five hundred bucks.

COLLEEN: Big deal. Hi, Mom. It's me. Me, Colleen. Brian, get off the extension. Yuch, he coughed right in my ear. What a freak. Did you get the mail yet? No, Mom, go get it. She didn't get the mail yet, can you believe her? Not Daddy's mail, my mail. Can't you be serious, stop kidding around. Open it up, what does it say? Okay, 'bye. All four schools!

MARIA THERESA: Which one are you going to?

COLLEEN: Saint Mary's, of course. Elizabeth, go ahead.

MARIA THERESA: Our Father, Who art in Heaven . . .

ELIZABETH: Cut it out, Maria, it's already decided. Mom, hi. Did you get the mail yet? Open it. I didn't? 'Bye, Mommy.

WANDA: Oh, Elizabeth.

COLLEEN: Shit. (*Covers her mouth quickly.*)

ELIZABETH: (*Steps away from girls, looking very sad.*) Then . . . I'm kidding. I did.

ALL: Saint Mary's, here we come.

(COLLEEN, MARIA THERESA, WANDA *return to their desks, pack up their books, listening while* ELIZABETH *speaks in monologue spot.*)

ELIZABETH: So that's it, I guess. Except that a couple of weeks ago, I was at a party. For some reason I began telling all these wild Catholic school stories. I hadn't thought about that part of my life, for a long time, but all the memories came back. We laughed for hours. Then as I was leaving, someone I didn't know very well, a public school refugee, asked me what I thought about God, now. I said I didn't think anything about Him except that maybe He wasn't a guy and left. When I got home, I couldn't get to sleep. The tail end of "Miracle on 34th Street" was on. The little girl was driving in a car and she had her eyes shut tight. She was saying over and over in the sweetest MGM voice, "I believe, I believe," over and over. I turned it off. I pulled my blanket up and I shut my eyes tight. I remembered how I used to believe in miracles, falling asleep with some question in my mind. And that night, it seemed the whole process was beginning again. Because I found myself asking, into the dark distance, a vaguely familiar question, "Are you there, Are you there?"

(*Lights come down slowly on* ELIZABETH.)

THE END

WATERBABIES

Adam LeFevre

WATERBABIES premiered at the Actors Theatre of Louisville, where it received the 1995 Heideman Award. It was directed by Simon Ha; the set design was by Stephanie R. Gerckens; the costume design was by Kevin R. McLeod; the lighting design was by Kathleen Kronauer; the production stage manager was Sarah Nicole Spearing; and the dramaturg was Corby Tushla. The cast was as follows:

LIZ Elizabeth Dwyer
EMMA Jennifer Bohler

Lights up.

A small office in the newly constructed wing of a YMCA complex in a medium-sized American city.

An institutional metal desk with chair, a small couch, a bookcase with a few books for and about children. On the wall, a big daisy made out of construction paper, each petal a different color, each bearing the name of a child—Becky, Andrew, Travis, etc.—and a painting, a seascape, perhaps a print of a Winslow Homer.

Emma sits quietly on the couch. In her lap a swaddled little body gently writhes.

Enter Liz, as if turning from one corridor into another. She holds a scrap of paper in her hand, referring to it as she talks to herself.

LIZ: Right, down the third green hallway. That was the third green hallway. First blue door on the left. Whose left? God, I don't have a clue where I am. Blue door. (*She turns and sees Emma.*) Oh! Hi. Water babies! Am I here?

EMMA: He's almost down.

LIZ: Uh oh. Nap time? Am I late?

EMMA: His eyes are open. I don't know.

LIZ: There was construction everywhere. Central Avenue closed entirely. The arterial backed up to Henshaw. Flashing arrows funneling traffic into one lane. Normally nice people, they get behind a wheel in a situation like that, presto! swine. Total maniac piglets. And forgive me, this new wing, it's gorgeous, but it's not the Y I remember. These color-coded corridors, I cannot fathom.

EMMA: (*Speaking to her bundle.*) No, no. Shh.

LIZ: Ooops.

EMMA: Don't do this to me. It's my life now.

LIZ: I'll whisper.

EMMA: Don't worry. Once he's down, he sleeps like a . . . like a . . . lo . . . like a law . . . Damn! Like a lull . . .

LIZ: Is this a bad . . .

EMMA: Lobster! A lobster. He sleeps like a lobster. There. Bingo.

LIZ: Cause if this is a bad time . . .

EMMA: It's not good or bad, long as it floats.

LIZ: . . . I could come back. No problem. I've got errands to do, and Jim, my husband Jim's got the baby at home. He takes Wednesday afternoons off now, which is such a blessing. A legitimate breather for me, and he gets his one-on-one Daddy time with Duncan. Am I talking too loud? How old's your little guy?

EMMA: He's . . . He's about . . . Oh God, I don't know. You know those days when everything . . .

LIZ: Boy, do I. I mean, having a kid . . .

EMMA: Everything is just so . . .

LIZ: Changes everything, doesn't it?

EMMA: Boneless. Unbraided. Blended in? Something with a *B* in it.

(*To bundle.*)

Lullabye-bye, Snookums. Sneepytime.

LIZ: What's his name?

EMMA: Oh God. Okay. It's . . . It's . . . Lo . . . Law . . . Lolaw . . .

LIZ: It's not important.

EMMA: It's his *name,* for Christsake! I'll get it.

LIZ: Why don't I come back?

EMMA: Blob! No! Bob! Bob. This is my boy, Bob.

(*She gently chucks him under the chin.*)

Bobby, blobby. Li'l puddin' face. Wow, he's really under now. I'm losing my ambivalence about the immediate future. What is it you want?

LIZ: I called you, remember? I have some questions about Water Babies.

EMMA: Oh, yes. Water Babies.

LIZ: Just some quick ones, you know, about the philosophy of the time-frame, you know. What's developmentally appropriate specifically vis-à-vis Duncan, who's pretty advanced, according to our doctor, physically. It's amazing, really. He'll be eleven months next week, and he's *this* far from walking. Because I've read if you wait too long, with some kids—and unfortunately, we only just heard about your program from my friend, Diane, who, by the way, said you just had a *knack* with the little ones. *Enchantress,* in fact, was the word she used. Anyway, I read if you start too late it can be traumatic and actually instill a fear, you know, of the water and create an obstacle the child then later on down the road has to overcome. If you wait, that is. If you wait too long. Before you start. So, I was just concerned that at eleven months we may have missed the boat, so to speak, with Dunkie. But I don't know, of course. Because this is not . . . my area. So.

(*A pause.*)

I guess your Bobby's a water baby.

EMMA: It's in the blood.

LIZ: So, how old was he when he started?

EMMA: Oh God, here we go again. Okay, wait. I'll get it. Bob was . . . When we met he was already nearly this size, so that would make him . . . It's conceivable he was younger, by a breath or two. Maybe. But you know he's not really mine so none of this is written in stone.

LIZ: Oh. He's adopted.

EMMA: Listen. You hear that?

LIZ: No.

EMMA: He doesn't get that from me. Does your son speak?

LIZ: Oh, yes. Lots of words. Doggie. Horsey. Moomoo.

EMMA: Horsey and Moomoo. Wow. Think I should worry about Bob?

LIZ: No. I mean, well . . . *How* old is he? No. I mean, no. Each one is just different. Each has his or her own way. Like my sister-in-law's little boy, Wade. He didn't say a word till he was nearly three and a half years old. Then, all of a sudden, one morning, this torrent of language just poured forth from this child's mouth—all these words they had no idea where he'd even heard them, as if they'd been dammed up inside his little brain and finally on this particular day, the dam just burst.

EMMA: This morning I thought I heard him say *waffle.* But he was just choking.

LIZ: Dunkie says *waffo.* And *maypo suppo.*

EMMA: I had to give him a real smack on the back.

LIZ: He calls it *maypo suppo.*

EMMA: Calls what *maypo suppo*?

LIZ: Syrup. Maple syrup.

EMMA: Don't worry. He'll get it.

LIZ: I'm not worried.

EMMA: Bob doesn't talk. He kind of transmits. You gotta stay on your toes.

LIZ: Have you been doing this a long time?

EMMA: What?

LIZ: Teaching infants to swim.

EMMA: Oh. I've been involved in aquatic education all my life. When I was a kid, I tried to teach myself to breathe through my eyes. I just thought I could do it.

LIZ: Aw. That's cute.

EMMA: No, I was absolutely serious about it. I sensed inside me this skill, this ancient, lost skill which I was sure I could salvage from the deep of my memory. I practiced in the bathtub. Kept my mouth and nose just below the surface of the water, and concentrated on bringing air in through my tear ducts, and around my eyes. I never got it. Swallowed a lot of water too. But I learned . . . that the breath . . . cannot be contained. It must circulate, always and forever. And that I could not disappear . . . into what contained *me* . . . and remain . . . myself.

LIZ: Wow, so you've really developed a philosophy, haven't you. It's not just the doggie paddle and back-float anymore.

EMMA: The brain is 80 percent water. Does that answer your question? That wasn't your question, was it. Damn. I'm sorry. What is it you want to know?

LIZ: Is Duncan too advanced for Water Babies? Jim is very gung-ho. I'm just . . . I may be a little over-protective, I guess. I just don't want anything bad to happen.

EMMA: Well, I don't know then. You see, it's like a dream. In a liquid environment, there are no guarantees.

LIZ: I mean, he's just a baby. I don't want him traumatized. I don't want him set back in any way. As a mother you know what I mean.

EMMA: No. No I don't. You think this is the Marines?

LIZ: No, of course not . . .

EMMA: Just what do you think I intend to do to little Dunkie?

LIZ: You misunderstand me . . .

EMMA: Roast him and eat him like a Peking Duck.

LIZ: No, please. I just . . .

EMMA: Lookit! Ol' Dunkie and me will get along just fine so long as he leaves the *moomoo doggie* out of it. We're swimmers here, not talkers.

LIZ: I'm not worried about *you.* I'm worried about the water.

EMMA: Oh, well. That's different. It is always wise to cast a cold and narrowed eye upon the water. Water can take you places from which, unless you're very careful, there is no return. Places so deep, so quiet, so beautiful, it's more than the human heart can bear. It's always good to pause at water's edge. Hesitation, as they say, is Wisdom's crippled child. For Duncan's sake, let's be perfectly quiet for a moment. No words in the world for awhile but water's words.

LIZ: I . . .

EMMA: Shh!

(*There's a considerable pause.* EMMA *cocks her ear toward* BOB.)

You hear that? Didn't that sound like *waffle?*

LIZ: I have to talk to Jim.

EMMA: How would he know?

LIZ: About Water Babies for Duncan. We just have to discuss it a little more before we can make an informed decision.

EMMA: That's a mistake. Men don't trust water. They can't fix it. It eludes them. Not their fault. Just the way it is. Jim'll steer you wrong on this, believe me. The hell with Jim is my advice. Though I'm sure he's an excellent man.

LIZ: We're a team. That's the way we do things. Sorry, I'll just have to get back to you when we decide what to do. Is it the same phone number?

EMMA: I should have told you. There's no space left in this session anyway. All filled up. Just before you arrived a baby crawled in here and formed a complete sentence. Crawled right up into my lap and said, you believe this, without a trace of a lisp or coo, said, "I shall test the deep." I mean, talk about *advanced.* I was just bowled over by the presence and self-possession of this little fry who couldn't have been more than a handful of moons old. So, I said, "Bless your soul, child, you're in! You're my last water baby." So, you see, there's just no room. Unless someone drops out. Or drowns.

LIZ: I'm sorry.

EMMA: Maybe next session.

LIZ: Maybe.

EMMA: Or maybe not. Your choice. I'm pro-choice.

(*To* BOB.)

Don't. Don't. Lullabye-bye. Lullabye-bye.

LIZ: He's waking up?

EMMA: Dreaming. I think he's dreaming. His eyes are open, but he looks very far away.

LIZ: Can I take a peek? I just adore babies.

EMMA: No. No!

LIZ: Okay. Is everything all right? Is your baby all right?

EMMA: Sometimes you have to listen with your feet to hear the S.O.S. from your heart. You don't understand, do you?

LIZ: I'm a mother. Like you. I just want my child to be healthy and happy and safe. That's why I came. That's why I wanted to talk to you. Because I thought you would be able to advise me.

EMMA: I did my best, my level best.

LIZ: Thanks for your time.

EMMA: It was nothing.

LIZ: I hope I can find my way out of here.

EMMA: Just keep turning as the colors change—blue to green, green to yellow, yellow to red, red to white. At the end of the white there's a big glass door. That's it. That's out.

LIZ: Thanks. Blue to green, et cetera. Thanks. Diane, my friend Diane, she says you're an extraordinary teacher. She recommended you. I thought you might like to know.

EMMA: Diane? I don't remember. So many babies, so many mothers. It's hard. I've already started to forget you. It just goes on and on.

LIZ: Goodbye. Good luck with all your water babies.

(*Exit* LIZ.)

EMMA: (*She looks down at the swaddled* BOB.) Luck. Luckabyebob. I remember it. Like an arrow. The first time I saw you. Flash of silver as you arced into the sunlight. The thrash sending white spray high over the gunnels into my bloodied sheets. Like being struck by an arrow. God. My heart stopped. Then it started beating backwards. I should've thrown you back. I should've thrown you back right then. Now it's too late. I've been struck by your silence. I need to know your secrets. Talk to me. Stop dreaming. Bob? Bob? Say *waffle. Waffle.* Say it. Say *waffle.*

CREDO

Craig Lucas

Credo *is dedicated to Robin Bartlett.*

CREDO was first produced at The Ensemble Studio Theatre Marathon 1995, 18th Annual Festival of One-Act plays. It was directed by Kirsten Sanderson (stage manager, Tamlyn Freund) with the following cast:

PERSON Marcia Jean Kurtz

(*Lights up.* PERSON *alone on stage.*)

PERSON: So it's Christmas eve,
I go out with the dog.
Jim and I have just broken up.
I've just been to an AA meeting
Where a woman got up
And said she had no friends,
Her best friend is her VCR
And it's broken.
I came home to the hole where the sofa was.
There's no Christmas tree either.
I can't stand the thought of sweeping up all the dead needles
And dragging the carcass out to the street
To join all the other dead trees
With what's happening to the rain forest.
I know the two aren't connected,
But anyway, I pull up a folding chair
And heat up a piece of cold pizza.
This, I think, is the low point.
The walls show little ghosts where the pictures once were.
I go out.

Did I tell you I didn't get my Christmas bonus?
Well, I wasn't expecting it,
But I haven't been able to take Apple to the vet about her problem,

So she dribbles a little across the lobby,
Past the doorman who isn't smiling at me;
I'm sure it's because I haven't given him *his* Christmas bonus,
But maybe's it's the trail of urine, too,
I don't stop to ask.
I smile bravely
And step outside where it has of course started to rain.
And people are running and looking very upset.
Surely the rain isn't that bad.
I turn:
There's been an accident on my corner.
I snap my head away,
I know if I look there'll be a baby carriage there
In the middle of the street.
I refuse to look.
They certainly don't need another person standing around, not doing anything.
I put my mind . . . Where can I put my mind?
Vienna.
Where Jim has gone with the woman he left me for.
You can't escape these thoughts.
All I know is her name.
Her name . . . is Carmella.
Apparently.
And I believe that she has had a sex change.
As far as I know, this has no basis in fact,
But I believe it as firmly as I believe
That there is nothing wrong with New York City
That can't be solved at least in part by keeping
Cardinal John J. O'Connor out of city politics
And back doing what he really does best
Which, if we are to take his word for it, is:
Exorcisms.

Where,
Where can I put my thoughts?

Ecuador.
My parents are in Ecuador.
They asked me to join them,
And I said
No, Jim and I would be spending the holiday together.
I hope that he and Carmella are caught
In the crossfire of some terrorist . . .
No, I don't.
Not really. But you know:
The sort of thing you see
On the evening news.
If you have a TV.
Or a phone.
Jim stopped paying the bills months ago,
As a kind of secret warning of what was to come.
But I refuse,
In my bones I refuse
To see myself as a victim.
I have gotten myself into this.
I allowed him to talk me into maintaining a joint bank account.
Everytime a little voice in my head would say
Watch out.
He's cute,
But he's not that nice.
Beneath it all,
Behind the charm,
His chin,
That first night,
And then again in Barbados,
Beneath it all
Is *him*.
I alone took each and every step
Which brought me here
To this street corner
In the rain
On Christmas eve

With my dog whose urinary infection
I cannot afford to fix.

And at that moment, my friends,
My dog squats.
And the worst thing that has ever happened to me
Unfolds before my very eyes.
A wire, loose plug from somebody's Christmas decorations
Carelessly strung in front of their little tea shop . . .
Electrocutes my dog.
And she falls immediately dead
On the sidewalk
In a sputter of sparks . . .
And the lights go out all down the front of the tea shop.
And a man comes out:
"What did you do?"
And I drop to my knees, unafraid,
Let me die, too,
Electrocute me.
And I embrace my dog, Apple,
Whom I have had for sixteen years.
She is my oldest friend.
She has seen me in my darkest, most drunken days.
She has been to every corner of my life, watched me make love.
She growled at the dogs on the dog food commercials.
She has been across the country and back.
Apple, I'm not afraid to say, is the purest,
Most uncomplicated expression of love I have ever known.
And she has been killed by an electric current
In the last sick days of her valiant existence.

The man stares at me from above.
"Oh my god" he says.
He can't believe it
Any more than I can believe it.
Come in, he says.

We carry Apple into the shop.
To me she smells good,
But to some people she does not.
It's been too cold to bathe her.
It's hard for one person to hold her in the shower.
She doesn't like the water.

The man offers me the only thing he has.
Tea.
We talk,
And he assures me that the accident on the corner
Did *not* involve a child.
And no one was killed.
What to do now with Apple?
I can't cry anymore.
I have cried so much the last two weeks
I can't cry for her now.
And I know . . .
In some way I see all at once that
Jim was not really good enough for me,
That I will meet someone else.
And even if I don't I will have
An extraordinary and rich and complicated life.
It is entirely up to me.
I will most likely survive all the roadblocks and the detours.
As my dad always says:
"Life can be rough, but think about the alternative."

But then again
He's never been sick a day in his life.
He hasn't ever had to struggle just to stand
Or been unable to stop himself from peeing
Where he knows he shouldn't
And doesn't want to,
But there it is in a stream,
Surprising him and me.
He's never had to look up

With big sorrowful eyes which say:
"I had no idea.
Don't yell."

No.
I only hope that I will go as quickly as Apple
When the time comes.
And if I don't,
I will absolutely,
I *know* I will face that bravely
And with dignity.
I know.
And if,
For some unforeseen but totally justified reason,
I can't,
And I am making a complete ass of myself,
Saying things I wouldn't ever say
And acting childishly
And turning into a prude
And a conservative
And am being a complete drag on everyone
For months and years,
I know my friends will forgive me.

And if for some equally valid and twisted,
But ultimately logical reason,
They don't
Or they can't,
Or they're all dead by then,
Or it's August and they're away,
Then I will forgive them,
Right?
The same way I forgave myself
For yelling at Apple the first time she peed
Before I realized what was going on.

And if . . .
Again, if I can't,

And everything is entirely for shit
And I can't even find my way to the end of a sentence . . .
And . . . you can fill in all the blanks . . .

That will be fine, too.

POOF!

Lynn Nottage

POOF! premiered at the Actors Theatre of Louisville on March 20, 1993. It was directed by Seret Scott; the set design was by Paul Owen; the costume design was by Kevin R. Mcleod; the lighting design was by Karl E. Haas; and the production stage manager was Julie A. Richardson. The cast was as follows:

LOUREEN Elain Graham
FLORENCE Yvette Hawkins

Darkness.

SAMUEL: WHEN I COUNT TO TEN I DON' WANT TO SEE YA! I DON' WANT TO HEAR YA! ONE, TWO, THREE, FOUR . . .

LOUREEN: DAMN YOU TO HELL, SAMUEL!

A bright flash. Lights rise. A huge pile of smoking ashes rests in the middle of the kitchen. LOUREEN, *a demure housewife in her early thirties, stares down at the ashes incredulously. She bends and lifts a pair of spectacles from the remains. She ever so slowly backs away.*

LOUREEN: Samuel? Uh!

(*She places the spectacles on the kitchen table.*)

Uh! . . . SAMUEL?

(*Looks around the stage.*)

Don't fool with me now. I'm not in the mood. (*Whispered.*) Samuel? I didn't mean it really. I'll be good if you come back . . . Come on now, dinner's waiting.

(LOUREEN *chuckles, then stops abruptly.*)

Now stop your foolishness . . . And let's sit down.

(LOUREEN *examines the spectacles.*)

Uh! (*Softly.*) Don't be cross with me. Sure I forgot to pick up your shirt for tomorrow. I can wash another, I'll do it right now. Right now! Sam? . . . (*Cautiously.*) You hear me!

(*Awaits a response.*)

Maybe I didn't ever intend to wash your shirt.

(*Pulls back as though about to receive a blow. A moment.*)

LOUREEN: Uh!

(*She sits down and dials the telephone.*)

LOUREEN: Florence, honey could you come on down for a moment. There's been a little accident . . . Quickly please . . . Uh!

(LOUREEN *gets a broom and a dust pan. She hesitantly approaches the pile of ashes. She gets down on her hands and knees and takes a closer look. A fatuous grin spreads across her face. She is startled by a sudden knock on the door.* LOUREEN *slowly walks across the room like a possessed child and lets in* FLORENCE, *who wears a floral housecoat and a pair of oversized slippers. Without acknowledgment* LOUREEN *proceeds to saunter back across the room.*

FLORENCE: HEY!

LOUREEN: (*Pointing at the ashes*).Uh!

(LOUREEN *struggles to formulate words, which press at the inside of her mouth not quite realized.*)

Uh!

FLORENCE: You all right? What happened?

(FLORENCE *sniffs the air.*)

Smells like you burned something?

(FLORENCE *stares at the huge pile of ashes.*)

What the devil is that?

LOUREEN: (*Hushed.*)

Samuel . . . It's Samuel, I think.

FLORENCE: What's he done now?

LOUREEN: It's him. It's him.

(LOUREEN *nods her head repeatedly.*)

FLORENCE: Chile, what's wrong with you? Did he finally drive you out your mind? I knew something was going to happen sooner or later.

LOUREEN: Dial 911, Florence!

FLORENCE: Why? You're scaring me!

LOUREEN: Dial 911!

(FLORENCE *picks up the telephone and quickly dials.*)

I think I killed him.

(FLORENCE *hangs up the telephone.*)

FLORENCE: What?

LOUREEN: (*Whimpers.*)

I killed him! I killed Samuel!

FLORENCE: Come again . . . He's dead, dead?

(LOUREEN *wrings her hands and nods her head twice mouthing "dead, dead."* FLORENCE *backs away.*)

No, stop it, I don't have time for this. I'm going back upstairs, you know how Samuel hates to find me here when he gets home. You're not going to get me this time. (*Louder.*) Y'all can have your little joke, I'm not part of it!

(*A moment.* FLORENCE *takes a hard look into* LOUREEN*'s eyes. She squints.*)

Did you really do it this time?

LOUREEN: (*Hushed.*) I don't know how or why it happened, it just did.

FLORENCE: Why are you whispering?

LOUREEN: I don't want to talk too loud something else is liable to disappear.

FLORENCE: Where's his body?

(LOUREEN *points to the pile of ashes.*)

LOUREEN: There! . . .

FLORENCE: You burned him?

LOUREEN: I DON'T KNOW!

(LOUREEN *covers her mouth as to muffle her words.*)

(*Hushed.*) I think so.

FLORENCE: Either you did or you didn't, what you mean you don't know. We're talking murder Loureen, not oven settings.

LOUREEN: You think I'm playing.

FLORENCE: How many times have I heard you talk about being rid of him. How many times have we sat at this very table and laughed about the many ways we could do it and how many times have you done it? None.

LOUREEN: (*Lifting the spectacles.*)

A pair of cheap spectacles, that's all that's left. And you know how much I hate these. You ever seen him without them, no! . . . He counted to four and disappeared. I swear to God!

FLORENCE: Don't bring the Lord into this just yet! Sit down now . . . What you got to sip on?

LOUREEN: I don't know whether to have a stiff shot of scotch or a glass of champagne.

(FLORENCE *takes a bottle of sherry out of the cupboard and pours them each a glass.*)

(LOUREEN *downs the glass of sherry. Then holds out her glass for more.*)

LOUREEN: He was . . .

FLORENCE: Take your time.

LOUREEN: Standing there.

FLORENCE: And?

LOUREEN: He exploded.

FLORENCE: Did that muthafucka hit you again?

LOUREEN: No . . . he exploded. Boom! Right in front of me. He was shouting like he does, being all colored, then he raised up that big crusty hand to hit me, and poof, he was gone . . . I barely got words out and I'm looking down at a pile of ash.

(FLORENCE *belts back her sherry and pours them another.* FLORENCE *wipes her forehead.*)

FLORENCE: Chile, I'll give you this, in terms of color you've matched my husband Edgar, the story king. He came in at six Sunday morning, talking about he'd hit someone with his car, and had spent all night trying to outrun the police. I felt sorry for him, forgot all about the fact that it was six in the morning. It turns out he was playing poker with his paycheck no less.

LOUREEN: You think I'm lying.

FLORENCE: I certainly hope so, Loureen. For your sake and my heart's.

LOUREEN: Samuel always said if I raised my voice something horrible would happen. And it did. I'm a witch . . . The devil spawn!

FLORENCE: You've been watching too much television.

LOUREEN: Never seen anything like this on television. Wish I had, then I'd know what to do . . . There's no question, I'm a witch.

(LOUREEN *looks at her hands with disgust.*)

FLORENCE: Chile, don't tell me you've been messing with them mojo women again? What did I tell ya.

(LOUREEN *stands and sits back down.*)

LOUREEN: He's not coming back. Oh no, how could he. It would be a miracle. Two in one day . . . I could be canonized, worse yet he could be . . . All that needs to happen now is for my palms to bleed and I'll be eternally remembered as St. Loureen, the patron of battered wives. Women from across the country will make pilgrimages to me, laying pies and pot roast at my feet and asking the good saint to make their husbands turn to dust. How often does a man like Samuel get damned to hell and go?

(LOUREEN *breaks down as though crying, as* FLORENCE *consoles her friend she realizes that she is actually laughing hysterically.*)

FLORENCE: You smoking crack?

LOUREEN: Do I look like I am?

FLORENCE: Shoot, I've seen old biddies creeping out of crack houses, talking about they were doing church work.

LOUREEN: FLORENCE, PLEASE BE HELPFUL, I'M VERY CLOSE TO THE EDGE! . . . I DON'T KNOW WHAT TO DO NEXT! DO I SWEEP HIM UP? DO I CALL THE POLICE? DO I . . .

(*The phone rings.*)

Oh God.

FLORENCE: You gonna let it ring?

(LOUREEN *reaches for the telephone slowly.*)

LOUREEN: NO!

(LOUREEN *holds the receiver without picking it up, paralyzed.*)

What if it's his mother? . . . She knows!

(*The phone continues to ring. They sit until it stops. They both breathe a sigh of relief.*)

I should be mourning, I should be praying, I should be thinking of the burial, but all that keeps popping into my mind is what will I wear on television when I share my horrible and wonderful story with a studio audience . . . (*Whimpers.*) He's made me a killer Florence, and you remember what a gentle child I was. (*Whispered.*) I'm a killer, I'm a killer, I'm a killer.

FLORENCE: I wouldn't throw that word about too lightly even in jest. Talk like that gets around.

LOUREEN: A few misplaced words and I'll probably get the death penalty, isn't that what they do with women like me, murderesses.

FLORENCE: Folks have done time for less.

LOUREEN: Thank you, just what I needed to hear!

FLORENCE: What did you expect, that I was going to throw up my arms and congratulate you. Why'd you have to go and lose your mind at this time of day, while I got a pot of rice on the stove and Edgar's about to walk in the door and wonder where his Goddamn food is. (*Losing her cool.*) And he's going to start in on me about all the nothing I've been doing during the day and why I can't work and then he'll mention how clean you keep your home. And I don't know how I'm going to look him in the eye without . . .

LOUREEN: I'm sorry Florence. Really. It's out of my hands now.

(LOUREEN *takes* FLORENCE*'s hand and squeezes it.* FLORENCE *regains her composure.*)

FLORENCE: You swear on your right tit?

(LOUREEN *clutches both of her breasts.*)

LOUREEN: I swear on both of them!

FLORENCE: Both your breasts Loureen. You know what will happen if you're lying.

(LOUREEN *nods.)*

(*Hushed.*) Both your breasts Loureen?

LOUREEN: Yeah!

(FLORENCE *examines the pile of ashes, then shakes her head.*)

FLORENCE: Oh sweet, sweet Jesus. He must have done something truly terrible.

LOUREEN: No more than usual. I just couldn't take being hit one more time.

FLORENCE: You've taken a thousand blows from that man, couldn't you've turned the cheek and waited. I'd have helped you pack. Like we talked about.

(*A moment.*)

LOUREEN: Uh! . . . I could blow on him and he'd disappear across the linoleum. (*Snaps her fingers.*) Just like that. Should I be feeling remorse or regret or some other "r" word? I'm strangely jubilant, like on prom night when Samuel and I first made love. That's the feeling!

(*The women lock eyes.*)

Uh!

FLORENCE: Is it . . .

LOUREEN: Like a ton of bricks been lifted from my shoulders, yeah.

(FLORENCE *walks to the other side of the room.*)

FLORENCE: You bitch!

LOUREEN: What?

FLORENCE: We made a pact.

LOUREEN: I know.

FLORENCE: You've broken it . . . We agreed that when things got real bad for both of us we'd . . . you know . . . together . . . Do I have to go back upstairs to that . . . What next?

LOUREEN: I thought you'd tell me! I don't know!

FLORENCE: I don't know!

LOUREEN: I don't know!

(FLORENCE *begins to walk around the room nervously touching objects.* LOUREEN *sits wringing her hands and mumbling softly to herself.*)

FLORENCE: Now you got me Loureen, I'm truly at a loss for words.

LOUREEN: Everybody always told me, "keep your place Loureen." My place, the silent spot on the couch with a wine cooler in my hand and a pleasant smile that warmed the heart. All this time I didn't know why he was so afraid for me to say anything, to speak up. Poof! . . . I've never been by myself, except for them two weeks when he won the office pool and went to Reno with his cousin Mitchell. He wouldn't tell me where he was going until I got that postcard with the cowboy smoking a hundred cigarettes . . . Didn't Sonny Larkin look good last week at Caroline's? He looked good, didn't he . . .

(FLORENCE *nods.*)

(FLORENCE *nervously picks up* SAMUEL*'s jacket, which is hanging on the back of the chair. She clutches it unconsciously.*)

LOUREEN: NO! *NO*! DON'T WRINKLE THAT, THAT'S HIS FAVORITE JACKET. HE'LL KILL ME. PUT IT BACK!

(FLORENCE *returns the jacket to its perch.* LOUREEN *begins to quiver.*)

I'm sorry.

(LOUREEN *grabs the jacket and wrinkles it up.*)

There.

(*She then digs into the coat pockets and pulls out his wallet and a movie stub.*)

Look at that, he said he didn't go to the movies last night. Working late.

(LOUREEN *frantically thumbs through his wallet.*)

Picture of his motorcycle, social security card, driver's license, and look at that from our wedding. (*Smiling.*) I looked good, didn't I?

(*She puts the pictures back in the wallet.* LOUREEN *holds the jacket up to her face.*)

There were some good things.

(LOUREEN *then sweeps her hand over the jacket to remove the wrinkles and folds it ever so carefully, and finally throws it in the garbage.*

And out of the mouth those words made him disappear. All these years and just words, Florence. That's all they were.

FLORENCE: I'm afraid, I won't ever get those words out. I'll start resenting you, honey. I'm afraid won't anything change for me.

LOUREEN: I been to that place.

FLORENCE: Yeah? But now I wish I could relax these old lines (*Touches her forehead.*) for a minute maybe. Edgar has never done me the way Samuel did you, but he sure did take the better part of my life.

LOUREEN: Not yet Florence.

(FLORENCE *nods.*)

FLORENCE: I have the children to think of. Right?

LOUREEN: You can think up a hundred things before . . .

FLORENCE: Then come upstairs with me . . . We'll wait together for Edgar and then you can spit out your words and . . .

LOUREEN: I can't do that.

FLORENCE: Yes you can. *Come on now.*

(LOUREEN *shakes her head.*)

Well I guess my mornings are not going to be any different.

LOUREEN: If you can say for certain then I guess they won't be. *I couldn't say that.*

FLORENCE: But you got a broom and a dust pan, you don't need anything more than that . . . He was a bastard and nobody will care that he's gone.

LOUREEN: Phone's gonna start ringing soon, people are gonna start asking soon, and they'll care. Maybe I should mail him to his mother. I owe her that. I feel bad for her, she didn't understand how it was . . . He was always threatening not to come back.

FLORENCE: I heard him.

LOUREEN: It would've been me eventually.

FLORENCE: Yes.

LOUREEN: I should call the police, or someone.

FLORENCE: Why? What are you gonna tell them? About all those times they refused to help, about all those nights you slept in my bed cause you were afraid to stay down here. About the time he nearly took out your eye cause you flipped the television channel.

LOUREEN: No.

FLORENCE: You've got it, girl!

LOUREEN: I can't just throw him away and pretend like it didn't happen. Can I?

(FLORENCE *nods.*)

Goodbye to the fatty meats and the salty food. Goodbye to the bourbon and the bologna sandwiches, Goodbye to the smell of his feet, his breath, and his bowel movements . . .

(*A moment.* LOUREEN *closes her eyes as though reliving a horrible memory, she shudders.*)

Goodbye.

(LOUREEN *walks over to the pile of ashes.*)

Samuel? . . . just checking.

FLORENCE: Goodbye Samuel.

(*They both smile.*)

LOUREEN: Chicken's warming in the oven, you're welcome to stay.

FLORENCE: Chile, I got a pot of rice on the stove. Kids are probably acting out . . . And Edgar, well . . . Listen, I'll stop in tomorrow.

LOUREEN: For dinner?

FLORENCE: Edgar wouldn't stand for that. Cards maybe.

LOUREEN: Cards.

(*The women hug for a long moment.* FLORENCE *exits.* LOUREEN *stands over the ashes for a few moments contemplating what to do. She finally decides to sweep them under the carpet, and then proceeds to set the table and sit down to eat her dinner.*)

THE END

THE WINGED MAN

José Rivera

THE WINGED MAN premiered at the Magic Theatre in San Francisco, California (Mame Hunt, Artistic Director), in November 1993. It was directed by Roberto Varea; the set design was by Lauren Elder; the costume design was by Chrystene Ells; the lighting design was by Jeff Rowlings; and the production stage manager was Lisa Larice. It was produced in an evening of one-acts by José Rivera called *Giants Have Us in Their Books.* The case of *The Winged Man* was as follows:

WINGED MAN	Sean San Jose Blackman
GIRL	Megan Blue Stermer
FRIEND	Michelle Pelletier
MOTHER	Margo Hall

CAST

DAYSI
THE WINGED MAN
WANDA
ALLYSHA

TIME: The present.

PLACE: A suburb.

1.

(A cave. Very dark. DAYSI *is entering the cave with her flashlight. She's a young high school student exploring the cave for her geology class. She stops, looks around, and makes a few notes in her notebook. She hears a* GROAN. *She stops writing and looks around. The* GROANING *stops. She wants to get out of there—but her fear is overcome by her curiosity. The* GROANING *starts. She follows the sound.*

Lights up on another part of the cave. We see a thin naked WINGED MAN *with large bloodied wings lying on the ground. There's a bullet hole in the* WINGED MAN*'s chest and only his hand against the wound keeps him from bleeding to death. One of his beautiful wings is badly broken. A pool of blood covers the cave floor. The* WINGED MAN GROANS.

The light from DAYSI*'s flashlight rakes the cave floor and comes to rest on the* WINGED MAN. DAYSI *screams and drops the flashlight. She picks it up. She looks at the* WINGED MAN. *He isn't moving. His eyes are closed. It's hard to tell if he's dead or alive.*

DAYSI *approaches the* WINGED MAN *cautiously. She bends down and very carefully touches his wings. The* WINGED MAN *groans weakly. She* GASPS. *She steps back. And then forward. She bends down again. Touches the* WINGED MAN*'s back. Strokes it. The* WINGED MAN *opens his eyes and looks at her. His eyes are beautiful. She almost* GASPS *again. Pulls back from him. Then she moves closer.*

Blackout.)

2.

(*Lights up on the cave. An hour later.*

The WINGED MAN *is lying with his head propped up against an improvised pillow. A tightly bound white cloth over his chest has stopped his bleeding. A blanket is draped over his nakedness.* DAYSI *is feeding the* WINGED MAN. *He takes the food and chews weakly.* DAYSI *gives him some water. He swallows greedily. He wants more and more. She laughs at his robust thirst.*

He looks at her and slowly holds out his hand to DAYSI. *She reaches out her own hand. Their fingers find each other and intertwine. They sit there a moment, just holding each other's hands. He opens his mouth to speak. She's dying to know who he is, what he is. She inches closer to him. A strange* GUTTURAL SOUND *comes out of the* WINGED MAN. *He seems to be trying to communicate with her but he can't. She tries to understand but she can't. She looks into his strange and troubled eyes. She smiles at his courageous attempt at speech. Suddenly he is gripped by terrible pain in his chest—over his wound—he* SCREAMS *and* SCREAMS. *It's unbearable to listen to.* DAYSI *does everything she can to calm him, ease his pain, stroking his forehead, kissing him, anything. The terrible pain subsides and the* WINGED MAN *calms down.* DAYSI *puts both arms around him. They look at each other.*

She holds him tight, rocking him back and forth. He cries very quietly. She is overcome with emotion and cries too. She kisses him.

Blackout.)

3.

(*Lights up on a kitchen table.*

DAYSI *sits at breakfast, wearing a white feather in her hair, staring into space. Her mother* WANDA *is with her.* WANDA *doesn't like the way*

DAYSI *looks. They look at each other silently. Something is preying on the girl's mind—but she can't articulate it yet. She starts to tremble.* DAYSI *calms down and then looks at* WANDA.)

DAYSI: I'm pregnant.

(WANDA *looks at* DAYSI. WANDA *slaps* DAYSI *across the face.*

Blackout.

In the blackout, DURING THE SCENE CHANGE, *we hear:*)

DAYSI'S VOICE: The baby's father. The baby's father is dead. The baby's father was either an angel from Heaven or, more likely, he was, he was of a race of, of winged men, of, of, human people . . . who . . . had . . . wings.

4.

(*Lights up on a high school hallway. A row of lockers.*

DAYSI *is at her locker.* ALLYSHA *comes along.* ALLYSHA *looks at* DAYSI, *who looks like she has a bad case of morning sickness.* DAYSI *leans against the locker, very weak, nauseous.*)

ALLYSHA: I hear ya got knocked up.

(*Beat.*)

DAYSI: Word travels fast.

(*Beat.*)

ALLYSHA: Okay who was it, Daysi? For real.

(*Beat.*)

DAYSI: You tell me.

ALLYSHA: Oh, you fucked an *angel?* You expect me to *believe* that? Okay, maybe he was *like* an angel, but come on. Who was it? Carlos? Ramon? Vinnie? Claudio? All of 'em? None of 'em? Were ya doing it all at once with a variety of gentlemen and now ya can't figure out who is the owner of the lucky sperm? I can understand that. But that's not like you, that's like me, or, like that's what some people *think* of me, but it's not what anyone thinks of *you,* least of all *me.* Ya know but ya not telling.

DAYSI: I fucked an angel.

ALLYSHA: Oh come on, Daysi, please, I'm ya best friend already. Ya don't have to play games with me. I've seen it all with ya. I'm cool. I don't judge. I just wanna help. Tell me who it is. You and I will go to this son-of-a-bitch, ask him why he didn't use a condom, then we're gonna shake the bastard down for money for an abortion, now who is he?

DAYSI: I'm having the baby.

ALLYSHA: Ya not having the baby.

DAYSI: It's a miracle baby, Allysha!

ALLYSHA: It's killing ya. Look at ya. Ya my best friend and I don't wanna see ya throw ya life away on some romance, ya much too young to be a mother, ya still a girl yaself, ya told me ya had plans and ya weren't gonna do the same bullshit ya mother did, and now ya telling me *this?* What am I, *stupid?*

DAYSI: I'm having the baby.

(*Beat.*)

ALLYSHA: Fine. How ya gonna pay for it?

DAYSI: I'll work.

ALLYSHA: At two bucks an hour!? Have ya priced formula? Have ya priced diapers? Get real. Babies are cash intensive. Ya on ya own, honey. Ya mother won't put up with having this illegitimate thing in her house—.

DAYSI: It's not a thing. It's a beautiful baby with wings.

(*Beat.*)

ALLYSHA: Great. I'm going to math. I have an appointment with REALITY. Ya wanna join me in reality, please call, okay?, ya have the number.

(ALLYSHA *leaves.* DAYSI *puts her hands over her mouth and nearly throws up. She gags, nearly falls over.* ALLYSHA *comes running back on, concerned.*)

Hey. I'm sorry. I'm being an asshole. Hey. I love ya. I'm here for ya. Whatever ya want, Daysi. I'm here for ya. A hundred percent. Okay? I love ya. I want ya to be happy. Okay?

(*No answer.*)

I think it's gonna be a beautiful baby.

(DAYSI *smiles weakly and takes* ALLYSHA*'s hand.*

Blackout.

In the blackout, DURING THE SCENE CHANGE, *we hear:*)

DAYSI'S VOICE: I bet he was of this ancient race. That pre-dates us all. That was around from the beginning. From earliest time. And they lived in harmony on the earth for millions of years. And they were happy here. Flying over the virgin world. Swooping, soaring. Secular angels. The—the source, you know, of our mythology regarding angels. The original vision. These winged people who survived millions of years until our kind came along with sticks and stones, then arrows, and howitzers, with guns and poisons, slowly, efficiently eradicating this magnificent species, killing them all until there was only one left. One.

5.

(*Lights up at a park bench.*

DAYSI *is sitting there. She's several months pregnant and showing. She and* ALLYSHA *feed pigeons out of bags of birdseed.* DAYSI *looks radiant, beautiful.*)

ALLYSHA: God, it's a beautiful day, I can't fucking believe it.

DAYSI: (*Feeding.*) Here chick chick chick chick chick. Here chick chick.

ALLYSHA: Is that what ya call pigeons? Chick? That don't sound right.

DAYSI: Here chick. Get your lunch.

ALLYSHA: Should be "here ya parasite-ridden flying sacks o' shit." That's more appropriate.

DAYSI: They're not. They're beautiful.

ALLYSHA: To *you*—in *your* condition—everything is beautiful.

DAYSI: Chicky chicky chicky.

(*Beat.*)

ALLYSHA: Ya mother says ya don't like to eat eggs anymore.

DAYSI: That's right.

ALLYSHA: Why is that?

DAYSI: Seems like cannibalism.

ALLYSHA: But ya not a bird!

DAYSI: I just don't like it! I see eggs on a dish, that soft yolk, see it punctured by a fork, start to bleed, all that potential lost, I get sad!

ALLYSHA: Ya mother says ya won't eat poultry! She says ya being weird!

DAYSI: Allysh', I'm *happy.* The morning sickness is over. I feel the baby kicking. And I just want to stay *happy* . . .

ALLYSHA: She says ya built a nest in ya room!

DAYSI: Just a little one.

ALLYSHA: Just a *little* one?! She says it covers your entire bed now, this whole friggin' fuckin' humungus nest with twigs and leaves and—!

DAYSI: I can't help it! It's an impulse! I just did it, that's all!

ALLYSHA: It's not normal. Tell me ya gonna dismantle it. Tell me that right now!

DAYSI: But it's gonna be. The baby's. The baby's nest. The baby's perch. Not a crib. No. He's not getting a crib! He's getting a beautiful, round, perfect nest his father wouldda been proud to see!

ALLYSHA: You are. *Persisting.* In this. *Madness.*

DAYSI: It's not. It's not madness.

(*Beat.*)

Let me show you something. Let me show you what nobody knows. I've been working overtime at White Castle so I could make enough money for this 'cause I know I wouldn't get any from Mom. I went to a radiologist. And I got me a magic picture of the fetus in my womb.

(*She reaches into a pocket and pulls out a tiny, fuzzy black and white ultrasound photo.*)

Ultrasound. Isn't it a miracle? The one place in your lifetime you're guaranteed privacy, and you can't even get that anymore! They have cameras that go into the darkness before birth and snap your picture! There he is. There's my baby. There's the son of the winged man.

(DAYSI *gives* ALLYSHA *the picture.*)

Can you see? I know it's fuzzy. But there. A head. Eye holes. Great magnificent brain. Heart, fingers, toes, genitals. And wings. Right there. Use your God-given eyes, Allysha. Use your eyesight. And check out these fucking beautiful wings on my son.

(ALLYSHA *stares at the picture. She is trying with all her might to see the wings. She finally does. She's shaken. She hands the photo back.*)

ALLYSHA: I don't see a frikkin' thing.

(DAYSI *takes the photo back. She starts to cry.*)

DAYSI: You're just saying that to be mean.

(*The two sit side by side in silence,* DAYSI *wiping her tears,* ALLYSHA *trying to control her shaking and fear.* DAYSI *starts to absently eat the birdseed. She likes the taste of it. She eats more and more, faster and faster,* ALLYSHA *watching her aghast.*

Blackout.

In the blackout, DURING THE SCENE CHANGE, *we hear:*)

DAYSI'S VOICE: One single beautiful man, the last of his kind, shot through the heart by some amazed hunter, some hick with a shotgun with visions of trophies in his head. And he wounded this man, who found a cave to die in, the last of his world, and he was quietly prepared to die there, until. Until me.

6.

(*Lights up on a tree.*

DAYSI, *nine months pregnant, sits on the branch of a tree, looking at the birds flying all around her. The* SOUNDS OF BIRDS *fill the air. Wind is blowing and she is enjoying the feeling of rushing air going through her hair.*

WANDA *enters.* WANDA *looks up at the* DAYSI.)

WANDA: Are you coming down for dinner? Are you going to spend another night in that tree? What's with you? You're going to be a mother any day now. That makes you squarely a woman, Daysi. A woman. WOMAN. Just like me. Once you have this baby, you're going to be no different than me. You'll have passed that borderland, that place in which your childhood is buried forever. You'll have to give up all the trappings of your childhood. You'll never play in the same way. The air in your lungs will never feel the same again. On the other side of the mirror a face will look back at you full of care and sleeplessness and the memory of pain. Now, I can understand you're afraid of that. But you should have thought of that before you got knocked up! Sitting up in a tree all day and night for weeks is not going to change that. It's not going to make the deep responsibility go away. That baby is going to need you desperately. That baby isn't going to want to hear your fantasies about some winged man you had a one night stand with. It's going to ask hard questions, Daysi. You're going to have to be honest with your baby and with yourself. And that honesty should start today, baby. Today. With you getting down off that tree and cease eating birdseed and dismantling that fucking nest in your bed! Put that fantasy away, child. A boy knocked you up. A real person. Not a miracle. Not fantasy. Get real, baby. Get off that tree. Start living your life.

(WANDA *waits.* DAYSI *opens her mouth and makes the same* GUTTURAL *sounds the* WINGED MAN *had made. The sounds are strange—and they get louder.* WANDA *puts her hands over her ears. The* SOUND OF BIRDS *fills the theatre.*

Blackout.

In the blackout, DURING THE SCENE CHANGE, *we hear:*)

DAYSI'S VOICE: I came along. And kept him alive for a couple of hours. And fed him. And watched over him. Then finally made love with him because I knew the line would end if he died, and I wanted a chance to save the species, to keep that race of winged humans alive just a little longer. Through me. What do you think of that?

7.

(*Lights up at the park bench.*

DAYSI, *no longer pregnant, enters pushing a stroller. We hear a* BABY CRYING. DAYSI *stops pushing the stroller. She looks around to make sure no one is watching her. She reaches into a pocket and takes out a can of* WORMS. *She starts feeding the worms, one by one, to the baby. The* CRYING STOPS.

Short SILENCE.

Then we hear HAPPY COOING SOUNDS *coming from the baby.* DAYSI *smiles.*)

DAYSI: Awwwwwwww. Chulo! Cute.

(DAYSI *reaches into the stroller. She holds up the bundled* BABY. *She kisses the* BABY*—then throws the bundle in the air.* DAYSI *waves goodbye as the* BABY *flies away.*

Blackout.)

END OF PLAY.

LIVES OF THE GREAT WAITRESSES

Nina Shengold

LIVES OF THE GREAT WAITRESSES, a finalist for the 1996 Heideman Award, premiered in a staged reading at Actors & Writers in Olivebridge, New York, in October 1995. Nina Shengold directed the following cast:

YETTA	Carol Morley
KAY	Nicole Baptiste
TAMMIE SUE	Sarah Chodoff
MELISSA	Sybil Rosen

SETTING: A greasy spoon.

YETTA, KAY, TAMMIE SUE, *prepping the breakfast shift. All in pink uniforms.*

LIGHTS UP *on* YETTA, *smoking a cigarette, soaking her feet. Late fifties, Bronx Jewish, a pit bull in lipstick.*

YETTA: I'm not an actress. I have a career.

(*She stubs out her cigarette.* BLACKOUT.

LIGHTS UP *on* KAY, *rolling flatware in napkins. Forties, black, born again.*)

KAY: You either got it, or you don't. If you don't, you won't ever. So don't even bother. Don't strain. Oh, there's things you can learn, sure. The fine points. The stance. "Heat that up for you?" "Toasted?" But honey—scratch that, make it hon—a truly great waitress is *born.*

You get what I mean? It's a feel thing. Deep under the bones of your bones. In your cells. Some reporter once asked Louis Armstrong what "swing" meant. Louis looked the guy dead in the eyeball and said, "If you gotta ask, you'll never know." *He* would've made a great waitress.

My very first diner, we had one. Flo Kelly. A goddess in Supp-hose. Flo was all waitress. She could fill two dozen shakers one-handed and never spill one grain of salt. She could carry eight Hungry Man specials lined up on her arm like a charm bracelet. Flo could serve pie à la mode so it looked like Mount Everest topping the clouds. She poured gravy like tropical rain. In Flo's maraschino-nailed fingers, the short-order carousel spun like the Wheel of Fortune, and never, not once, did a customer's coffee get cold.

Well, I mean to tell you, that diner was *hers.* If Jesus Himself Amen came in and sat down to supper, he would've tipped double. Then one Blue-Plate Special, right after the lunch rush, Flo hung up her hairnet, cashed in her checks, and went sunny-side up. And that's when the Lord took my order. I knew what I was. I was called.

(*She steps closer.*)

Look in my eyes. I know mysteries way beyond menus. I have felt the Lord's love pierce my heart like a skewer through gyros. I have seen Jesus weep ice-kold milk with a K.

(*She holds out her hand.*)

Heat that up for you? Hon?

(BLACKOUT.
LIGHTS UP *on* TAMMIE SUE, *filling up sugar shakers. Forties, dithery, slight Southern twang.*)

TAMMIE SUE: So this fella sits down at my counter. Scrawny, beat, banty thing, ugly as yesterday's homefries, and he's got the look. You all know that look.

(*She demonstrates.*)

There's this puppy dog whimpering back of his eyes, means he's looking for more than two eggs on a raft, wreck 'em, cuppa joe light. So I do what a girl's gotta do. I ignore him. No warmups, no sass, save my smile for the grandpas and wedding rings in the next booth. Comes the end of my shift, and this shriveled-up walnut, this cottage cheese curd, this crust of burnt toast is still sitting there. Dog in his eyes rolls right over and begs.

So I give him the deep-freeze. I shoot him a look that would flatten meringue.

(*She demonstrates.*)

And what's he do? Smiles at me. *Smiles.* Gatty teeth, great big space in the middle, looked just like a little ole kid with skinned knees on the playground.

Well, hell. That did melt me up. Kay's always telling me I got a heart as big as a Butterball turkey, and besides it's been way, way too long since my griddle got greased. So we go to the motor home up top his semi.

Well. I tell you that man had a mouth that could melt you like butter and syrup on top of a short stack of buckwheats. He did things with his fingers that should be illegal, or fattening. That little runt had him a secret self under his outfit. We've all of us got one, but this was a secret worth spreading around. And he did. He most certainly did. He could love you up one side and back down the other and still leave the middle part gasping for more. That man had a gift. Mashed potatoes and gravy. I left him a tip, that's the God's honest truth.

So the next time you find yourself checking out someone's dessert case, remember, it isn't the Dream Whip that counts. It's the peach in the pie.

(*She pours sugar straight into her hand, sticks her tongue in it.* BLACKOUT.

LIGHTS BACK UP *on* YETTA, *drying her feet off and pulling on flesh-colored knee-highs and nurse's shoes.*)

YETTA: We got us a new one today. Little blondie thing. Brains like a dishrag. Marty says to me, Yetta, give her a try. What try. Way she walks into the *room* I can tell you the broad ain't no waitress. She's got this two hundred and ninety pound bag slung over her shoulder, you just *know* that it's gonna be full of her face eight by ten. You *know* that she's gonna be hocking the customers, "Hi! I'm—"

(MELISSA, *twenty, walks on with a musical comedy smile. Brand new uniform.*)

MELISSA: (*Overlapping.*)—I'm Melissa. Our specials tonight are a light cappellini with sauce Margherita—

YETTA: Spaghetti and meatballs.

MELISSA: —a baked beef and pork terrine—

YETTA: Meat loaf.

MELISSA: —and I want to thank my parents, my agent, and God for believing in me.

YETTA: A question. Does *anyone* care what's the name of the person who's pouring your coffee cup? *Thank* you.

MELISSA: Gemini. Capricorn rising.

YETTA: My *breakfast* is rising.

MELISSA: "The quality of mercy is not strained."

(*Bright smile, starts to sing:*)

"Brigadoon, Brigadooooonn . . ."

YETTA: Am I right or right? Hopeless. First lunch rush, her head'll be spinning around like the milkshake machine. But she bats her big blues up at Marty and tells him yes, she's got experience. Marty, being A) dense and B) male, does not ask her what kind. So it's up to yours truly to break the kid in. Never mind I got migraines in both of my feet. Tammie Sue knows her ass from her elbow on good days, and Kay's gonna try to convert her. Born *once,* she can just about handle, forget born again. So I give her the counter, okay? Let her piss off the regulars. Marty's there working the register, maybe he'll know from "experience" next time around. Which I bet you good odds is the end of this shift.

(MELISSA *takes pad and pencil out of her apron, approaches an imaginary customer on the fourth wall with a big nervous smile.*)

MELISSA: Hi. Can I get you some breakfast? Um, coffee? Uh huh . . .

(*She writes on her pad, very slowly and clearly.*)

Is that "regular" meaning not decaf, or regular with cream and—Right. What? Oh, *menus,* I'm sorry . . . Right back.

(*She scuttles out.* YETTA *smirks.*)

YETTA: And we're off. And it doesn't get better. Clear through to the lunch rush she's mixing up eggs over easy supposed to be scrambled. She's bringing the Western the waffles. She's dropping forks right, left, and center. The decaf goes dry. Then she loses an order, a party of six, and they walk without paying.

(MELISSA *rushes out, breathless.*)

MELISSA: I'm sorry it's taking so long, I'm— . . . Hello?

(*She looks towards the exit, near tears.*)

YETTA: So I look over at Marty like, hey, get the hook, because Miss Eight by Ten flunked her audition. And Marty just flashes his not-quite-so-pearlies—the *breath* on that man, it could kill you—and says, "Listen, everyone's gotta start somewhere." I'll tell him where *I'd* like to start. With his head on a plate. A klug of him. I need a cigarette.

(*She reaches for one.* BLACKOUT.

LIGHTS UP *on* MELISSA, *untying her apron, alone.*)

MELISSA: This is my first day of work. Not here. Ever. My family had money and nobody made me. I came to this city to look for a job and nobody would hire me. It's kind of like being a virgin—I'm not any more, but I was—and I'm telling you, nobody wants to be first. Too much pressure. My roommate said, "Lie." So I did.

(*She sits.*)

People think if you haven't done something before, you're an idiot. People can't know what's inside you. You don't know yourself till you're given a chance. Then all of a sudden this new personality starts to swell under your skin, bursting through where you'd never expect it, and nothing you thought you were makes any sense. You're elastic. You're putty. You've been up for hours, making love to a man whose back ripples with muscles you've never felt, feeling your body expand and explode and dissolve into air, into something like stars, and it doesn't seem possible that you could open your eyes to the same old alarm clock and fit in the same pair of shoes.

I don't want to lose this. This newness, this urgent, sharp knowledge that everything matters. That being good matters. I want to do everything well.

I know, I'm a waitress. It's not what I've dreamed of, what anyone dreams of, but I make a difference. I do. There are lives on each stool at that counter. The old man who's ordered his Sanka and shredded wheat every morning for twenty-five years.

(*She nods toward someone in the audience.*)

Otto.

The woman who fought with her husband last night and treated herself to French toast with her friend who just had a mastectomy. Velma and Ruth.

The man who panhandled the price of his coffee. Muhammed.

I touch them. I give them the quiet sensation that once in their sad, uncontrollable lives, they wanted a small thing and got it. I brought it. I bore them a gift. And that matters.

(*She hangs up her apron, on a transparent hook hanging down from clear fishing line.*)

You watch me. I'm going to be brilliant. I'm going to be one of the greats.

(*The apron flies up like an angel.* LIGHTS UP *on all four of the women. Tableau.*)

THE END

DESDEMONA

A PLAY ABOUT A HANDKERCHIEF

Paula Vogel

DESDEMONA: A PLAY ABOUT A HANDKERCHIEF, was originally produced in association with Circle Repertory Company by Bay Street Theatre Festival, Sag Harbor, Long Island, New York, in July 1993. It was produced by Circle Repertory Company (Tanya Berezin, Artistic Director; Abigail Evans, Managing Director), in New York City, in November 1993. It was directed by Gloria Muzio; the set design was by Derek McLane; the costume design was by Jess Goldstein; the lighting design was by Michael Lincoln; the fight direction was by Rick Sordelet; the original music and sound design were by Randy Freed, and the production stage manager was Fred Reinglas. The cast was as follows:

EMILIA	Fran Brill
DESDEMONA	J. Smith-Cameron
BIANCA	Cherry Jones

CHARACTERS

DESDEMONA: Upper-class. Very.
EMILIA: Broad Irish Brogue.
BIANCA: Stage Cockney.

PLACE: A back room of the palace on Cyprus.

TIME

Ages ago.

The prologue takes place one week before Desdemona's last day on Cyprus.

NOTE TO DIRECTOR

Desdemona was written in thirty cinematic "takes"; the director is encouraged to create different pictures to simulate the process of filming: change invisible camera angles, do jump cuts and repetitions, etc. There should be no blackouts between scenes.

Desdemona was written as a tribute (i.e., ripoff) to the infamous play, *Shakespeare the Sadist* by Wolfgang Bauer.

PROLOGUE

A spotlight in the dark, pinpointing a white handkerchief lying on the ground. A second spotlight comes up on EMILIA, *who sees the handkerchief. She pauses, and then cautiously looks about to see if she is observed. Then, quickly,* EMILIA *goes to the handkerchief, picks it up, stuffs the linen in her ample bodice, and exits. Blackout.*

Scene I

A mean, sparsely furnished back room with rough, whitewashed walls. Upstage left there is a small heavy wooden back entrance. Another door, stage right, leads to the main rooms of the palace. There are a few benches lining the walls, littered with tools, baskets, leather bits, dirty laundry, etc. The walls bear dark wooden racks which neatly display farm and work equipment made of rough woods, leathers, and chain.

In the center of the room, there is a crude work table with short benches. As the play begins, DESDEMONA *is scattering items and clothing in the air, barely controlling a mounting hysteria.* EMILIA, *dark, plump, and plain, with a thick Irish brogue, watches, amused and disgusted at the mess her lady is making.*

DESDEMONA: Are you sure you didn't see it? The last time I remember holding it in my hand was last week in the arbor— you're sure you didn't see it?

EMILIA: Aye—

DESDEMONA: It looks like—

EMILIA: —Like any body's handkerchief, savin' it has those dainty little strawberries on it. I never could be after embroiderin' a piece of linen with fancy work to wipe up the nose—

DESDEMONA: It's got to be here somewhere—

EMILIA: After you blow your nose in it, an' it's all heavy and wet, who's going to open the damn thing and look at the pretty stitches?

DESDEMONA: Emilia—are you sure it didn't get "mixed up" somehow with your . . . things?

EMILIA: And why should I be needin' your handkerchief when I'm wearing a plain, soft shift which works just as well? And failing that, the good Lord gave me sleeves . . .

DESDEMONA: It's got to be here! (DESDEMONA *returns to her rampage of the room.*) Oh—skunk water! (*A man's undergarment is tossed into the air behind* DESDEMONA*'s shoulder.*) Dog piddle!!

EMILIA: I'm after telling you m'lady—

DESDEMONA: Nonsense! It's got to be here! (*There is a crash of overturned chain.* DESDEMONA*'s shifts are thrown into the air.*) God damn horse urine!!!

EMILIA: It was dear, once upon the time, when m'lady was toddling about the palace, and all of us servants would be follerin' after, stooping to pick up all the pretty toys you'd be scatterin'—

DESDEMONA: Emilia, please—I can not bear a sermon.

EMILIA: There was the day the Senator your father gave you your first strand of pearls from the Indies—you were all of five—and your hand just plucked it from your neck—how you laughed to see us, Teresa, Maria, and me, scrabbling on all fours like dogs after truffles, scooping up the rollin' pearls— (*There is a ripping noise.*)

DESDEMONA: Oh, shit. (*Two halves of a sheet are pitched into the air.*)

EMILIA: But you're a married lady now; and when m'lord Othello gives you a thing, and tells you to be mindin' it, it's no longer dear to drop it willy nilly and expect me to be finin' it—

DESDEMONA: Oh, piss and vinegar!! Where is the crappy little snot rag! (DESDEMONA *turns and sees* EMILIA *sitting.*) You're not even helping! You're not looking!!

EMILIA: Madam can be sure I've overturned the whole lot, two or three times . . . It's a sight easier hunting for it when the place is tidy; when all is topsy-turvy, you can't tell a mouse dropping from a cow pie—(DESDEMONA *returns to the hunt:* EMILIA *picks up the torn sheet.*)—Now see, this sheet here was washed this morning. Your husband, as you know, is fussy about his sheets; and while it was no problem to have them fresh each night in Venice—I could open the window and dunk them in the canal—here on Cyprus it takes two drooling orderlies, to march six times down to the cistern and back again. (EMILIA *regards the sheet carefully.*) It's beyond repair. And now that your husband commands fresh sheets, my Iago has got it in his head to be the lord as well; he's got to have fresh sheets each night for his unwashed feet.

DESDEMONA: Emilia, please—I may puke. (DESDEMONA, *in frustration stamps on the clothes she's strewn from the basket.*) It's got to be here, it's got to be here, it's got to be here—Emilia—Help me find it!

EMILIA: You're wasting your time, m'lady. I know it's not here.

DESDEMONA: (*Straightening herself.*) Right. And you knew this morning that my husband wasn't mad at me. Just a passing whim, you said.

EMILIA: Ah, Miss Desdemona . . . not even a midwife can foretell the perfidiosity of men.

DESDEMONA: Give me strength. Perfidy.

EMILIA: That, too.

DESDEMONA: It can't have walked off on two feet!

EMILIA: Mayhap m'lady dropped it.

DESDEMONA: Oh, you're hopeless. No help at all. I'll find it by myself. Go back to your washing and put your hands to use.

EMILIA: Yes, m'lady.

Scene 2

EMILIA *and* DESDEMONA. EMILIA *scrubs sheets.*

DESDEMONA: Will it come out?

EMILIA: I've scrubbed many a sheet, but this is the worst in my career . . . It's all that Bianca's fault. I paid her well for the blood, too. "And be sure," I says, "it's an old hen—one on its last gasp—young chick blood's no good for bridal sheets, it's the devil to come out. Madam's sheets," I says, "are the finest to be had in Venice, and we don't want them ruined and rotted from the stain." And Bianca swore, "I've an old hen on crutches that will wash out clear as a maidenhead or a baby's dropping." Ah, but that chick wasn't a week old. And what with it bakin' in the sun for a month now—but if anyone can, Mealy will scrub it virgin white again.

DESDEMONA: Oh, hush about it. I can't stand to think on it . . . barbaric custom. And my best sheets. Nobody displays bridal sheets on Cyprus.

EMILIA: There aren't any virgins to be had on Cyprus.

DESDEMONA: Half the garrison came to see those sheets flapping in the breeze.

EMILIA: Why did the other half come?

DESDEMONA: To pay their last respects to the chicken! (*They laugh.*)

Scene 3

We hear EMILIA, *in a good humor, humming a tune such as "When Irish Eyes Are Smiling,"* Another clatter of heavy metal things being tossed onto the floor.*

DESDEMONA: JESUS! WHAT IS THIS?

EMILIA: (*In disbelief.*) You didn't find it! (DESDEMONA *crosses to* EMILIA, *holding a long, crooked bit of iron with a wicked point.*)

DESDEMONA: No—this!!

EMILIA: 'Tis a hoof-pick.

DESDEMONA: A hoof-pick? What is it used for?

EMILIA: After all your years of trotting m'lady's bum over field and farrow, and you've never laid your eyes on the like? When your mount picks up a stone in its foot, and it's deep, you take the pick and hold on tight to the hoof—and then you dig it in and down to the quick and pry it out—

DESDEMONA: You dig *this* in? Good lord—

EMILIA: Aye, takes a goodly amount of sweat and grease—it's work for a proper man, it is. (DESDEMONA, *absorbed in fondling the hoof-pick, stretches out on the table.*)

DESDEMONA: Oh me, oh my—if I could find a man with just such a hoof-pick—he could pluck out my stone—eh,

* Special Note on Songs and Recordings: For performance of such songs, arrangements, and recordings mentioned in this play that are protected by copyright, the permission of the copyright owners must be obtained, or other songs, arrangements, and recordings in the public domain substituted.

Emilia? (*They laugh.*) Emilia—does your husband Iago have a hoof-pick to match? (EMILIA *turns and looks, then snorts.*)

EMILIA: What, Iago? (DESDEMONA *puts her hand on the base and covers it.*)

DESDEMONA: Well, then—this much?

EMILIA: Please, mum! It's a matter o' faith between man and wife t—

DESDEMONA: —Ahh—not that much, eh? (DESDEMONA *covers more of the pick.*) Like this?

EMILIA: Miss Desdemona!

DESDEMONA: Come now, Emilia—it's just us—

EMILIA: Some things are private!

DESDEMONA: It's only fair—I'm sure you know every detail about my lord—

EMILIA: (*Shrugging.*) When the Master Piddles, a Servant holds the Pot—

DESDEMONA: (*Persisting.*) This much "hoof?"

EMILIA: Not near as much as that!

DESDEMONA: This much? (*Pause.*)

EMILIA: (*Sour.*) Nay.

DESDEMONA: Good God, Emilia, I'm running out of—

EMILIA: —The wee-est pup of th' litter comes a'bornin' in the world with as much—(DESDEMONA *laughs.*) There. Is m'lady satisfied?

DESDEMONA: Your secret's safe with me.

Scene 4

EMILIA, *scrubbing.* DESDEMONA *lies on her back on the table, feet propped up, absent-mindedly fondling the pick, and staring into space.*

Scene 5

We hear the sound of EMILIA, *puffing and blowing. Lights up on* DESDEMONA *getting a pedicure.*

DESDEMONA: Where is she? It's getting late. He'll be back soon, and clamoring for me. He's been in a rotten mood lately . . . Headaches, handkerchiefs, accusations—and of all people to accuse—Michael Cassio!

EMILIA: The only one you haven't had—

DESDEMONA: —And I don't want him, either. A prissy Florentine, that one is. Leave it to a cuckold to be jealous of a eunuch—

EMILIA: (*Crowning.*) —Bianca would die!

DESDEMONA: Then we won't tell her what I said, will we? (EMILIA *becomes quiet.*) What Bianca does in her spare time is her business.

(EMILIA*'s face clearly indicates that what* BIANCA *does in her spare time is* EMILIA*'s business, too.* DESDEMONA *watches* EMILIA *closely.*) You don't much like Bianca, do you, Mealy? (*No response.* EMILIA *blows on* DESDEMONA*'s toes.*) Come on, now, tell me frankly—why don't you like her?

EMILIA: It's not for me to say . . .

DESDEMONA: Emilia!

EMILIA: It's just that—no disrespect intended, m'lady, but you shouldn't go a'rubbin' elbows with one o' her class . . . Lie down with hussies, get up with crabs . . .

DESDEMONA: Her sheets are clean. (*Pause.*) You've been simmering over Bianca for some time, Mealy, haven't you?

EMILIA: (*Rancorously.*) I don't much like to see m'lady, in whose em-ploy I am, traipsing about in flopdens, doin' favors for common sloppots—Bianca! Ha! She's so loose, so low, that she's got to ad-ver-tise Wednesday Night Specials, half-price for anything in uniform!

DESDEMONA: Well, purge it out of your blood; Bianca will soon be here—

EMILIA: —Here! Why here? What if someone sees her sneaking up to the back door? What will the women in town say? A tart on a house call! How can I keep my head up hanging out the wash and feedin' the pigs when her sort comes sniffin' around—

DESDEMONA: —She's coming to pay me for last Tuesday's customers who paid on credit. And to arrange for next Tuesday—

EMILIA: (*Horrified.*) Not again! Once was enough—you're not going there again! I thought to myself, she's a young unbridled colt, is Miss Desdemona—let her cool down her blood—but to make it a custom!—I couldn't let you go back again—risking disease and putting us all in danger—

DESDEMONA: —Oh, tush, Mealy—

EMILIA: —You listen to me, Miss Desdemona: Othello will sooner or later find out that you're laying for Bianca, and his black skin is goin' to blister off with rage!! Holy Jesus Lord, why tempt a Venetian male by waving red capes? My Iago would beat me for lookin' at the wrong end of an ass! (*Very worked up.*) Your husband will find out and when he does! When he does!! (EMILIA *makes the noise and gesture of throat cutting.*) And then! And then!! AIAIaiaiaiahhh!! My lady!! What's to become of me! Your fateful hand-maid! Where will I find another position in this pisshole harbor!

DESDEMONA: Stop it, Mealy! Don't be—silly, nothing will happen to me. I'm the sort that will die in bed.

EMILIA: (*Beseechingly.*) You won't leave your poor Mealy stranded?

DESDEMONA: You'll always have a position in this household . . . Of some sort. (MEALY*'s face turns to stone.*) Oh, come now, Mealy, haven't I just promoted you?

EMILIA: Oh, m'lady, I haven't forgot; not only your scullery maid, but now your laundress as well! I am quite sensible of the honor and the increase in pay—of two pence a week . . . (EMILIA *suddenly turns bright and cheery.*)—and whiles we are on the subject.

DESDEMONA: —Oh, Christ, here it comes.

EMILIA: But m'lady, last time an opening came up, you promised to speak to your husband about it in Venice; I suppose poor old Iago just slipped your mind—

DESDEMONA: —Look, I did forget. Anyway, I recommended Cassio for my husband's lieutenant. An unfortunate choice. But that subject is closed.

EMILIA: Yes, mum. (EMILIA *starts to return to her laundry. There is a knock at the door, and* DESDEMONA *brightens.*)

DESDEMONA: There she is! Emilia, let Bianca in—No, no wait—(*To* MEALY*'s annoyance,* DESDEMONA *arranges herself in a casual tableau. The knock repeats.* DESDEMONA *signals* EMILIA *to go answer the door.* EMILIA *exits through the door to the palace, and then quickly returns.*)

EMILIA: M'lady, it's your husband. He's waiting for you outside.

DESDEMONA: (*Frightened.*) Husband? . . . Shhhittt . . . (DESDEMONA *pauses, arranges her face into an insipid, fluttering innocence, then girlishly runs to the door. She flings it open, and disappears through the door. We hear a breathless* DESDEMONA, *off.*) Othello! (*And then, we hear the distinct sound of a very loud slap. A pause, and* DESDEMONA *returns, closes the door behind her, holding her cheek. She is on the brink of tears. She and* EMILIA *look at each other, and then* EMILIA *looks away.*

Scene 6

DESDEMONA *and* EMILIA. DESDEMONA *frantically searches.*

DESDEMONA: It's got to be somewhere!!—Are you quite sure—

EMILIA: —Madam can be sure I overlooked the whole lot several times.

DESDEMONA: Um, Emilia—should, should you have "accidentally" taken it—not that I'm suggesting theft in the slightest—but should it have by mistake slipped in with some of your things—your return of it will merit a reward, and all of my gratitude. (DESDEMONA *tries to appear casual.*) Not that the thing itself is worth anything—it's a pittance of musty linen—but still . . .

EMILIA: (*With dignity.*) I've never taken a thing, acc-identiy or not. I don't make no "acc-idents." Mum, I've looked everywhere. Everywhere. (*Quietly.*) Is m'lord clamoring about it much? (*They eye each other. Pause.*)

DESDEMONA: Which position, Mealy?

EMILIA: (*Puzzled.*) Which position?

DESDEMONA: For your husband.

EMILIA: Oh, Miss Desdemona! I won't forget all your—

DESDEMONA: —Yes, yes, I'm sure. What opening?

EMILIA: It's ever so small a promotion, and so quite equal to his merits. He's ensign third-class, but the budget's ensign second-class.

DESDEMONA: Very well, the budget office. Can he write and account and do—whatever it is that they do with the budget?

EMILIA: Oh, yes—he's clever enough at that.

DESDEMONA: I really don't understand your mentality. Emilia. You're forever harping on how much you detest the man. Why do you beg for scraps of promotion for him? Don't you hate him?

EMILIA: I—I—(*With relish.*) I *despise* him.

DESDEMONA: Then?

EMILIA: You see, miss, for us in the bottom ranks, when man and wife hate each other, what is left in a lifetime of marriage but to save and scrimp, plot and plan? The more I'd like to put some nasty rat-ridder in his stew, the more I think of money—and he thinks the same. One of us will drop first, and then, what's left, saved and earned, under the mattress for th' other one? I'd like to rise a bit in the world, and women can only do that through their mates—no matter what class buggers they all are. I says to him each night—I long for the day you make me a lieutenant's widow!

Scene 7

EMILIA *and* DESDEMONA. *We hear the sounds of scrubbing between the scenes.*

DESDEMONA: Please, my dear Emilia—I can count on you, can't I? As one closest to my confidence?

EMILIA: Oh, m'lady—I ask no greater joy than to be close to your ladyship—

DESDEMONA: Then tell me—have you heard anything about me? Why does Othello suspect Cassio?

EMILIA: Oh, no, m'lady, he surely no longer suspects Cassio; I instructed Iago to talk him out of that bit of fancy, which he did, risking my lord's anger at no little cost to his own career; but all for you, you know!

DESDEMONA: You haven't heard of anything else?

EMILIA: No Ma'am. (*But as* DESDEMONA *is to* EMILIA*'s back,* EMILIA *drops a secret smile into the wash bucket.* EMILIA *raises her head again, though, with a sincere, servile face, and turns to* DESDEMONA.) But if I did know anything, you can be sure that you're the first to see the parting of my lips about it—

DESDEMONA: Yes, I know. You've been an extremely faithful, hard-working servant to me, Emilia, if not a confidante. I've noticed your merits, and when we return to Venice—well—you may live to be my *fille de chambre* yet.

EMILIA: (*Not quite sure what a* fille de chambre *is.*) I'm very grateful, I'm sure.

DESDEMONA: Yes—you deserve a little reward, I think—(EMILIA*'s face brightens in expectancy.*)—I'll see if I can wheedle another tuppence out of my husband each week . . . (EMILIA *droops.*)

EMILIA: (*Listlessly.*) Every little tiny bit under the mattress helps, I always says to myself. (*A pause.* DESDEMONA *paces, comes to a decision.*)

DESDEMONA: Mealy—do you like the dressing gown you've been mending?

EMILIA: It's a lovely piece of work, that is, Miss. I've always admired your dresses . . .

DESDEMONA: Yesss . . . yes, but isn't it getting a bit dingy? Tattered around the hem?

EMILIA: Not that anyone would notice; it's a beautiful gown, m'lady . . .

DESDEMONA: Yes, you're right. I was going to give it to you, but maybe I'll hang on to it a bit longer . . .

(EMILIA, *realizing her stupidity, casts an avaricious, yet mournful look at the gown that was almost hers.*)

EMILIA: Oh, m'lady . . . It's—it's certainly a lovely cloth, and there's a cut to it that would make one of them boy actors shapely . . .

DESDEMONA: (*Peeved at the analogy.*) Hmmmm—tho', come to think of it, it would fit Bianca much neater, I think . . .

EMILIA: Bianca! Bianca! She's got the thighs of a milch cow, m'lady!

DESDEMONA: (*Amused.*) I've never noticed. (EMILIA, *sulking again, vigorously scrubs. In conciliation.*) No, come to think of it, I believe you are right—it's not really Bianca's fashion. It's all yours. After tonight.

EMILIA: Oh, Miss Desdemona!!

Scene 8

The same. In the darkness we hear EMILIA *singing a hymn: "la la la la—Jesus; la-la-la-la—sword; la-la-la-la—crucifix; la-la-la-la—word." Lights come up on* DESDEMONA *lying stretched out on the table, her throat and head arched over its edge, upside down. A pause.*

DESDEMONA: You really think his temper today was only some peeve?

EMILIA: I'm sure of it; men get itchy heat rash in th' crotch, now and then; they get all snappish, but once they beat us, it's all kisses and presents the next morning—well, for the first year or so.

DESDEMONA: My dear mate is much too miserly to give me anything but his manhood. The only gift he's given me was a meager handkerchief with piddling strawberries stitched on it, and look how he's carrying on because I've lost it! He guards his purse strings much dearer than his wife.

EMILIA: I'm sure my Lord will be waitin' up for you to come to bed. Full o' passion, and embracin' and makin' a fool o' himself—You just see if your Mealy isn't right.

DESDEMONA: Yes, of course you're right. Good old Mealy, I don't know what I'd do without your good common sense. Oh, it's the curse of aristocratic blood—I feel full of whims and premonitions—

EMILIA: Perhaps it was something m'lady et?

DESDEMONA: (*First she smiles—then she laughs.*) Yes—that must be it! (DESDEMONA *laughs again.* MEALY *can't understand what is so funny.*)

Scene 9

EMILIA *and* DESDEMONA.

EMILIA: Ambassador Ludovico gave me a message and is waitin' a response.

DESDEMONA: What does my cousin want? (EMILIA *digs into her bodice.*)

EMILIA: It's somewhere in here . . . wait—(EMILIA *searches.*)

DESDEMONA: Oh, good Lord, Mealy, you could lose it in there! (DESDEMONA *runs to* EMILIA, *peers in her bosom, and starts to tickle her.*)

EMILIA: Miss Desde—! Wait, now—no, STOP!! Here it is now—(EMILIA *finds a folded paper. She hands it to* DESDEMONA, *and then peers over* DESDEMONA*'s shoulder.*)

DESDEMONA: (*Sighing.*) Oh, Ludovico, Ludovico. "Deeply desiring the favor, etcetras." " . . . Impatient until I can at last see you in private, throwing off the Robes of State to appear as your humble friend." He's just too tiresome.

EMILIA: What response are you wanting me to give?

DESDEMONA: Oh, I don't know. Let the old lecher wait. I told him it was entirely past between us, and then he bribes his way into being appointed Ambassador! (DESDEMONA *in a lo-*

quacious mood. EMILIA *gives her a rubdown.*) Ah, Emilia, I should have married Ludovico after all. There's a man who's always known the worth of ladies of good blood! A pearl for a pinch, a brooch for a breast, and for a maidenhead . . . (DESDEMONA *breaks into laughter.*) Ah, that was a lover!

EMILIA: I don't know how those sainted sisters could let such is-sagnations go on in their convent—

DESDEMONA: —assignations. Really, Emilia, you're quite hopeless. However can I, the daughter of a senator, live with a washerwoman as *fille de chambre?* All fashionable Venice will howl. You must shrink your vowels and enlarge your vocabulary.

EMILIA: Yes, mum. As-signations, as it were. (*Muttering.*) If it were one o' my class, I could call it by some names I could pronounce. I've put many a copper in their poor box, in times past, thinkin' them sisters of charity in a godly house. Not no more. They won't get the pairings of my potatoes from me, runnin' a society house of ass-ignations!

DESDEMONA: Oh, those poor, dear sisters. I really don't think they knew anything about the informal education their convent girls receive; for one thing, I believe myopia is a prerequisite for Holy Orders. Have you ever noticed how nuns squint? (*Beat.*) Each Sunday in convent we were allowed to take visitors to chapel; under their pious gaze Ludovico and I would kneel—and there I could devote myself to doing him à la main—(DESDEMONA *gestures.*)—right in the pew! They never noticed! Sister Theresa did once remark that he was a man excessively fond of prayer.

Scene 10

EMILIA*'s* credo.

EMILIA: It's not right of you, Miss Desdemona, to be forever cutting up on the matter of my beliefs. I believe in the

Blessed Virgin, I do, and the Holy Fathers and the Sacraments of the Church, and I'm not one to be ashamed of admittin' it. It goes against my marrow, it does, to hear of you, a comely lass from a decent home, giving hand jobs in the pew; but I says to myself, Emilia, I says, you just pay it no mind, and I go about my business. And if I take a break on the Sabbath each week, to light a candle and say a bead or two for my em-ployers, who have given me and my husband so much, and who need the Virgin's love and protection, then where's the harm, say I? (*Breath.* EMILIA *gets carried away.*) Our Lady has seen me through four and ten years of matreemony, with my bugger o' a mate, and that's no mean feat. Four and ten years, she's heard poor Mealy's cries, and stopped me from rising from my bed with my pillow in my hand to end his ugly snores 'til Gabriel—(EMILIA *stops and composes herself.*)—Ah, Miss Desdemona, if you only knew the peace and love Our Lady brings! She'd help you, mum, if you only kneeled real nice and said to her—and said—(EMILIA *can't find the words that such a sinner as* DESDEMONA *should say as polite salutation to Our Lady.* DESDEMONA *erupts into laughter.*)

Scene II

EMILIA *eats her lunch.* DESDEMONA *plays in a desultory fashion with a toy. Then, frightened.*

DESDEMONA: Emilia—have you ever deceived your husband Iago?

EMILIA: (*With a derisive snort.*) That's a good one. Of course not, miss—I'm an honest woman.

DESDEMONA: What does honesty have to do with adultery? Every honest man I know is an adulterer . . . (*Pause.*) Have you ever thought about it?

EMILIA: What is there to be thinkin' about? It's enough trouble once each Saturday night, than to be lookin' for it. I'd never cheat, never, not for all the world I wouldn't.

DESDEMONA: The world's a huge thing for so small a vice.

EMILIA: Not my world, thank you—mine's tidy and neat and I aim to keep it that way.

DESDEMONA: Oh, the world! Our world's narrow and small, I'll grant you—but there are other worlds—worlds that we married women never get to see.

EMILIA: Amen—and don't need to see, I should add.

DESDEMONA: If you've never seen the world, how would you know? Women are clad in purdah, we decent, respectable matrons, from the cradle to the altar to the shroud . . . bridled with linen, blinded with lace . . . These very walls are purdah.

EMILIA: I don't know what this thing called "purr-dah" means, but if it stands for dressing up nice, I'm all for it . . .

DESDEMONA: I remember the first time I saw my husband and I caught a glimpse of his skin, and oh, how I thrilled. I thought—aha—a man of a different color. From another world and planet. I thought—if I marry this strange dark man, I can leave this narrow little Venice with its whispering piazzas behind—I can escape and see other worlds. (*Pause.*) But under that exotic facade was a porcelain white Venetian.

EMILIA: There's nothing wrong with Venice; I don't understand why Madam's all fired up to catch Cyprus Syph and exotic claps.

DESDEMONA: Of course you don't understand. But I think Bianca does. She's a free woman—a new woman, who can make her own living in the world—who scorns marriage for the lie that it is.

EMILIA: I don't know where Madam's getting this new woman hog-wash, but no matter how you dress up a cow, she's still got udders. Bianca's the eldest one of six girls, with teeth so horsy she could clean 'em with a hoof pick, and so simple she has to ply the trade she does! That's what your Miss Bianca is!

DESDEMONA: Bianca is nothing of the sort. She and I share something common in our blood—that desire to know the world. I lie in the blackness of the room at her establishment . . . on sheets that are stained and torn by countless nights. And the men come into that pitch-black room—men of different sizes and smells and shapes, with smooth skin—with rough skin, with scarred skin. And they spill their seed into me, Emilia—seed from a thousand lands, passed down through generations of ancestors, with genealogies that cover the surface of the globe. And I simply lie still there in the darkness, taking them all into me; I close my eyes and in the dark of my mind—oh, how I travel!

Scene 12

EMILIA *and* DESDEMONA. DESDEMONA *is recklessly excited.*

EMILIA: You're leaving?!! Your husband?!!

DESDEMONA: It's a possibility!

EMILIA: Miss Desdemona, you've been taking terrible chances before but now—if my Lord catches you giving him th' back wind, he'll be after murdering both of us for sure—

DESDEMONA: Where's my cousin Ludovico? Is he in his room?

EMILIA: He said he was turnin' in early to get some rest before th' morning—

DESDEMONA: Yes—he'll catch the first tide back. Well, there's no harm in trying.

EMILIA: Trying what!

DESDEMONA: Trying on the robes of the penitent daughter. Ludovico can surely see how detestable this island, this marriage, this life is for me. (DESDEMONA *has worked herself to the point of tears. Then she smiles.*) Perhaps a few tears would move him to intercede with my father on my behalf. If the disgrace of eloping with a Moor is too great for Venetian society, a small annual allowance from Papa and I promise never to show my face in town; and then . . . who knows . . . Paris! Yes, I'll go write Ludovico a note right away, asking to see him tonight.—Mealy—just in case—could you pack a few things for me?

EMILIA: And what if your husband discovers—

DESDEMONA: I'll leave first thing in the morning.

EMILIA: If I may make so bold to suggest—

DESDEMONA: What, what—

EMILIA: That you by all means sleep with your husband tonight. So's he won't suspect anything. While you and he lie together, and if your cousin agrees, Mealy could pack up your things quiet-like in your chamber.

DESDEMONA: Yes, that's good. My life rests on your absolute discretion, Emilia.

EMILIA: No one will hear a peep out o' me. But my lady—

DESDEMONA: Now what is it?

EMILIA: What becomes of me?

DESDEMONA: Oh, good heavens, Mealy—I can't think of trivia at a time like this. (*Smoothly.*) I tell you what. Be a good girl, pack my things—and of course, should I leave tomorrow, I can't very well smuggle you on board, too—but I will send for you within the week. And your services will be remembered in Venice; with freer purse strings—who knows? Eh, my *fille de chambre?* (*At this sop to her feelings,* EMILIA *becomes fierce.*)

EMILIA: That won't do, m'lady. If you leave me behind, I'll not see you again, as your laundress, much less as your "fee der schomer"—(DESDEMONA, *realizing the power that* EMILIA *now has, kneels beside* EMILIA.)

DESDEMONA: All right. I'll intercede with my cousin on your behalf. I'll plead with him to take you, too. But I can't promise anything. Are you sure it's what you want? (EMILIA *nods.*) You'd leave your husband behind? (EMILIA *nods vigorously.*) Then—not a word. (DESDEMONA *rises, and in turning to go.*) Oh, Emilia—since you're just dawdling over that laundry—why not stop and peel some potatoes for Cook. When my husband comes in, he'll want his usual snack of chips before he turns in—just the way he likes them—(DESDEMONA *shudders.*)—*greasy.*

EMILIA: But Miss, it's not my place no more to peel potatoes! I'm promoted now! I'm no mere (*With disgust.*)—SCULLERY MAID.

DESDEMONA: Now, Mealy, just this once—

EMILIA: —You said I wouldn't have to do potatoes anymore!

DESDEMONA: (*Harshly.*) —I can leave you rotting on Cyprus all together, you know. Do as you're told. Peel the potatoes, and then look sharp and have that wash on the line by the time I return. Do I make myself clear?

EMILIA: Yes, m'lady.

DESDEMONA: (*Sweetly.*) And Emilia, dear—if Bianca comes when I'm gone, let me know immediately—I'll be in my chamber.

EMILIA: Very good, Miss Desdemona. (DESDEMONA *exits.* EMILIA *grudgingly gets up, and finds the barrel of potatoes. On the bench there is a paring knife.* EMILIA *brings everything back to the table, sits, and begins paring potatoes—venting her resentment on gouging out eyes, and stripping the skin from a potato as if flaying a certain mistress alive. Then, she snorts out in contempt.*) Fee der shomber! (*Then* EMILIA *pauses and wonders if* DESDEMONA *might not be for real in her offer—and questions the empty room with;*) Feeyah der schomber? (*Before* EMILIA'S *eyes, she visualizes splendid dresses, the command of a household of subservient maids, a husbandless existence—all the trappings that go with the title.* EMILIA *begins energetically, resolutely, and obediently to slice the potatoes.*)

Scene 13

EMILIA *is hanging up the wash.* BIANCA *knocks several times. Then enters.*

BIANCA: Gaw Blimey!

EMILIA: And where is' you've lost your manners? Lettin' the door ajar and leavin' in drafts and the pigs—

BIANCA: Aw'm sorry, Aw'm sure . . . (BIANCA *closes the door. Hesitates, and then with friendly strides, goes toward the clothesline.*) 'Ow do, Emilia!

EMILIA: I'd be doin' a lot better if ye'd stop your gaddin' and lend a hand with these things.

BIANCA: Oh. Right you are, then. (BIANCA *goes briskly to the clothesline, and works. Silence as the women empty the basket.* EMILIA *leaves* BIANCA *to finish and starts in on her sewing. Pause.*) Well, it's—it ain't 'arf swank 'ere, eh? (BIANCA *indicates the room.*)

EMILIA: (*Snorts.*) Swank? What, this? This is only the *back* room. The palace is through those doors—

BIANCA: Oh. Well, it's swank for a back room wotever it 'tis. Aw niver got to see it much; the Guv'nor in the owld days didn't leet me near, said Aw made the men tomdoodle on their shifts; like as they'd be dis-tracted by me atomy. Aw think it's sweet o' him to gi' me such credit; me atomy ain't that bleedin' jammy—but then, the owld Guv was the first to gi' me the sheeps' eye 'imself—very sweet on me, 'e was. So you see, Aw'd niver got close to the place before. Aw fink it's swank!

EMILIA: (*Icily.*) I'm sure you do.

BIANCA: Yes, it's quite—wot do ye call it—lux-i-o-rious.

EMILIA: Lux-i-o-ri-us!! If I was you, I'd large my voc-abulary, an' shrink me vowels.

BIANCA: (*Offended.*) 'Ere now! Wot bus'ness is me vowels to you?! Leave me vowels alone—

EMILIA: —I'm after talking about your voc-abulary—your patter—not your reg-ularity.

BIANCA: Oh. (*Keeping up a friendly front with difficulty.*) Right. Well, then, is Desdemona 'ere?

EMILIA: (*Sharply.*) *Who?*

BIANCA: Uh—Des-de-mona . . .

EMILIA: Is it m'lady you're referrin' to as if she were your mess mate?

BIANCA: Look 'ere—Aw'm only doin' as Aw was towld. She tells me to call her Desdemona, and she says Aw was to call and settle up accounts for last Tuesday night for those johns who paid on tick—oh, you know, who paid on credit, as yew la-de-da Venetians would say.

EMILIA: (*Softly hissed.*) You listen to me, lassie: you're riding for a fall the likes of which you never got paid for by your fancy men. The mistress of this house is not at home, nor will be to the likes of you. What m'lady does in the gutter is her own business, same as yours, but what happens here is the common buzz of all.

BIANCA: (*Stunned.*) Wot! Miss Desdemona herself is callin' us mates; Aw niver—

EMILIA: —then she's gullin' you, as sure as 'tis she's gullin' that ass of a husband who's so taken with her; but let me tell you, you'll go the way like all the other fancies she's had in Venice . . . *I* should know. We all of us servants in her father's house talked on end about Miss Desdemona. —For a time, she wanted to be a saint, yes! A nun with the sisters of mercy. At age twelve she was washin' the courtyard stones for penance, with us wiping up behind her. Then she was taken with horses, thank Jesus, and left sainthood behind—and then in turn again, she thought she was dyin'—stopped eating, and moped, and talked all dreamy and a little balmy-like—until her father finally saw sense and sent her to the convent to be bred out of her boredom. You're nothin' but the latest whim, a small town floozy with small town slang, and if she's lucky, she'll tire of you before the master finds out. (*Significantly.*) *If* she's lucky.

BIANCA: (*Somewhat subdued.*) So wot am Aw t'do, Emilia? Aw arsks you—

EMILIA: —Then ask me by "Miss Emilia" to you—(*With great dignity.*) I'll have you know, I've hereby been promoted to "fee der shimber" and if I was you, I'd keep on my right side.

BIANCA: (*Impressed, scared.*) Oh—"fee dar shimber"—Aw niver met one o' those before—Aw arsks yer pardon, Miss Emilia, Aw'm sure.

EMILIA: That's a bit of all right. You just listen to me: I know what side of me bread is buttered; behind this whimsy-cal missus is a power of a master—so you mind yourself; the smell of your sin's goin' to catch m'lord's whiffin' about, and he's as jealous as he's black. If m'lord Othello had a mind to it, he could have that little lollin' tongue of yours cut clean out of your head, with none of the citizens of Cyprus to say him nay. And then what would you do for your customers! If he catched you degineratin' his wife—

BIANCA: (*Starting to cry with fear.*) Aw swear, Miss Emilia, Aw'm not degineratin' m'lady; we was just mates, that's wot; if Missus Desdemona wants to lark and gull her smug of a husband, that's her business, then, ain't it! Aw done as she towld me, an' that's all—she's a good lady, an' al, and Aw've just been friendly-like to her—

EMILIA: —Don't be a little fool hussy. There's no such creature, two, three, or four-legged, as "friend" betwixt ladies of leisure and ladies of the night. And as long as there be men with one member but two minds, there's no such thing as friendship between women. An' that's that. So turn yourself around, go out and close the door behind you, and take all traces of the flophouse with you—includin' your tall tales about your "friendships" with ladies—

BIANCA: (*Anger finally conquering fear.*) You can call me wot you like, but Aw'm no liar! Aw'm as 'onest a woman as yerself! And wot's more, mebbe you can wipe yer trotters on women who have to crack their crusts by rolling blokes in Venice, but 'ere it's differnt.—Aw have a place 'ere and Aw'm not ashamed t'own it—Aw'm nice to the wives in town, and the wives in town are rather nice to me. Aw'm doin' them favors by puttin' up wif their screwy owld men, and Aw like me job! The only ponk Aw has to clean up is me own. (*Starts to leave but.*)—And wot's more, Aw likes yer lady, whefer you think so or not. She can see me as Aw am, and not arsk for bowin' and scrapin'—she don't have to be nobby, 'cause she's got breedin', and she don't mind liking me for me own self—wifout th' nobby airs of yer Venetian washerwomen! Aw'm at home 'ere in my place—you, you Venetian washerdonna—you're the one out o' yer element! (BIANCA *stalks to the door, but before she can reach it,* DESDEMONA *enters.*)

DESDEMONA: Emilia.

Scene 14

The same. DESDEMONA, EMILIA, *and* BIANCA.

DESDEMONA: Emilia. I thought I told you to tell me the instant Miss Bianca arrived. Well?

EMILIA: I didn't want to be botherin' m'lady with the ambassador—

DESDEMONA: —I want none of your excuses for your rudeness to our guest. My dear Bianca! I've been waiting impatiently—I could have just died of boredom. (DESDEMONA: *bestows a warm hug on Bianca.*)—May I kiss you? (DESDEMONA *"kisses"* BIANCA *by pressing both sides of their cheeks together.*)

BIANCA: (*Stammering.*) Aw'm not worthy of it, m'lady—

DESDEMONA: Oh, Bianca, so stiff and formal! —What have I done that you should be so angry with me?

BIANCA: (*Quickly.*) Nofing! Your lady's been all kindness to me . . . but mayhap . . . Aw'm not the sort o' mate for one o' your company!

DESDEMONA: Nonsense! I'll decide my own friendships . . . (DESDEMONA *looks meaningfully at* EMILIA. *To* BIANCA.) You must excuse my entertaining you in such a crude barn of a room; my room's much cozier, but I don't know when my . . . my . . . "smug"—is that right? (*Bianca nods.*)—when he'll return. (DESDEMONA *laughs.*) Right now Othello's out in the night somewhere playing Roman Orator to his troops. (DESDEMONA *guides Bianca to the table: they sit side by side.*) Emilia . . . Ask Miss Bianca if she'd like some wine. (*To* BIANCA.) It's really quite good, my dear. (EMILIA *glumly approaches* BIANCA.)

EMILIA: Well, are you wantin' any?

DESDEMONA: Emilia! "Would you care for some wine, Miss Bianca?"

EMILIA: (*Deep breath, red.*) "Would you care for some wine, Miss Bianca?"

BIANCA: Why thank you—D-desdemona, Aw could do w' a sneaker—

DESDEMONA: (*Laughs.*) How I love the way you talk! . . . Emilia, fetch the wine and two goblets. That will be all.

EMILIA: Yes, mum. (EMILIA *exits and* BIANCA *relaxes.*)

DESDEMONA: My poor Bianca; has Emilia been berating you?

BIANCA: Well, Aw don't know about that, but she's been takin' me down a bit. Aw don't thinks she likes me very much.

DESDEMONA: Oh, what does that matter! Why should you want her friendship—you don't have to care what anyone thinks about you—you're a totally free woman, able to snap your fingers in any one's face!

BIANCA: Yea, that's wot all right—but still, Aw likes people to like me.

DESDEMONA: Oh, well, you mustn't mind Emilia. She's got a rotten temper because her husband—her "smug"—is such a rotter. Oh, Iago! (DESDEMONA *shudders.*) Do you know him?

BIANCA: (*Smiling, looking away.*) Aw know 'im by sight—

DESDEMONA: You know the one, then—the greasy little man. He's been spilling his vinegar into her for fourteen years of marriage, until he's corroded her womb from the inside out—and every day she becomes more and more hallowed out, just—just a vessel of vinegar herself.

BIANCA: (*Disturbed.*) Wot a funny way of lookin' at it—(BIANCA *is bewildered.*)

Scene 15

BIANCA *and* DESDEMONA.

BIANCA: So you don't fancy Iago, then, do you?

DESDEMONA: Detest him. But of course, I don't have anything to do with him—I only need suffer his wife's company. Poor old Mealy—

BIANCA: —"Mealy?" (BIANCA *laughs, her fear of* EMILIA *diminishing.*)

DESDEMONA: Yes, I've nicknamed her that, because I suspect it annoys her. Still, it fits. (DESDEMONA *and* BIANCA *giggle.*) Alas, when Othello and I eloped it was on such short notice and my husband's so stingy with salary that the only maid I could bring was my father's scullery maid.

BIANCA: Yer scullery maid! Not—not yer—wot-de-ye-call it—"Fee dah—Feyah der—"

DESDEMONA: *"Fille de Chambre!"* Heavens, no! I keep her in line with the prospect of eventual advancement, but she's much too unsuitable for that—why she doesn't speak a word of French, and she's crabby to boot. Still, she's devoted and that makes up for all the rest.

BIANCA: Wot makes you fink she's devoted?

DESDEMONA: Ah, a good mistress knows the secret thoughts of her maids. She's devoted.

BIANCA: Well, it's a cooshy enough way to crack a crust . . .

DESDEMONA: Crack a crust?

BIANCA: Oh—beg yer pardon; Aw mean t'earn a livin'—

DESDEMONA: (*Enthralled.*) "Crack a crust!" How clever you are, Bianca!

Scene 16

DESDEMONA, BIANCA, *and* EMILIA. EMILIA *stands before* DESDEMONA, *bearing a pitcher and two mugs on a tray.*

EMILIA: Wine, m'lady . . .

DESDEMONA: Ah, excellent. (EMILIA *serves* DESDEMONA *first with all the grace she can muster; then she negligently pushes the wine in the direction of* BIANCA.)

BIANCA: Thank you, Mealy.

DESDEMONA: (*Toasting* BIANCA.) Now, then: to our friendship!

BIANCA: T' yer'ealth—(DESDEMONA *delicately sips her wine, as* BIANCA *belts it down so that the wine trickles from the corner of her mouth.* EMILIA *is aghast. As* BIANCA *wipes her mouth with her hand, she notices* EMILIA*'s shock and blurts.*) 'Scuse me guttlin' it down me gob—

DESDEMONA: Oh, tush, Bianca. Mealy, haven't you mending to carry on with? (EMILIA *silently seats herself apart and picks up the drawers.*) I tell you, Bianca, it's a disgrace. My husband refuses to buy new linen for his drawers, so Emilia must constantly mend the old. (*Confidentially.*) He's constantly tearing his crotch-hole somehow.

BIANCA: (*Amused.*) And how does that happen?

DESDEMONA: (*Demurely.*) I have no idea. —More wine, dear?

Scene 17

The same. BIANCA *and* DESDEMONA, *drinking.* EMILIA *sews.*

DESDEMONA: How about another . . . round?

BIANCA: All right, then. (DESDEMONA *pours generously.*)—But not so much! Aw could get lushy easy. (BIANCA *sips her wine:* DESDEMONA *knocks it back, and wipes her mouth with her hand. They laugh.*)

Scene 18

DESDEMONA *and* BIANCA, *drinking. They are giggling helplessly, spluttering.* EMILIA *sews.* DESDEMONA *starts to choke on her wine from laughing.*

Scene 19

The same. DESDEMONA *and* BIANCA *try to control themselves. Then* DESDEMONA *holds up the hoof-pick, and* BIANCA *and* DESDEMONA *explode in raucous laughter.* EMILIA *is furious.*

Scene 20

The same.

BIANCA: Listen, luvs, where's yer five-minute lodging?

DESDEMONA: My . . . what?

BIANCA: Yer Durry Lane? Yer—where's yer bleedin' crapper! Yew know—where do yew make water?

EMILIA: M'lady makes her water in a hand-painted Limoge pot, a holy sight with angels havin' a grand time—it's not for the like of you!

DESDEMONA: There's an outhouse in the back by the shed . . . careful of the muck and the pigs.

BIANCA: 'Ta. Be back in a few . . . Aw've got t' go see a bloke about a horse. (BIANCA *exits.*)

EMILIA: And you're after havin' yourself a proper time.

DESDEMONA: Oh, Mealy, I'm sorry—we were just having fun—

EMILIA: At my husband's expense. You finagled that out o' me, and then you went and told it to My Lady of the Public Square . . .

DESDEMONA: It . . . It just . . . slipped out. (DESDEMONA *goes into another gale of laughter. Then.*)—Mealy—I'm going to ask her about Cassio!

EMILIA: Why must you be knowin' every man's size?! (DESDEMONA *laughs again.*)

DESDEMONA: —No, I mean I'm going to tell her that Othello suspects him.

EMILIA: Are you daft from the wine?

DESDEMONA: Why not? Maybe we can get to the bottom of this . . .

EMILIA: Why is it mattering? Tomorrow morning we're leaving with the ambassador—

DESDEMONA: —Yes, yes, but I can find out why—

EMILIA: —I don't understand why m'lady is in such a rush to havin' her throat slashed our last night on Cyprus—

DESDEMONA: —Look, I'll just tell her that my husband is under some false impression, and ask her for—

EMILIA: —And why should she be believin' you?

DESDEMONA: She'll believe me! She'll believe me because . . . I'll give her . . . I'll give her . . . my word of honor.

EMILIA: And just how much goat cheese does that buy at market? —I know the world! I've seen flesh buckets fightin' for their fancy men in the streets in Venice, and a pretty sight it was!

DESDEMONA: Oh, Mealy—

EMILIA: —You'll be bleedin' on the wrong time of the month! Those trullies, all of them, carry slashers down in their boots—(BIANCA *throws open the door and sticks her head in;* EMILIA *and* DESDEMONA *are startled.*)

BIANCA: Did-jew miss me?

Scene 21

BIANCA, DESDEMONA, *and* EMILIA.

BIANCA: 'Ere now—let me settle w' you fer Tuesday night—let's see . . . (BIANCA *rummages in a pocket of her dress.*) It were six pence a john, at ten johns makes fer . . . five bob, an' tuppence fer tips. (EMILIA *gasps.*)

DESDEMONA: I can hear what you're thinking Mealy—Holy Mother, I made more in twenty minutes than you do in a week of washing!

EMILIA: Five bob . . .

DESDEMONA: How large now the world for so small a vice, eh, Mealy?

EMILIA: I'm—I'm not to be tempted, Miss Desdemona.

DESDEMONA: Brave girl!

BIANCA: 'Ere's the brass ready. Tuppence for tips is bleedin'-well for a Tuesday.

DESDEMONA: Really?

BIANCA: It so be as how Wednesday is pay-day 'ere; Tuesday nights are the cooshiest layin', but the stingiest payin'—

EMILIA: Aye, "Men earns their money like Horses and spends it like Asses" . . .

DESDEMONA: Never mind Mealy, Bianca; she's over there calculating what price fidelity. Now about next week—

EMILIA: —You two can cackle with laughter at me if you like, but it's a duty for me to stop your ladyship from gettin' into danger—

BIANCA: (*Offended.*) Danger! Wot danger! She helped me out on me Adam an' Eve Night—there's no danger; Aw gave her me lambs; the feisty, firkin' lads come on th' other nights, not on Tuesday. It don't take no elbow grease; Tuesday's just lying back and Adam an' Evein' it—

EMILIA: I don't understand your "Adam and Eve" and I don't think I want to . . .

DESDEMONA: Oh yes you do, Mealy; "Adam and Eve" is what you and Iago did on your wedding night . . .

BIANCA: She just might fink it means fallin' asleep—(EMILIA *vigorously stitches the hem.*)

DESDEMONA: She's right, tho', Bianca, she's only trying to protect me; how about if we leave next Tuesday night open. If I can sneak away into the darkness of your boudoir, then I'll send word by Emilia—

BIANCA: Right, then, but you understand me, Miss Desdemona, there'll be no firsky johns when you comes clandecently; just the meek ones who are low on pocket-brass, or the stingy-mingy-gits who don't want to pay for nothin' wild; an' there'll be a fresh bed, an' the room so dark that your own husband wouldn't know you—

DESDEMONA: —Oh, Bianca—what a thought—do you think he'd come? I'd die for sure—(DESDEMONA *laughs.*)—And wouldn't he be mad if he's paid for what he got for free at home!!

BIANCA: Well, the room's bleedin' black—blacker than he is. (BIANCA *and* EMILIA *laugh together,* DESDEMONA *is affronted.*)

DESDEMONA: I beg your pardon?

BIANCA: No, no—all my Tuesday johns are reg'lars—Aw know 'em all. So if you want, let me know—it'll be treacle next to wot Aw had today—

DESDEMONA: —Do tell, Bianca—

EMILIA: —Hasn't m'lady had enough—

DESDEMONA: —Oh, hush, Mealy—just mend your crotches, and don't listen.

BIANCA: All right, then. Aw have this one john who comes once a week for an L & B—

DESDEMONA: "L & B?"

BIANCA: In th' Life, it's known as a lam an' brim—first they lam you, an' mayhap you lam them, then you brim 'em—(DESDEMONA *looks blank.*) You know—first they beat you, an' then you beat them, and then you give 'em wotever—an Adam an' Eve, or a Sunny-side Over—

DESDEMONA: (*Dawning.*) You mean men actually pay to beat you? And to be beaten?

BIANCA: Oh, well, it costs 'em a pretty penny, Aw can tell you; there's nothin' doin' for less than two bob.

DESDEMONA: (*Eyes wide.*) My. Well, carry on.

BIANCA: Well, there's this one john, an owld mate, who's been on tick for some weeks, an' 'e's got quite a bill. But Aw feels sorry for 'im, 'is wife really lams 'im at 'ome, an' Aw figure 'e needs t' get it off 'is chest—So 'e comes in, an' Aw says: "Tom—you owe me over two quid, now; when's it coming'?" "Gaw, Bianca," 'e says, "Aw just been out o' Collar, an'—"

DESDEMONA: —"Out of Collar?"

BIANCA: Wot yew call un-deployed . . . "Bianca," 'e says, "Gawd luv yew, me owld woman an' Aw've had a row an' Aw'm all done in. Aw'll pay th' soddin' bill, some'ow; but fer now, fer owld times," 'e says—well Gawd's Wounds, wot was Aw t'do? "Right, then, Tom," Aw said, an' Aw lays down on the bed—'cause 'e liked me to go first—an' 'e puts the straps on me—"Tom," Aw says, "listen, luv, th' straps are bleedin' tight—" An' before Aw knew wot, 'e was lammin' me fer real!! 'E did me fer a jacketin' such as Aw thought would be me last L 'n' B!! Aw bite me teeth not to scream, 'cause the bobbies won't put up with no row, no matter how many quid Aw pay 'em . . . Well, Tom finally gets it over wif, an' it's *my* turn. "Aw'm sorry, Bianca," 'e says, "if Aw got a bit rough." "Oh, it's nofin', Tom," Aw says—'cause Aw'm determined t' get me own back . . . So Aw tie 'im down on th' bed—'e's a big strapper o' a bloke—An' then Aw lam th' *pudding* out o' 'im—!! An' 'e's 'ollerin' like it's th' Second Coming. Then after Aw gi' 'im a royal pasting, Aw go through 'is togs, an' in the back pocket—Aw find a soddin' crown! "You been 'olding out on me, Tom! Aw've had it wi' yer dodges an' flams—wot kind o' a soup kitchen do yew fink me?"—An' Aw let into 'im again!!—"Bianca—let me go, an' Aw'll niver flam to ye again!" "BLEEDIN'-RIGHT!" Aw says. So Aw copped 'is brass, takes up the belt, an' let 'im loose—straight into the street 'e runs, naked as a blue-jay—Aw had to throw 'is togs after 'im. "Yew Owld Stringer!" Aw yelled: —"'Ere's yer togs, an' fer yer change, take this!" (BIANCA *raises her fist and slaps her elbow; excited, she catches her breath.*)

DESDEMONA: Jesus. Weren't you scared?

BIANCA: Aw'd be lyin' if Aw said nay. Aw though it was me last trick. You can't be too careful, there's a lot of maggot-brained doodles in me bus'ness. But Aw can take care o' meself.

DESDEMONA: Doesn't—doesn't it hurt?

BIANCA: Naw—not usual. It's stingy-like, but it's all fakement.

(BIANCA *looking into* DESDEMONA*'s eyes, gets an idea.*) . . . Aw c'n show you if you likes . . . C'mon, it won't hurt you none—

DESDEMONA: Well . . . yes, all right, Bianca, show me.

Scene 22

The beating scene. EMILIA, BIANCA, *and* DESDEMONA.

EMILIA: Are you out o' your mind? Lettin' a strumpet strap you in your own house like a monk in Holy Week?

DESDEMONA: Turn around, Emilia, and mind your own business. Go on, turn around, and say your beads. Pay no attention. (*To* BIANCA.) Sorry—please continue. (EMILIA *says her beads through the following.*)

EMILIA: Hail Mary Full of Grace the Lord is with Thee—

BIANCA: Get up on the table wi' yer tale end up—

EMILIA: Holy Mary, Mother of—(EMILIA *turns and sees* DESDEMONA *spread-eagled.*)—GOD!!!

BIANCA: Right now. Aw'll just take a strap 'ere—an' Aw'll just brush you wi' it—but when Aw let's go, you move yer tail up—all right?

DESDEMONA: I—I think so; it's rather like rising to the trot on a horse—

BIANCA: Right then. One-up, Two-down; all right, now, One: (DESDEMONA *moves up.*) Two-: (BIANCA *lightly straps* DESDEMONA *as she moves down.*) One-: (DESDEMONA *moves up.*) An' Two-: (DESDEMONA *moves down; a strap.*)—Does it hurt?

DESDEMONA: No—no, it doesn't really.

BIANCA: Right then. Let's have some sound e-ffecks. One; Two—(DESDEMONA *screams,* EMILIA *clutches her rosary.*)—NO!!—not that loud! The bobbies would be in on yew so fast yew wouldn't get yer panties up—just a moan enow to get 'im excited . . . Right, then? Now: One-Two; One-Two; One-Two; One-Two; One-Two; One-Two!! (DESDEMONA *perfects her synchronized moans, building to a crescendo, at which point she breaks into peals of laughter.*)

DESDEMONA: It's smashing!—Mealy—you really must try it!

Scene 23

As before.

BIANCA: Aw want you t'take this in th' right way, now; but if you weren't born a lady, you'd a been a bleedin'-good blowzabella. One o' the best. An'—well, no matter what fate holds, there's always room fer you in me shop. (*Bashful.*) Aw means it, too—

EMILIA: —Holy Mother, if anyone had so much as whispered in Venice that you'd be makin' a bonnie whore, there'd be a blood duel to settle in the streets!

BIANCA: Aw'm payin' yer lady me respecks as one professional t'anofer. You—you got as much notion of me craft as a donkey has of Sunday.

EMILIA: Why, thank you—at least someone has noted me merit.

DESDEMONA: (*Gently.*) I'm very complimented, Bianca . . . and I really did enjoy Tuesday night—but I don't think I'd better risk covering for you again.

BIANCA: —You're—you're not brimmin' fer me anymore?

DESDEMONA: No—I don't think I'd better.

EMILIA: (*To herself.*) Heigh-ho! On to the next—

BIANCA: (*Trembling.*) But—but we c'n still be mates, wot?

DESDEMONA: Of course we can! I want that very much. I never tire of hearing your stories. They're so lively, so very funny.

What else have I got for amusement's sake. (BIANCA *is disturbed.* EMILIA *smiles.*)—but you haven't told me yet about your evening off with Cassio last Tuesday . . . did you enjoy yourself?

BIANCA: You don't want to 'ear about it none, it's not anyfing amusing—

DESDEMONA: Now, just tell me all about it, Bianca; you can tell me your secrets, too. Woman to woman. What did you two do?

BIANCA: (*Shy.*) We just talked.

EMILIA: (*Snorting.*) *All* night?

BIANCA: Yes! 'E's differnt, you know. 'E's a gen'l'man, 'e is—an' 'e makes the rest o' the blokes round 'ere look like the ninny-hammers they are—

EMILIA: Oh, he's diff'rent, all right. You'd think after all week of tom-foolin' with the like of hicks, you'd have more sense than to go prancin' about with some *nancy* town stallion.

BIANCA: Wot! Nancy! Nancy, is it? Who're you callin' "Nancy?"

DESDEMONA: Now, Mealy, don't tease her—

EMILIA: —the way I see it, it's no acc-i-dent for himself to be an army man—

BIANCA: —Aw tell you wot, M'lord Cassio 'twill make a smug more obligin' in bed than the one you've got—

DESDEMONA: (*Warningly.*)—Ladies, ladies—

EMILIA: —Well, you'll never find out what it is to be havin' the like of a proper husband in the bed.

BIANCA: Mayhap Aw will, too. Aw'm ready to let my way of life go fer wash the second 'e arsks me.

DESDEMONA: What!

BIANCA: Aw'm giving 'alfe me brass each week to the priest, Father Donahue, so's 'e c'n pray fer me sins an' t'gi' me apsolution—Aw'm ready t' say yes whenever 'e arsks me 'and—an' Aw c'n go to th' altar as unstained as you were on yer weddin' night.

EMILIA: (*Seeing* BIANCA *in a new light.*) So—you're after goin' to the priest reg-ular? (*Impressed.*) That's a lot of money.

BIANCA: Bleedin'-right.

DESDEMONA: (*Crestfallen.*) Oh, Bianca—oh, surely you're—you're not the type that wants to get married? (*Depressed,* DESDEMONA *goes and pours herself another mug of wine.*)

BIANCA: Wot's wrong wif that? Aw'm still young, an' Aw've got a tidy sum all saved up fer a dowry. An' m'lord Cassio's only got t'arsk fer a transfer to th' garrison 'ere; we'd make a bleedin-jolly life of it, Aw c'n tell you. Aw'd get us a cottage by th' sea, wif winder-boxes an' all them kinds of fings, an' 'e could go to th' tipple'ouse as much as 'e likes, wifout me sayin' nay. An' then—then Aw'd be bearin' 'im sons so's to make 'im proud—

EMILIA: (*Triumphantly.*) There! There's your new woman, m'lady! Free! Does for herself!

BIANCA: Why, that "new woman" kind o' fing's all hogwash! (EMILIA *nods her head in agreement.*) All women want t' get a smug, it's wot we're made for, ain't it? We may pretend differnt, but inside very born one o' us want smugs an' babies, smugs wot are man enow t' keep us in our place.

DESDEMONA: (*Quietly into her wine.*) I don't think I can stand it . . .

BIANCA: 'Scusin' my cheek, but you're a lucky lady, an' you don't even know it. Your 'ubby might be wot you call a bit doo-lolly-tap-tap up 'ere—(BIANCA *taps her head.*)—but th' maritle knot's tied good 'n' strong. Every time Aw 'ear—

(*Dreamily.*) "Til deaf do us part"—Aw starts t' snurfle. Aw can't 'elp it. If only Cassio would say them words an' make me th' 'appiest o'—

EMILIA: —And what makes you think m'lord Cassio—who's Venetian born, an' wears silk next to his skin, not none of your Cyprus scum, is goin' to be marryin' a tried-on strumpet?

BIANCA: 'Coz a gen'l'men don't lie to a bird—Aw should soddin'-well know where ofs Aw speak. Besides, m'lord Cassio gi' me a "token o' 'is es-teem"—

EMILIA: Hmmpf! And I'm after supposin' you gave him the same, as you've given tokens of esteem to all your customers—a scurvy clap—that's your token. (DESDEMONA *becomes curious.*)

DESDEMONA: —Hush, Mealy. (*To* BIANCA.) Never mind her, Bianca—I believe you. What type of token did Cassio give?

BIANCA: (*As enthused as a teenage girl.*) It's a real flashy bit o' goods. It's a muckenger so swank Aw don't dare blow me beak in it. (*Confidentially.*) So Aw carry it down in me knockers an' next to me 'eart.

DESDEMONA: (*Lost.*) —A swank . . . muck . . .

BIANCA: —Wot Aw mean is, it ain't yer typic sneezer. (BIANCA *gropes into her bodice, and tenderly takes out an embroidered handkerchief; proudly.*) 'Ere it is, now.

DESDEMONA: (*Starting.*) —Why—(DESDEMONA *looks carefully, then in relief.*) Oh, thank God, Bianca, you've found it. I'm saved. (DESDEMONA *stops.*) But what—whatever are you doing with my handkerchief?

EMILIA: (*To herself.*) Oh, Jesus, he gave it to Cassio!

BIANCA: (*Blank.*) *Your* handkerchief? *Yours?!* (*Dangerously.*) What's Cassio doin' wi' your hand-ker-chief?

DESDEMONA: That's precisely what I want to find out—EMILIA—

BIANCA: (*Fierce.*) —Aw bet. So—you was goin' t' 'elp me out once a week fer Cassio? (*Advancing.*) You cheatin' hussy—Aw'll pop yer peepers out—(BIANCA *lunges for* DESDEMONA; EMILIA *runs.*)

EMILIA: —She's got a knife!—

DESDEMONA: —Listen, Bianca—

BIANCA: When Aw'm gulled by a woman, she don't live to do it twice—

DESDEMONA: —Bianca, I swear!—(BIANCA *sees the hoof-pick and picks it up, slowly advancing on* DESDEMONA, *who backs away toward the clothesline.*)

BIANCA: —Aw'll carve you up into cag-meat an' feed you to the pigs—Aw'll gag yer puddings out yer gob, you'll choke so hard—

DESDEMONA: —I never!—(BIANCA *swipes at* DESDEMONA *with the pick; the two clench each other; breaking away,* DESDEMONA *falls, and picks up a wine bottle in defense.*)

BIANCA: Yer gonna snuff it, m'lady—so say yer prayers, yew goggle-eyed scab o' a WHORE ['ORE]. (DESDEMONA *ducks behind the hanging clothes, with* BIANCA *following. We hear a scuffle, grunts, and screams.* EMILIA *runs for the palace door, calling.*)

EMILIA: —GUARD!—GUARD—!! (EMILIA *flings the door open. Then she realizes she can't call the guard, and quickly closes the door behind her, turning to face the room with grim desperation. Softly.*) Jesus.

BIANCA: (*Off.*) —BLOODY!—

DESDEMONA: (*Off.*) —MEALY!! (EMILIA *runs away from the door, taking out her crucifix.*)

EMILIA: Oh, Jesus. Oh, Jesus. (*And then, we hear a scream, a splash—and the sound of a bottle breaking. Slowly a dark, wet stain spreads on a cloth drying on the clothes-line. For a moment, there is silence.* BIANCA, *looking grim and fierce, strides out from behind the clothes, holding the hoof-pick. She looks at* EMILIA, *who backs away. There is a pause. Then,* DESDEMONA *steps from behind the hanging clothes, holding a broken wine bottle. The torso of her gown is splashed with dark, indelible burgundy. Softly:*) O, thank Jesus—

DESDEMONA: Bianca! . . . Bianca, I never did.

BIANCA: Leave me alone . . . Aw've lost me chance of a smug! (BIANCA *erupts into weeping, starts to wipe her nose with the handkerchief.*)—There! Take yer filthy linen! Aw wouldn't blow me nose on it—

DESDEMONA: Bianca—I never did. I never did.

BIANCA: Aw loved 'im—

DESDEMONA: —Bianca—

BIANCA: —An' Aw lost 'im—

DESDEMONA: —Bianca—

BIANCA: —An' oh, oh, the cottage by the sea . . .

DESDEMONA: If it makes a difference, I didn't.

BIANCA: —You gulled yer 'usband an' you gulled me! An' Aw thought we was mates! (BIANCA *starts to leave;* EMILIA *calls after her.*)

EMILIA: I told you there's no such thing as friendship with ladies—

BIANCA: —You!! Washerdonna!! Shut yer potato-trap! Don't you be so 'igh an' mighty smart!! (*Reaching the door,* BIANCA *opens it, and turns.*) And just where was your Iago last Tuesday night! (*Triumphantly,* BIANCA *slams the door behind her. A very long pause. Then,* DESDEMONA *tries to sound casual.*)

DESDEMONA: Um, EMILIA *dear, just—just where was Iago last Tuesday night?*

EMILIA: (*Distressed.*) He . . . he said . . . he said that he was on guard duty . . . (EMILIA *begins to cry.* DESDEMONA *sits beside her, and tentatively puts her arms about* EMILIA. *Then,* DESDEMONA *rocks her maid.*)

Scene 24

Lights up on DESDEMONA *and* EMILIA, *seated at the table, drinking wine, saying nothing.*

Scene 25

DESDEMONA *and* EMILIA, *at table, staring ahead into air.* DESDEMONA *wearily looks into her cup, and pours herself and* EMILIA *another cup of wine. They look at each other, nod to each other, and drink together.*

Scene 26

DESDEMONA *is drinking.* EMILIA *grasps her own mug. Then, in a low voice.*

EMILIA: Do you know which one he was?

DESDEMONA: No . . . I don't think so. There were so many that night.

EMILIA: Aye, you were having a proper time at it. Travelin' around the world!! (*Pause.*)

DESDEMONA: There was one man . . . (*Hesitating.*) It might have been him.

EMILIA: (*Laughs harshly.*) My husband's a lover of garlic. Was that the man you're remembering?

DESDEMONA: No—it's not that—although . . .

EMILIA: Well, what is it you remember!

DESDEMONA: There was one man who . . . didn't last very long.

EMILIA: Aye. That's the one.

Scene 27

The same.

EMILIA: When I was married in the Church, the knot tied beneath the Virgin's nose, I looked forward to the bed with as much joy as any girl after a hard day. And then Iago—well, he was still a lad, with the softness of a boy, and who could tell he'd turn into the man? (EMILIA *pauses to drink.*) But all that girl-nonsense was knocked out of me by the nights. Night followin' night, as sure as the day's work came after. I'd stretch myself out on the bed, you see, waitin' for my good man to come to me and be my mate—as the Priest said he could—but then. But then I saw it didn't matter what had gone on between us—the fights, my crying, a good meal or a cold one. Days could pass without a word between us—and he'd take his fill of me the same. I could have been the bed itself. And so, you see, I vowed not to be there for him. As he'd be lying on me in the dark, I'd picture up my rosary, so real I could kiss the silver. And I'd stare at the Blessed Cross itself, while he was somewhere doin' his business above, and I'd say the first wooden bead, and then I'd finger the next bead in my mind, and then onto the next—(EMILIA *stops.*) But I never did make it to the medallion. He'd be all through with me by the time of the third "Hail Mary." (*Pause.*) Does my lady know what I'm saying?

DESDEMONA: I'm not sure. I . . . I don't think it's . . . happened to me like that.

EMILIA: Ah, well, men are making fools of themselves over you. The Ambassador is traipsing from the mainland just to hold onto your skirt; and your husband—(EMILIA *stops herself.*)—Well, maybe it's all different for the likes of you. (DESDEMONA *says nothing.*) And then, maybe not. It's hard to be seeing, when you're young and men watch you when you pass them by, and the talkin' stops between them. But all in all, in time you'll know. Women just don't figure in their heads—not the one who hangs the wash, not Bianca—and not even you, m'lady. That's the hard truth. Men only see each other in their eyes. Only each other. (*Beat.*) And that's why I'm ready to leave the whole pack of them behind and go with you and the Ambassador. Oh, to see my husband's face tomorrow morning! When he finds out that I can get along by myself, with no thanks to his plotting and hatching!—But it's leave him now or be countin' my beads through the years, waitin' for his last breath!

DESDEMONA: (*Quietly.*) Emilia—I'll be honest with you, even if it puts me in risk to do so . . . You're to stay behind tomorrow. I've asked my cousin for my own safe passage. I wish to go alone with Ludovico. (EMILIA *stands very still.*) I am in your hands. You can run and tell my husband all—but I don't want to trifle with your feelings and desert you with the first tide. This way, you see, I'm only temporarily leaving you behind. But I promise I'll need your service in Venice as much as tonight. So, you're to follow me when all household matters are in hand, taking with you whatever my husband permits. As a token of my esteem—here—(DESDEMONA *takes off a ring, and gazes at it wistfully.*) I want you to have this. It's a memento given me by Ludovico for—well, never you mind what for. Little did he think it would wind up 'round the finger of an honest woman. (DESDEMONA *gives the ring to* EMILIA.)

EMILIA: This ring is for me? but it's of value, m'lady—(EMILIA *tries to return it;* DESDEMONA *insists.* EMILIA *makes a decision.*) Listen, Miss, you've gone and leveled with me, and I'm after doing the same with you—(EMILIA *blurts.*)—M'lady, don't go to your husband's bed tonight. Lie apart—stay in my chamber.

DESDEMONA: Why? Whatever for? It would raise suspicion.

EMILIA: I'll say you're ill—with woman sickness.

DESDEMONA: But why?

EMILIA: Because . . . because . . . oh, m'lady, you know how easy it is to be seduced by a husband's soft word, when it's the like of angry words he pours down upon your head—

DESDEMONA: (*Very still.*) Emilia—what have you done?

EMILIA: I took the handkerchief.

DESDEMONA: You took the handkerchief . . . I thought you did.

EMILIA: It was to be a joke, you see; my husband put me up to it, as a lark, he said, just to see—

DESDEMONA: (*Very softly.*) —Iago—Oh, my sweet Jesus—

EMILIA: And he was laughing about it, ye see, and he was as gay as a boy; he said he'd just . . . hide it for a while, all in jest—

DESDEMONA: Oh, no—he . . . he must have . . . planted it on Cassio—that's why . . .

EMILIA: It was just for a lark!

DESDEMONA: Emilia—what has your husband been thinking!

EMILIA: I don't know what he thinks. (DESDEMONA *twists the handkerchief.*)

DESDEMONA: What use is this to me now? If I return it, my husband will say that my lover gave it back to me!!

EMILIA: Miss Desdemona—oh my lady, I'm sure your husband loves you!

DESDEMONA: How do you know that my husband—!

EMILIA: —More than the world! He won't harm you none, m'lady—I've often seen him—

DESDEMONA: —What have you seen?!

EMILIA: I've seen him, sometimes when you walk in the garden, slip behind the arbor just to watch you, unawares . . . and at night . . . in the corridor . . . outside your room—sometimes he just stands there, Miss, when you're asleep—he just stands there—

DESDEMONA: (*Frightened.*) Oh, Jesus—

EMILIA: And once . . . I saw . . . I came upon him unbeknowin', and he didn't see me, I'm sure—he was in your chamber room—and he gathered up the sheets from your bed, like a body, and . . . and he held it to his face, like, like a bouquet, all breathin' it in—(*The two women pause: they both realize* OTHELLO*'s been smelling the sheets for traces of a lover.*)

DESDEMONA: That isn't love. It isn't love. (*Beat.*) Why didn't you tell me this before?

EMILIA: (*Carefully.*) I always thought it was not my place. (*The two women do not speak for a moment.* EMILIA *looks toward the palace door.*) Well, what are we to be doin' now?

DESDEMONA: We have to make it to the morning. You'd better come with me—it's not safe for you, either. (EMILIA *says nothing.*) We'll have to leave all behind. It's not safe to pack. (DESDEMONA *thinks, carefully.*) Now listen, carefully, Emilia. I'll go to my own chamber tonight. You're to wait up for my husband's return—tell him I'm ill and I've taken to my own bed. He's not to disturb me, I'm not well. I'll turn in before he comes, and I'll . . . pretend to sleep if he should come to me. (*Pause.*) Surely he'll not . . . harm a sleeping woman.

EMILIA: I'll do it.

DESDEMONA: Good. I'd better go to bed. (DESDEMONA *starts toward the palace door and stops.*)

EMILIA: Would you like me to brush your hair tonight? A hundred strokes?

DESDEMONA: Oh, yes, please, Emilia . . .

Scene 28

EMILIA *brushes* DESDEMONA*'s hair.* DESDEMONA *leans back, tense, listening to the offstage palace.*

EMILIA: Now, then—(EMILIA *starts.*) One, two, three, four, five, six—

Scene 29

The same.

EMILIA: Forty-five, forty-six, forty-seven—

Scene 30

DESDEMONA *and* EMILIA. EMILIA *reaches the hundredth stroke.*

EMILIA: Ninety-seven . . . ninety-eight . . . ninety-nine . . .

(*They freeze. Blackout.*)

END OF PLAY

WORKOUT

Wendy Wasserstein

CHARACTER

WOMAN

(A woman enters a small room wearing leotards and a midi sweattop. She turns on disco music and lies on the floor. She begins to exercise, and begins to talk.)

Ready for your workout? We'll start with buttock tucks. These are my favorite. Now lie back, breathe deep. Big breath. Mmmmmm. Relax, feet forward. Remember, make the muscles burn.

(She begins to bounce her buttocks.)

And lift and lower. And lift and lower. Squeeze it. Squeeze it. Push up, release. Push up and release. Really squeeze it, Denise. Lift up, lift up and bounce bounce bounce.

(She begins doing leg lifts.)

This is what I like to think about when I'm doing my workout. I think about how I got up at four-thirty in the morning and ran for five miles. And how great that run felt. Keep bouncing, up down up down. I like to think about the brewer's yeast I gave my children for breakfast. Squeeze it! Squeeze it! And how proud I am that the words "french toast" are never used in our house. I think about my husband's stamina. It's better now than when we first got married because we're organized. Work deep. Work deep!

(She does lifts in fire hydrant position.)

And I think about the novel I'm writing between nine and eleven this morning. And the chain of appliance stores I'm opening at twelve. I just think it's so important that we take charge of our own appliances. Last week I restored the electricity for the city of Fresno. And a year ago I couldn't use a can opener. Just keep bouncing, Denise. And one, and two. And this afternoon after my yoghurt shake . . .

(*She goes into a split.*)

Ooooooooooooh I felt the burn that time. I'm going to learn Serbo-Croatian so I can star in the Marshall Tito story, which I am also producing, directing, writing, editing, and distributing. I'll need all my strength. Let's do twenty more. Denise, put the gun down. Your life isn't my fault! Be angry with your buttocks. Let them know your feelings.

(*She squats, elbow to knee.*)

At five o'clock I'm going to my daughter's dance recital, where my husband will announce his candidacy for governor—I hope you all will vote for him—and I will announce the publication of my new workout book for children under six and their pets. On our way home, the entire family will stop at the home of a woman friend of mine for women's friendship and tofutti ice cream. Release, release, we're almost there. Don't give in. Push it. Push it.

(*She begins doing jumping jacks.*)

And then my very favorite part of the day. Tuck in. Feel it all over. The children are outside playing nonviolent baseball with radishes and zucchinis, my husband is preparing his part of the family meal and debating with Connie Chung and the six o'clock news team by satellite. Just two more. Get ready to release. And it is time for my moment. Just me.

(*She stops exercising for the first time.*)

And I sit for the first time in the day. On my favorite chair, with my favorite quilt. And I take a deep breath, and I cry. (*She pauses.*) But just a little.

(*She stands up.*)

And then I tuck in my stomach and pull up from the chair. Vertebra by vertebra. And I take a deep inhalation and exhale. And now we're ready for fifty more jumping jacks. And one, and two, and three, let's go, Denise.

(*She continues jumping happily.*)

END

THE ROLE OF DELLA

John J. Wooten

THE ROLE OF DELLA premiered at 12 Miles West Theatre Co. in October 1995. It was directed by John J. Wooten; the set designer was John Hindman; the lighting designer was Dan Feith. *The Role of Della* was produced as part of *Roadside Attractions,* a one-act festival sponsored by 12 Miles West. The cast was as follows:

EMMA WINNS	Rhonda Watson
ELIZABETH RYAN	Beth Fischer
MS. STEWART	Michele Tauber

CAST

EMMA
ELIZABETH
WOMAN

TIME: Now

PLACE: An audition studio

Lights up on an audition studio. EMMA *stands in front of a table. She carefully examines a few head shots, which are spread about the table. She notices one of interest and slowly sits down in a chair in front of the table.* ELIZABETH *slowly sticks her head into the room.*

ELIZABETH: Excuse me. (*Startled, Emma quickly puts the head shot on the table. She begins to rise.*) No, don't get up. I'm a little early. There was no monitor out front. I saw the door open. I didn't know if I should come straight in . . . or if I should wait . . . I'll come back in a few minutes. (*Starts out*)

EMMA: Do you have your audition card?

ELIZABETH: Oh, yeah. (*With a smile.*) I wouldn't lose this. I had to get here at 6 A.M. to wait in line and I still barely got a slot. Some girl offered me fifty dollars for this card. Just for a chance to audition. It's like a zoo out there.

EMMA: Hand it to me, please.

ELIZABETH: Sure. (*She crosses to her. Offers hand.*) I must say it's a great pleasure to meet you, Ms. Stewart. I've heard great things about your theatre.

EMMA: (*Shakes hand.*) Thank you. The card.

ELIZABETH: Oh, right. (*She hands Emma the audition card.*) Sorry. Just a little nervous.

EMMA: That's all right. I understand.

ELIZABETH: John Wyatt says hello.

EMMA: Really.

ELIZABETH: He's doing great. He just booked . . .

EMMA: Do you have a head shot and resume?

ELIZABETH: Of course. (*She hands* EMMA *her resume.*)

EMMA: (*Takes a moment, looks at the headshot.*) No, I need your headshot. (ELIZABETH *laughs.*) Is something funny?

ELIZABETH: I don't understand.

EMMA: (*Deliberately slow.*) I need your headshot.

ELIZABETH: This is my headshot.

EMMA: No.

ELIZABETH: Yes, that's me.

EMMA: Really? You've gained a few pounds since this picture was taken, haven't you?

ELIZABETH: I beg your pardon?

EMMA: What role are you interested in?

ELIZABETH: Della.

EMMA: Della? Really? The young ingenue?

ELIZABETH: (*A beat.*) Yes.

EMMA: (*Chuckles to herself.*) Okay. Why not. What piece are you doing?

ELIZABETH: Uh . . . Today, I

EMMA: Can you move back a little, please?

ELIZABETH: Sure. Sorry. (*She moves back, away from table.*) Good morning. My name is Elizabeth Ryan. Today, I will be doing a selection from . . .

EMMA: Just do the monologue.

ELIZABETH: Right.

EMMA: You only have two minutes, you know?

ELIZABETH: Yes. (*She turns and takes a breath. She turns back around, and begins.*) "Oh, we would get into terrible arguments, my mother and I."

EMMA: Do I have something on my face?

ELIZABETH: Pardon?

EMMA: Why are you looking at me?

ELIZABETH: Is it okay if I direct my piece to you?

EMMA: What do you think?

ELIZABETH: (*Begins again, awkwardly directing piece to chair.*) "Once, when I was twelve or thirteen, I told her that God was a moronic fairytale—I think I'd spent an entire night . . ."

EMMA: Do you have anything else?

ELIZABETH: Excuse me?

EMMA: Do you have another monologue? (ELIZABETH *looks confused.*) Anything? . . . I've already heard that twice today.

ELIZABETH: Really?

EMMA: Yes, and I was glad Agnes killed the baby.

ELIZABETH: (*Taken aback.*) I'm sorry. If you'd like to give me a direction with it, I'd be happy to . . .

EMMA: This is not an acting class, Elizabeth. Besides, what you need is an interpretation class. *Agnes of God* is not a melodrama.

ELIZABETH: No, of course not. I wasn't trying to . . .

EMMA: Don't make excuses. Just do something else.

ELIZABETH: I don't have anything else prepared. I thought that piece was appropriate.

EMMA: Actors do not think, Beth. They act. Those who think, think. Those who act, act. Those who think they can act, spend more time thinking than acting.

ELIZABETH: Of course. Can I please try again?

EMMA: No. Tell me a story . . . Something funny.

ELIZABETH: Funny?

EMMA: Yes. Make me laugh.

ELIZABETH: Just like that?

EMMA: You want this job, don't you? You want to play Della?

ELIZABETH: Of course.

EMMA: Then make me laugh. Are you an actress or aren't you?

ELIZABETH: Okay . . . Let's see . . . When I was a little girl, my friend Carol and I found this old doll's house in her attic. We sneaked it carefully downstairs and cleaned it off. Carol had a pet mouse, Binkey. So we dressed Binkey up in this white Barbie dress and . . .

EMMA: (*Ignoring her.*) So, I see here that you've listed Sandy in *Grease* as one of your credits.

ELIZABETH: Oh, yes. It was a great experience. Working with Paul Jones. Do you know him?

EMMA: Didn't anyone ever tell you not to lie on your resume?

ELIZABETH: I didn't.

EMMA: Oh, come now.

ELIZABETH: I didn't. I swear I didn't.

EMMA: There's no character listing here by *The Glass Menagerie.* Was it done in the absurdist style or did you play the gentleman caller?

ELIZABETH: I played Laura.

EMMA: That must have been some time ago.

ELIZABETH: Last summer.

EMMA: I'm sorry, I didn't mean to interrupt your little story.

ELIZABETH: That's okay . . . Uh, where was I . . . So, after we dressed Binkey up in the Barbie costume, we placed him inside the doll house and he crawled right into the miniature bathroom as if he wanted to take a bath . . .

EMMA: Add a Southern accent.

ELIZABETH: (*Adding a Southern accent.*) . . . Then he got stuck in the miniature hall closet and we had to shake the doll house up and down and then Binkey popped out but he was all hyper and we couldn't catch him so he ran downstairs and Carol's mom was having this big ritzy dinner party and Binkey ran right at . . .

EMMA: Let's see a little Spanish.

ELIZABETH: . . . la grande jefe de mi madre, pero cuando la senorita jefe . . .

EMMA: No. I don't want Spanish dialogue. I want a Spanish accent. Comprende?

ELIZABETH: Oh . . . I can't do a Spanish accent.

EMMA: Then at least show me you have some energy . . . Act the story out.

ELIZABETH: (*A beat. Elizabeth proceeds to act out everything she says.*) So, Carol's mother's boss screamed, leaped up onto the couch and pulled up her dress. Well, she wasn't wearing underwear . . .

EMMA: Faster.

ELIZABETH: . . . Then Carol's mother's boss's husband tried to grab her but instead he knocked her off into the double salsa sour cream dip and . . .

EMMA: Faster!

ELIZABETH: . . . and Binkey got scared and ran out into the front yard and the whole party went outside to look for him except Carol's mother's boss's husband and Carol's mother's boss who was crying, not because of the double salsa dip or even the flashing incident.

EMMA: No words!

ELIZABETH: Pardon?

EMMA: No words. (*Completely enthralled in the story, Elizabeth then acts out the rest of the story without words. This includes a chase scene, fainting, a cat, a dog, maybe even death. Elizabeth finishes with a loud laugh. She can't help but applaud herself.*)

EMMA: (*A beat. Dryly.*) Couldn't think of anything funny, huh?

ELIZABETH: (*A long beat. On the verge of tears.*) Why are you being so rude to me.

EMMA: (*Innocently.*) Rude. Am I being rude? I'm sorry, Elizabeth. Please continue your quaint little rodent story.

ELIZABETH: I don't want to. I'm leaving.

EMMA: Leaving. You sure? You still have a few seconds left.

ELIZABETH: If you didn't think I was right for the role you should have just said so.

EMMA: Right? You're perfect. I just wanted to make sure you could handle all the terrible things Della must endure.

ELIZABETH: Really?

EMMA: Sure.

ELIZABETH: And?

EMMA: There is no doubt in my mind that you think you would be perfect for this role. I don't think I've ever seen an actress quite like you before.

ELIZABETH: Thank you!

EMMA: But out of fairness I have to finish out the day. I'll call you tomorrow. Mind you, it will be late. Between midnight and 4 A.M. Make sure you're awake and by the phone. If you don't pick up after the first ring, I'll offer Della to someone else.

ELIZABETH: Don't worry. I won't sleep a wink.

EMMA: Good.

ELIZABETH: Anything I should know about the character? Keep in mind?

EMMA: Leave the wig at home. It doesn't fit.

ELIZABETH: Wig?

EMMA: And learn a Spanish accent and combine it with the Southern. You can talk faster too.

ELIZABETH: Even faster?

EMMA: Pace is everything.

ELIZABETH: Okay. I'll work on it tonight.

EMMA: Alright. Run along now. I'll be in touch . . . (ELIZABETH *smiles and turns to go.*) Wait! Your number is 555-8798?

ELIZABETH: Yes.

EMMA: Just wanted to make sure.

ELIZABETH: Thank you. Thank you so much!

EMMA: No, thank you. (ELIZABETH *exits.* EMMA *watches her off. She picks up* ELIZABETH*'s head shot, crosses to the waste basket and throws the head shot away, giggling to herself. A woman enters with coffee and takeout bag.*)

WOMAN: Hi, can I help you?

EMMA: (*Startled.*) Yes. (*A wide-eyed smile suddenly appears.*) Hi, I'm a little early. I saw the door open. Should I wait outside? . . . I'll wait outside.

WOMAN: No, that's okay. Do you have your audition card?

EMMA: Yes. (*Hands her* ELIZABETH*'s card.*) Here you go . . . I must say it's a pleasure to meet you, Ms. Stewart. I've heard great things about your theatre.

WOMAN: Well, thank you. We try.

EMMA: (*Trying to be sincere.*) John Wyatt says hello.

WOMAN: John! How is he?

EMMA: Great.

WOMAN: Do you have a picture for me?

EMMA: Sure do. (*Crosses to bag and pulls out her resume.*)

WOMAN: It's like a zoo out there.

EMMA: I know. I had to get here at 6 A.M. just to get an audition card. I didn't think I was going to get to see you. (*Elizabeth hands the woman her resume.*)

WOMAN: What piece are you doing?

EMMA: A short selection from Agnes of God.

WOMAN: (*Smiles.*) In that case, you better move back a few steps.

EMMA: Of course. (*Emma backs up.*) Good morning. My name is Emma Winns.

WOMAN: Wait . . . Uh, what role would you like to be considered for, Emma?

EMMA: (*A beat.*) Della.

BLACKOUT

CONTRIBUTORS' BIOS

EDWARD ALBEE is the internationally renowned author of *Who's Afraid of Virginia Woolf.* He has written the Pulitzer Prize–winning plays *A Delicate Balance, Seascape,* and *Three Tall Women.* Other works include *The Death of Bessie Smith, The Zoo Story, Tiny Alice, The Lady from Dubuque,* and *All Over.*

LEE BLESSING is the award-winning author of *A Walk in the Woods, Eleemosynary,* and *Independence.* His plays have been widely produced across the U.S. at numerous theaters, including Actor's Theatre of Louisville, the Eugene O'Neill National Playwrights Conference, Philadelphia Festival for New Plays, and on Broadway. New York's Signature Theatre Co. devoted an entire season to his works.

LAURA CUNNINGHAM is a novelist and journalist as well as a playwright. Her plays have been produced at Steppenwolf Theatre and on Theatre Row. She is the author of the memoir *Sleeping Arrangements.* Her works have been published in *The New Yorker, The New York Times,* and other publications.

MARY GALLAGHER's plays, including *Little Bird, Father Dreams, Chocolate Cake, Dog Eat Dog, How to Say Goodbye, Buddies,* and *¿De Dónde?*, have been published by Dramatists Play Service, and have been produced all over the U.S. and in many foreign countries. She also writes novels, most recently *The Mooch,* and screenplays.

MADELEINE GEORGE's plays *Sweetbitter Baby* and *The Most Massive Woman Wins* were produced off-Broadway in the 1993 and 1994 Young Playwrights Festivals. She is a member of the Dramatists Guild.

VELINA HASU HOUSTON's award-winning, critically acclaimed plays are internationally produced. Besides her signature play *Tea,* her plays include *Kokoro, Asa Ga Kimashita, Necessities, Hula Heart* (commission), *Cultivated Lives* (commission), and others. She writes critical essays and for film and TV, and heads the playwriting program at USC's School of Theatre.

TINA HOWE is the author of *Coastal Disturbances, Painting Churches,* and *Museum.* Her work has been produced in New York on Broadway, off-Broadway at the Public Theatre and Second Stage, and regionally. Honors include Obie and Outer Critics Circle awards and a Guggenheim fellowship. She teaches at NYU.

SHERRY KRAMER's plays include *The Law Makes Evening Fall, Napoleon's China, The Wall of Water, What a Man Weighs,* and *Things That Break.* Her plays have been produced in New York, regionally, and abroad. Her honors include grants from the NEA, the New York Foundation for the Arts, the McKnight Foundation, and the Weissberger and Jane Chambers awards. She is an alum of New Dramatists.

CASEY KURTTI's plays *Catholic School Girls* and *Three Ways Home* have been produced Off-Broadway and throughout America, Australia, and Canada. Her critically acclaimed Daytop Village Production of *The Concept* has toured America and was seen in Russia in 1994. Her screenwriting credits include PBS; *Missing in America,* ABC; Emmy-nominated *Girlfriend* and *Divas* on HBO; and *Women on Parole.*

ADAM LEFEVRE's *Waterbabies* received the 1995 Heideman Award. Other plays include *Yucca Flats; The Crashing of Moses Flying By; Americansaint; Grant at Windsor*; and *Ethiopian Tooth*. He published a book of poems. *Everything All At Once,* with Wesleyan University Press, and makes his living as an actor on stage, screen, and TV.

CRAIG LUCAS is the author of *God's Heart, Blue Window,* and *Missing Persons* (1995 Drama Desk nominee for Best Play). He has received Guggenheim and Rockefeller Grants, the Outer Critics Circle Award, the Obie Award, and a Tony nomination for Best Play (*Prelude to a Kiss*). Screenplays include *Longtime Companion,* and the adaptations of his plays *Reckless* and *Prelude to a Kiss.*

LYNN NOTTAGE is a playwright from Brooklyn. Her plays include *Crumbs From the Table of Joy, Por'Knockers,* and *Las Meninas.* They have been produced in theatres across the country, including Second Stage, The Vineyard, Steppenwolf, Dance Theatre Workshop, and the Actor's Theatre of Louisville. Nottage is a recipient of Playwriting Fellowships from New Dramatists, the New York Foundation of the Arts, and Manhattan Theatre Club. Ms. Nottage is a graduate of Brown University and the Yale School of Drama.

JOSÉ RIVERA is the author of *Cloud Tectonics,* which premiered at the 1995 Humana Festival at the Actor's Theatre of Louisville. His play *Marisol,* winner of a 1993 Obie award for Outstanding Play, premiered at the Humana Festival in 1992. Other plays include *The House of Ramon Iglesia, Each Day Dies with Sleep,* and *The Promise.*

NINA SHENGOLD's short plays, including *Finger Food, Women & Shoes,* and *Daughter of the Bride,* have been produced by theatres all over the country. She won the ABC Playwright Award and the L.A. Weekly Award for her full-length *Home-*

steaders, and a Berrilla Kerr Foundation grant for her new play *Grown Women.*

PAULA VOGEL is a playwright, screenwriter, and professor. Her plays include *The Baltimore Waltz* (nominated for the Pulitzer Prize in 1992), *Hot 'n' Throbbing, And Baby Makes Seven,* and *Desdemona.* She has headed Brown University's Playwriting Workshop since 1985. Awards include two NEA Playwriting fellowships, two MacDowell Colony fellowships, and the Rhode Island Governor's Arts Award.

WENDY WASSERSTEIN is the author of *The Sisters Rosensweig, The Heidi Chronicles, Uncommon Women and Others,* and *Isn't It Romantic.* Honors include the Pulitzer Prize, Tony Award, and Drama Desk Award. A graduate of the Yale School of Drama, she is author of the children's book *Pamela's First Musical,* and is a contributing editor to *New York Woman* and *New Woman* magazines.

JOHN J. WOOTEN's credits include *Dover Won't Get Out* and *The Limbo Room* for Life Repertory Company; *Friends Till the End,* which won the 1992 Village Gate One-Act Festival; and *Trophies,* which ran off-Broadway at the Cherry Lane Theatre. He was awarded a playwriting fellowship by the New Jersey State Council on the Arts, and recently finished *Uncommon Enemies,* a Civil War-era psychological thriller.

ABOUT THE EDITORS

NINA SHENGOLD and ERIC LANE are editors of *Take Ten: New 10-Minute Plays* for Vintage Books. For Penguin Books, they edited *Moving Parts: Monologues From Contemporary Plays, The Actor's Book of Scenes From New Plays,* and *The Actor's Book of Gay & Lesbian Plays,* which was nominated for the Lambda Literary Award for excellence in gay and lesbian publications in the U.S. In addition, Ms. Shengold edited *The Actor's Book of Contemporary Stage Monologues,* and Mr. Lane edited *Telling Tales: New One-Act Plays.*

NINA SHENGOLD won the ABC Playwright Award and the L.A. Weekly Award for her play *Homesteaders,* and received a Berilla Kerr Foundation grant for her work-in-progress *Grown Women.* Her one-acts have been performed all over the country. Ms. Shengold's TV scripts include Hallmark Hall of Fame's *Blind Spot,* starring Emmy nominee Joanne Woodward, and the upcoming *Silent Night.* A founding member of the theatre company Actors & Writers, she lives in upstate New York with her daughter Maya.

ERIC LANE's plays have been performed at theatres in New York and around the country. Works include *The Gary & Rob Show, The Heart of a Child,* and *Dancing on Checkers' Grave.* Mr. Lane wrote, directed, and produced *Cater-Waiter,* a short film starring David Drake and Tim Deak, which is currently hitting the festival circuit. He is artistic director of Orange Thoughts, a not-for-profit theater and film company in New York City.

Honors include a Writer's Guild Award (for TV's *Ryan's Hope*), two Yaddo residencies, the first La Mama Playwright Development Award, and finalist in the O'Neill Center National Playwrights Conference (*Times of War*).

Grateful acknowledgment is made to the following for permission to reprint these previously published plays:

Three Tall Women by Edward Albee. Copyright © 1994 by Edward Albee. Reprinted by permission of Dutton Signet, a division of Penguin Books USA Inc.

Independence by Lee Blessing. Copyright © 1985 by Lee Blessing. Copyright © 1983 as unpublished dramatic composition by Lee Blessing.

CAUTION: The reprinting of *Independence* included in this volume is reprinted by permission of the author and Dramatists Play Service, Inc. The amateur and stock performance rights in this play are controlled exclusively by Dramatists Play Service, Inc., 440 Park Avenue South, New York, NY 10016. No amateur or stock production of the play may be given without obtaining, in advance, the written permission of the Dramatists Play Service, Inc., and paying the requisite fee. Inquiries regarding all other rights should be addressed to Judy Boals, c/o Berman, Boals & Flynn, 225 Lafayette Street, Suite 1207, New York, NY 10012.

Beautiful Bodies by Laura Cunningham. Copyright © 1987 by Laura Cunningham. All rights reserved. Reprinted by permission of the William Morris Agency, Inc., on behalf of the author.

CAUTION: Professionals and amateurs are hereby warned that *Beautiful Bodies* is subject to a royalty. It is fully protected under the copyright laws of the United States of America, and of all countries covered by the International Copyright Union (including the Dominion of Canada and the rest of the British Commonwealth), and of all countries covered by the Pan-American Copyright Convention and the Universal Copyright Convention, and of all countries with which the United States has reciprocal copyright relations. All right, including professional, amateur, motion picture, recitation, lecturing, public reading, radio broadcasting, television, video or sound recording, all other forms of mechanical or electronic reproduction, such as information storage and retrieval systems and photocopying, and the rights of translation into foreign languages, are strictly reserved. Particular emphasis is laid upon the matter of readings, permission for which must be secured from the Author's agent in writing. Inquiries concerning rights should be addressed to William Morris Agency, Inc., 1325 Avenue of the Americas, New York, NY 10019, Attn: Peter Franklin.

Bedtime by Mary Gallagher. Copyright © 1997 by Mary Gallagher. Reprinted by permission of Mary Gallagher. For all other rights contact: Mary Harden, c/o Harden-Curtis Associates, 850 Seventh Avenue, #405, New York, NY 10019.

The Most Massive Woman Wins by Madeleine George. Copyright © 1994 by Madeleine George. Reprinted by permission of Rosenstone/Wender on behalf of the author. For all other rights inquiries should be addressed to the author's agent: Ronald Gwiazda, Rosenstone/Wender, 3 East 48th Street, New York, NY 10017.

Tea by Velina Hasu Houston. Copyright © 1987 by Velina Avisa Hasu Houston. Reprinted by permission of Velina Hasu Houston. For all other rights contact: Mary Harden, c/o Harden-Curtis Associates, 850 Seventh Avenue, #405, New York, NY 10019.

Appearances by Tina Howe. Copyright © 1981 by Tina Howe. Reprinted by permission of Flora Roberts, Inc. For all inquiries contact: Flora Roberts, Inc., 157 West 57th Street, New York, NY 10019.

David's Redhaired Death by Sherry Kramer. Copyright © 1991 by Sherry Kramer. Reprinted by permission of Sherry Kramer. For all other rights contact: Sherry Kramer, 2525 Sheridan, Springfield, MO 65804, Tel: 417-881-1740.

Catholic School Girls by Casey Kurtti. Copyright © 1978, 1989 by Casey Kurtti. Reprinted by permission of Ellen Hyman Agency on behalf of the author. For all other rights contact: Casey Kurtti, c/o Ellen Hyman Agency, 90 Lexington Avenue, New York, NY 10016, Tel: 212-689-0727.

Waterbabies by Adam LeFevre. Copyright © 1996 by Adam LeFevre. Reprinted by permission of Adam LeFevre. For all other rights inquiries should be addressed to the author's agent: Jason Fogelson, William Morris Agency, 1325 Avenue of the Americas, New York, NY 10019.

Credo by Craig Lucas. Copyright © 1995 by Craig Lucas. All rights reserved. Reprinted by permission of the William Morris Agency, Inc., on behalf of the author.

CAUTION: Professionals and amateurs are hereby warned that *Credo* is subject to a royalty. It is fully protected under the copyright laws of the United States of America, and of all countries covered by the International Copyright Union (including the Dominion of Canada and the rest of the British Commonwealth), and of all countries covered by the Pan-American Copyright Convention and the Universal Copyright Convention, and of all countries with which the United States has reciprocal copyright relations. All rights, including professional, amateur, motion picture, recitation, lecturing, public reading, radio broadcasting, television, video or sound recording, all other forms of mechanical or electronic reproduction, such as information storage and retrieval systems and photocopying, and the rights of translation into foreign languages, are strictly reserved. Particular emphasis is laid upon the matter of readings, permission for which must be secured from the Author's agent in writing. Inquiries concerning rights should be addressed to William Morris Agency, Inc., 1325 Avenue of the Americas, New York, NY 10019, Attn: Peter Franklin.

Poof! by Lynn Nottage. Copyright © 1995 by Lynn Nottage. Reprinted by permission of Lynn Nottage. The live stage production rights to this play are represented by Broadway Play Publishing Inc. For all other rights contact: Peter Hagan, Writers and Artists Agency, 19 West 44th Street, New York, NY 10036.

The Winged Man by José Rivera. Copyright © 1996 by José Rivera. Reprinted by permission of José Rivera. For all other rights contact: Joyce Ketay Agency, 1501 Broadway, Suite 1910, New York, NY 10036.

Lives of the Great Waitresses by Nina Shengold. Copyright © 1994 by Nina Shengold. Reprinted by permission of Nina Shengold. For all other rights inquiries should be addressed to the author's agent: Phyllis Wender, Rosenstone/Wender, 3 East 48th Street, New York, NY 10017.

Desdemona by Paula Vogel. Copyright © 1993 by Paula Vogel. All rights reserved. Reprinted by permission of the William Morris Agency, Inc., on behalf of the author.

CAUTION: Professionals and amateurs are hereby warned that *Desdemona* is subject to a royalty. It is fully protected under the copyright laws of the United States of America, and of all countries covered by the International Copyright Union (including the Dominion of Canada and the rest of the British Commonwealth), and of all countries covered by the Pan-American Copyright Convention and the Universal Copyright Convention, and of all countries with which the United States has reciprocal copyright relations. All rights, including professional, amateur, motion picture, recitation, lecturing, public reading, radio broadcasting, television, video or sound recording, all other forms of mechanical or electronic reproduction, such as information storage and retrieval systems and photocopying, and the rights of translation into foreign languages, are strictly reserved. Particular emphasis is laid upon the matter of readings, permission for which must be secured from the author's agent in writing. Inquiries concerning rights should be addressed to William Morris Agency, Inc., 1325 Avenue of the Americas, New York, NY 10019, Attn: Peter Franklin.

Desdemona was originally produced in association with Circle Repertory Company by Bay Street Theatre Festival, Sag Harbor, Long Island, NY, July 1993. Produced by the Circle Repertory Company, New York City, Tanya Berezin and Abigail Evans, Producers.

Workout by Wendy Wasserstein. Copyright © 1995 by Wendy Wasserstein. Reprinted by permission of Phyllis Wender on behalf of Wendy Wasserstein. For all other rights contact: Phyllis Wender, Rosenstone/Wender, 3 East 48th Street, New York, NY 10017.

The Role of Della by John J. Wooten. Copyright © 1995 by John J. Wooten. Reprinted by permission of Rosenstone/Wender on behalf of John J. Wooten. For all other rights inquiries should be addressed to the author's agent: Ronald Gwiazda, Rosenstone/Wender, 3 East 48th Street, New York, NY 10017.